GLOBAL
DILEMMAS

Contributors:

Richard N. Cooper

Jorge I. Domínguez

Paul M. Doty

Elliot J. Feldman

Douglas A. Hibbs

Stanley Hoffmann

Samuel P. Huntington

Herbert Kelman

Michael Nacht

Joseph S. Nye, Jr.

Gary R. Orren

Robert D. Putnam

Sidney Verba

Raymond Vernon

GLOBAL DILEMMAS

Edited by

Samuel P. Huntington

and

Joseph S. Nye, Jr.

Published by

The Center for International Affairs

Harvard University *and*

University Press of America

University Press of America, ® Inc.

4720 Boston Way
Lanham, MD 20706

3 Henrietta Street
London WC2E 8LU England

Library of Congress Cataloging in Publication Data
Main entry under title:

Global dilemmas.

    Includes bibliographies.
    1. World politics—1975-1985—Addresses, essays,
lectures. I. Huntington, Samuel P. II. Nye, Joseph S., Jr.
III. Cooper, Richard N. IV. Harvard University. Center
for International Affairs.
D849.G57   1985   327'.09'047   85-7374
ISBN 0-8191-4525-4 (alk. paper)

Co-published by arrangement with the
Center for International Affairs, Harvard University

The Center for International Affairs provides a forum for the expression of responsible views. It does not necessarily agree with those views.

Chapter 1 is an article extracted from Robert D. Putnam and Nicholas Bayne, *Hanging Together, The Seven-Power Summits*, Cambridge: Harvard University Press, 1984. ©1984 by Heinemann/Royal Institute of International Affairs. Used with permission.

Chapter 11 was originally published in the Political Science Quarterly, Summer 1984. ©1984 by The Academy of Political Science. Used with permission.

The Center For International Affairs Executive Committee, 1984–85

The Center for International Affairs is a multidisciplinary research institution within Harvard University. Founded in 1958, the Center seeks to provide a stimulating environment for a diverse group of scholars and practitioners studying various aspects of international affairs. Its purpose is the development and dissemination of knowledge concerning the basic subjects and problems of international relations. Major Center research programs include national security affairs, U.S. relations with Europe, Japan, Africa, and other areas of the world, nonviolent sanctions in conflict and defense, international economic policy, and other critical issues. At any given time, over 160 individuals are working at the Center, including faculty members from Harvard and neighboring institutions, practitioners of international affairs, visiting scholars, research associates, post-doctoral fellows, and graduate and undergraduate student associates.

CONTENTS

Preface   ix

Part I Ethics and politics in foreign   I
        policymaking

   1   The lessons of western summitry   3
        ROBERT D. PUTNAM

   2   Ethics and foreign policy   23
        RICHARD COOPER AND
        JOSEPH S. NYE, JR.

Part II Security dilemmas of the nuclear age   43

   3   The search for security in an increasingly   45
        insecure world
        MICHAEL NACHT

   4   Arms control at bay   60
        PAUL M. DOTY

Part III The interplay of economics and   77
          politics in industrial democracies

   5   Political and economic equality: a theoretical   79
        and empirical comparison
        SIDNEY VERBA AND
        GARY ORREN

   6   Macroeconomic performance, macroeconomic
        policy, and electoral politics in industrial
        democracies
        DOUGLAS A. HIBBS   123

7   Patterns of failure in government   138
    megaprojects: economics, politics, and participation
    in industrial democracies
    ELLIOT J. FELDMAN

Part IV Regional politics: Latin America   159
         and the Middle East

8   The foreign policies of Latin American states   161
    in the 1980s: retreat or refocus?
    JORGE I. DOMÍNGUEZ

9   Overcoming the psychological barrier: an   199
    analysis of the Egyptian–Israeli peace process
    HERBERT KELMAN

Part V The prospects for prosperity,   225
        freedom, and stability

10 Old rules and new players: GATT in the   227
    world trading system
    RAYMOND VERNON

11 Will more countries become democratic?   253
    SAMUEL P. HUNTINGTON

12 The future of the international political   280
    system: a sketch
    STANLEY HOFFMANN

Preface

The Center for International Affairs was founded in 1958 by four Harvard faculty members—Robert Bowie from law, Henry Kissinger from political science, and Edward Mason and Thomas Schelling from economics—to encourage interdisciplinary social science research on fundamental problems in international affairs. In the words of the first annual report, "Our capacity to achieve the promise and avoid the perils of the modern age depends first, on deeper knowledge of the forces making for change, and second, on increased understanding of the impact of these forces in the international order. The required studies can seldom be done by government or officials immersed in pressing current activities. The Center for International Affairs was founded in the belief that Harvard has unusual resources for basic research of this kind."

Over the years the topics have changed, but Center work has always focused on basic research in the fundamental problems of international affairs and on their implications for public policy.

In the 1950s the world was nuclear, bipolar, and starkly divided. There were potential flash points in Berlin and elsewhere in the old world and also in the slums and stagnant economies of third world countries. Many of the latter were struggling to feed exploding populations as they emerged from colonialism and began to manage their own affairs. In this context, the Center focused its research on three broad concerns: bipolar strategic relations in the nuclear era; conditions and developments in the two camps; and economic development to promote prosperity and security in poor countries. Although different labels were used, something like this trinity of interwoven themes formed the organizing framework for most of the work conducted at the Center in the early years.

In addition to the core faculty members, research associates from Harvard and other universities joined the Center for limited periods to conduct their own research along these themes. Each year there were also a dozen practitioners from different countries—diplomats, civil servants, and military officers—who spent an academic year in advanced study and research at the Center. These Center Fellows brought their practical experience to the research conducted at the university and used the facilities of the university for their professional and personal growth.

Over the course of the 1960s the Center grew rapidly, in numbers of faculty, research associates, and Fellows. Equally important was the evolution of the research programs. In the early 1960s, interest in Western European integration led to the study of functional groupings and incipient supranational institutions in other regions. Comparative analysis of economic development in various regions of the third world was enriched by studies of social and political development as well. In the strategic area much formative work on arms control was conducted at the Center. The study of European—American alliance relationships grew into a deeper attention to the politics of modern Europe.

In the 1970s new strands of research were added to these persistent themes. Transnational studies highlighted phenomena as diverse as the Scandinavian and Nordic systems, Canada–U.S. relations, international information media, and multinational corporations. Attention was devoted to analysis of regional developments in Africa, Latin America, and the Middle East. The problems of interdependence were studied both in developing areas and in relations among developed countries. The focus on the U.S.–European relationship became enriched by the growth of interest in the U.S.–Japan relationship and trilateral relations among the developed parts of the globe.

By the time of the Center's 25th anniversary in 1983 the number of research topics had become even more complex. Much work was being done on the interaction between economic policy and performance and democratic politics in industrialized societies. A new national security program focusing on U.S. national security problems had been launched to supplement the 1970s emphasis on arms control. Expanded attention was also being given both to the European Community and to European security dilemmas. International economic issues were also coming to the fore. In almost all these research efforts, a central focus of attention was the interaction between domestic politics, foreign policy, and the international environment. Throughout its history, the Center has always conceived of the term "international" in its title to encompass not only the relations among nation states in the strict sense, but also the broad patterns of comparative social, political, and economic change occurring within societies.

In a sense the essays in this volume represent what the faculty on the Executive Committee of the Center regard as central issues for research in international affairs during this decade. Some issues carry over from themes that have been central to the Center's research programs since its founding; other issues represent the evolution of new areas of interest and concern. All have the common theme of concern with relating fundamental research in international affairs with public policy issues. Preliminary drafts of these papers were discussed at the Center's 25th anniversary conference in Cambridge in June 1983. This conference, made possible by a generous grant from the Scaife Family Charitable Trusts, was attended by over three hundred past and current Center members.

We begin the volume with a section on the problems of formulating policy in advanced industrial societies. Robert Putnam surveys the politics of western economic summits over the years, while Richard Cooper and Joseph Nye analyze the ethical problems in formulating foreign policy in countries with the tradition of oscillating between realism and idealism, such as the United States. These essays are followed by a section on an issue that has been central since the first days of the Center, the security dilemmas of the nuclear age. Michael Nacht sketches the problems of searching for security in an increasingly insecure world, and Paul Doty assesses the potential and limitations of efforts to deal with such dilemmas through arms control.

Security dilemmas, of course, are not the only problems of the modern world. It has been argued that equality and the search for equality is the pressing issue of the 20th century just as liberty was in the 19th century. The political intentions and prospects which arise from the search for greater political and economic equality are described in part three by Sidney Verba and Gary Orren. Their study is followed by two other pieces on the interplay of economics and politics in the industrial democracies. Douglas Hibbs analyzes the relationship between macroeconomic performance and electoral politics in industrial democracies; Elliot Feldman looks at the patterns of failure in government megaprojects in advanced industrial democracies and the reasons why these failures occur. The interaction of development and security issues takes different forms in different regions. In part four, Herbert Kelman looks at the overcoming of psychological barriers in the Egyptian–Israeli peace process, and Jorge Domínguez analyzes the domestic and international factors affecting the foreign policies of Latin-American states in the 1980s.

Finally, in part five, efforts are made to evaluate the implications of current trends for prosperity, freedom, and stability in the world. Raymond Vernon looks at the changing international economic order, in particular the way in which domestic economic changes have put pressure on the rules of the international trading system. Samuel Huntington provides an analysis of the prospects that more countries, particularly in the Third World, will develop democratic institutions, and Stanley Hoffmann looks at the overall evolution of the international political system.

A reading of these essays will indicate how much the world has changed since the Center was established in 1958, as well as provide an indication of how Center faculty members see the world evolving in the 1980s and what they regard as fruitful avenues for research. The Center has demonstrated a capacity for innovation in adapting to changes in the world around it both in terms of its research programs and in development of new activities such as its student programs and workshops. This flexibility is a major source of strength. Underlying that strength is the commitment to fundamental research on long-range problems of international affairs that is the heart of the Center's program. In this volume, we not only celebrate a quarter century of the Center's existence, but offer a representative sample of the work underway as we enter our next quarter century.

Samuel P. Huntington
Joseph S. Nye, Jr.

I

Ethics and politics in foreign policymaking

ROBERT D. PUTNAM
The lessons of western summitry

RICHARD COOPER AND
JOSEPH S. NYE, JR.
Ethics and foreign policy

1

The lessons of western summitry

ROBERT D. PUTNAM

Professor of Government and Chairman of the Government Department, Harvard University

Origins of the summits

An exhaustive search for the historical antecedents of Western summitry might begin with the Bath summit of 973, when King Edgar of the West Saxons was rowed up the River Avon by the other four participating monarchs. But the modern origins of the annual economic summits held over the last decade among the leaders of the major industrial democracies can be traced to a top-secret meeting in the White House Library on March 25, 1973.

During that winter a hectic series of transatlantic meetings among financial officials had failed to forestall the final collapse of the Bretton Woods international monetary order. Hoping to coordinate the stances of the key Western governments in the aftermath, u.s. Treasury Secretary George Shultz invited his counterparts from Britain, France, and Germany to meet privately with him, each accompanied only by one senior aide. The ministers insisted on a maximum of discretion and a minimum of preparation, partly because of the risk of protest from excluded countries and partly because of their own sense that in a turbulent world they needed to close ranks as political leaders, escaping from the technical pettifoggery of bureaucrats.

Over the ensuing months, this "Library Group" continued to meet quietly, seeking to sort out international monetary questions in the uncharted waters of floating exchange rates. Even in their earliest sessions, however, their discussions ranged across the spectrum of international and domestic political economy. In these relaxed encounters, free from the normal constraints of international negotiations and domestic rivalries, a climate of camaraderie and mutual trust developed, along with a sense of confidence in their own expertise and a remarkable frankness in expressing frustrations with political and bureaucratic adversaries back home. It was, for most of the participants, an experience unique in their professional lives. Over the course of the next year or two the group expanded to include the Japanese (and occasionally the Italians); the problems sparked by the first oil shock —

3

inflation, recession, and international debt—rose on their agenda; and the original participants gradually moved on to other positions. But nearly a decade later they would still recall with nostalgia their sense of solidarity, exclusiveness, and shared power, as they sat secretly together at the control panel of the world economy.

The key figures in the Library Group were remarkable leaders, and it was hardly surprising when in 1974 two of them, Helmut Schmidt and Valery Giscard d'Estaing, ascended to the posts of Chancellor and President, respectively.[1] Nor was it surprising that they carried to their new responsibilities the idea of confidential and informal conversations among the West's key political leaders, as detached as possible from normal bureaucratic channels. When in 1975 Giscard launched the idea of an economic summit, he had solid backing from Schmidt. Shultz (by then an unofficial advisor to President Ford) helped to ensure American participation. Reflecting their shared image of the summit as a kind of super Library Group, Schmidt is reported to have explained, "We want a very private, informal meeting of those who really matter in the world."

Beyond these personal predilections, the institution of economic summitry was encouraged by several structural features of contemporary international relations. In the first place, economic interdependence has increasingly entangled foreign and domestic politics.[2] International trade and finance have gradually dissolved the barriers between national economies. In today's world, the tradeoff for price stability in Hamburg may be unemployment in Harlem. The *projet* of a French socialist president is constrained by decisions of American monetary authorities. These trends pose an ever-sharper dilemma for democratic political leaders by threatening their autonomy to respond to domestic constituencies. If they are to avoid recourse to costly protectionist measures, they must cooperate with their counterparts abroad in an effort to manage the mutual interference that is the price of interdependence.[3]

Thus, metaphorically, a national leader needs to play a two-level game.[4] Across the international table sit his foreign counterparts, while around a second table behind him sit spokesmen for key domestic interests. The political complexities of this two-level game are staggering, quite apart from the technical economic complexities. Moves rational for a player at one board (such as raising energy prices or limiting automobile imports) may be quite irrational for him at the other board, but major inconsistencies between moves in the two games are not tolerated by other players or by kibitzers. Any key player at the international table dissatisfied with the outcome may upset the game board, but a leader who fails to satisfy an adequate number of his fellow players at the domestic table risks being evicted from his seat.

To the founders of Western summitry, only heads of government seemed well placed to try to resolve this tension between international economics and domestic politics. For a generation of leaders who had them-

selves come of age during the Great Depression, the dangers of a return to
economic nationalism were vivid.

A second part of the explanation for the move toward summitry was
the shift in relative power among the United States, Europe, and Japan.
For the first quarter-century after 1945 the United States had been powerful
enough alone to serve as custodian of the world economic order, but by the
early 1970s the Americans seemed neither willing nor able to assert global
leadership. The end of American hegemony was epitomized by the collapse
of the Bretton Woods system, followed almost immediately by the first oil
shock and the worst downturn in economic activity since the 1930s. The
collective clipper of the Western economies had suddenly entered stormy
seas, the captain had disappeared, and the ship's mates scuttled around the
helm in wary confusion. To restore the stability that United States predominance had earlier assured, a new system of collective leadership would
need to be jury-rigged, bringing together the leaders of the key Western
countries.[5]

Giscard, Schmidt, and their counterparts believed that heads of government could make a unique contribution to international coordination,
beyond the capacity of conventional officialdom. International economics
could no longer be considered "low politics," left to bloodless diplomats, to
cunning central bankers, to distant international organizations, or to the
haphazards of the market. As politicians, the heads could rise above the
petty concerns of narrow-minded technicians. (Giscard and Schmidt, for
example, would later conspire to create the European Monetary System
over the objections of most of their monetary experts.) Moreover, only heads
of government could overcome the increasing fragmentation of international
negotiation along functional lines, with trade issues handled by trade specialists, financial issues by the "international money mafia" of finance ministry officials, and so on. Only the heads could impart the kind of momentum
to international discussions that could offset the risks of economic nationalism.

Thus, the founding fathers of summitry defined the *scope* of the new
institution in ambitious terms. However, they were almost equally committed to simplicity in the *process* of summitry. Recalling their Library Group
experience, they aimed at a summit with little pomp, little preparation, and
little institutional underpinning. Indeed, so strong was the antibureaucratic
sentiment among the founders that they assigned responsibility for what
minimal preparation was deemed necessary to "personal representatives"
(later dubbed "sherpas") whose links with the summiteers themselves were
more important than their place in the official hierarchy.

In fact, this combination of ambitious objectives and simple procedures—however attractive it has been to summiteers themselves throughout
this period—proved impractical right from the outset. This history of Western economic summitry, as we shall see, reflects a constant struggle to

reconcile these irreconcilable desires. When the first several summits made clear that substantial accomplishments required substantial preparation, the summiteers of the late 1970s accepted American ideas for deepening the institutional base of summitry. By the beginning of the 1980s, however, the pendulum had begun to reverse course, and discontent with bureaucratic degeneration of the summit process became widespread. Finally, with the near collapse of the summit as an institution following the Versailles meeting of 1982, a new generation of summiteers accepted that procedural simplicity would require radically lower substantive expectations. In short, one lesson of the last decade is that summits can be simple or substantial, but not both.[6]

The first summits: 1975–1976

The first Western economic summit was held in the isolated Château de Rambouillet over the wet autumn weekend of November 15–17, 1975. Those present included the leaders of the United States, Japan, West Germany, France, the United Kingdom, and Italy.[7] The recession induced by the first oil crisis had passed its trough, and the leaders expressed confidence that their existing policies were adequate to sustain recovery. On trade issues, they sought with some success to stiffen Prime Minister Wilson's resistance to protectionist pressures within his Labour Cabinet. The centerpiece of Rambouillet, however, was an agreement to restore some order to the international monetary system, reconciling long-standing Franco–American differences about the exchange rate regime. The proposed revisions to the IMF Articles of Agreement were ratified by the IMF Interim Committee in Jamaica two months later.

The participants had tried to cast this first summit as an intimate and informal "fireside chat," faithful to its Library Group antecedents. In fact, however, the notion of casual, unofficial preparations did not last out even this first round of summitry, either within governments or between them. As one ex-sherpa privately recalls,

> I learned very soon that it was not possible to act entirely on my own. Too many ministries were involved and too many subjects on which I was not expert, and I began to coordinate my activities with the regular departments—that's always a delicate thing in government.

Moreover, the monetary agreement supposedly struck at the summit had in fact been meticulously prepared beforehand in marathon transatlantic negotiations between Edwin Yeo of the U.S. Treasury and his French counterpart, Jacques de Larosière, meeting almost weekly during the two months before the summit. So complex and delicate was the accord that neither the other sherpas nor the heads of government were allowed to see the joint Franco–American memorandum that formed the basis of the summit agreement. So much for the notion of a casual Library Group summit!

Nevertheless, the summit was crucial to the successful monetary accord in three ways, which well illustrated how these meetings would be useful on other issues in later years. The Rambouillet summit:

- provided an action-forcing deadline for the experts;
- offered political "cover" against domestic criticism, in this case helping Giscard fend off complaints from orthodox Gaullists;
- imparted the necessary momentum to subsequent international deliberations.

President Giscard had not intended that the summit should be a regular annual affair, but Rambouillet was widely considered a success, and the Ford White House, girding itself for an election year, could not resist the temptation to call a follow-up session in early 1976. Hastily prepared and with little substantive justification, the Puerto Rico summit of June 27–28, 1976, had more the flavor of a beach outing than a serious deliberative meeting of the leaders of the Western world.[8] The summiteers agreed that the economic revival then underway called for a relatively austere policy mix. The only visible accomplishment of the summit was captured in one newspaper headline: "Summit Leaders Endorse Ford's Economic Policy."[9]

By the following winter, the optimism of the Puerto Rico declaration proved excessive. The recovery stalled, and unemployment in the West began to rise toward a new postwar record. Meanwhile, a new Administration was taking office in Washington, offering both a new approach to summitry and a prescription for the economic slowdown.

Institutionalizing the summit: 1977–1980

Instead of what one European summiteer termed (admiringly) "an open-hearted gossip among friends," the Carter people proposed that the summit should cap an institutionalized process of intensive consultation and policy coordination. "We can't bring the President halfway around the world for a seminar," said Ambassador Henry Owen, appointed by President Carter to work full time on summit activities. Drawing on the work of several Trilateral Commission task forces, the Americans argued that bureaucrats were part of the solution, not part of the problem. Under the aegis of these Trilateralists, the rhythm of summit preparations accelerated. The sherpas settled into an annual pattern of three full preparatory sessions, in which the key points of the summit communiqué were prenegotiated, beginning about four months before the summit itself, together with a follow-up session six months afterward. "The sherpas' group became a new kind of international institution," reported one participant. "It was the collective sense that emerged there about issues and priorities and bargains that determined the summit agenda."

Summitry became a year-round, results-oriented enterprise, spilling well beyond the confines of a single weekend gathering of heads of government. The summit preparations exerted a gravitational pull on virtually all ongoing discussions of any significant international issue. The line between follow-up for the last summit and preparation for the next became blurred, as did the line between summitry and ordinary intercourse among governments. The summit process came to involve most of the major international economic organizations, including the OECD, the IMF, and the GATT, as well as bilateral and multilateral contacts among the summit countries. In short, the summit became the focus of Western economic diplomacy. The new approach was symbolized by changes in the venue of summitry: Instead of being surrounded by the luxury of country homes and beachfront hotels, the summits of the late 1970s were held in work-a-day sites in London, Bonn, and Tokyo.

Without question, the single most important factor that encouraged the institutionalization of summitry after 1976 was steady pressure from the Americans. Indeed, even before the advent of Jimmy Carter's Trilateralists, Secretary of State Kissinger had advocated a relatively structured approach to Western summitry, with "cooperative decisions" and systematic follow-up. But in retrospect it seems inevitable that regardless of the attitudes of the Americans, the summits would have become more formal, more elaborate, and more bureaucratized. As one European alumnus of the Library Group observed, "Most institutions have started as a 'library group,' but almost all library groups, if they survive, become institutions." In later years the ills of institutionalized summitry would be blamed on the innovations of the Carter years, but during the late 1970s this more systematic approach to summitry was widely hailed. Even a somewhat skeptical Le Monde, for example, welcomed what it termed " institutionalized Trilateralism."[10]

In substantive terms, the incoming Carter Administration proposed to use summit-linked negotiations to apply Keynesian policies on a global basis. Recovery was sought through a coordinated program of reflation, led by the "locomotive" economies of the United States, Germany, and Japan. This suggestion received considerable support from Britain and the other weaker countries, as well as the OECD and many private economists, who argued that it would overcome international payments imbalances and speed growth all around. On the other hand, the proposal was resisted by the Germans and the Japanese, who complained that prudent and successful economic managers should not be asked to bail out irresolute and spendthrift governments.

The London summit of May 6–8, 1977, provided only interlocutory responses to the main items on the agenda. Although the Germans and Japanese avoided commitments to fiscal expansion, they did agree to ambitious growth targets. A heated controversy about Jimmy Carter's nuclear nonproliferation policy was defused by an agreement to begin a joint study of the nuclear fuel cycle. No substantive progress was made on trade issues, although United States trade envoy Robert Strauss and his colleagues received marching orders to proceed with the Tokyo Round trade negotiations. In the short run the London summit was described by many commentators as a "failure"; but over the next several years all these initiatives would come to fruition.

By early 1978 the American locomotive was moving under full steam, reducing unemployment, but also engendering a massive trade deficit and triggering a steady decline in the dollar. Many foreign observers shared Schmidt's worries about the Americans' uncontrolled appetite for imported oil and their apparent unconcern about monetary stability. All sides conceded that the world economy was in serious trouble, but it was not clear which was more to blame — tight-fisted German and Japanese fiscal policies, or slack-jawed United States energy and monetary policies.

In early April the neutron bomb controversy brought personal relations between Jimmy Carter and Helmut Schmidt to a new low. However, the institutional machinery of summitry continued to hum, and at virtually this same moment the outlines of a possible economic policy package deal for the forthcoming summit began to emerge. The Germans would agree to specific reflationary measures, amounting to one percent of GNP, and in return, the Americans would commit themselves to a series of energy initiatives, particularly the decontrol of domestic oil prices. Secondary but still important elements in the Bonn accord would include a Japanese commitment to export restraint and reconfirmation of an earlier agreement on domestic growth, American recognition of the risks of inflation, and acquiescence by the other countries (particularly the reluctant French) to a successful conclusion of the Multilateral Trade Negotiations. At the summit itself in Bonn on July 16–17, 1978, after some intense bargaining about the details, this package was approved, the clearest case of a summit deal that left all participants happier than when they arrived.

Remarkably, virtually all the crucial pledges of the Bonn summit were redeemed. The Germans and Japanese delivered additional reflation, the Americans (somewhat belatedly) delivered anti-inflationary policies and lower oil imports, and the others ratified the Tokyo Round agreement, liberalizing world commerce. At the time, most international economic observers, including such defenders of orthodoxy as the IMF and the Basle club of central bankers, welcomed the policies agreed at Bonn.

In retrospect, however, opinions differ on the economic merits of the Bonn package. Many Germans and Japanese (though not all) now argue that their stimulus measures contributed to subsequent budget deficits and inflation, although other experts maintain that additional stimulus was the right medicine in July 1978, and attribute the subsequent inflation to exogenous factors, especially the Iranian revolution and the second oil crisis. All agree that oil price decontrol in the United States was a success. This is not the place to resolve these questions of economic assessment. For present purposes, it is important to note two crucial features of this rare case of genuine international policy coordination.

First, the Bonn package involved a linkage among several different sectors—trade, energy, and fiscal policy—a linkage that was fundamentally political, so to speak, and not functional. Because in the modern state such distinct sectors are normally handled by different bureaucracies and respond to different domestic constituencies, cross-sector trade-offs rarely can be accomplished without the active involvement of the chief executive. Yet without such cross-issue linkage, important positive-sum international games may never be concluded.[11] For example, there was no possible German concession within the energy field that could have induced the American energy concession.

A second feature of the politics of the Bonn accord is even more revealing: Agreement was possible only because a powerful minority within each key government actually favored on domestic grounds the policy that was being demanded internationally. In the German case, for example, a political process that had been catalyzed by foreign pressures but orchestrated by expansionists within the Schmidt government, led to a situation in which a revision of German economic policy would have been highly likely, even if in the end the international pressure had eased. In effect, despite Schmidt's public protests, the Chancellor let himself be pushed into a policy that he probably favored on domestic grounds, but would have found costly and perhaps impossible to pursue without (in the words of one of his closest advisors) the "tailwind" provided by the summit.

A broadly similar analysis applies to the politics of the Japanese contribution, as pro-stimulus Japanese officials exploited American pressure. Without internal divisions in the Japanese government, it is unlikely that the foreign demands would have been met, but without the external pressure, it is even more unlikely that the Japanese expansionists could have overridden the powerful Ministry of Finance.[12]

In the American case, too, internal politicking reinforced, and was reinforced by, the international pressure. Key officials within the Administration strongly favored a tougher energy policy. Indeed, during the summit preparations several American negotiators had privately urged their German counterparts to put more pressure on the Administration to reduce oil imports. After the summit, the President's commitment to his colleagues at Bonn played a central role in the heated intramural debate about the Administration's energy policy, and was probably crucial in the final decontrol decision.

In short, in each case the domestic advocates of the internationally desired policy were able to use the summit process to shift the internal balance of power in their favor. In the end, each leader was doing what he believed to be in his own and his nation's interest, even though not all his aides agreed. Yet without the summit he probably would not (or could not) so readily have done what he was doing. In that sense, the deal struck at Bonn represented a successful meshing of domestic and international pressures.

The Bonn meeting closed a cycle of summits concerned primarily with fostering recovery from the recession induced by the first oil shock. In retrospect, the first quartet of summits can be seen to have focused on coordinating the economic policies of the participants in increasing scope and detail. Bonn, however, represented the end of an era for the demand management school of economic policy within the summit process. Severe international payments imbalances had been corrected, unemployment was headed down, and concern began to shift to the stubborn problem of inflation. Within less than a year, Jimmy Carter had turned toward more restrictive policies, Margaret Thatcher had ousted Labour, and the rise of the Ayatollah Khomeini and an emboldened OPEC had transformed the agenda of world economic problems and, with it, the nature of summitry.

By the time the summiteers gathered in Tokyo on June 28–29, 1979, energy and inflation dominated their thoughts. Monetary restraint became the new orthodoxy, and the leaders had little difficulty in agreeing on the slogan of "nonaccommodation" of the oil price shock. In the summit deliberations on energy, however, chaos prevailed. The sherpas' preliminary work had been overtaken by turbulence in the spot market and by shifting national policies. For the first time, summiteers had to grapple with the unpredictable twists of an immediate crisis, and the Japanese chairman, Masayoshi Ohira, was unprepared to guide the debate. Midway through the first day, the plenary discussion stumbled to a halt.

In the language of game theory, the Western nations found themselves in a classic "prisoner's dilemma": All would benefit if they could reduce their collective demand for imported oil, but each nation individually would be better off if it did not limit consumption, regardless of what the others did.[13] The logic of collective action in this case required that each country make a credible, mutually binding commitment to reduce oil imports.[14] In principle, the summit was a particularly useful venue for addressing this dilemma. First, all the major countries whose involvement was necessary were represented, yet their number was small enough for the responsibility of each to be clear. Second, the visibility and authority of the summiteers made their mutual commitments more credible, for it is costly to renege on a commitment by the head of government.

After much bilateral and multilateral haggling, the Tokyo summiteers finally reached agreement on individual oil import targets for 1979–80 and for 1985, as well as on a variety of other energy initiatives. In retrospect, officials in the participating countries, as well as impartial observers at the International Energy Agency, believe that the Tokyo decisions did have a significant impact on national energy policies, strengthening the hands of conservationists. However, the effects were more symbolic than practical. Given the haze of uncertainty surrounding estimates of future demand, and given the realities of the prisoner's dilemma, each country sought to minimize its commitment. As a result, the agreed targets were too high to constrain imports effectively (with the possible exception of the Japanese, who had been unprepared for the turn of events in Tokyo), and consequently the collective gains were minimal. In the final analysis, government energy policies were less important in accounting for the subsequent reduction of demand than the direct effect of price rises and the unexpectedly severe world recession.

The risks of an unscripted summit discussion had become manifest at Tokyo. Consequently, the preparations for the next meeting, held in Venice on June 22–23, 1980, were more meticulous than ever before. A wide measure of agreement was reached ahead of time on a long-term energy program and on other economic issues, leaving frustratingly little room for any contribution by the leaders themselves. This harmony among the allies on economic policy contrasted sharply with their discord over political issues. Their divergent reactions to the Soviet invasion of Afghanistan had crystallized and exacerbated the deepening transatlantic (and especially German–American) rift over East–West relations. On the fringes of the summit, Carter and Schmidt had an angry exchange about the NATO double-track missile decision, but thanks to a ham-handed Soviet propaganda initiative on the eve of the summit, the summiteers were able to agree on a collective statement condemning the occupation of Afghanistan. In historical perspective, the Venice meeting was notable primarily as a harbinger of an era in which disputes over East–West matters would begin to rival economics on the summit agenda.

Deflating expectations: 1981–1983

By summit time 1981, the cast of characters had radically changed. Five of the eight summiteers who gathered in Ottawa on June 19–21 were newcomers, led by Ronald Reagan and François Mitterrand. The ideological dialect between the affable conservative homilist and the contemplative socialist intellectual would dominate the summits of the early 1980s, just as the summits of the late 1970s had been structured by the force field between Jimmy Carter and Helmut Schmidt. The issues that had preoccupied earlier summits—German and Japanese reflation, the weak dollar, and energy—were replaced by an entirely new set of controversies that would dominate the Reagan–Mitterrand era—United States interest rates and the strong dollar, East–West trade, and the East–West military balance.

The concern of the non-Americans about currency instability and high real interest rates increased as their economies plunged uenxpectedly into the longest and deepest recession in half a century, but there was less unanimity on the causes and cures. In the new ideological climate, few of the leaders were prepared to call for a looser American monetary policy, and most thought exchange rate intervention would offer at best temporary relief. Complaints about the United States budget deficit mounted, even among Reagan's closest allies, and their frustration over the gridlock in American fiscal policy intensified.

Traditional transatlantic differences over East–West trade had become even sharper with the advent of "economic warriors" in the new American Administration. Even outspoken anti-Communists like Margaret Thatcher were dismayed by the suggestions of retroactivity and extraterritoriality implicit in the Reagan Administration's assault on the proposed trans-Siberian pipeline. There was less overt resistance to American suggestions for halting the leakage of militarily relevant Western technology, but here too progress proved difficult.

Like the introduction to a sonata, the Ottawa summit contained an exposition of virtually all the themes that would be developed in subsequent summits of the early 1980s. However, the new leaders were too fresh in office to begin thinking of adjustments to their programs. Virtually every participant returned home to announce that no policy changes were contemplated as a result of the summit—"No change in direction," said Treasury Secretary Regan. "Not one line," averred Mitterrand.

Strenuous efforts were made in the run-up to the 1982 summit to address the two central controversies. On international monetary affairs, the sherpas achieved a delicate accommodation of the Franco–American dispute. On the one hand, a joint study would be undertaken about the effectiveness of past currency interventions; and on the other, the Group of Five finance ministers, together with the Managing Director of the IMF, would periodically conduct "multilateral surveillance" of their respective economic policies. The key to this double-barreled compromise was that it enabled the two sides to agree on procedures, while continuing to disagree about where those procedures were likely to lead.

Meanwhile, a separate group of negotiators sought to resolve the differences over East–West trade. The Americans pushed for strict curbs on credits to the Soviet bloc, in return for which the President would lift the threat of an embargo against Western equipment and technology intended for the Soviet pipeline. However, the Europeans were chary of the prospect of East–West economic warfare. The foreign ministries of France, Germany, and the United States sought language that might narrow the differences, but resistance to compromise remained strong in Mitterrand's Elysée Palace, Schmidt's Chancellery, and Reagan's White House.

As the leaders arrived for the Versailles summit on June 4–6, 1982, there was talk of a package deal, linking American concessions on monetary policy to greater European caution on East–West trade. However, the situation did not resemble at all the comparable stage of the 1978 summit; now there was far from universal agreement on the contours of the package. When Mitterrand hailed the fragile compromise on monetary matters as the first step in "reform of the international monetary system," Secretary Regan retorted that the French President "didn't read the fine print." Meanwhile, Mitterrand backed away from a preliminary agreement on East–West credit, and the summiteers themselves spent a marathon, nerve-wracking, nitpicking final session, seeking phraseology to bridge their disagreement.

The final declaration went some way toward meeting the American demands, but the gossamer fabric of compromise began to unravel as soon as the summiteers left for home. The Germans proclaimed that the accord permitted East–West "business as usual," and Mitterrand ruled out any change in French policy. The impression that the Europeans were reneging gave ammunition to hard-liners in the White House, who had felt all along that the President had been bamboozled (and badly advised). On June 18, far from relaxing the pipeline sanctions as the Europeans had hoped, Reagan extended his ban to United States subsidiaries and licensees abroad. A firestorm of protest swept Europe, as the pipeline decision followed on the heels of an acrimonious conflict over European steel exports. The usually sober *Financial Times* concluded that "the components of the Western Alliance are coming apart."[15]

Summitry had clearly exacerbated the conflict, not restrained it. What had gone wrong?

First, the issue of East–West economics had been poorly prepared for the summit. In a classic failure of diplomacy, neither side fully understood the depth of feeling on the other, and no one on the American side had both the technical expertise and the political clout to strike a deal and make it stick. Moreover, each of the presidents disavowed efforts by his own foreign minister to reach a compromise, Mitterrand during the summit itself and Reagan two weeks later. The involvement of the heads of government had clearly made things worse—a powerful indictment of summitry.

A further serious mistake, shared again by both sides, was the failure to recognize that both the monetary agreement and the accord on East–West trade could endure only so long as their essential ambiguities were left unchallenged. The most that could be hoped for at Versailles was the beginning of a slow process of mutual adjustment, but that process was aborted by the escalating sequence of divergent press briefings. In the "global village," rhetoric intended primarily for internal consumption can have international consequences.

Most fundamentally, foreign and domestic forces in 1982 were not pushing in the same direction, as they had been in 1978. Virtually no one in the Reagan Administration (at least in 1982) favored international monetary reform, and virtually no one in power in Bonn or Paris wanted to use economic leverage against the Soviets. Indeed, the domestic pressures (particularly on the East–West issue) encouraged the leaders' own obstinate instincts.

On the other hand, the summit confrontation and its bitter summer sequel obscured the areas of agreement that had in fact been achieved. The monetary accord represented a certain accommodation between the French and Americans, and in fact this compromise itself survived the post-summit polemics. Moreover, almost immediately after Versailles the economic policies of the two governments began independently to converge, as Mitterrand was forced to devalue the franc and tighten his fiscal policy, while the Federal

Reserve (worried about the international debt crisis) loosened American monetary policy. On East–West trade, by the following winter the new Secretary of State Shultz had succeeded in knitting together a set of joint studies which allowed the Americans to climb down from their exposed position. In effect, although the twin agreements reached at Versailles were overturned two weeks later, these agreements represented a point of equilibrium among the contending forces to which the alliance would return. In short, Versailles would prove to be a substantive success, though a procedural disaster.

Ever since the Venice summit of 1980, discontent about institutionalized summitry—about the proliferation of preparatory activities, about the bloated, prenegotiated communiques—had been mounting among the participants. The new summiteers, unlike their predecessors, viewed summitry as a set routine, not something they had molded to fit their own backgrounds and personalities. Six of the eight summiteers in 1977 and 1978 had been ex-finance ministers, but of those who would gather in 1983 (and 1984), none were. Moreover, the leaders of the successor generation were generally less internationalist in outlook, more insular and domestically oriented, than their predecessors. In terms of substance, as opposed to appearance, they tended to take summitry less seriously. They devoted less of their own energies and those of their closest aides to summit preparations than their predecessors did. The summit was now seen less as an institution for managing differences among the allies than as a kind of international jousting match, with each summiteer presented as a national paladin, vigorously (and usually victoriously) defending national interests against obtuse and even malevolent foreigners.

Finally, international policy concertation (like all forms of intervention in the free market) was ideologically uncongenial to the more conservative newcomers. Rightward political trends during 1983 reinforced this attitude (and incidentally evicted the last of the founding fathers, Helmut Schmidt). In the new climate of opinion, summitry seemed part of the problem, not part of the solution. As the German business daily *Handelsblatt* editorialized,

> The internationalization of economic problems fostered by the economic summits all too often can exempt governments and politicians from the duty of putting their own house in order more decisively.[16]

Instead of coordinating an interlocked but nationally differentiated set of macroeconomic policies, the summits of the 1980s offered a simpler, more uniform prescription: control inflation by checking monetary growth and reducing budget deficits.

This transformation in outlook was widespread, but it was most marked in the United States. Jimmy Carter's Trilateralists had had an expansive view of summitry, but the Reaganites feared that summitry might ensnare the President in international commitments that would cut across domestic priorities. Before his first summit, Reagan's sherpa had insisted that "there will be no concrete conclusion, no numbers in the communique, no specific policy agreements." After his third summit, the President himself—asked if he had changed any of his views as a result of the encounter—would reply with disarming candor, "Not really." "You don't go to the summit for the purpose of changing your mind or making policy deals," explained one of Reagan's aides. "Nobody in that group has any political accountability except to his people back home."

To be sure, in the first two years of the Reagan–Mitterrand era, despite their complaints about institutionalized summitry, both presidents had tried to use the summit process to achieve important policy objectives, such as changing United States monetary policy or curbing East–West trade. But the Versailles fiasco made clear the hazards of excessive ambition in this new era. Another visible failure might doom the whole summit enterprise and (not incidentally) discredit the participants. Consequently, 1983 saw a joint effort to lower expectations and muffle controversy, a kind of conspiracy to avoid catastrophe.

It was not the first time that aspirations for a less structured summit had been expressed, but they were more nearly realized in 1983. Formal preparations for Williamsburg began later and focused less on substance and more on logistics and public relations. This simplified approach was possible, first, because lowered expectations allowed lighter preparation. Second, negotiations on many of the issues in the background to the summit were decentralized to other forums—East–West economics to the OECD, the IEA, COCOM, and NATO; trade issues to trade ministers; monetary and macroeconomic issues to finance ministers; and so on. In short, despite denigration of "bureaucratic" preparations, much of what would be proclaimed at Williamsburg had been carefully elaborated by officials beforehand. The summit itself was "debureaucratized," but the treatment of the issues was not.

By the time that the leaders met in the colonial Virginia capital on June 28–30, 1983, most of the previous year's controversies had been shelved. The "Shultz studies" had served as the basis for a "nonaggression pact" between the White House and the Elysée Palace over East–West trade, and a week before the summit Reagan declared that there was now "peace among us" on the issue. The Administration's two-year all-out assault on this issue had had "consciousness-raising" effects in Europe, but it was hard for most observers to see gains sufficient to offset the damage that had been done to Western solidarity.

The shifts in French and American economic policy, the conservative political trends in most of the participating countries, and the belated, but powerful United States economic recovery had all combined to leave the French isolated on most economic issues. Some weeks before the summit, Mitterrand had caused a stir by calling for "a new Bretton Woods," but as the leftist French daily *Liberation* observed, to pound on the table you need a fist, and "France doesn't have one."[17] To be sure, on interest rates and the budget deficit, the Americans were attacked even by their ideological allies in Britain, Germany, and Japan, but Reagan and Regan remained unmoved. Two days after the summit, CEA Chairman Feldstein wrote plaintively that "perhaps Williamsburg has made a contribution toward raising everyone's awareness of the importance of the dollar's high value and the role the anticipated budget deficits are playing in creating this problem,"[18] but there is no evidence that the message was received in the White House or the Treasury. The visitors returned to Bonn, London, and elsewhere, complaining privately about the Americans' "disastrous," "dogmatic," and "selfish" attitude.

The most striking achievement of Williamsburg was the joint statement on defense, arms control, and the Euromissiles. This declaration marked a new stage in the long-term trend toward an increasing quotient of "political" deliberations at the "economic" summit. The statement occasioned a debate of almost unprecedented vigor among the heads, concerning both the implicit geographical extension of the Atlantic Alliance to include Japan and the relative firmness or flexibility of the West's bargaining position in the Geneva Euromissile talks. In the end, however, the summiteers agreed on language that repeated well-established Western positions. On the other hand, the endorsements by France and Japan, neither of which had taken part in the NATO double-track decision, were symbolically important. Whatever the declaration's short-term impact on the Euromissile controversy, it was probably more significant as a landmark in the growing involvement of Japan in Western security discussions, which is one of the most notable side benefits of the first decade of Western summitry.

Summits: so what?

Any observer of the Western summits is bound to ask "So what?" Have the summits played a significant role in the international political economy, or have they been evanescent public relations spectaculars? Have the summits helped reduce tensions among the allies, or have they made things worse? Generalizations are difficult, for summits have a more protean character than other international institutions. They have changed in shape, in function, and even in importance, in response to the changing personal predilections of the participants around the table. Nevertheless, some things are clear from the record of the last decade.

First, the original concept of an informal, personalized Library Group for the world's leaders was unrealistic. Heads of government cannot meet secretly and informally, cannot divorce themselves from their official machinery, cannot hope to range widely across complex problems in 48 hours without detailed preparation. Preliminary negotiations have been essential to nearly all summit successes, from the Rambouillet monetary accord to the battle averted at Williamsburg over East–West trade.

On the other hand, face-to-face encounters at the summit can sometimes lubricate international relations. "You would think twice about taking actions against a friend," observes one ex-summiteer. Moreover, the prospect of meeting their colleagues forces chief executives to focus on the international dimension of problems they usually see in domestic terms. The Italians have a word for it: well-placed observers there say that the most important effect of the summits has been to *sprovincializzare* ("deprovincialize") Italian leaders, a phenomenon paralleled in other summit countries. For example, one Reagan aide notes that "the qualms that [German Chancellor Helmut] Kohl had on the political statement [about the Euromissiles in 1983] probably did a lot by way of educating the President."

It is also unrealistic to cast the summit as a kind of grand assizes of the Western world, a supranational forum rendering collective decisions on the great problems facing the industrial democracies. As the summits of 1977–78 or of 1981–83 illustrate, these encounters must be seen as episodes in a continuing process of international accommodation that flows across a variety of institutions, rather than as climactic, free-standing moments of decision. Summits are stages in a marathon, not isolated sprints.

Moreover, as one distinguished summiteer frankly points out,

> Every nation goes there, first, to explain its own problems, and secondly, to see how far it can get others to help it with its own problems. I doubt if many of us go there saying, "Here is the central problem of the world economic strategy. What measures should we all take to improve it?" Basically, we are most concerned about our own domestic problems.

On the other hand, summits at their most effective have represented precisely the recognition by these politicians that they could not solve their own problems without addressing world problems. If no significant domestic pressure for an internationally cooperative line of policy exists, summitry cannot create it, but where it does exist, the summit process can amplify its effectiveness.

Much of what is important about summits does not happen at the summit and is not specified in the summit communiqué. As Henry Nau, one of Reagan's summit team, has written: "The real test of summits is their impact on perspectives and policies over time, not their drama and specific decisions when they occupy center stage in the public eye."[19] To understand summitry, as to understand a good magic show, one must often glance away from the center of attention; one must look for the indirect effects of the summit process in other international arenas and especially in domestic decision-making.

By engaging the prestige and the power of the highest authorities in each country, summits energize the policy process, both nationally and internationally. For example, the summits of Rambouillet, Bonn, and Tokyo provided essential impetus to negotiations on monetary reform, trade, and energy, respectively. In 1983 widely shared concern about the prospect of

a second successive "failed" summit encouraged accommodation on international monetary issues and especially East–West trade. Summits have
often been important less for what happened *at* them than for what happened
in anticipation of them.

As a rule, national leaders go to summits to get international legiti-
mation for their present policies, not to discuss changing those policies. By
definition, this sort of mutual reinforcement does not lead governments to
pursue policies that they would not otherwise wish to conduct, but it can
help them to pursue policies that would otherwise be more difficult to
implement domestically. Examples of this use of summitry range from Wilson on trade and Giscard on flexible exchange rates at Rambouillet to the
Germans, British, and Italians on Euromissile deployment at Williamsburg.

Formal policy commitments made at the summit have not been common, but they have sometimes been used very effectively in subsequent
bureaucratic battles. As one American summit participant noted,

> If a president commits himself to something at a summit, and you
> can cite that in a meeting, that's a damn powerful argument. The rest of
> the government may not always be impressed, but the president is.

Without adequate domestic resonance within each government, international pressure alone cannot produce agreement, no matter how sensible
a package may seem in purely economic terms. Summits cannot impose
cooperation; they can only facilitate it by shifting a closely balanced domestic
equilibrium. This is the lesson of the 1977–78 negotiations over the Bonn
package, and by contrast, the 1982 negotiations over monetary policy and
East–West trade.[20] Thus, ironically, international cooperation may be made
easier, not harder, by divisions within governments.

Generally speaking, the summit process tends to strengthen the hands
of the more internationalist factions within each of the participating governments. Aside from the Bonn package, this pattern has been illustrated
repeatedly on questions of protectionism and trade liberalization. This, of
course, is why domestic advisors in more than one government have cas-
tigated the summit process as a kind of "internationalist conspiracy," a
critique that was almost as common among domestically oriented liberal
Democrats in the Carter White House as it is among conservative Reagan-
auts.

A rather different critique sometimes offered of summitry is that it
short-circuits the regular diplomatic process and undermines the traditional
international institutions.[21] However, actual instances are hard to find in
the historical record. The most successful Western summits have in fact
been closely tied to actions in the existing institutions. Several summits,
such as those of 1975, 1978, and even 1982, have given useful impetus to
ongoing diplomatic negotiations. A more accurate criticism is that the summits have not succeeded in launching new international negotiations, but it

is notable that at Williamsburg both major protagonists sought to use the summit in this way, the French for international monetary reform, the Americans for a new trade round. It may be true that the effectiveness of many of the conventional international organizations, such as the OECD and the GATT, has declined in recent years, but if so, summitry is not to blame. More important factors have been the waning of American leadership and the divisive impact of economic adversity. Conversely, there is no evidence that the recent scaling down of summit ambitions is rejuvenating traditional channels of economic diplomacy.[22]

The history of Western summitry makes clear that the politics of international policy coordination is even more complex than the economics of interdependence. Faced with this dilemma, recent summiteers have lowered their expectations. In a world without interdependencies, this sort of congenial live-and-let-live anarchy could ensure international comity. However, in the real world of the 1980s, uncoordinated actions can leave everyone worse off. For example, the absence of coordination among the major governments after the second oil shock seems to have led to competitive deflation and to a steeper decline than any single government anticipated.[23] Moreover, in the absence of policy coordination, world markets impose convergence more brusquely and less efficiently. France learned this lesson in 1981–82, and it may well be that the United States will be taught the same in 1984–85. Heads of government cannot achieve miracles. If they attempt too much, they may fall short. But there are some problems which none but they can tackle and which they can solve only if they work together.

NOTES

This essay draws heavily on Robert D. Putnam and Nicholas Bayne, *Hanging Together: The Seven-Power Summits* (Cambridge: Harvard University Press, and London: Royal Institute of International Affairs and Heinemann, 1984).

1. Besides Shultz, Schmidt, and Giscard, other alumni of this little group include Paul Volcker, Chairman of the Federal Reserve, Karl-Otto Poehl, President of the Bundesbank, and (somewhat later) Jacques de Larosière, Managing Director of the International Monetary Fund.
2. See Richard N. Cooper, "Economic Interdependence and Foreign Policy in the Seventies," *World Politics*, v. 24 (January 1972), pp. 159–181. Subsequent work on the political dimension of economic interdependence includes Miriam Camps, *The Management of Interdependence: A Preliminary View* (New York: Council on Foreign Relations, 1974); Andrew Shonfield and others, *International Economic Relations of the Western World, 1959–1971* (London: Oxford University Press, for the Royal Institute of International Affairs, 1976), esp. vol. I, pp. 93–137; Robert O. Keohane and Joseph S. Nye, Jr., *Power and Interdependence: World Politics in Transition* (Boston: Little, Brown, 1977); Fred Hirsch and Michael Doyle, "Politization in the World Economy: Necessary Conditions for an International Economic Order," in Fred Hirsch, Michael Doyle, and Edward L. Morse, *Alternatives to Monetary Disorder* (New York: McGraw-Hill, 1977); Robert J. Gordon and Jacques Pelkmans, *Challenges to Interdependent Economies: The Industrial West in the Coming Decade* (New York: McGraw-Hill, 1979); and Miriam Camps and Cather-

ine Gwin, *Collective Management: The Reform of Global Economic Organizations* (New York: McGraw-Hill, 1981).

3. On problems of international policy coordination, see, for example, Marina v.N. Whitman, *Reflections of Interdependence: Issues for Economic Theory and U.S. Policy* (Pittsburgh: University of Pittsburgh Press, 1979); Ralph C. Bryant, *Money and Monetary Policy in Interdependent Nations* (Washington, D.C.: Brookings Institution, 1980); Richard N. Cooper, "Economic Interdependence and Coordination of Economic Policies," in *Handbook for International Economy*, Ronald Jones and Peter B. Kenen, eds. (New York: North Holland, 1984); and the works collected in *International Economic Policy: Theory and Evidence*, Rudiger Dornbusch and Jacob A. Frenkel, eds. (Baltimore: Johns Hopkins University Press, 1979). Some monetarist theorists of the "rational expectations" school are skeptical about the utility of international policy coordination.

4. Economists and political scientists have recently begun to apply game-theoretic concepts to the analysis of the international economy. See, for example, Bryant, *Money and Monetary Policy in Interdependent Nations*, esp. pp. 453–481; Cooper, "Economic Interdependence and Coordination of Economic Policies," and the works cited therein; Robert O. Keohane, "u.s. Foreign Economic Policy Toward Other Advanced Capitalist States," in *Eagle Entangled: u.s. Foreign Policy in a Complex World*, Kenneth A. Oye, Donald Rothchild, and Robert J. Lieber, eds. (New York: Longman, 1979), pp. 107–09; Arthur A. Stein, "Coordination and Collaboration: Regimes in an Anarchic World," *International Organization*, v. 36 (Spring 1982), pp. 299–324.

5. On the so-called "theory of hegemonic stability," see Robert O. Keohane, *Beyond Hegemony: Cooperation and Discord in the World Political Economy* (Princeton: Princeton University Press, 1984); Charles P. Kindleberger, *The World in Depression, 1929–1939* (Berkeley: University of California Press, 1973); Marina v.N. Whitman, "Leadership without Hegemony," *Foreign Policy*, no. 20 (1975), pp. 138–64; Robert Gilpin, u.s. *Power and the Multinational Corporation: The Political Economy of Foreign Direct Investment* (New York: Basic Books, 1975); Stephen D. Krasner, "State Power and the Structure of International Trade," *World Politics*, v. 28 (1976), pp. 317–47; and Timothy J. McKeown, "Tariffs and Hegemonic Stability Theory," *International Organization*, vol. 37 (Winter 1983), pp. 73–91. See also *America as an Ordinary Country: u.s. Foreign Policy in the Future*, Richard Rosecrance, ed. (Ithaca: Cornell University Press, 1976), and David P. Calleo and Benjamin M. Rowland, *America and the World Political Economy: Atlantic Dreams and National Realities* (Bloomington: Indiana University Press, 1973).

6. Empirical scholarship on the Western summits is still rare. Relevant works include George de Menil and Anthony M. Solomon, *Economic Summitry* (New York: Council on Foreign Relations, 1983); Elke Thiel, "Economic Summits from Rambouillet to Venice," *Aussenpolitik*, vol. 32 (1981), pp. 3–14, and "Economic Conflict Before and After Versailles," *Aussenpolitik*, v. 33 (1982), pp. 356–369; Henry H. Fowler and W. Randolph Burgess, *Harmonizing Economic Policy: Summit Meetings and Collective Leadership: Report of the Atlantic Council's Working Group on Economic Policy* (Boulder, Colorado: Westview Press, 1977); Charles Robinson and William C. Turner, co-chairmen, Harald B. Malmgren, rapporteur, *Summit Meetings and Collective Leadership in the 1980's* (Washington, d.c: The Atlantic Council, 1980); J. Robert Schaetzel and H. B. Malmgren, "Talking Heads," *Foreign Policy*, no. 39 (Summer, 1980), pp. 130–142; *Western Summits and Europe: Rivalry, Cooperation, and Partnership*, Cesare Merlini, ed. (London: Croom Helm, 1984). Several interesting works have appeared in German, French, and Japanese: Dieter Hiss, "Weltwirtschaftsgipfel: Betrachtungen eines Insiders [World Economic Summits: Observations of an Insider]," in *Empirische Wirtschaftsforschung: Konzeptionen, Verfahren und Ergebnisse*, Joachim Frohn and Reiner Staeglin, eds. (Berlin: Duncker and Humblot, 1980); Rainer Hellmann, *Weltwirtschaftsgipfel woze?* [Whither Economic Summits?] (Baden-Baden: Nomos, 1982); Marie-Claude Smouts, "Les Sommets des pays industrialisés," *Revue de Droit International* (1980), pp. 668–685; George

de Menil, "De Rambouillet à Versailles: un bilan des sommets économiques," Politique Etrangère, no. 2 (June 1982), pp. 403–417; Yoichi Funabashi, *Philosophy of the Summits* [in Japanese] (Tokyo: Asahi Shinbun-sha, 1980).

7. The Italian Prime Minister had been included on the guest list over French resistance. As hosts the next year, the Americans succeeded in adding the Canadian Prime Minister, and in 1977 the President of the European Commission joined the group, albeit as a kind of second-class citizen. Thereafter the membership list in this exclusive club was closed.

8. One unannounced purpose of the meeting was to allow Ford, Schmidt, Giscard, and Callaghan to discuss responses to the growing power of the Communists in Italy.

9. *San Juan Star*, June 28, 1976, as cited in George de Menil and Anthony M. Solomon, *Economic Summitry* (New York: Council on Foreign Relations, 1983), p. 20.

10. *Le Monde*, Paris, July 19, 1978.

11. See Robert D. Tollison and Thomas D. Willett, "An Economic Theory of Mutually Advantageous Issue Linkages in International Negotiations," *International Organization*, vol. 33 (Autumn, 1979), pp. 425–49.

12. See I. M. Destler and Hisao Mitsuyu, "Locomotives on Different Tracks: Macroeconomic Diplomacy, 1977–1979," in *Coping with U.S.-Japanese Economic Conflicts*, I. M. Destler and Hideo Sato, eds. (Lexington, Mass.: D. C. Heath, 1982), pp. 271–93.

13. The original "prisoner's dilemma" refers to a pair of accomplices held in separate cells, each of whom is told that if he confesses and implicates his partner, he will be let off lightly, but if he is silent, while his partner confesses, he will be severely punished. If both prisoners remain silent, they will both escape punishment, but unable to coordinate their stories, each has a powerful incentive to confess, and thus both end up being punished.

14. The classic analysis of this dilemma is provided in Mancur Olson, *The Logic of Collective Action* (Cambridge: Harvard University Press, 1965).

15. *Financial Times*, London, June 30, 1982.

16. *Handelsblatt*, Düsseldorf, June 4–5, 1982.

17. As cited in *New York Times*, May 21, 1983.

18. *New York Times*, June 2, 1983.

19. *Washington Times*, December 26, 1983.

20. Potential transnational coalitions are not always consummated, as evidenced by the failure of the internal critics of the Reagan Administration's fiscal policy in 1983–84 to join forces with the foreign critics. This is one more illustration of the fact that summitry in the 1980s has less "bite" in national policy-making than was characteristic of the 1970s.

21. See J. Robert Schaetzel and H. B. Malmgren, "Talking Heads," *Foreign Policy*, no. 39 (Summer, 1980), pp. 130–42.

22. One development worth following is the new "multilateral surveillance" mechanism, involving the Group of Five finance ministers and the IMF Managing Director. This body is, of course, the lineal descendant of the Library Group. If the innovation succeeds in taking over the business of international economic policy coordination, it may mark the reversal of the process by which Western summitry was originally instituted. The enhancement of the Group of Five partially reverses the 1975–77 decisions that added Italy, Canada, and the European Community to the charmed circle, and bureaucratically, it represents the reconquest by finance ministries of some of the turf that summitry had forced them to relinquish to chief executives, foreign ministries, and other economic agencies.

23. See OECD *Economic Outlook*, no. 33 (July, 1983).

2

Ethics and foreign policy

RICHARD N. COOPER

Maurits C. Boas Professor of International Economics, Harvard University

JOSEPH S. NYE, JR.

Clarence Dillon Professor of International Affairs, Harvard University

The United States is famous (or notorious) for introducing moral considerations into foreign policy. Indeed, some scholars have identified moralism as one of the unique characteristics of American policy.[1] Idealists have applauded America's commitment to promoting its values in world politics. Realists have deplored the effects of moralism, arguing that moral righteousness often blinds the mind to potentially disastrous policy consequences. To some extent, the applause and condemnation in the realist–idealist debates over American foreign policy are beside the point. Given the nature of American political culture, there will always be a demand for moral expression in foreign policy. To ignore it in one period is likely to lay the grounds for exaggerating it in the next. By trying to banish moral arguments, realists have abdicated the responsibility to discipline moral arguments to standards of clarity, consistency, and causal analysis. The appropriate question is not how to avoid, but how to handle morality in foreign policy.

Obviously we must start with certain normative assumptions. Since we are writing about American foreign policy, we assume the acceptance of democratic procedures, and the values of a modern liberal democracy. This still leaves wide room for moral disagreements over the values to be expressed in American foreign policy. In moral reasoning, there are always some basic normative premises. Some people merely state these premises and refuse to discuss or examine their consistency or the logic of the policy positions derived from them. This is primitive assertion rather than moral reasoning. Our interest is with arguments about morality and American foreign policy that go beyond primitive assertion. We will look first at the implications of four different moral perspectives, and then at the different roles of the citizen and the statesman.

23

Four approaches to ethics in international politics

International politics is not a particularly hospitable ground for moral argument. Different cultures have different views of right and wrong; there is no overall government to balance the sometimes conflicting claims of order and justice; and there is an extra complexity of causation that arises from having to consider three levels of analysis (the individual, the state, and the systems of states). Broadly speaking, there are four schools of thought about ethics and international politics: the skeptics, the realists, the cosmopolitans, and the state moralists.[2]

The *skeptic* sees international politics as an amoral realm. Obligation exists only where there is community which defines and recognizes rights and duties. Such communities exist only in weak forms at the international level, and this prevents international morality.

The *realist* accepts some moral obligation, but believes it is limited primarily to the instrumental value of order. The world of sovereign states is a world of self-help without the moderating effects of a common executive, legislature, or judiciary. In such a domain, the range of moral choices is severely constricted and order must precede justice. The government which attempts to indulge its moral preferences may fail in its duties to maintain the balance of power and preserve order. As Hans Morgenthau has written,

> The state has no right to let its moral disapprobation . . . get in the way of successful political action, itself inspired by the moral principle of national survival. . . . Realism, then, considers prudence . . . to be the supreme virtue in politics.[3]

The skeptics and realists play a useful role in reminding us that justice depends upon a degree of order and community, and that international moral crusades can lead to disorder, injustice, and consequences that are immoral even by the standards of the crusaders. But while it is true that international politics is less hospitable ground for moral argument than is domestic politics, it does not follow that morality is irrelevant in the international realm. Both statesmen and citizens constantly make moral judgments about international affairs. Survival may come first; but much of the international politics is not about survival. Choices among alternative courses of action must be made on many other issues, large and small, and these choices can be (and are) affected by moral values. Statesmen face choices with moral significance, and citizens often wish their leaders to express moral values in those choices. There are no strong institutions to enforce norms; but crude international institutions of law and diplomacy do preserve some degree of order and influence the attitude of governments. Moreover, many citizens hold multiple loyalties to several communities at the same time. They may wish their governments to follow policies which give expression to the rights and duties engendered by other communities in addition to those structured at the national level.

The *cosmopolitan* approach stresses the common nature of humanity. States and boundaries exist, but this does not endow them with moral significance. *Ought* does not follow from *is*. As David Luban has written,

> The rights of security and subsistence . . . are necessary for the enjoyment of any other rights at all. No one can do without them. Basic rights, therefore, are universal. They are not respectors of political boundaries, and require a universalist politics to implement them; even when this means breaching the wall of state sovereignty.[4]

While the cosmopolitan approach has the virtue of accepting transnational realities and avoids the sanctification of the nation-state, it also has serious drawbacks. First, since morality is in part about choices, then to underestimate the significance of states and boundaries is to fail to take into account the main features of the milieu in which choices must be made. As Stanley Hoffmann notes,

> Moral politics is an art of execution; principles unaccompanied by practical means or by an awareness of possible trade offs remind one of Peguy's famous comment about Kant—"his hands were pure, but he had no hands."[5]

Applying ethics to foreign policy is more than merely constructing philosophical arguments; it must be relevant to the domain in which moral choice is to be exercised. The other problem with the cosmopolitan approach is ethical; it discards the moral dimension of national politics. There are rights of people to live in communities and to express their own political choices autonomously. A pure cosmopolitan view which ignores these rights of self-determination fails to do justice to the difficult job of balancing rights in the international realm.

The fourth approach stresses *morality* among states and the significance of state sovereignty and self-determination. In this view, the rights of states are a collective form of their citizens' individual rights to life and liberty. The nation-state may be seen as a pooled expression of individual rights. It represents, as Michael Walzer sets forth,

> . . . the rights of contemporary men and women to live as members of a historic community and to express their inherited culture through political forms worked out among themselves. . . .[6]

Thus, there is a strong presumption against outside intervention. However, this presumption is not absolute. Foreigners have an obligation not to intervene unless the lack of fit between a government and the community that it represents is radically apparent. For example, Walzer would allow intervention to prevent massacre and enslavement; to balance a prior intervention in a civil war; or to assist secession movements that have demonstrated their representative character. This presumption and its exceptions are analogous to many of the existing rules of international law.

An alternative formulation of the state-moralist viewpoint is offered by John Rawls. Recognizing that people live in states, he asks what rules the states would choose or would have chosen for just relations among themselves if they did not know in advance how strong or wealthy they would be. The principles that Rawls derives—self-determination, nonintervention, and obligation to keep treaties—are again analogous to existing principles of international law.[7]

The virtues of the state-moralist approach is that it takes account of the reality of the way that international politics is at present structured, and conforms quite closely to existing principles of international law. The weakness in the approach is the weakness of the concept of self-determination. Who is the self that determines?

How do we know when there is a radical lack of fit between government and people? Must an oppressed group fight and prevail to demonstrate its claim to speak as a people worthy of international recognition? If so, is not might making right? Or as a critic asks,

> In Walzer's world, are there not self-identified political, economic, ethnic, or religious groups (for example, capitalists, democrats, communists, Moslems, the desperately poor) who would favor foreign intervention over Walzer's brand of national autonomy (and individual rights) if it would advance the set of rights, values, or interests at the core of their understanding of justice? . . . Why should Walzer's individual right to national autonomy be more basic than other human rights, such as freedom from terror, torture, material deprivation, illiteracy, and suppressed speech . . . ? Walzer's ideal is but one normative, philosophical conception among others, no more grounded and often less grounded in people's actual moral attitudes (and social identities) than other conceptions.[8]

In short, the state-moralist approach is particularly weak when it treats self-determination and national sovereignty as absolute principles which must come first in a lexical ordering of moral principles. In practice, peoples do want self-determination and autonomy, but they want other values as well. There is a constant problem of trade-offs and balancing moral desires.

The difference between cosmopolitans and state moralists is a difference over balancing national and transnational values. Since sophisticated cosmopolitans admit the political significance of boundaries, and sophisticated state moralists admit the possibility of duties beyond borders, the two positions tend to converge in practice. But they start with different presumptions, and thus specify different conditions for qualifying or overriding their presumptions as they are applied to particular cases. While we start our arguments from a state-moralist base, it is a qualified form of that position, and many of the qualifications lead to a position that could also be reached, albeit in a somewhat different manner, by some cosmopolitans and by some realists.

In common practice, many people judge morality by referring to the motives, the means, and the consequences of actions. It is easy to agree on the moral quality of actions which are good or bad on all three scores. And we might agree to rank low those acts which have good consequences that inadvertently and unforeseeably grew out of bad intentions. But there is less agreement about the ranking of two acts which both rest on good intentions, but one uses good means and produces bad consequences while the other uses bad means but produces good consequences. In practice, we judge particular means in terms of auxiliary principles such as double effect (having unintended but foreseeable consequences), omissions being (sometimes) less culpable than acts, and a general sense of proportionality. None of these principles is without pitfalls which are spelled out in the literature of moral philosophy, but used carefully, they allow us to introduce some order into our moral dilemmas.[9]

Ends, means, and consequences are all important in weighing competing moral claims. An action that passes the test on motives, means, and consequences still may be judged morally inferior if it precludes an alternative course of action with lower (moral) costs and/or higher moral benefits. Right versus wrong is often less difficult to handle than right versus right. This is doubly true in international politics where there is less agreement about what is right and where the consequences of actions are typically highly complex and often more difficult to estimate than in well-ordered domestic politics. But once again, the difficulty of moral reasoning in foreign policy does not justify our avoiding it; rather we must work harder to do it better.

Citizens and statesmen

Another complication in thinking about ethics and foreign policy is being clear about the different levels of analysis and relationships involved. We often speak of a state acting morally or immorally when we refer to its behavior toward the citizens of other states. But what do we mean when we speak of a state acting—all the citizens or just the top leaders? Do the citizens and the statesmen have the same moral duties to foreigners? And what are the obligations that citizens and statesmen owe to each other?

When we speak of states, we are referring to collectivities, and collective responsibility is a difficult concept. Different people have different degrees of responsibility for state actions and deserve different degrees of blame or approbation. Moreover, institutions such as governments develop standard operating procedures which take on a life of their own. For example, in assigning moral responsibility for the Soviet Union's shooting down of a Korean civil aircraft with the loss of 269 lives, does one conclude that the interceptor pilot was to blame for obeying orders or that his immediate supervisors were to blame for giving orders, or that the top leaders were to blame for permitting procedures to exist that failed to allow adequately for uncertainty and mistakes? Whatever one's views about the allocation of blame, we are not prevented from making a moral judgment that the Soviet action was wrong.

It is perfectly appropriate to make moral judgments about the consequences of actions by institutions. Our awareness of the complexities of collective responsibility draws our attention to questions of structural factors that constrain moral choices in particular cases, and it may allow us to exonerate a person who is acting in a state role in a manner that we would not accept if he were acting simply as an individual. For example, if the Director of the CIA went to Managua as a tourist and shot three civilians on the street, we would judge him guilty of murder. If he followed presidential orders and consulted with Congress before approving a covert action in which the probability of deaths was high, and in which three Nicaraguan civilians were in fact killed, we would face a more complex moral judgment in which he would share only a portion of any blame. In short, we judge people acting in institutional roles somewhat differently from those acting as individuals.

On the other hand, while the standards of judgment are more complex, the standards for officials are not completely different. Filling an institutional role does not exonerate a person from all observance of normal moral standards. A burden of proof still rests on the individual who claims exemption, and the quality of the arguments he uses must be carefully judged in terms of motives, alternative means, probable consequences, and competing moral claims. Just as we found it was not enough for an official to say that anything is acceptable "because international politics is an amoral realm," it is equally unacceptable to justify any action simply on the grounds that one is acting in an official role rather than as an individual. In fact, some role-based defenses ("I was only following orders, only carrying out policy") have been judged inadmissable for highly placed individuals since Hitler's atrocities and the Nurenberg trials focused new attention on issues of collective responsibility. The statesman, bureaucrat, or soldier may claim to be judged by a different standard than the individual is, but he is not excused from asking moral questions about whether the action, the procedure, the policy, and the role are justifiable before he acts in a manner that deviates from normal moral rules, which typically are and should be defined for officials acting in any institutional role. Institutional roles nonetheless complicate our moral choices. Careful moral reasoning about foreign policy must pay particular attention to arguments given for any deviation from the normal moral rules that govern individual behavior to a different behavior allegedly (and possibly) justified by reasons of state.

The perspective of the citizen

To be human is to have views about right and wrong behavior. Inevitably the moral views of individuals will—and should—influence their views on foreign policy, both of their own country and of others. What are the obligations that citizens owe each other when they introduce their ethical concerns into foreign policy preferences? One can argue that there should be no restrictions. Whatever an individual citizen's sentiments, if they are to influence his country's foreign policy constructively, they must be consistent and well considered. These might be called rules of reason. The moral views of most individuals are a bit of a jumble. Principles often conflict. If applied uncritically to foreign policy, they lead to contradictory actions. A requirement for consistency is not a call for simplicity. On the contrary, moral sentiments must necessarily be highly complex to deal with numerous circumstances that are morally ambiguous on any simple view. But they should not lead to contradictions in actions, for contradictory actions can have serious costs of their own, especially when undertaken by a nation. They lead to uncertainty elsewhere in the world about the guiding principles of a nation's foreign policy, and to a reputation for unreliability in the eyes of other nations.

To have a constructive influence on foreign policy, an individual's moral views should also be well thought out in terms of their foreseeable consequences. Too often actions based on normal moral rules and good intentions have morally offensive consequences in the complex arena of world politics. The full consequences of actions usually cannot be predicted with certainty; but neither are we totally ignorant about the future results of a certain course of action. Citizens can ask one another to consider the full range of likely consequences.

Foreign policy must reconcile the often conflicting moral views of many individuals, a task that becomes immeasurably more difficult as the number and diversity of views increase. In this sense, the responsible citizen in a democracy should be aware of the costly and sometimes dangerous effects that may result if all citizens press for their personal moral solutions to all issues and refuse to compromise with the views of others. In short, there should be a degree of tolerance for the divergent moral views of others — a condition that is necessary for democracy to function in the domestic realm as well.

What norms and procedures can protect against such problems? Democratic theory is a start, but alone is not sufficient. If the majority of citizens wish to reflect a moral preference in foreign policy, there should be a presumption in favor of that expression. But given the danger of mass hysteria (or indifference), long-run interests may be neglected. And the practice of building majorities by log rolling may undercut the common interest. Simple pursuit of pressure-group interests can lead to lowest-common-denominator solutions which may risk long-run prudential interests as well as lead to immoral consequences.

Arthur Schlesinger has suggested a rule that as many issues as possible be disposed of on prudential grounds.[10] This approach may help to reduce the amount of heated moral debate, but still begs the question of strong moral preferences and the definition of prudence. One could argue that moral debate and pressure might be qualified by a Rawlsian-type rule of reason. A citizen should press a moral concern upon his government's foreign policy only so long as he would admit the legitimacy and wisdom of other citizens pressing analogous concerns. Such an approach helps to prevent the degeneration of the democratic principle as a means of considering the role of ethical concerns in foreign policy. In short, the obligation that citizens owe one another when introducing their moral preferences into foreign policy is prudential attention to the realities of international life and a respect for the positions and circumstances of others when they urge actions which may jeopardize common interests.

The perspective of the statesman

If individuals will and should apply their moral views to foreign policy, qualified only by democratic practice and a rule of reason, what of the foresighted political leader and executor of foreign policy, the statesman? How are officials limited in what they may do for moral reasons by their obligations to their constituents? The obligation of a statesman is to maintain and improve the well-being of the people he represents, in all of the dimensions that are relevant to them. His objectives would thus normally encompass their physical security and economic well-being, but must also include their psychological security and well-being. He must, insofar as possible, consider *all* the consequences of the actions he directs, now and in the future. He should act as a guardian or trustee for the interests of those he represents.

As Niebuhr and others have pointed out, a trustee is not entitled to sacrifice the interests of others.[11] He must act prudentially on their behalf. And a prudent statesman approaching his task with utter realism must take moral sentiments into account in weighing his actions. There are three major reasons why this is so.

First, the realistic statesman must consider the influence of his current actions on the ability of his successors to exercise a degree of discretion appropriate for the management of foreign policy. To ignore systematically the moral sentiments of the citizenry will undermine trust not only in him, but in his office. It will lead to loss of public support for foreign policy, so necessary especially in a democracy, but also in other forms of government.

Second, since the psychological well-being of his country's citizenry is part of the statesman's responsibility, he must take the self-respect of the citizens as citizens directly into account, quite apart from the possible ultimate loss of their support.

Third, an important element in the ability of any country to carry out its foreign policy objectives is its reputation abroad. This reputation rests in part on consistency and reliability in behavior. Underlying this is the confidence of other nations that our nation will carry out its commitments. The ability to make credible commitments can aid the statesman enormously in pursuit

of his current and future objectives. Confidence and credibility depend upon
a number of factors—by no means only on morality—but the establishment
of trust among nations is immeasurably easier if they share common moral
values, and if those moral values are seen to motivate foreign policy actions.
With trust based on shared moral sentiment, certain commitments become
credible that would not otherwise be possible (e.g., placement of tactical
nuclear weapons in densely populated friendly nations). It must be recognized that the influence of moral sentiment on foreign policy also makes
certain commitments inoperative as instruments of foreign policy, because
moral inhibitions will make it impossible to carry them out. One of the
prudential judgments a country (as represented by a series of statesmen)
must face is how to strike a balance between these conflicting considerations.
But any such balance is likely to result in some influence of moral sentiment
on a country's foreign policy.

The statesman also faces two crucial considerations that will greatly
influence the evaluation of expected outcomes of possible courses of action.
The first concerns the weight he attaches to the consequences of actions
which may occur in the far future as opposed to those he may have to
confront in the short term. The second concerns the weight he attaches to
uncertainty that is inevitable in his attempt to forecast consequences of
actions.

In the assessment of consequences it is reasonable to give outcomes
anticipated far in the future less weight than those expected to occur in the
near future. A discount should be applied both to future costs and to future
benefits, with the discount to grow in proportion to the distance into the
future. While there are difficult moral problems in the process of balancing
current and future moral claims, not to apply some discount would lead to
the intuitively unacceptable result that any finite cost would be worth paying
now for any benefits, however small, that are expected to last indefinitely
into the future. But what discount rate should be applied? (A 3% discount
per annum implies that the "worth" of outcomes 24 years from now is
assessed today at half that future value, and the "worth" of outcomes half
a century from now is assessed today at under one-fourth of that future
value.) And how frequently should the rate be altered? No doubt, if a people
finds its survival threatened, it will and should take actions for preservation
which may have high long-run costs. In more tranquil periods, a lower
discount rate is appropriate. The statesman must make the crucial judgment
about how to weigh present against future, taking into account the considered preferences of his country's citizenry. But he should not vary the
discount to be applied to the future arbitrarily from one decision to another.
As elsewhere in foreign policy, considerable advantages result from consistency and reliability within a framework of expectations that each country
establishes.

A second crucial choice concerns the extent to which a country should
accept or avoid risky courses of action. Future consequences of today's

actions can never be ascertained with certainty, but they can be predicted with varying degrees of confidence. One course of action may show a better expected outcome than another but be subject to a greater range of uncertainty of prediction. Should it be undertaken or not? How much risk is acceptable? Again, the statesman must decide how much risk to run, taking into account the (typically conflicting) proclivities of the citizenry.

Does this prudential approach exhaust the statesman's use of morality in foreign policy? Is there room for the statesman to interject his own moral standards into his decisions and actions in foreign policy? If two courses of action are assessed to be completely equivalent in their net benefit to the nation, taking into account all expected future as well as present consequences, the choice between them from the trustee's point of view is a matter of indifference, and he might decide between them on the basis of his personal moral code as well as on the basis of any other criterion. But apart from this hairline case, once one allows the trustee to interject his personal moral code (when it differs from the public's) into his decisions, it will by definition in the short term involve the trustee in sacrificing the interests of his country's citizens.

As Hoffmann and others have pointed out, statesmen as trustees must sometimes violate their individual moral codes for reasons of long-range consequences such as protecting the public order that makes adherence to normal moral rules possible for most individuals in a society.[12] A statesman who is perfectly consistent by individual moral standards may often find himself in conflict with his responsibilities as trustee. For example, Secretary of State Henry Stimson held the noble personal moral view that "gentlemen do not read one another's mail."[13] Moral consistency would have required Stimson to oppose the creation of the NSA and its predecessors. Yet breaking diplomatic and naval codes in the 1930s probably altered the outcome of the Second World War, and in any case greatly shortened it.

It does not follow from this discussion of the trustee's role that the statesman's personal moral views have no role in foreign policy. For one thing, the statesman is a moral educator as well as a trustee. Part of his role is to help the community define more sharply its usually diverse moral preferences and understanding of issues. The educator helps the citizenry to define and evaluate particular situations.

By "educating his electorate," the statesman may reduce the tension between his personal moral views and his obligations as a trustee. For example, a leader may view institutionalized racial injustice in South Africa as morally repugnant. He may also see prudential reasons (e.g., Soviet influence, security of sea routes, nonproliferation) for not breaking off relations with the white South African government. But he may believe it right to expend some of his country's political influence on the racial issue rather than husbanding it all for use on the security issues. He may combine moral and prudential arguments to persuade the public to see the trade-offs in the same manner that he does, taking into account the fact that his educative efforts will themselves have consequences for his ability to execute the nation's foreign policy. Should he fail, however, his trustee role limits the extent of his personal moral intervention. If the statesman finds a situation morally repugnant in terms of his conscience and personal integrity, he can continue his efforts at public education or he can resign as trustee.

This position should not be interpreted to mean that the statesman must yield to the public passions and angers of the moment. As Edmund Burke pointed out two centuries ago, the trustee in representative government must consider the long-run interests of his country's citizens, not merely their current preferences, even if he thus risks electoral defeat. As an "educator" the statesman can sharpen and clarify his country's interests so that they are understood by the people. But as statesman-trustee, his positions must appeal to the citizens' cooler judgments and moral sentiments. If his educational efforts fail despite ample time and widely disseminated information, the democratic premise favoring the public's considered views must ultimately limit the statesman.

Second, the exception that we allowed above—where two courses of action are equivalent in benefit—is defined narrowly, but in practice encompasses a relatively wide range of situations because of uncertainty in calculating consequences in the complex international system. Many situations arise where prudential considerations could point either way. For example, in deciding whether to give asylum to a prominent refugee from China, the statesman must consider the effects on relations with China and the balance of power in East Asia. But he must also consider the effects on America's reputation as a country that defends the rights of individuals, and the long-run effects of opening one's country to blackmail once it departs from an established standard in support of individual liberty. Since the uncertainty about consequences and net benefit is likely to be large, the actual leeway to decide the issue on a personal moral proclivity toward the rights of individuals may be quite substantial in practice.

Finally, the statesman's moral roles are not fully exhausted by his obligations to those for whom he acts as trustee. His primary obligations are to his own people, but he has a residual cosmopolitan obligation to respect the rights of other peoples in situations where there are equivalent choices among means to promote his own people's interests. This residual obligation may shrink almost to zero in the realm of survival and necessity— for example in a situation of impending enemy attack. (Even in such a situation there are moral—not to mention prudential—questions concerning the future of humanity if the statesman chose to respond with a preemptive nuclear strike.) But as Wolfers has pointed out, much of international politics is not in the realm of necessity, and even in the definition of security interests, the statesman can make moral choices among means.[14] In the "just war" theory, his obligations to respect the rights of those beyond his borders include factors such as just cause, reasonable chance of success, proportionality of costly means to the end values pursued, and discrimination between combatants and civilians. He may follow such an approach for prudential reasons or in reflection of the moral preferences of his country's citizenry. But even faced with an indifferent citizenry, he might accept a moral obligation to choose means which reduce the loss of rights or life imposed on others. In retrospect, many Americans wish their trustees in the 1930s had taken greater electoral risks to rescue more Jews from Hitler's genocide.

There are serious risks to admitting exceptions to the trustee theory. Insofar as public opinion in the statesman's country admits some obligation to foreigners (such as "just war" theory), there is no problem. But if the trustee role is weakened to allow the statesman to follow his personal moral code, how can we be sure that his actions or inaction will have good consequences? Suppose the statesman is a cosmopolitan religious fundamentalist who, in judging issues of war and peace, places no value on the souls or lives of atheists. Would we still wish to weaken the trustee theory to admit idiosyncratic moral preferences? The checks and balances of the Constitution provide some protection, but it is safer in a democracy, on balance, to restrict the statesman to the role of trustee, albeit with a Burkean degree of flexibility, while allowing the citizen wide leeway for asserting moral preferences in foreign policy.

Thus, even taking the above qualifications into account, we see that the statesman's exercise of *personal* moral choice will be highly constrained in foreign policy because of his institutional role. This is not to say that morality plays no role in a statesman's attitudes and actions. As a matter of fact, his transition from normal rules to consequentialism requires careful moral reasoning. Nor does it mean that morality plays no role in foreign policy. The citizen is not so constrained, and citizens may demand that their trustees express widely held moral values in national policy. But the statesman must temper this popular preference by introducing prudential considerations.

Problems of intervention and autonomy

We will exemplify these concepts by considering problems of intervention, but first it is important to clarify the concept. An important aspect of competing moral claims in a world of nation states is national autonomy and self-determination. For example, if the government of a country needing land reform were so weak that the only way to effect reform would be for an outside government to establish a colonial administration to carry through the objective, most people today would argue that such outside intervention would not be justified. Or, to cite an example given by Michael Walzer, even if it were possible for Swedes to add a chemical to Algerian drinking water which would make Algerians behave like Swedish social democrats, such an action would not be justified.[15]

Part of what we owe to others in recognition of their special status as humans is respect for their autonomy. Autonomy cannot be absolute, but as Jonathan Glover notes, a concern for basic human rights includes a presumption in favor of autonomy. [16] Even if one argues that moral obligation is owed only among individuals, nation states can be seen as communities of pooled individual rights. At the same time, national autonomy may sometimes conflict with the autonomy of individuals and groups within a nation. Moreover, unlike the legal concept of sovereignty, in practice national autonomy is often highly qualified.

Thus moral proscriptions against outside involvement cannot be absolute. Walzer argues that the state is the arena where self-determination is worked out and from which foreign armies have to be excluded. He says there should be a presumption of legitimacy of internal processes unless there is a radical lack of fit between government and community. But the rules allowing foreigners to intervene and thus disregard the presumption against outside involvement are as important as the presumption itself. These rules are rightly restrictive when one focuses, as Walzer does, on extreme forms of intervention associated with large-scale use of lethal force. But these rules for war do not give much guidance for the approach to issues such as human rights or economic assistance.

When we consider outside involvement in the socio-economic realm, it is important to remember that true national autonomy is rarely encountered. Sovereign nations do not fully control their destinies. First, the workings of the international economy typically have important effects across national boundaries even in the absence of any overt governmental intervention. In a few cases, these transnational economic effects may even have life and death consequences for impoverished people in poor countries that are just as significant and more likely to occur than military action. [17]

Second, nation states are not billiard balls, hard and closed unto themselves and merely ricocheting off one another. As argued earlier, many citizens in many states have multiple loyalties both below and above the national level which give rise to various senses of community. Citizens may welcome outside involvement in their national affairs—up to a certain point.

Third, few countries are fully self-sufficient, and outside assistance and involvement can help to turn a merely theoretical autonomy today into a greater real autonomy in the future. Some outside involvement now may strengthen the national capacity to influence its own destiny in the future. If this strengthens a state, it may reduce the chances of future outside interventions.

Finally, self-determination is not a precise concept. It is one thing to say that every group has the right to choose its own sovereign, but how is such a choice to be decided? In reality, democratic procedures are not used in many countries. But even the observance of democratic principles is not enough because the decision of where (within what boundaries) and when (now or later) and on what agenda (what is excluded?) one votes will often lead to radically different outcomes. In other words, there is always a certain degree of moral arbitrariness in the decisions about which rights of self-determination are observed and which are not.[18] We can think of degrees of self-determination in proportion to the extent to which sectors of a society are able to participate in determining national views. Self-determination can be seen as an attribute of societies, while sovereignty is an attribute of states. When a small and unrepresentative elite sets national policies which are against the interests of large parts of the population, national autonomy may conflict with self-determination. Thus the respect for autonomy of the state cannot be absolute.

Not only is there a porousness and relativism about the concept of national autonomy, but the concept of outside involvement is similarly complex. One can imagine a variety of dimensions of intervention with respect to method, scope, purpose, degree, and duration.

From a moral point of view, the degree of coercion involved in outside involvement is very important. Governments have coercive powers. One can imagine a wide spectrum of actions by outsiders ranging from declarations or speeches aimed at the citizenry in another country, to full-scale military invasion. (See Table 1.) In between one would find such actions as support for the ruling government, economic or military assistance to the government, (usually covert) economic or military assistance to opposition groups, and small-scale military intervention. We use the term "intervention" broadly to refer to the entire spectrum of deliberate outside involvements in another country's domestic affairs. In international law and diplomacy, it is used more narrowly to refer to the more coercive end of the scale—where an outsider "interferes coercively in the domestic affairs of another state."[19] Although the narrower use of the term is sanctified in legal usage, we believe the broader definition is appropriate for a discussion of the morality of intervention against a background of respect for autonomy, without in any way meaning to suggest that the degree of coercion is not an important variable.

We may judge some outside involvement to be immoral, regardless of the degree of coercion, if the intentions were malevolent: for example, if the purpose were to exercise domination or if the consequences were predictably bad on all counts of relevant criteria. But if we judged the intentions and consequences to be good, then we would focus on the means of outside involvement, particularly the degree of coercion because of its costs in terms of autonomy. Whether one is looking at a broad or narrow definition of intervention, one would look at questions of "proportionality"—the costs of outside involvement in relation to the danger being averted or the severity of the wrong being righted. In assessing proportionality, one must look both at the possible unintended consequences as well as the intended ones. Assessment of proportionality must include the long-term effect on an existing system of international rules if one violates them in a particular case, especially if great coercion is used.

Table 1. Intervention

High outsider coercion:
low local choice

Military invasions . . . .

Limited military action . .

Blockade . . . .

Support of opposition . . .

Military advisors . . . .

Economic assistance . . .

Broadcasts to country . . .

Speeches . . . .

Low outsider coercion:
high local choice

Military intervention

Once one departs from an absolute prohibition against military intervention, it is essential that good moral reasoning protect against abuse. It is not adequate moral reasoning for a statesman to justify extreme violation of national autonomy protected by international law against such intervention, by invoking a low-probability hypothetical future ("they might have gone Communist and that might have tipped the balance of power"). Nor is it adequate to justify intervention because the moral imperative of preventing an abstraction like "totalitarian rule" demands it, if the conditions for totalitarianism do not exist and are unlikely to develop. Even if there is some risk of tipping the balance of power or tolerating the installation of totalitarian rule, consistent moral reasoning requires an explanation of why a statesman intervenes in one case and does not intervene in other equally egregious cases of present or potential danger.

One can protect against spurious justification based on intended consequences by requiring that the calculation of these consequences be subjected to a broad and careful causal analysis; by deciding to observe rules where the calculation of consequences involves large uncertainties; and by developing procedures to ensure impartiality in those cases where a departure from normal rule is judged to be justified.

Among the duties that we owe to citizens of a foreign country is not to kill them or take away their autonomy without compelling justification. The prohibitions against military intervention in international law help to reinforce these minimal duties. Thus it makes sense to start with a state moralist position favoring nonintervention unless Walzer's rules of disregard apply (e.g., genocide, counterintervention, etc.). Alternatively, the cosmopolitan who contemplates military intervention because of the severity of the injustices being suffered by the population of a foreign country must consider the competing moral claim of national autonomy as well as prudential concerns for maintaining the interstate legal order. Similarly, the realist contemplating military intervention must weigh the degree of threat to his country's interests resulting from a change in the balance of power against the same competing moral and prudential claims. The consequences considered must include the long-term effect on the institutional framework of international law which not only contributes to interstate order but reinforces important moral duties to foreigners.

Even if the severity of the security threat is real or the deprivation of human rights is egregious, careful causal analysis is needed to calculate consequences. The prospects of success at reasonable costs in terms of lives and local autonomy must be weighed. Unintended consequences must be estimated. Will it be possible to withdraw quickly? Is it reasonable to believe that proportionality can be maintained once intervention has begun? If the purpose is to replace a government, what is the probability that the successor government will be better? And if the only way to ensure the improvement is to maintain a presence that approaches imperial rule, will not the costs in terms of lost local autonomy be disproportionate to the ends sought? Such considerations are analogous to those required by traditional "just war" theory.

Another consideration is the assessment of probable consequences of not intervening. Are there alternatives? What are their risks and costs? What about responsibility for our past actions? Should we intervene to counter the effects of past interventions, particularly if the net effect is to increase local autonomy over the long run? Central America comes to mind. Similarly, in some instances where a high degree of outside intervention by others exists, to refuse to counterintervene means, in Talleyrand's phrase, that intervention and nonintervention may amount to the same thing. The distinction between acts and omissions may vanish in such instances.

All such assessments of consequences are highly problematic. We can never know the full consequences of our actions. The more tenuous or uncertain the causal reasoning about consequence, the more hesitant one should be about departing from the rules against coercive intervention. The costs to the system of rules, local autonomy, and human lives from a military intervention is likely to be more immediate and certain than the hypothesized benefits and dangers averted. There should be a "clear and present danger" test. When the uncertainties are large and the dangers appear only at the end of a long hypothetical causal chain, the presumption in favor of nonintervention is reinforced.

If, despite such careful analysis, it seems that coercive intervention is still justified, it is essential to take steps to assure the preservation of impartiality. The higher one goes on the scale of coercion, the greater the presumption should be in favor of multilateral efforts in order to "buy" insurance against the dangers of national hubris and egoism. Multilateral actions, consultation with allies, and public diplomacy in international organizations are all cumbersome, but they help the statesman to protect himself against the danger of disregarding impartiality too easily when he judges consequences. One can admit that the prohibitions against even military intervention are not absolute, but still insist, once one departs from the rules, that special care must be taken to protect the quality of moral reasoning about competing moral claims.

Nonmilitary intervention

The same considerations apply to less coercive degrees of outside involvement in the domestic affairs of other countries. Even when intervention is not so clearly proscribed by legal rules, the difficult tasks of weighing competing moral claims must be faced. The presumption in favor of local autonomy still stands, but we may choose to override it when our relatively noncoercive actions are commanded by obligations of Samaritanism, responsibility for the effects of our past actions, or by a desire to promote true national autonomy in the other country in the face of internal or external threats to it. We still must consider proportionality and the severity of the situation. For example, are people starving? If so, and the local government is ignoring their plight, higher degrees of involvement would be justified than if conditions were not so severe. Similar arguments can be made in favor of intervention when political liberty and order are at stake. Are the prospects for enhancing political liberty particularly promising? In the absence of outside intervention is violent disorder highly likely? If so, a higher degree of international involvement may be justified.

A second factor to be considered is the degree of existing transnational interdependence. When there is a high degree of transnational interdependence, noninvolvement is not possible. One may need to be actively involved to counter the unwanted effects of his or her other activities. In addition, where there is a high degree of interdependence, there is also likely to be a higher degree of leverage and capability to affect a situation. In short, where it is not possible to be uninvolved, as for example in the United States' historical relationship to Central America, some deliberate outside involvement may be justified to redress the negative effects of other forms of involvement. Indeed, such new involvement may not lead to a net reduction in overall autonomy.

The justifiable degree of relatively noncoercive international involvement should be assessed in terms of the effects on individual and local autonomy within another country. Some communities may be structured in such a way that large portions of the population which are strongly affected by national decisions are not able to participate in the process or even significantly affect it. In such instances, a degree of outside involvement which tends to strengthen the weaker parties by promoting devolution and decentralization or otherwise providing them with resources, may actually increase the capability of an indigenous political process to achieve autonomous trade-offs in a fashion which reflects the wishes of a large portion of the population. Conversely, however, the outside involvement cannot extend to the point that it is the outsider rather than the indigenous population which has the strongest effect on these decisions.

Finally, one must consider procedures to ensure impartiality in balancing competing moral claims even in relatively noncoercive outside involvement. It is all too easy for humans to unconsciously weigh their own interests more heavily when balancing competing moral claims. This is particularly true for outside governments where power politics and idealism often create a complex mix of motives. Thus, it is important that a procedure for making such judgments include the perspective of the country in which the intervention occurs. This argues for both a high degree of local involvement in decision-making and for an explanation of policy judgments which is accessible and acceptable to local audiences. It also suggests the value of involvement of international agencies as a means of protecting against cultural imperialism, conscious or unconscious, in processes of implementation. As with military intervention, while the rules are not absolute, the presumption should be in favor of the negative obligation to respect the autonomy of others, and special care must be taken to preserve impartiality in the moral reasoning used to justify outside involvement.

Conclusions

Ethics and foreign policy are inextricably intertwined for Americans. To deplore this fact, as did the mainstream conventional wisdom of post World War II realism, is to abdicate responsibility for disciplining moral reasoning in this domain. We do not need a new debate between realism and idealism; instead, we need to marry realist insights about the dangerous consequences of too simple an application of the rules of individual moral behavior in the complex domain of international politics, with insights about the limited but real moral obligations to fellow citizens and foreign peoples that arise from the effects of interdependence and the admission of a (weak) sense of common humanity.

At the same time, we need to avoid the complete double standard of behavior permitting a statesman to totally avoid customary norms of morality because of the allegedly amoral nature of international politics or the license which is implied by too simplistic a view of the trustee's role. As a matter of fact, quite the opposite is true: we have seen that total skepticism about ethics in international politics is not justified, and that the statesman's role does not grant full exoneration from normal moral standards. While the statesman must appeal to a critical level of consequentialist reasoning, the grounds on which he justifies his transition from normal rules to consequences must be held up to careful scrutiny. Simply consequentialist arguments are not enough.

International politics is not like domestic politics, and ethical considerations in foreign policy are more complex than in domestic policy. But they exist. The role of ethics in foreign policy is modest, but it is also inescapable. Neither politics nor morality really stops at the water's edge. They just become more complicated. The dangers of shallow moralism do not justify equally shallow cynicism. What is required are further efforts to refine our moral reasoning in this particularly difficult domain.

NOTES

1. Dexter Perkins, "What Is Distinctly American about the Foreign Policy of the United States?" in Glyndon Van Dusen and Richard Wade, eds., *Foreign Policy and the American Spirit* (Ithaca: Cornell University Press, 1957). See also: George Kennan, *American Diplomacy* (New York: Mentor Books, 1952), and Robert Osgood, *Ideals and Self-Interest in America's Foreign Relations* (Chicago: University of Chicago Press, 1953).
2. Charles Beitz, "Bounded Morality," *International Organization* 33, Summer 1979, pp. 405–424.
3. Hans J. Morgenthau, *Politics Among Nations* (New York: Knopf, 1955), p. 9.
4. David Luban, "The Romance of the Nation State," *Philosophy and Public Affairs*, 9 (Summer 1980), p. 392.
5. Stanley Hoffmann, *Duties Beyond Borders* (Syracuse: Syracuse University Press, 1981), p. 144.
6. Michael Walzer, "The Moral Standing of States," *Philosophy and Public Affairs*, 9 (Spring 1980), p. 211.
7. John Rawls, *A Theory of Justice* (Cambridge: Harvard University Press, 1971), p. 378.
8. Gerald Doppelt, "Statism Without Foundations," *Philosophy and Public Affairs*, 9 (Summer 1980), pp. 401–403.
9. Jonathan Glover, *Causing Death and Saving Lives* (Harmondsworth: Penguin, 1977), Chapters 6 and 7.
10. Arthur Schlesinger, Jr., "National Interests and Moral Absolutes," in Ernest Lefever, ed., *Ethics and World Politics* (Baltimore: Johns Hopkins University Press, 1972), p. 22.
11. Reinhold Niebuhr, *Moral Man and Immoral Society* (New York: Scribner, 1932); see also the criticism in J. E. Hare and Carey B. Joynt, *Ethics and International Affairs* (New York: Saint Martins, 1982), pp. 27–33.
12. Hoffmann, *Duties Beyond Borders*, pp. 17 ff.
13. James Bamford, *The Puzzle Palace* (New York: Penguin, 1982), p. 46.
14. Arnold Wolfers, "Statesmanship and Moral Choice," in *Discord and Collaboration* (Baltimore: Johns Hopkins University Press, 1962), Chapter 4.
15. Walzer, "The Moral Standing of States," op. cit.
16. Glover, *Causing Death and Saving Lives*, p. 74.
17. For examples, see Robert O. Keohane and J. S. Nye, "Transgovernmental Relation and International Organization," *World Politics* XXVII (October 1974).
18. Stanley French and Andres Gutman, "The Principle of Self-Determination," in Virginia Held et al., *Philosophy, Morality and International Affairs* (New York: Oxford University Press, 1974).
19. R. J. Vincent, *Nonintervention and International Order* (Princeton: Princeton University Press, 1974), p. 13.

II

Security dilemmas of the nuclear age

MICHAEL NACHT

The search for security in an increasingly insecure world

PAUL M. DOTY

Arms control at bay

3

The search for security in an increasingly insecure world

MICHAEL NACHT

*Associate Professor, School of Public Affairs,
University of Maryland*

Security is the freedom to act. It is the ability to pursue objectives without fear of being threatened by opposing forces. In the modern world of nation states, no state is totally secure. Security is a relative concept. The freedom of action of any state is necessarily limited by the finite nature of the resources and capabilities of the state as well as by the ability of other states or groups of states to block its given course of action. Coercion on the other hand is the ability to restrain or dominate. It is the use of force or threats of force to nullify an individual will or to compel the selection of a particular course of action. Security and coercion therefore are intimately related. Security is the power not be coerced.

The dominant perception today is that we feel less secure than we *recall* having felt 25 years ago. Security seems more elusive and complex than it once appeared to be. For many Americans there is a sense of a declining ability to protect and promote United States national interests, no less the interests of the international community. We tend to forget or at least to minimize, however, the difficulties we faced in the past.

Remembrance of conditions past

A quarter-century ago, when the Center for International Affairs was founded, evidence of insecurity was in fact abundant. In military terms the United States was still reeling from *Sputnik*, the first orbiting earth satellite, launched by the Soviet Union in October 1957. The Soviets had demonstrated technological prowess, especially with respect to ballistic missile technology, far beyond what most Western analysts thought they were capable of achieving. Considerable anxiety pervaded the American defense community that we were being overtaken by the Soviets. This anxiety immediately stimulated the establishment of the post of the President's

45

Science Advisor and other organizational responses underscoring the significance of science and technology for national policy. A major impetus was provided for the rapid development and then deployment of United States land-based and sea-based ballistic missiles. Moreover, a high-level advisory body, the Gaither Commission, expressed grave concerns about the vulnerability of American nuclear forces to a Soviet first strike. The Commission called for the commitment to a major civil defense program and highlighted what its members thought to be a serious "missile gap" between the United States and the Soviet Union. This "gap," it should be recalled, subsequently became a major issue in the 1960 Nixon–Kennedy presidential campaign.

Arms control efforts, especially bilateral negotiations between the superpowers, were in a rudimentary stage of development. Distrust between Washington and Moscow ran very deep. Official contacts at high levels were minimal. And the formidable stumbling block of on-site inspection, required by the United States and routinely rejected by the Soviet Union (with the exception of the Antarctica Treaty of 1959), seemed at the time to be a permanent impediment to the regulation of the nuclear arms competition.

In broader issues of foreign policy there was much for Americans to feel insecure about. The Soviet Union's alliance with the People's Republic of China appeared from Washington to be quite stable. This combined Sino–Soviet threat posed serious political and military challenges to the United States on the Asian mainland and in many of the newly independent countries of the Third World. American passivity during the Hungarian Revolution provided convincing proof that Eastern Europe was an acknowledged *de facto* sphere of Soviet influence. Crises over the status of Berlin and the islands in the Taiwan Straits, each on more than one occasion, raised the serious prospect of war with the Soviets and with the Chinese.

Nor were relations rosy between the United States and its European and Japanese allies. American failure to back the French and British initiatives in the Suez crisis of 1956 contributed to the return to power of Charles DeGaulle in France, the acquisition of a French nuclear force, and the subsequent withdrawal by France from the integrated military command structure of the North Atlantic Treaty Organization (NATO). European economic integration had moved forward with painful slowness and political integration on the Continent remained merely the fantasy of a few European visionaries and American scholars. The credibility of American security guarantees for its European allies was probed continuously by unconvinced policy "influentials" on both sides of the Atlantic. Across the Pacific, the redefinition of the United States–Japan Security Treaty in 1960 guaranteed United States military base rights on Japanese territory. But it came at the expense of an extraordinary outpouring of anti-American Japanese popular sentiment which necessitated the canceling of President Eisenhower's scheduled trip to Tokyo near the end of his eight-year tenure in the White House.

In addition, on the economic front, the periodic recurrence of troubling recessions in the United States was felt with great force among most of America's allies, and frictions over trade and monetary policies were a hardy perennial of alliance relationships.

These difficulties notwithstanding, however, we look today upon the late 1950s and early 1960s as a far more stable period than the present one. A quarter-century ago Americans were optimistic about their future with firm expectations that their lives would be easier and more affluent than those of their parents. This optimism reflected an appreciation of an international economic system dominated by the United States. America retained its extraordinary influence in world markets. The Bretton Woods system, which stipulated a formula of fixed exchange rates for international monetary transactions consistent with American preferences, was functioning well. The Keynesian model of macroeconomic management commanded widespread support in the United States and throughout the Western economies. Economic considerations as such remained largely outside the "high politics" of international security concerns.

While the West was being persistently challenged by the forces of communist expansionism, there was a common (though not universal) understanding among all segments of American society—politicians, scholars, journalists, businessmen, the uniformed military, the clergy, the scientific community, labor unions—that the containment policy fashioned by the United States in the late 1940s was effective. A combination of prudent use of military force and political and economic assertiveness on a global scale was the most appropriate way to protect American and Western interests.

If we had a special meter to measure the level of political, economic, military, and psychological security of the American people, we could pose two questions: First, where is the needle on the meter today relative to 25 years ago? Second, in what direction is the needle moving? No real data can be offered to answer these questions since our security meter is purely imaginary. But one can cite a number of developments, past and prospective, which strongly suggest that the needle would be pointing today to less rather than more security and that it would be moving in the direction of increased insecurity.

To explain this erosion in perceived security there are seven developments and issues worthy of examination:

1. America is in search of itself
2. The United States–Soviet competition breeds insecurity
3. Alliance fragmentation is increasing
4. Economic policies are now high politics
5. Soviet weaknesses are a source of concern
6. Military technology breeds insecurity
7. Political instability pervades the poorer countries

Sources of insecurity in the 1980s

1. America is in search of itself

The sense of a nation's security is derived as much from psychological sources as from the more tangible economic and military assets it can apply to further its national interests. Given the political and military traumas experienced by the United States in the last two decades, it is not at all surprising that in attitudinal terms the American body politic has become far less optimistic about itself and its role in the world than it was prior to 1960.

Perhaps the most significant of these traumas has been the assassination of several national leaders, notably President John Kennedy, Martin Luther King, and Senator Robert Kennedy. These individuals, despite their human failings and at times ineffectual policies, symbolized a better and hopeful future for important segments of American society. Their brutal murders, especially President Kennedy's, have left many unanswered questions. Were they in fact killed by lone assassins or victims of large conspiracies? Were elements of the United States government in any way involved in the murders? Were foreign powers, particularly the Soviet or Cuban governments, behind the killings? Why were these American leaders killed? If these men were indeed assassinated by lone gunmen, what does this tell us about the nature of American society and its proclivity toward violence? If officials or former officials of the American government have answers to these questions, why have they not come forward and revealed their knowledge?

Many of these questions may well have been answered to the satisfaction of some Americans, but they haunt most of the rest of us. This seemingly endless search for answers has had several major consequences. It has, first of all, cast doubt on our ability to produce effective leaders and to sustain a leadership role in the world. In the 1984 Democratic Party primary elections, for instance, the voter appeal of the Reverend Jesse Jackson for American Blacks and of Senator Gary Hart for middle-class white professionals has not been unrelated to the search for successors to King and Kennedy, respectively. Yet somehow leadership seems to be eluding the American people. None of the prominent contemporary figures on the national scene, nor any of the presidents since Kennedy, are seen to have the ability to inspire the people the way we now believe our leaders of the early 1960s could. While President Reagan has sought through ideological consistency and military assertiveness to correct this image, he has apparently only partially succeeded. Depite an extraordinarily attractive personality and exceptional abilities as a public communicator, his acknowledged lack of substantive expertise in many areas and his absence of diplomatic accomplishments have introduced inherent limitations in his leadership potential.

Absence of leadership has been coupled with a continued sense of self-doubt and self-restraint stemming from the memories of Vietnam. Although it has been claimed that Americans have placed the Vietnam experience behind them, this assertion is palpably incorrect. Popular and congressional debates over the introduction of American forces abroad, whether they be marines in Lebanon or army units in Central America, automatically trigger references to the Vietnam analogy whether or not this reference is warranted. For many in Congress, the Vietnam lesson has been to curb the war-making powers of the President. For the uniformed military, there is a pronounced reticence to become embroiled in combat abroad unless there is unmistakable evidence of broad public support plus a willingness on the part of the political leadership to take full responsibility for what happens on the ground. And for many members of the electorate, the use of military force is seen in virtually all instances as an inappropriate response to what are indigenous economic, social, and political grievances. Whereas the generation of Americans born during and immediately after World War II grew up with the heroic image of United States marines raising the American flag at Mt. Suribachi on Iwo Jima, those born since 1960 recall the last American helicopter lifting off the roof of the American embassy in Saigon in April 1975 and the image of other American helicopters crashing into each other in the Iranian desert during the aborted hostage rescue mission. In short, failure has replaced success and ineptitude has been substituted for heroism in the imagery of American combat.

To these memories can be added the Watergate crisis, which produced the first resignation of a sitting president in American history, and the ongoing debate about the proper role of the United States intelligence community, initiated by the Church Committee investigations of the mid-1970s. The cumulative effect of these developments has been the weakening of American self-confidence and the questioning of America's role in a complex and turbulent global environment.

2. The United States – Soviet nuclear competition

A second major source of insecurity which is likely to be with us at least through the balance of the 1980s is the widespread belief that the United States has lost its nuclear advantage over the Soviet Union. This realization has, ironically, produced two dissimilar if not contradictory concerns. Those individuals of a more conservative political bent, particularly fearful of Soviet military power and the unquenchable thirst of Russian expansionism, see the Soviet leadership possessing a window of opportunity to exploit their military advantages (such as in heavy intercontinental ballistic missiles and intermediate-range ballistic missiles) for political gain. Coercion of America's European and Japanese allies, Soviet expansion in the oil-rich Persian Gulf region, or perhaps even direct use of Soviet conventional forces in some third area with its nuclear forces poised to deter American use of its own nuclear arsenal are among the most frequently cited scenarios. Variations on these themes are examined and re-examined by officials and private analysts of the American defense community.

At the opposite end of the spectrum are the views of numerous public interest groups and concerned citizens who are less alarmed by the Soviet threat than by the seemingly uncontrollable character of the Soviet–American arms competition. Unlike many defense policy experts who see the super-power nuclear balance as reasonably stable, increasing segments of the American public perceive an arms race that is careening out of control and appears to be propelling us all toward nuclear war. This fear has unleashed formidable popular criticism of the fundamental strategic, economic, and moral premises of American nuclear policy.

A major source of this criticism has been a growing appreciation of how vast the nuclear arsenals have become—from perhaps 300 United States weapons and a few dozen Soviet bombs at the time of the Korean War to an aggregate superpower accumulation today of approximately 50,000 warheads. For others, who are aware of the increasing precision and control of nuclear delivery vehicles, there is special emphasis on the acquisition of enhanced nuclear war-fighting capabilities and the adoption of doctrines and declaratory policies which appear to be legitimizing the engagement of limited nuclear war. Whereas many in the professional defense community applaud such developments as strengthening nuclear deterrence, the dominant public interpretation is that the likelihood of nuclear war is increasing significantly.

Moreover, the absence of progress in negotiated arms control agreements is widely viewed to be a danger signal that United States–Soviet relations are in a state of extremely serious decline. The realization that not a single superpower arms control agreement has entered into force in the last decade despite a multiplicity of negotiating efforts has contributed significantly to the heightened sense of concern about the future controllability of the nuclear competition.

The net effect of these divisions between defense specialists and the public and indeed within the community of experts itself has been to call into question the basic utility of nuclear weapons. What in fact are the uses of these weapons? How significant are they in advancing the political influence of the state? To what extent will the United States–Soviet nuclear balance determine the outcome of a superpower crisis? Is the principal or sole use of nuclear weapons to deter the initial use of these weapons by one's adversary? Can nuclear weapons deter a conventional attack? If there is skepticism that the answer to this last question is positive, what does this tell us about the credibility of American nuclear guarantees to the European and Japanese allies of the United States? In broader terms, is the very concept of "extended deterrence" fatally flawed?

Overall it would appear that the American public and congressional sentiments which to a large degree mirror public attitudes seek simultaneously a United States nuclear posture second to none, a stable strategic relationship with the Soviet Union, and significant progress in nuclear arms control and reductions. As United States policies have seemingly been unable to satisfy any of these objectives, frustration and insecurity have been the natural by-products.

3. Alliance fragmentation

The structure of America's post-World War II allied relationships was shaped in a period of extraordinary United States military and economic domination over much of the rest of the world. While the period 1945–1965 is often looked upon today with nostalgia as a "norm" from which we have mistakenly strayed, this contention is unjustified. In reality, the two decades following the Second World War presented unique opportunities for the United States as the only major power to escape unscathed from the global conflagration. It was only a matter of time for new military and economic power centers to appear or reappear and to challenge the primacy of American political influence.

In Western Europe, slowly but surely the Federal Republic of Germany has emerged as the linchpin of the North Atlantic Treaty Organization reflecting the nation's political and geographic centrality as well as its military and economic strength. But Germany retains special ties with the East, given that it is a divided nation. *Ostpolitik* means something quite tangible to most Germans in human, cultural, and economic terms which "détente" never meant for most Americans. The inevitable desire of most West Germans to maintain and enhance relationships with East Germany necessitates a reasonably relaxed political atmosphere in Europe which can only be sustained if German–Soviet relations are on an even keel. Automatically, then, increased United States–Soviet tensions place the West Germans in the awkward position of seeking to conform to American policy preferences in order to maintain alliance cohesion while simultaneously striving to reduce these very tensions to further their interests in and with the East.

It is surely legitimate to inquire how long this balancing act can last. After all, the mean lifetime of alliances in international politics during the modern nation-state system has been estimated by some political scientists as slightly more than two years. Yet NATO celebrated its thirty-fifth anniversary in 1984! What is astonishing is how NATO has survived so many crises: the rearmament of West Germany and its entrance into NATO in 1955; the rift caused by American unwillingness to support Anglo–French actions in the Suez crisis of 1956; the withdrawal of France from the integrated military command structure of the alliance in 1966; the aborted effort to create a multilateral nuclear force (MLF); frequent tensions in Greek–Turkish relations, notably over Cyprus in 1974; Soviet incursions into Hungary in 1956 and Czechoslovakia in 1968, as well as the crisis over Solidarity in Poland in 1980–81; and, most recently, the strenuous Soviet political and diplomatic attempt to prevent NATO (and especially Germany) from accepting the deployment of Pershing II intermediate-range ballistic missiles and ground-launched cruise missiles at the end of 1983.

NATO has indeed been "at the crossroads" virtually throughout its existence. Peering ahead, we see that increased strain may well arise from two sources. First, new generations in allied countries are less familiar than their predecessors with the origins of the alliance and may well feel less beholden to American largesse as the basis for their own security. Second, differences over out-of-area policies could further undermine alliance cohesion. While NATO is a defensive alliance established to protect the territorial integrity of its member states, this has not prevented American policymakers and legislators from seeking allied support for United States policies in the Middle East, Central America, and elsewhere. It is in these regions distant from Central Europe that United States–European interests are most divergent, and where differences could become sufficiently acrimonious to undermine the raison d'être of the alliance. For these issues coupled with increasing American impatience for the Europeans to shoulder a greater share of the defense burden are stimulating the questioning of American incentives to maintain alliance relationships. Similarly with respect to Japan the economic competitiveness of United States–Japan relations is as much a source of American pressure for an increased Japanese defense effort as strategic considerations are.

In short, the centrifugal forces among the allies are gaining strength, creating perceptions of greater alliance fragmentation. It is, however, the nature of the Soviet threat, the nuclear stalemate between the superpowers, and the commonality of economic interests among the allies despite their competitive tendencies that cumulatively serve as the centripetal forces which are preserving alliance cohesion.

4. Economic policies as high politics

It has been reported by those who were close to him that Henry Kissinger, when serving as President's Assistant for National Security Affairs, boasted on more than one occasion of his ignorance of and disinterest in economic theory and economic policies. Whether or not this is accurate is of little moment; rather it suggests an important element of change in international relations. For perhaps the first quarter-century since the end of World War II the American dominance of the world economy, the confidence of Western economists in their ability to anticipate and thereby manipulate micro- and macroeconomic behavior, and the primacy of the nation state in world politics permitted students of "power politics" to relegate issues of trade, investment, and monetary policy to a distinctly subordinate role as shapers of American foreign policy.

This is today clearly no longer the case. Instead, aspects of economic policy are among the most dynamic forces of contemporary world affairs and are a principal source of heightened insecurity. As was demonstrated in the deep economic recession of 1981–83, American economic weakness has global repercussions which are highly disadvantageous to virtually all sectors of the world economy. What makes the contemporary period especially stressful is that elements of weakness have been identified, in steel and other "smokestack" industries, which may well require major structural changes in the American economic system. The vociferous debate over the virtues and vices of a national industrial policy, irrespective of which perspective prevails, suggests that the consensus over how to run the United States economy has broken down.

The Keynesian model for managing macroeconomic behavior has come under attack from a variety of sources in business, government, and academe. And the Reagan administration's experiment with "supply side economics," an experiment that has come to be criticized by both supporters and detractors of this approach, has led to the accumulation of record budget deficits which virtually all agree is a time bomb that will, if not drastically reduced, someday shatter American economic prosperity.

This disagreement over macroeconomic policy reflects a deep decline in the confidence of the economics profession to articulate sound economic policies. With growing specialization among professional economists and heavy reliance on sophisticated quantitative methods of analysis, a serious divergence is developing between the national and global economic problems that demand careful attention and the proclivities and modes of analysis of those best equipped to address these issues.

One such global economic problem is the extraordinarily shaky status of the international banking community and the unprecedented indebtedness of many less developed countries. Despite dire predictions of an international economic collapse looming just over the horizon, few effective measures have been devised to ameliorate this problem. Instead, complex schemes of debt rescheduling have been invoked to defer rather than rectify the highly overexposed positions of more than a dozen major developing countries and the numerous financial institutions to which they are in debt.

Moreover, energy security, once an unknown term, has now become a permanent feature of international affairs that concerns statesmen whether energy supplies are soft or tight. Despite major strides in energy conservation and the diversification of oil supplies over the last decade, there is an acute recognition of the enormous disruptive potential particularly to the economies of Western Europe and Japan should there be a prolonged interruption in oil exports emanating from the Persian Gulf states. This is a vulnerability largely unknown before 1973.

Finally, in institutional terms it is now commonplace to acknowledge the power of large numbers of multinational and transnational institutions and processes which vastly complicate and largely erode the power of the nation state. In sum, the relatively straightforward days of balance of power diplomacy, if they ever did exist, are now relegated to the historical scrap heap of statesmanship. The complex and demanding world of contemporary economic and political statecraft is now itself a major source of insecurity.

5. Soviet weaknesses as a source of concern

Some students of the evolution of the Soviet state claim that the society Lenin had firmly established by 1924 has undergone one unending crisis. Chronic food shortages, gross economic inefficiency, internal purges and terror, the ravages of war, and a political system seemingly bent on stifling its highly creative and talented populace have been prominent features of the Soviet landscape for 60 years. The question now is whether there are indeed fresh challenges facing the Soviet leadership which could produce a major confrontation with the West.

Despite an enormous investment in military hardware since the mid-1960s, it appears as though the Soviet Union is experiencing serious difficulty realizing tangible political gain from the accumulation of its military power. The achievement of nuclear parity with the United States has only stimulated the cantankerous Americans to push ahead in a quest to regain some measures of strategic superiority. The presence of large Soviet conventional forces in Eastern Europe has not prevented periodic challenges to Russian control, nor has the Soviet military shadow over Western Europe intimidated NATO governments into backing away from the decisions to modernize both nuclear and conventional forces. Indeed it can be argued that heavy-handed Soviet diplomacy, particularly in West Germany, has weakened the European peace movement and produced exactly the form of NATO cohesion that the leaders in Moscow were seeking to disrupt.

Elsewhere Soviet military power has brought few rewards in relations with China or Japan, and Soviet troops remain actively engaged in conflict in Afghanistan where no clear termination point is in sight. In the developing world, despite important gains through the Vietnamese victory in 1975 and in sub-Saharan Africa, Soviet influence is spotty at best. The Middle East has been a noteworthy area of Soviet failure in which Moscow's leverage has been largely reduced to the promotion of its interests through coordination with Syria. In the Western hemisphere, even if promotion of revolutionary movements through Cuban proxies serves Soviet policy aims and is becoming increasingly stressful for the United States, the Cuban connection is a multibillion dollar investment for the Soviets that they are ill equipped to underwrite. And beyond these region-specific considerations, it must be plainly evident to Soviet leaders that the appeal of Soviet communism as a model for the developing world has long ago been reduced to negligible levels.

If Soviet foreign policy aims are being frustrated in spite of their achievement as a military superpower, domestic difficulties are equally formidable. The Soviet economic system is simply not providing the growth and quality output demanded by the successive five-year plans in order for the Soviet government to make its presence felt in the world economy. Chronic problems of worker absenteeism, alcoholism, management inefficiency, and transportation and communication bottlenecks strongly suggest that major structural reform is required for the Soviet economy to perform up to the expectations of its leadership. Yet the political risks to the leadership inherent in this reform induce a powerful reluctance to proceed with the needed remedies.

The problem of managing a weak economic system is compounded by incipient tensions between the Great Russians and non-Russian Soviet minorities. While no tangible evidence of a major "nationalities problem" has yet materialized, it is a permanent challenge for the ruling Russians to govern a society in which they are increasingly becoming a minority people.

The burden of empire abroad and ineffective institutions at home must be keenly felt by the aging members of the Politburo. These burdens have inculcated a low risk-taking propensity, but who knows how long this can be sustained? As the United States–Soviet rivalry has spread from a regional to a global context, the opportunities for direct superpower conflict would appear to be increasing. Under such circumstances, should the United States seek to exacerbate Soviet weaknesses or not? Would a highly vulnerable Soviet leadership be a more or less dangerous adversary for Washington? The very uncertainty caused by deeply embedded Soviet weaknesses is itself no cause for comfort in the West.

6. Military technology breeds insecurity

It was noted earlier in the discussion of the United States–Soviet nuclear competition that the movement to more discriminating military technologies is creating among the public the impression that nuclear-war fighting capabilities are being acquired whose net effect will be to increase the likelihood of nuclear war. In fact these technologies are part of a broader pattern of development which could have revolutionary in contrast to evolutionary effects on international politics.

What we are now witnessing is the development and subsequent deployment of a whole range of military systems—land-based, sea-based, air-based, and eventually space-based—sharing the common virtues of high accuracy and information precision. The inexorable consequence of these deployments is an increased sense of vulnerability, not merely of population centers which have long been vulnerable to attack, but of all fixed targets whose coordinates can be determined by the potential attacker. Increased vulnerability is not in fact limited to fixed targets but extends to classes of mobile targets whose movements can be monitored with regularity and therefore predictability.

When military forces judge themselves to be vulnerable to attack, they instinctively respond to frustrate the attacker. Such responses involve countermeasures to confuse the attacking forces, defenses to protect the intended targets, and mobility and deception to make the "target acquisition" problem as difficult as possible. This dynamic of measure-countermeasure-counter-countermeasure is as old as military competition itself. What is new, however, is that more than ever before armed forces will have a capacity to strike what they are aiming at with minimum "collateral damage."

The introduction of these technologies of precision and control exacerbate organizational and political aspects of defense policymaking. Witness the excruciating decade-long struggle on the part of four successive American presidential administrations to identify an acceptable resolution to the Minuteman intercontinental ballistic missile (ICBM) vulnerability issue. Scores of basing modes have been examined and then rejected for failure to satisfy strategic, operational, budgetary, or political criteria. In short, advances in military technologies which are producing conditions of more vulnerable forces are not easily overcome in a military sense and are very expensive as well.

To gain perspective it is worth noting that the last truly revolutionary developments in military technology emerged shortly after World War II. The confluence of nuclear weapons, ballistic missiles, and solid-state electronics produced the age of the nuclear missile and the "offense-dominance" of the contemporary United States–Soviet nuclear balance in which deterrence rather than defenses has kept the peace. The effort by President Reagan to stimulate advances in strategic defenses is designed to extricate the United States from this maddening relationship, but it is a very long way from an earnest expression of presidential hope to an operationally effective battle management system.

It is likely that such initiatives will proceed, irrespective of their short-term promise. We are already witnessing the earliest stages of military competition in space with crude antisatellite devices, with strategic defenses probably not far behind unless an arms control regime can be fashioned to curtail the competition (which seems most unlikely). Wherever one looks, from Central Europe to Central America to open ocean areas to space, the battlefield is becoming increasingly complex, making obsolete tomorrow the strategies and tactics that were thought today to be highly effective. While the United States and the Soviet Union, and other nations to a lesser extent, search for major technological breakthroughs that could fundamentally alter existing military relationships, substantial feelings of apprehension accompany the search.

7. Political instability in the developing areas

Surely among the most noteworthy developments in international politics in the second half of the twentieth century has been the collapse of the colonial empires and the emergence of scores of independent sovereign states in Asia, Africa, and, to a lesser degree, in Latin America. The experience of many of these states in the last two decades has been marked by considerable political, social, and economic instability. More than one hundred of these states are governed by some type of authoritarian regime which functions in an environment devoid of any form of legitimized political succession. Many of these regimes seem unable or unwilling to satisfy the basic human needs of large percentages of their populace. Nor in many instances are they able to prevent the coalescing of opposition forces which often look to Moscow or Beijing for material, if not ideological, support.

From Castro's succession to power in Cuba in 1959 through the fall of the Shah of Iran in 1979, it has been repeatedly demonstrated that regime changes in developing countries can have a direct bearing on American interests as well as on the lives of the citizens of these states. Often, though not always, regime change is accompanied by the adoption of policies by the new regime that are seen as adverse to American strategic concerns. This is sometimes the case because the United States has actively supported the *ancien régime* and is therefore seen as the enemy by the new ruling elite.

In the course of these experiences, prior to, during, and subsequent to the regime change, all too often Washington has been able to exercise few effective levers to promote positive (as defined by the United States) socio-economic and foreign policies. The United States is frequently captive of its own anticommunist rhetoric and is effectively manipulated by the government under siege to support it militarily and economically despite its own antidemocratic policies. Then, if the authoritarian regime falls to socialist or Soviet-aided groups, America finds it difficult to establish relationships which simultaneously satisfy congressional critics, United States foreign policy interests, and the preferences of the new regime.

Authoritarian regimes conduct oppressive policies which generate grievances among the people who often are attracted to models of socialist and communist economic and political systems. The central failing of the United States has been an inability to help provide an attractive alternative for the people by effectively promoting democratic social values. This was the problem Washington had to wrestle with in Southeast Asia in the 1960s, and this is the problem being faced in Central America in the 1980s. No one wishes to repeat the searing experience in Vietnam, but, as noted earlier, diverse and often mutually exclusive "lessons" have been learned from this 15-year trauma. Invoking the Vietnam analogy with respect to contemporary problems in El Salvador and elsewhere in Central America triggers vehement expressions of support and outrage.

The United States continues to search for a mix of economic, political, diplomatic, and military tools it can apply in the developing world to promote not only its own interests but what it believes to be the best interests of the majority of the people in these countries. We know from experiences that (1) these countries are extraordinarily diverse; (2) American inattention, passivity, or deliberate inaction are no guarantee of positive results; and (3) deep American military involvement can also bring about disaster. Managing political change in the developing world is among the most demanding challenges facing any American administration, and it is not at all obvious that a set of effective policies are now or will shortly be forthcoming.

Conclusion

In this brief and sweeping review of the principal alterations to international relations in the past quarter-century, we have identified seven areas which are themselves sources of anxiety and concern. But these areas can serve as well as an agenda upon which to build security.

First, the United States must move beyond the traumas of the 1960s and 1970s and seek to define its role in the world, sensitive to changing international conditions, articulating its policies with self-confidence but without stridency. This will probably require a new generation of leadership willing to strike out in fresh directions and unwilling to accept the "constraints" which are an ever-present rationale for avoiding bold initiatives. A modest demonstration of successful leadership would go a long way toward dispelling the memories of recent failures.

Second, every effort must be made to provide effective means of regulating the United States–Soviet nuclear arms competition. Given the enormity of this undertaking, it may well be wise to step back from seeking complex and comprehensive negotiated agreements and instead strive to reach accords, formally or implicitly, in which each side yields a single system or capability of value to itself. By reducing individual threats, even one at a time, progress in arms control could be achieved which would be recognized as tangible albeit limited contributions to national security.

Third, Americans must accept the diversity inherent in alliance relationships. The maintenance of security ties with our NATO and Japanese allies is not a matter of American charity, but rather are commitments in accord with United States national interests. It would be wise therefore to go a long way to accommodate change within the existing alliance framework since virtually all alternatives to the present fundamental arrangements are less attractive than what we have been living with for many years.

Fourth, we must make a better effort to integrate foreign economic and national security policies. Indeed the very distinction is not merely meaningless but downright misleading. Economic competition with our allies can have highly corrosive effects on our security relationships. We and our allies must take great pains therefore to adopt political strategies for our economic activity so that to the extent feasible our trade, investment, and monetary interactions produce "positive-sum" and not "zero-sum" results.

Fifth, we must be careful not to humiliate the Soviet people or to adopt policies which would generate a "trapped" feeling among the Kremlin leadership. Strength, perseverance, and consistency must be the hallmark of American policies toward the Soviet Union. As Soviet policies adapt to changing circumstances we must position ourselves to take advantage of opportunities to reduce tensions, and not be motivated by a simplistic desire to see Soviet weaknesses worsen. The superpower relationship is simply too dangerous to substitute brinksmanship for foreign policies.

Sixth, we must maintain an integrative perspective of where advances in military technologies are taking us. Every new weapon is not necessarily needed or desirable. Emphasis should be placed on minimizing the vulnerability of existing systems to remove the temptation of our adversaries to strike even under conditions of deep crisis. Moreover, a concerted effort should be made to define concretely those areas of military competition in space which can best be curtailed through negotiated or tacit agreement.

Let us not enter an open-ended arms race in space without having thought through the consequences of the competition.

Seventh, we need to ensure that more effective use is made of our economic and military aid in developing countries so that grievances to regimes extant are attenuated rather than exacerbated. Without country-specific, highly focused, micro-managed assistance policies, the United States has little hope of inculcating its social and political values in the developing world.

When the Center for International Affairs was founded, it was already dimly perceived that global interdependence was an emerging international phenomenon. It was hoped, indeed expected, that interdependence would breed security. Interdependence has in fact arrived, but security is more elusive than ever. In all likelihood, many of the conditions we face today will continue without being overtaken by either global anarchy or nuclear war. The challenge is to manage them a little better rather than a little worse.

It has been said that optimism is a state of mind, whereas pessimism is a character trait. In the real world of international relations this is about as optimistic as we can afford to be.

4

Arms control at bay

PAUL DOTY

Mallinckrodt Professor of Biochemistry
Center for Science and International Affairs, Harvard University

It can be easily argued that the year 1958, which saw the beginning
of the Center for International Affairs, was also the year in which strategic
arms control between East and West began. Prior to that year, there had
not only been no arms control agreements but none of the attempts could
be said to contain the seeds of later success. Not so in 1958. In the fall of
that year, two conferences were held in Geneva that do indeed mark the
beginning of nearly continuous negotiations involving the Soviet Union and
the United States (sometimes together with the United Kingdom) in efforts
to control nuclear weaponry.

The Conference on Surprise Attack adjourned in failure after six weeks
during which it was not possible to agree on agenda. Nevertheless, the ghost
of this conference has remained with us ever since in that its theme, to
reduce the likelihood of first strike, is ever present in the twenty-five years
of negotiations that have followed. The other conference, On the Discon-
tinuence of Nuclear Weapons Tests, began a process that led to the Partial
Test Ban Treaty of 1963, subsequent related treaties in 1974 and 1976 that
remain unratified by the United States, and the likelihood that further
negotiation will proceed in the future.

In its early years, the Center contributed substantially to the maturing
of strategic analysis and arms control conceptions that have structured the
way we think about the radically new dilemmas of the nuclear age. The
triad of land-based missiles, submarine-based missiles, and long-range bombers
took form in the 1960s. Their deployment permitted the phasing out of the
vulnerable and poorly controlled bomber force of the 1950s and a reduction
by half of the megatonnage on line. The doctrines of assured destruction
and flexible response that governed these new forces were a clear improvement over massive retaliation. Although eventual improvements in ballistic
missile accuracy were anticipated, the hardening of silos kept the land-based
missiles invulnerable for another decade or more. The Limited Test Ban
Treaty of 1963 slowed the development of nuclear weapons by several years
and created seismic detection capabilities that would in time make possible

more severe restrictions on weapons tests. President Johnson hoped to cap these developments by negotiating ceilings on the major strategic weapons, but this was to await the Nixon–Kissinger period.

In retrospect, the problem of nuclear weapons in Europe was not well handled. Failures at the political level led to France undertaking her own development. Thousands of battlefield weapons were sent to Europe without forethought as to how their use would improve security. And the attempt to find a limited nuclear role for West Germany via the multilateral force failed. However, the Non-Proliferation Treaty of 1968, imperfect though it was, seems to have played an important role in slowing the spread of nuclear weapons states far beyond what anyone thought possible a few years before. The SALT I ABM Treaty and the Interim Agreement putting a ceiling on strategic missiles was a landmark in showing that agreements could be reached in limiting central forces and that tempting but dangerous technological developments could be jointly restrained. With the success of satellite photography and electronic surveillance in counting the vehicles that launch nuclear weapons and in determining the characteristics of launchers being tested, the way seemed open to agreements that would decisively limit and then reduce the nuclear arsenals.

This did not happen. No further arms control agreements of significance were reached after 1972. The negotiation of SALT II was repeatedly delayed and finally completed in 1979, too late to stem the proliferation of warheads through MIRVing in the 1970s and too modest in its scope to win ratification in the Senate before the Soviet invasion of Afghanistan postponed such action indefinitely.

Our purpose is to examine some aspects of this failure to develop an expanding arms control regime, especially to see how the political process was unable to adapt to the increasing rate of technological change, and then to survey the present scene and to peer hesitantly into the different futures that further developments in weaponry or possible revival in arms control may bring.

I

Because arms control has not progressed in the last decade, it has been seen by many observers as becoming less relevant, even irrelevant. Yet the absence of any alternative approach to controlling the arms race and the recent rise of public interest in arms control has kept it high on the international agenda. Indeed, with the decline in the state of East–West relations, arms control discussions have come to carry the main burden of what remains of East–West diplomacy.

In a formal sense, arms control agreements are made or not made according to whether the following four conditions can be met:

1. There is sufficient communication between the two parties and sufficient incentive to identify an area of potential agreement.

2. One side (the USSR) is willing to accept a negotiated agreement.
3. The other side (United States) is willing to accept a negotiated agreement.
4. The diplomatic and technical means can be found to define the framework in which the agreement can be sought and the means by which verification of compliance can be insured.

The first requirement implies that state relations are such as to permit rational, credible discourse. The hostility during most of the Cold War period (1947–54) was so intense as to preclude such discourse. The second requirement is essentially met by agreement within the Politbureau of the USSR. Of course, military and foreign ministry groups lower in the hierarchy contribute, but prolonged opposition from many sectors along the decision chain is not as pronounced as in the United States. The third requirement is much more difficult to meet because many groups in the United States can block the consensus required. This can occur either in the policy formulation stage or in the ratification stage. At either juncture, the unwillingness of key agencies of the Executive or the unwillingness of thirty-four Senators out of a Congress of 535 members can be fatal. Behind such identifiable impediments lie whole sets of complex, shifting political groupings willing to put single issues ahead of agreement.[1] The fourth requirement is usually difficult to meet, but with sufficient refinement of the area to be covered, resourcefulness with respect to verification, and much hard work a way can usually be found. Generally, there are a number of routes to a given goal and relatively few goals which seem unreachable.

The dozen agreements and treaties that were enacted between 1959 and 1973 met these requirements. But what of the many possibilities for agreement that were not reached? It will be useful to review the most salient opportunities, ones which if grasped would have profoundly altered the course of the nuclear competition.

At the outset of the nuclear age, the seminal question of control of the atom was faced in the two policies advanced by the United States and the USSR. These were profoundly different and as a result the first requirement could not be met. Although much of the difference could be covered by the contrast between "control first" and "disarmament first," it is hardly realistic to assume that two such different societies with little previous contact (outside limited military collaboration during World War II) and now faced with a sudden quantum jump in the dimensions of warfare could have found common ground.

The next opportunity came a few years later when the possibility of constructing thermonuclear devices of nearly unlimited destructive power, thousands of times greater than the Hiroshima device, became evident. In the grip of the Cold War, meaningful communications hardly existed and little was to be expected. The intense internal debate on the American side over proceeding with research and development was tilted by the Soviet

Union's first nuclear explosion in August 1949. In January 1950, President Truman ordered work to begin. Progress was rapid: the first thermonuclear explosion occurred in 1952 and a series of developments yielded the first practical H-bomb test at Bikini in the spring of 1954. Soviet tests occurred in the same time-frame, indicating that they had made their decision to proceed no later than the United States. With the Korean War beginning in 1950 and the subsequent evidence of Stalin's paranoid behavior at this time, no other outcome seems to have been possible.

The seeming inevitability of the H-bomb development was matched within a few years by developments at the other end of the scale of nuclear explosions, battlefield nuclear weapons. It is interesting that a number of influential persons who opposed the H-bomb development did so, in part, because such a crash effort would delay the development of tactical nuclear weapons for battlefield use. This direction was favored because it seemed more urgent and practical to keep aggressors at bay by threatening their armies with certain destruction if they invaded than by threatening massive retaliation. And there was the practical incentive, too: since the possibility of matching Soviet conventional troop strength in Europe was remote, battlefield nuclear weapons could substitute for manpower. Thus, with little opposition and little forethought as to the consequences of actual use, battlefield weapons were developed in the 1950s and about 7,000 were deployed in Western Europe in the early 1960s. In the same period, the late 1950s, and with no opposition or no consideration of negotiation, intermediate-range nuclear-armed ballistic missiles were developed and deployed in Europe by both sides. The United States missiles were withdrawn a few years later, but the Soviet ss-4s and ss-5s remained.

These three failures of diplomacy, one a failed negotiation and two cases where neither side proposed to negotiate, have permanently shaped the structure of the nuclear world. They were taken in a climate where there was virtually no United States–Soviet contact, when Soviet policy was either paranoid or recklessly aggressive, and when the nuclear balance was greatly in the American favor. The outcome could hardly have been other than what it was. There was no political framework which could have handled the explosion of technological advance that was thrust upon the two emerging superpowers.

II

As the 1960s began to unfold, United States–Soviet contacts improved. Despite the Cuban missile crisis and the Vietnam War, this improvement was to continue until 1973. Changing political considerations played a major role, but four technical developments propelled the two sides toward some form of cooperation as well. The first was the worldwide protest against the radioactive fallout resulting from United States and Soviet nuclear weapons tests in the atmosphere. The second was the practical possibility of the nuclear arsenals evolving toward survivable weapons that would not invite a preemptive strike in times of crisis. The third was the development of satellite reconnaissance and electronic surveillance that removed much of the uncertainty from each side's view of the other's strategic forces. The fourth was the shared interest in preventing other countries from becoming nuclear.

The intersection of these several developments reversed the pattern of 1945–60. Between 1963 and 1973, ten agreements or treaties dealing with nuclear matters were made between the United States and the USSR and often involving other parties as well. There were some examples from each of the major categories that make up modern arms control: (1) *arrangements* to reduce the risk of nuclear war, (2) *bans* of weapons and deployments that may increase the risk of war, and (3) *limitations* of allowed weapons that will create or preserve a balance of forces. The Hot Line Agreement of 1963 and its modernization in 1971, the Non-Proliferation Treaty of 1968, and the Prevention of Nuclear War Agreement of 1973 fall in the first category, "arrangements." The Limited Test Ban Treaty of 1963, the Outer Space Treaty of 1967, the Seabed Arms Control Treaty of 1971, and the earlier Antarctic Treaty (1959) are in the "bans" category. The ABM Treaty and the Interim Agreement to limit strategic ballistic missiles of 1972 (SALT I) represent the "limitations" approach to controlling central strategic forces with an aim to reaching balanced reductions.

In all of these cases, the four requirements noted earlier were met. By the standards of the nuclear age, this period saw a relatively harmonious relation develop between political conceptions of United States–Soviet common interests and the mastery of technical developments so that these became the instruments of policy formulation and negotiation. Even so, some important opportunities were missed. The Limited Test Ban, which restricted nuclear tests to underground, did eliminate the health risks due to fallout and did briefly interrupt the refinement of nuclear weapons. But a comprehensive treaty banning all tests could have been concluded if a compromise between the three on-site inspections the Soviets would allow and the seven which the United States wanted could have been made. Had such an agreement been reached and had it held, the course of nuclear weaponry would have been radically changed. At the other end of this period, SALT I failed to include a ban or regulation on MIRVing and thereby allowed a radical change in nuclear forces to proceed in the 1970s, a change that is widely regretted. On balance, however, this period of 1963–73 saw the greatest progress toward mutual control over nuclear forces that has occurred in the post-World War II years. This is not the place to dwell on the evolution of the political side of the United States–Soviet relation that had made this possible, but the coincidence of improved relations and some progress on the nuclear question is clear and stands in sharp contrast to the 1950s and to the period since 1973.

III

The development of detente, which President Kennedy had called for in his American University speech of June 1963, reached its peak a decade later but did not last. Sharp differences over the meaning of the concept, the long drawn-out retreat of the president over Watergate, the ejection of Soviet influence in Egypt followed by the October 1973 war, and the expansion of Soviet military influence in Africa showed the structure of detente could not bear the weight of unfolding events. The erosion of the United States–Soviet relation has continued to this day and with it we have seen a cumulative failure of the arms control process, whether viewed as an instrument to facilitate the relation or as a serious joint attempt to reduce the risks of nuclear war.

The ebb and flow of developments in military technology were at a high point in this period: if these new possibilities were to be restrained, it would impose a greater than usual demand on the political process just as it was becoming weaker. The first issue was the MIRVing of half the United States land-based ICBM force and all of its sea-based force, thereby trebling its inventory of strategic missile warheads. Predictably, the Soviet Union followed. Now both sides have about 8,000 warheads on line. This sudden affluence in warheads inevitably provoked deep changes in strategy and doctrine. Since the important urban, industrial, and military targets of the 1960s were already covered, the new weapons required new targets. In this way, the conceptions of nuclear war-fighting were born. Assured destruction remained as the irreducible, fall-back doctrine, but now, with many warheads of increasing accuracy, a new vista of possible military and military-related targets numbering in the tens of thousands were reachable. Deterrence was expanded to include deterring the war-fighting capabilities of the other side by deploying our own weapons directed at many critical parts of the Soviet military system.

This outlook was abetted by the continuing improvement in the accuracy of delivery of missile warheads. Surgical strikes against military targets became the norm of military planners. Although higher accuracy may in time lead to the deployment of smaller yield weapons that would produce less collateral damage, the destruction that would occur in built-up areas remained enormous. More importantly, the silos of the land-based missiles, despite their being hardened, would soon become vulnerable to highly accurate warheads. In earlier times, when accuracy was measured in many hundreds of meters, these silos were safe because they could survive such near misses: now, with much higher accuracy, that protection was gone. In the 1980s, the two sides would be entering a particularly dangerous counterforce era when, with enough accurate warheads on MIRVed ICBMs, either side could threaten the land-based forces of the other side and whatever part of the submarine force was in port by using only a fraction of its own force. Such a threat could provoke the side receiving it to launch its own forces on warning since otherwise they may be lost. Many hold the view that such a successful disarming strike could not be accomplished in a practical way because of the inability to rehearse it. But opinions are divided on this with the result that this possibility becomes a part of the thinking of military planners and publics alike. Such a situation was simply not possible a decade earlier and hence was not then a part of the nuclear lexicon.

Still another new weapon was to arise in the 1970s and will be deployed in very large numbers in the 1980s if unrestrained. This is the cruise missile in its several forms: air-launched (ALCM), ground-launched (GLCM), and sea-launched (SLCM). After several years of lying undeveloped, the attractions of this weapon were recognized by the Air Force in its search for a way to overcome the heavy air defense of the Soviet Union which increasingly threatened bomber penetration of its borders. ALCMs launched from well outside national borders can accomplish delivery with relatively small losses. Of course, the prescription can be followed by the other side as well. As a result, the United States is now directing new efforts to finding ways to protect itself against Soviet ALCMs that would greatly multiply the current threat of a rather limited bomber force.

Thus, military research and development yielded a bumper crop of new weapons in the 1970s at a time of declining United States–Soviet relations. The one hope of mobilizing restraints against this lay in erecting proper limits in SALT II. Such negotiations were to have begun in 1973, when it was visualized that a treaty on limiting strategic weapons once each four years may indeed lead to substantial and beneficial arms control. This did not happen. The Vladivostok Agreement (1974) provided a framework for SALT II. But delays in implementation, aided by the deteriorating atmosphere in United States–Soviet relations and internecine warfare within the Ford Administration, led to no product. The Carter Administration entered office with a less divided interest in making progress but stumbled by seeking an agreement embodying much more severe limits than those in the Vladivostok Agreement rather than completing what was left unfinished from the Ford Administration. As a result, it took a year to get SALT II negotiations back into a meaningful phase and then another year to reach the agreement itself in June 1979. With relations with the Soviet Union continuing to worsen, ratification was certain to be difficult. Nitze and then Rowny had resigned from the delegation over points that became the core of right-wing opposition: allowance of continuation of much greater Soviet ICBM throw-weight (despite an approximate compensation in much superior United States bomber loadings), insufficient constraint on the Soviet Backfire bomber, and the claim that Soviet superiority was legitimized and growth in Soviet forces assured. The pro-treaty forces were less than completely enthusiastic because the reductions required were so modest and under the treaty warhead numbers could grow considerably. After months of debate, often embittered by other disagreements in the United States–Soviet scene, it appeared that a close but favorable vote may have been had in early 1980. But the Soviet invasion of Afghanistan reversed that expectation and President Carter withdrew the treaty from consideration.

Thus, in January 1981, a new administration took office in the wake of a new low in United States–Soviet relations and a continued failure in arms control. Now the linkage between the two was more firmly established.

IV

During the first year of the Reagan Administration, it became clear that policy toward the Soviet Union and arms control was undergoing a sharp change. The Soviet Union was to be treated as untrustworthy, every practice was to be reexamined to see if reciprocity existed, and the Soviet Union was to be prevented from attaining high technology from the West beginning with United States contributions to the gas pipeline to Western Europe. In arms control, the SALT II treaty would remain unratified, other arms control negotiations were to end, the old policy of incrementalism was to be replaced by one seeking deep cuts in strategic weapons in a "fair, balanced and verifiable manner." The negotiations to be continued were those on intermediate nuclear forces (INF) and those on reductions of strategic weapons (START). A substantial acceleration in defense expenditures was put in motion so that the position of inferiority into which the United States had fallen would be rectified before the end of the decade. It was alleged that this build-up would induce Soviet willingness to reach agreements at the negotiating table.

Well into the fourth year of the Reagan Administration, these approaches have not borne fruit. United States–Soviet relations have worsened even more, the INF negotiations have been terminated by the Soviet side, and the Soviets have set no date for resuming the START negotiations. Insofar as successful arms control negotiations are presumed to require a considerably higher level of useful governmental contact, this result is predictable. But the unfolding of events has been somewhat more interesting and complex. We consider five aspects in some detail.

1. INF

The INF negotiations began in October 1980 and ended in December 1983 when the Soviets walked out over the beginning of NATO deployments of Pershing II missiles and ground-based cruise missiles. In retrospect, this negative outcome could have been anticipated from the outset. The failure lay in the inability of the two sides to find sufficient common ground to make agreement through compromise possible. The first requirement for agreement mentioned earlier could not be met, not through insufficient communications at the negotiating level, but through the failure to relate the negotiations to a larger framework in which trade-offs may have produced sufficient incentives to reach agreement here.

The differences were basic. The United States position was that negotiations be limited to missiles of intermediate range, that all such systems world-wide be included, and that the French and British nuclear weapons that could reach the Soviet Union not be counted. The Soviet Union had about 800 warheads on intermediate-range missiles at the outset of the negotiations and about 1,400 at the end. NATO forces had none. Only the eighteen land-based missiles of the French fell within the intermediate-range category and these, like the submarine-launched missiles, were not subject to NATO control and could not be negotiated. The same applied to the British. However, even if these forces had been included, they totalled only 162, making the ratio of Soviet to Western warheads more than eight to one. Hence, there was little incentive for the Soviets to negotiate away their advantage. The Soviet position was that aircraft capable of delivering nuclear weapons at intermediate range should be included. And, further, they insisted that if such aircraft were included a balance already existed which should not be disturbed but taken as a base from which reductions were to be made. No such balance existed by Western counting; the missile- and aircraft-deliverable weapons favored the Soviet side by more than four to one. Moreover, the means by which aircraft capable of nuclear delivery can be counted and continuously verified have never been developed.

Looking behind the official positions, the differences were even more profound. The Soviets insisted that the nuclear lineup consists of the central nuclear forces of intercontinental range, for which they claim parity exists, and regional or theater balances of which that in Europe is the only one under negotiation. Here they assume there has been a balance for two decades or more and that their ss-20 missiles being introduced are only to replace older missiles. The introduction of new NATO missiles capable of reaching Russia would upset these balances just as much as the Soviet introduction of missiles in Cuba would. The NATO position is that the Soviet missiles targeted on Western Europe were tolerable when the United States had a clear superiority in central systems but that when that disappeared in the late 1970s, the imbalance in Europe should be addressed. Furthermore, the view in NATO was that all NATO countries were to be equally protected and weapons that targeted Western Europe targeted the alliance. Hence, the Soviet missiles in Europe served as a means to intimidate Europe while no comparable force was targeted on the Soviet Union.

Clearly, no compromise was evident. Now that negotiations have ended, the United States government believes that the Soviets will see the steady deployment of United States missiles as sufficiently distasteful to return to negotiate some kind of balance that permits some NATO deployment and limits theirs. The Soviets indicate that this is futile, that United States missile deployment in any number circumvents the existing balance. It is unlikely that any compromise can be found within the present negotiating

framework. The obvious way to expand the framework is to merge the INF
and START negotiations so as to include all weapons systems with ranges
exceeding, say, 1,000 miles. This would surely lead to a more complicated
negotiation and require considerable time, but it may be the only way out.
Neither side shows any interest at present. As has happened before, the
burdens of negotiation have now become so great and complex that no
forward motion can be expected until there is a political settlement of some
outstanding differences. At present, this course is even more remote because
of the level of hostility which surrounds the relation and the paucity of
governmental contacts that preclude exploring trade-offs that could loosen
the logjam.

2. START

START addresses a much wider range of problems and hence allows a
much wider framework for negotiation. Moreover, it addresses the central
balance where parity or near-parity exists. The Reagan Administration con-
tends that parity has disappeared and can only be regained by a substantial
military build-up over a period of seven years or more. The Soviets fear
this development would upset the parity that they insist exists already.
Hence, they have an incentive to negotiate an agreement that would prevent
the unfolding of the planned United States build-up. Meanwhile, their own
programs, that are likely in time to match or surpass those of the United
States, are going ahead.

When the START negotiations finally began in June 1982, the United
States position showed a marked change. The goal was to move far beyond
SALT II by shifting to counting ballistic-missile warheads and aiming to
reduce those to 5,000 on each side. Moreover, since missiles were the more
threatening weapons, their reduction should be sought first by imposing
severe reductions here and postponing negotiations on bombers. In a continuation of its earlier policy, the Soviet Union approached the negotiation
as another SALT-like step, in which launchers would be reduced from the
2,250 limit in SALT II to 1,800, and maintained that such agreements have
as a prerequisite a ban on United States intermediate-range missiles in
Europe.

After a year of sparring, the United States introduced significant changes
in its position in June and October 1983, in part as a result of the recom-
mendations of the Scowcroft Commission and in part due to pressure from
members of Congress who tied their continued support of the MX missile
to further changes. As a result, the severe reduction on numbers of launchers
was removed so as to allow small, single-warhead ICBMs to be introduced.
Bombers, together with the limit on the number of ALCMs they could carry,
were moved up for concurrent negotiation with the missiles. The 5,000
missile-warhead limit remained and some attention to approaching equal
destructiveness in the forces was required. The October changes proposed
that the reduction schedule to reach the 5,000 missile-warhead limit be at

least as rapid as five percent of total warheads per year, and that if replace-ment was desired such new missiles be compensated for by an additional withdrawal of warheads. The bombers and ALCMs could be treated in the same way, although it was suggested that replacements be allowed on a one-for-one basis or a separate trade-off against Soviet missile throw-weight could be negotiated.

All in all, this represented a substantial change in the United States position. It was even hinted that the reduction to 5,000 warheads could be revised. However, by the time this was presented at Geneva, the hostility had reached a very high level due to Soviet beliefs that the shooting down of the Korean airliner had been so exploited by the United States as to embarrass them severely and the NATO deployments scheduled for December seemed on course. One observer stated that the Soviets "would have turned down their own draft proposal if we had offered it to them." As a result, they left the negotiations refusing to agree on a date for their reconvening. Once the deployments began in December, the Soviets claimed that an essential requirement of their negotiating had been destroyed and that the new situation which the NATO deployments produced removed the basis on which they had proposed a 1,800 launcher limit. Their price for returning to the negotiation is now set at no less than the removal of weapons already deployed in Europe, a most unlikely event.

Thus, despite the greater room for maneuver and the great amount of relevant work done in SALT II, no agreement has been reached and the present stagnation threatens to last for some time. As with INF, only a settlement of some major political differences is likely to reopen negotiations on these central issues.

3. Freezes

The mood in the United States public has undergone remarkable changes since the beginning of the Reagan Administration. Its origins probably date from the failure to ratify SALT II: for many concerned citizens, this marked the end of a long period of hope that the tensions and risks of the nuclear age would be diminished by cumulative agreements. The arrival of the Reagan Administration brought with it a confrontational, hardline approach to the Soviet Union. For many, this was taken to be incompatible with the arms control goals that eventually emerged. And so, little was expected. The administration pronouncements on nuclear issues were widely viewed as frightening and seemed an indulgence that ignored the spreading rec-ognition that nuclear war was to be avoided at almost any cost rather than be planned for in the normal course of events. This disillusionment with administration planning evoked even stronger opposition from many Eu-ropean publics. The nuclear protector had threatened to become the nuclear instigator.

In the United States, these feelings found expression in the nuclear freeze movement. Loose coalitions of groups created a network that has survived for several years and shows signs of being a force in the 1984 elections. Freezes have long played a role in the history of arms control, often under the term of moratoria. That this now became a rallying post for many people of diverse views is a credit to its capturing the feeling that "enough is enough," that the consequences of nuclear war are far more devastating than many had ever thought, and that a "comprehensive" freeze seemed an easy formula for stopping a senseless arms competition. And "stopping it" seemed to suggest a more quickly attainable goal than the complicated reductions that the administration was trying to negotiate. One has to stop running before turning around, and stopping or freezing became a clearly defined objective in the minds of many.

The comprehensive freeze that was adopted as the prescription of the freeze movement was far from simple.[2] It was defined as a bilateral, verifiable freeze on all further testing, production, and deployment of nuclear weapons. Since there are roughly a hundred different weapons being tested, produced, or deployed by the two superpowers, this is a substantial list on which to reach agreement on establishing the existing numbers and the means of verifying that no further production and deployment will occur.[3]

Despite the progress made in SALT II, those deliberations covered less than half the weapons involved and did not address production. So the "stopping" covers a much wider range of weapons than those now under consideration. Nevertheless, this approach has the advantage that, if negotiable, it would prevent compensating for the weapons being limited by deployments that were allowed, a major drawback of the classical arms control approach. However, the time required to negotiate such a comprehensive freeze seems to stretch into many years by any standard.

In contrast to this assessment, the quickness with which such a freeze might be put in place is widely hailed as one of its great attractions. How to deal with this dilemma? One way is to ease up on the verification requirement; the other is to revert to a moratorium while negotiations go on. Neither of these is likely to be attractive to both the administration and the Senate. Hence, the only apparent alternative lies in reducing the menu of what is to be frozen, that is, a limited freeze. If this were reduced to the weapons covered in SALT II plus the new bombers (Backfire, Blackjack, and B-1B) and/or a ban on testing nuclear weapons, and if such a package could be negotiated in a year or so, it would be a very substantial accomplishment. However, the leaders of the freeze movement seem to be moving in a somewhat different way. Their preference seems to be for a moratorium on the testing and deployment of ballistic missiles and a cessation of underground nuclear tests, to be enforced by congressional action that would put funding for these items in escrow if the Soviet Union undertook the same obligations. However, this route is open to several objections: moratoria are inconsistent with the low state of trust now existing between the two countries because a well-prepared breakout can offer real short-term advantages to the initiator; the verification required for a short moratorium may involve some compromises that would be inappropriate for a prolonged period; the complete test ban still has substantial problems such as defining what is a nuclear test and hence a moratorium could lead to claims of violation.

Returning to the comprehensive freeze, there remains the difficult problem of negotiating a mutually acceptable time for the onset of such a regime and the more difficult problem of specifying how replacements and modernization are to be handled. If a B-52 bomber crashes it cannot be replaced with a newly made B-52 since that technology has been scrapped. If the freeze were limited to a short period, such as a year, a total freeze might be acceptable, but if it were for an indefinite period, many problems would arise and require negotiated settlement. This difficulty unmasks a deeper difference between those who favor a freeze and those who prefer the more traditional arms control approach. In the latter, there is a real concern over modernization and replacements. Despite reduction schedules, allowance needs to be made for retaining the reliability of the remaining force and for the replacement of allowed weapons with those deemed more survivable and hence less at risk in a crisis. Supporters of a freeze tend to underrate this dimension. Hence, the duration of a freeze assumes quite different importance in the two points of view.

If both sides were starting afresh, the comprehensive freeze with its inevitable exceptions may make as much sense as the system-by-system approach that leaves many weapons unrestrained. In the real world, much progress useful in a future agreement would be cast aside for a new menu of problems not yet well understood. The disillusionment with the failure to reach agreement in the last decade is understandable: it remains unclear that any advantage is to be gained by switching to the comprehensive freeze with its heavy burden of negotiation before any progress on reductions or evolution toward more stable forces could be undertaken.

The Reagan Administration is opposed to any freeze of this kind. Yet all the Democratic candidates support it in a none too well-defined manner. Should the Democrats come to power with the mandate to reach an early agreement that would show some progress, they could settle for the limited freeze described above. This form of a freeze would indeed be a major accomplishment if carried out soon enough to allow time to deal with the problems of long-term modernization and verification within the four-year term. Yet the opposition that such an agreement would meet in the Senate, despite possible shifts in the next election, would be daunting. Again, political limits without some accommodation of Soviet–American differences will prevent agreement being reached.

4. Cruise missiles

Neither the present stagnation nor the limited freeze address the two most pressing issues being forced by developing technology: the cruise missile and the militarization of space.

Because of their inherent smallness of size, cruise missiles are extremely difficult to detect and verify except when associated with visible carriers that are also controlled. If ALCMs can be restricted to heavy bombers, they can be satisfactorily verified, provided that all ALCMS can be classed as nuclear. Should conventionally armed versions be assigned to other uncontrolled aircraft, the problem of discrimination would become virtually impossible.

GLCMs are unlikely to be developed with intercontinental range; hence, the problem lies in the intermediate-range missile category. Should such negotiations resume, verification of the kinds of GLCMs now being deployed in Europe should not prove very difficult because of the visibility of the truck that carries four missiles and the retinue that accompanies it. The problem lies in insuring that the GLCMs are not deployed in other ways.

The most difficult verification problem lies with sea-based cruise missiles (SLCM). Pre-modern versions having ranges of 600 km are now deployed by the Soviet navy by the hundreds, primarily for ship attack. It is likely that modern SLCMs with much longer range for land attack will be deployed on ships as well as special submarines and possibly on attack submarines as well. The United States Tomahawk program calls for the deployment of 1,000 land-attack cruise missiles on attack submarines beginning in mid-1984. Similar missiles with conventional warheads will be based on naval ships. Again, discrimination will present a most difficult challenge. The most difficult, however, would be the verification of any limits on submarine-launched land-attack cruise missiles. Further, such deployments complicate the mission of attack submarines since their primary purpose is to intercept shipping at whatever risk, not to remain out of action as would be required for a reserve nuclear force. In any event, the time is rapidly approaching when their deployment on both sides can be so diverse and their confusion with conventionally armed missiles of the same characteristics so unavoidable that the limits of arms control may have been passed by. Left unattended, this problem will present great uncertainties to both sides and may block arms control in the future when there is more interest than now in achieving it. This deserves urgent attention before the point of no return is passed.

5. Space

The military use of space has increased over two decades to the point where it is now an important part of the security systems of the two sides, and other countries are beginning to move in the same direction. Reconnaissance from space has now become a standard, accepted practice. It benefits the United States in three ways. Because of the inherent differences between open and closed societies, we have much more to learn from reconnaissance than do the Soviets. Satellites are inherently fragile and, due to their predictable paths, are quite vulnerable to attack. The protection provided by modest hardening and maneuverability is of limited value and purchased at very high cost. Finally, since the United States is likely to be more dependent on the military use of space than the Soviet Union, its ability to adequately deter possible Soviet interference with its satellites by threats of reciprocal action is limited. Thus, the international sanctioning of military space activities has been of particular benefit to the United States.[5]

In this situation, there was little incentive for the United States to develop anti-satellite weapons (ASAT) since the major effect would probably be to stimulate the Soviets to do the same, leading to a net disadvantage for the United States. With the exception of a minor effort (1964) long since abandoned, the United States restrained from such developments despite a low-keyed, on-again-off-again Soviet program. This ended when President Ford initiated a United States ASAT program (February 1976). The Carter Administration carried this forward but with the explicit policy of seeking an arms control agreement at the same time. Such negotiations were held in 1978–79. The Soviet Union initially opposed the United States position of seeking to ban the testing and deployment of ASAT weapons and then reversed their position so quickly that the United States seemed unable to adjust before the meetings were suspended, allegedly to allow full attention to ratifying SALT II. The talks have not been resumed. Apparently, a draft treaty remains with the usual amount of unsettled points but showing some progress in the direction of "non-use" and "rules of the road" agreements.

The Soviet Union responded to this discontinuation of the talks by taking their proposals to a wider forum, the United Nations, first in 1981 and then in substantially changed form in 1983. The latter draft treaty bans ASAT tests and calls for the elimination of ASAT systems already existing as well as the prohibition of the use of force against space objects or against targets on earth from space. Its enforcement and verification provisions are nearly nonexistent and it is flawed by prohibiting the use of any manned spacecraft for military purposes, a feature that would outlaw both the United States shuttle and the Soviet Salyut system. Assuming that some parts of this draft treaty are dispensable and that others are open to negotiations, it would seem that an agreement could be reached if both sides were seriously interested.

Although the Reagan Administration still has the matter under review as of this writing, press leaks indicate that it is considered unverifiable and talks will not be resumed. If this is so, a great opportunity will be lost. With the testing of an F-15-launched ASAT missile by the United States and the continued development and testing of a ground-launched ASAT missile by the Soviets, the stage is set for developing over the next decade ASAT weapons that would be moderately effective against satellites in low earth orbit and other ASAT weapons that could reach the much higher stationary orbits where the United States has a preponderance of assets. The problems of verification are quite varied. Some are not particularly demanding and a restricted form of treaty could be designed about them. Other verification problems are difficult and will become more so with the passage of time.

Here, the national interest should require the striking of a bargain between the value of additional measures that would be in our interest if they are likely to be verifiable and the value of abandoning such measures because we cannot now be certain of verification.

The objections to negotiating an ASAT treaty have a deeper base in the desire of the Reagan Administration to avoid interference with its long-range program for strategic defense ("Star Wars"). The president's call in March 1983 for a research and development program aimed at "our ultimate goal of eliminating the threat posed by strategic nuclear missiles" must of necessity examine all sorts of interception of ballistic missiles in their post-boost phase or of the warheads in the mid-course or terminal part of their trajectory. Such testing will be indistinguishable from the testing of ASAT weapons in many cases. Hence, the conflict and the likelihood that an arms race in space will come about.

This is regrettable on several scores. The failure to seek an arms control solution to the vulnerability of satellites in a period in which they are becoming increasingly essential to our security and no other means based on defense or deterrence is adequate represents a triumph of policy uninformed by technical reality. More importantly, this divorce from technical reality threatens to generate a new race in strategic defense which could lead to the deployment of space systems costing in the range of ten to fifty times that of any now deployed and vulnerable to relatively inexpensive means of destruction. As a recent report states: "The prospect that emerging Star Wars technologies, when further developed, will provide a perfect or near-perfect defense system, literally removing from the hand of the Soviet Union the ability to do socially mortal damage to the United States with nuclear weapons, is so remote that it should not serve as the basis of public expectation or national policy . . ."[6] Most informed persons believe that the futility of this course will be recognized within a few years at most and that the momentum developed will be turned to "less than perfect" defense, which really means defense of land-based missiles where improvement over present capabilities is clearly possible. But this course would collide with the SALT I Treaty on Antiballistic Missiles which has been a bulwark in holding back expensive excursions into a technology whose performance under wartime conditions would always be uncertain and whose existence would destabilize the delicate equilibrium we now have.

V

This reconnaissance of the broad front at which technology and politics meet in the effort to build a safer, less threatening future provides little comfort. The conditions of the one period (1963–73) in which progress was made have not returned. While history cannot repeat itself, it seems evident that two strikingly different cultures, organized under governmental regimes that have very little in common, cannot reach accommodations that are clearly in their mutual interest if the prevailing atmosphere is so hostile and distrustful that meaningful, differentiated communication and exploration is not possible. Until this is in some way reversed, it is unlikely that the accumulating problems on the nuclear menu can be taken up in a manner that might lead to resolution. Priorities that allow for some accommodation must first be established at the political level on both sides before diplomacy and technology can liberate East and West from an increasingly dangerous stagnation.

NOTES

1. Such matters are analyzed by Steven E. Miller, *International Security*, *8*, no. 4 (1984), 67–90.
2. Randall Forsberg, *Scientific American*, *247*, 1982, 52 – 61.
3. Howard Stoertz, Jr., *International Security*, *8*, no. 4, (1984), 91–110.
5. Paul B. Stares in *National Interests and the Military Use of Space*, ed. W. Durch (Cambridge, Mass.: Ballinger, 1984).
6. A. Carter, "Directed Energy Missile Defense in Space," Office of Technology Assessment, April 1984.

III

The interplay of economics and politics in industrial democracies

SIDNEY VERBA AND GARY ORREN

Political and economic equality:
a theoretical and empirical comparison

DOUGLAS A. HIBBS

Macroeconomic performance,
macroeconomic policy, and electoral politics
in industrial democracies

ELLIOT J. FELDMAN

Patterns of failure in government
megaprojects: economics, politics, and
participation in industrial democracies

5

Political and economic equality:
a theoretical and empirical comparison

SIDNEY VERBA

Carl H. Pforzheimer University Professor,
Harvard University

GARY R. ORREN

Associate Professor of Public Policy, Kennedy School of Government,
Harvard University

Inequality is a wellspring of conflict in most societies. One group looks at another, finds it more affluent, more powerful, more secure—and concludes that things are not as they should be. It may resolve to redress the inequality. Sometimes, too, the other group looks back at the less affluent, less powerful, less secure and, fearing they will want such redress, takes steps to forestall it. In either case, conflict is likely to follow.

This generalization is sound, but not particularly helpful. We need to define the issue much more precisely. Here, however, is where inequality causes confusion. Inequality is everywhere: among individuals, families, classes, ethnic groups, regions, and nations. It may concern many different valued "goods": wealth, power, security, prestige, leisure, or love. Inequality may be based on results or on opportunity; it may be measured in relative or absolute terms; the units that are equal or unequal can be individuals or groups; and on and on.

The result is that conflict over inequality is multidimensional. The position of any participant in such a conflict will typically be ambiguous. An individual may be at once higher than some in relation to a particular value, lower than others in relation to another. One's position may differ

The authors are indebted to their collaborators in an international project on attitudes toward equality: G. Donald Ferree, Jr., Ikuo Kabashima, Steven Kelman, Ichiro Miyake, and Joji Watanuki. Further analyses of these data by these collaborators and the present authors are in progress.

depending upon whether the unit of comparison is individuals, classes, or ethnic groups. An individual from a disadvantaged group may be highly advantaged within that group. All this makes inequality not less pressing, but rather more complex. It is a mercurial issue capable of spawning many varied conflicts. And the conflicts are intertwined since inequality in one sphere affects the degree of inequality in another.

This essay deals with the metamorphosis of inequality issues into political conflict. The multidimensionality of inequality is part of the story, as is the nexus among different realms of inequality. Yet coherence demands that we focus on one aspect of the issue to the exclusion of others. The focus will be on comparing political inequality and economic inequality. The purpose is to understand the differences in how the problem of inequality is posed in each domain and how those differences lead to varying patterns of conflict. In particular, we will suggest why it is that conflict is more intense when rooted in an issue of political rather than economic equality.

Differences between income and influence

Political equality refers, most basically, to the distribution of power or influence over collective decisions. Economic equality refers to the distribution of material goods, in particular income and wealth. The relationship between the economic domain of income and the political domain of influence lies at the heart of equality. Equality in one domain can in principle remain independent of the extent of equality in the other. One can be wealthy yet lack political influence, or be influential in politics but not particularly affluent. In general, however, the two go hand in hand: the wealthy are likely to be influential in politics; the influential likely to be wealthy. The relationship is causal and reciprocal: wealth can help one obtain influence; influence can be the key to wealth.[1] For this reason, one cannot clearly separate conflicts over economic equality from conflicts over political equality.

Yet the contest over economic equality takes a different form from that over political equality because equality means something different in each case. The difference involves the extent to which equality in each domain represents a constant-sum game, is favored by social norms, and is measurable.[2]

A constant-sum game. A constant-sum game is one in which a gain for one contestant means a loss for others. Constant-sum games are often called zero-sum. A variable-sum game is a contest in which all can gain, or, at least, one person's gain is not necessarily another's loss; here the competition can be more benign. In part, the distinction between a constant-sum and a variable-sum contest depends upon the availability of the desired goods—in this case, income or influence. If the amount is limited, the contest is usually constant-sum. If the amount of goods is growing or capable of growing, as in an expanding economy or, perhaps, an expanding political system, the contest may be variable-sum. The nature of the contest also depends upon how the contestants evaluate their own positions. Those who constantly compare their own lot with that of their opponents see the contest as constant-sum: their opponents gain, they lose, even if in an absolute sense they have not changed. If one's absolute position is what counts, then— given a growing pie to divide—all can gain at once.

Neither the contest over income nor that over influence is a pure constant-sum or a pure variable-sum game. For political influence, the contest is constant-sum vis-à-vis one's adversaries, those who oppose one's goals or favor alternative goals. A gain in influence by those who take an alternative view represents a loss in one's own influence. One's absolute position depends solely upon how one stacks up against one's opponents. Yet in relation to one's allies the contest is variable-sum. When their influence increases, so does one's own, at least indirectly. Thus, much depends on whose influence is being compared with whose.

In an expanding polity the influence of all groups could grow at once. If government programs were steadily expanding and each societal group carved out a special area of concern of little interest to other groups, each contestant could increase its influence within its own area without detracting from the others.[3] However, given a limited governmental budget, a crowded political agenda, and the fact that in times of economic constraint government programs favoring one group will limit resources available for others, an expanding political pie is impossible. Benign conflict, where each group can dominate its area of interest without threatening other groups, would therefore be unlikely. In times of economic contraction, the contest for political influence across groups tends to be sharpest. Similarly, James Tobin has referred to the constant-sum nature of the vote market: "The aggregate supply of votes is intrinsically inelastic. Allowing a free market in votes could not augment the power of the electorate as a whole; it would serve only to redistribute it differently."[4]

The contest over income differs from that over influence. An expanding polity, in which all groups gain, is simply a pipedream. Yet an expanding economy, in which the income of all groups can increase together, is eminently feasible. Furthermore, in the realm of income some inequality is needed to provide incentives for economic progress, although the proper amount is a matter of debate. When the rich get richer, the poor do not necessarily get poorer; they may actually gain. Therefore, the contest need not be virulent. Unlike influence, however, there is less to be gained from an improvement in the income of others who share one's point of view. The income is theirs, not one's own.[5]

Under certain circumstances, the contest over income may approximate a constant-sum game. In a stagnant economy, if one group gains, others lose.[6] Thus, at least in the short run, income conflict may intensify. Furthermore, even if income can improve in an absolute sense for all at the same time, income may be subjectively closer to a constant-sum contest. The deciding factor here is one's satisfaction with one's income, which appears to be based on one's relative position. The proportion of the population satisfied with its income has stayed about the same, even as real percapita income has risen.[7] Since this satisfaction depends on one's rank in the income hierarchy, another's gain is one's own loss.

Hence, in comparing the contests over income and over influence, it is impossible to classify one as strictly constant-sum and the other as strictly variable-sum. Both are to some extent constant-sum. The pie is not necessarily expanding, and, in any case, people compare slices. Nevertheless, conflicts over influence are more likely to take on the character of a constant-sum contest than are conflicts over income. One group may gain income without taking it directly from another; thus groups are not likely to see themselves in direct competition for the same earnings. But where there is political conflict over government policies, each group is in a constant-sum contest with others who want to steer the government in a different direction.

Ideal and reality. As Huntington makes clear, in politics and economics the reality of equality and the ideal of equality generate tension within individuals and groups.[8] The relationship between ideal and real can also generate conflict among groups. Groups may differ in their ideals, in their perceptions of reality, or in how they see the gap between ideal and reality. An important difference between income and influence inheres in their relation to social ideals or norms. The norm of equality is often more powerful in relation to political influence than to wealth. In most modern democracies, national ideals do not promote economic equality to the same degree that they insist on political equality. Many people subscribe to the view that economic rewards should be based roughly on effort and talent; income should not be equal. Indeed, it is argued that full economic equality would harm society by removing incentives for work and investment. Disparities in influence, though recognized and probably deemed inevitable, are more widely deplored as unjust.

However, the commitment to political equality as an ideal may be more apparent in the abstract than in the specific influence hierarchies that people consider fair. The ideal of equal influence is hard to reconcile with the desire to increase one's own influence beyond that of others. This might result in a much more qualified commitment to political equality than the general norm would imply. People may wish for equality but—to paraphrase George Orwell—would like to be a bit more equal than others. That position is understandable in light of the constant-sum characteristics of the struggle for political position. In politics, unlike economics, each group's relative position is crucial. No group considers itself well-off until it has reached the top.

Thus, while there is little consensus on the distribution of either income or influence, the disagreement in one domain concerns the ideal, while in the other, the disagreement concerns both the reality and the extent to which the ideal ought to be realized. With respect to income, groups agree on what the situation is but disagree on how wide an income gap between the top and the bottom of the hierarchy is proper. In relation to influence, they agree that the distribution should be equal, as long as it is skewed in their favor, but disagree on the actual distribution. Therefore, in politics both norms and perception of influence are in dispute, perhaps the latter even more than the former. In addition, jockeying for position is often more intense in the political domain than in the economic since influence hinges on rank. As for income, the gap among groups or occupations is considered more important than the ranking; hence, conflict is usually far more benign.

Furthermore, the disparity between ideal and real may spill over from one domain to the other. Political ideals, which tend to be more egalitarian than economic ideals, may pose a challenge to economic inequality. Conversely, economic reality, which tends to be hierarchical, may affect the extent to which the ideal of political equality can be achieved. The first challenge we recognize easily as embodying the notion of social and economic citizenship. This is the right to equal treatment in social and economic matters as an extension of one's basic political equality as a citizen. When political rights were extended to encompass universal male suffrage, many observers—some who favored such extension and some who opposed it—believed that the tension between the new political equality and economic inequality would lead to government intervention in order to level economic conditions. Full political democracy, it was believed, would not tolerate the continuation of free-market capitalism and its consequent inequalities.

In fact, political democracy has modified but not eliminated economic differentiation. It has led to the welfare state, not the egalitarian state. The extent to which the economy has remained unequal, in reality and as an ideal, varies across democracies, but inequality remains.[9] One reason the egalitarian ideal of political democracy has had less impact on the reality of economic inequality than many observers expected is that the existence of economic hierarchy erodes equality in the political sphere. The reality of unequal economic position provides some citizens and groups with a disproportionate share of the resources necessary for effective political action. And this mutes the effect of formal political equality. The result is a constant and uneasy tension between the two spheres. Inequality in the economic sphere affects politics, as those with more economic resources use them for political purposes. Political equality, in turn, produces a constant challenge to economic inequality as disadvantaged groups try to use the state to redress their disadvantage.

Measuring inequality. It is impossible to determine conclusively which domain—economics or politics—is more equal in a society. The main reason is that there is no common metric. In fact—and this is another important difference between politics and economics—there is no agreement upon a metric in politics as there is in economics. Income is much easier to measure than is influence. Again, the distinction is not absolute. What ought to count as income is ambiguous, and much income can be hidden or obscured. Nevertheless, individuals or groups are fairly easily compared in terms of their monetary income, either in absolute dollars or in their share of total income. Although precise measurement of a group's income may be difficult, it is usually possible to make a rough approximation and determine who is better off than whom. But for influence there is no clear metric, no government statistical service to collect data, and no government agency like the Internal Revenue Service in the United States to compel precise recording or reporting. The problem is even more severe when the influence is not of individuals but of groups or segments of society. The major debate over the power structure in societies concerns the amount of influence actually held by various actors; the debate is over "who governs?" not over "who should govern." For want of an accurate measure, the debate may never end. Our argument is that the problem of the absence of a standard metric for measuring influence has important substantive consequences.

These three major differences between income and influence lead us to expect differences in the nature of conflict over equality in the political and economic domains. The constant-sum nature of the conflict over political influence makes relative position crucial, leading individuals and groups to want to reduce the sway of those groups they see as influential, particularly groups taking different policy positions. The mere fact of other groups' power causes their own weakness. The situation is less clear-cut with respect to income. Much depends on the state of the economy and on individual perceptions. A constricted economy or a sense of comparative deprivation may make income a relative good, like influence. As a result, individuals would want to cut the income of those perceived to have the most. Yet one can also consider one's income in absolute terms. Another's gain may not be seen as a loss for oneself; indeed, it might even be a benefit to the economy and indirectly to one's own income.

The precision with which income and influence can be measured also affects the conflict in both domains of equality. The issue of who wields the most influence is more subjective, and thus more controversial, than is the question of who earns the most. Contenders in the political struggle will view the world differently, since there is no objective referent. Each side undoubtedly will see the other as more powerful than the other views itself; each will see itself as weaker than it is viewed by the other. What seems to one side as the redress of a disadvantage will seem to the other like an increase of an existing advantage. Thus, controversy over perceptions plays a more significant role in connection with influence than with income.

Finally, we expect that disputes over equality of income are more likely to involve how much equality there ought to be rather than the actual distribution of income shares. The apple of discord over income is the proper size of the gap between those at the top and those at the bottom. In the realm of influence, on the other hand, there is more normative agreement, consensus on the ideal of political equality combined with a self-protective view of who should be most influential, but greater conflict over the question of who, in fact, is the most influential.

The three characteristics of political influence—the general agreement on an ideal of equality of influence, the uncertainty as to who has the most influence, and its constant-sum nature—give the conflict over influence a particular cast. A group that is perceived to be more influential than other groups is also perceived to be illegitimately so, because it violates the general ideal of influence equality. It also poses a threat to other groups. Given the constant-sum nature of influence, one group's strength is another's weakness. Since relative position is what counts, the contenders will want not merely to reduce the distance between those at the top and those at the bottom, as they do in relation to income, but to change the order of the hierarchy. Finally, add to this the uncertainty as to who is in fact influential. Each group sees the world differently. Typically, each sees its antagonists as influential and itself and its allies as weak. The result is a common agreement that influence ought to be equally distributed coupled with a sharp disagreement as to what changes in the influence hierarchy have to take place to achieve this common goal.

Data

The discussion so far has been very general. Our analysis will have a much more specific base: a comparative study of the beliefs and values of leaders in Japan, Sweden, and the United States. These three nations are, as democracies, all committed to political equality; they are, as (more or less) welfare states, committed to some economic equality; and they are, as relatively affluent and peaceful societies untroubled by major extremist movements, able to afford both. But "how much equality" remains an important issue in each country. The nations differ substantially in their degree of economic equality and, though one cannot say this with any precision for reasons just given, in political equality as well. However, we are not concerned with these differences. Rather we are concerned with similarities across the three nations—not in substantive positions on equality but in the relationship between political and economic equality.[10] We are interested in whether the two domains of equality differ from each other in the same way in each nation, and in a way that is consistent with the general distinctions we have just drawn.

In each of the three nations, samples of leaders in a variety of social sectors were surveyed via mailed questionnaires.[11] In each country, about ten groups were chosen. About 300 usable questionnaires were returned by each of the leadership groups; the return rates ranged from fifty-two percent to sixty-seven percent for the various groups.

The sample consists of leaders from those sectors for whom the issue of equality is important, who are likely to take part in political struggles over it, and who represent a wide range of views on the subject. The conflict over equality involves either the attempt of one segment of society to protect a distribution favorable to itself or the attempt of another to improve its share of the distribution. Thus, we surveyed both established groups and challenging groups: groups whose position in the distributional scheme is fairly well settled and groups who challenge that distribution. The groups chosen vary somewhat from country to country, but categories overlap a good deal.

The established groups in each country include business leaders, leaders of organized labor, and leaders of farm organizations. As challengers, we chose leaders of the women's movements in each country, leaders of civil rights groups in the United States, and leaders of the Buraku Liberation League, representing a group greatly discriminated against in Japan. Leaders of the major political parties in each country were interviewed. We also chose sectors of society that play a mediating role on the issue of equality, that is, leaders in the media and intellectuals. Finally, in the United States and Japan, we sampled "future leaders": students at prestigious colleges and universities. (See Appendix for a more detailed description of the leadership groups in each country.)

The data to be discussed here come from two questions asked of our leaders, one dealing with income equality and the other with influence equality. On income equality, we provided a varied list of occupations and asked what the leaders thought the "average annual earnings" were for people in those occupations and what, in their opinion, someone in each of those occupations "should earn." Figure 1 reproduces the question on income posed in the United States.

Several characteristics of the income question should be noted. In the first place, we asked about income, not about wealth. This is, we believe, appropriate given our concern with the distribution of rewards for work. If we had asked about assets rather than earnings, the results might have been quite different. The distribution of wealth is more highly skewed than the distribution of earnings is. We asked about earnings for particular occupations so that the leaders would have a concrete referent to which they could respond—which we believe they would not have had if we had asked about more abstract categories such as the "bottom five percent of families." By linking earnings to occupations, we assume that respondents answered in terms of the salary and wages received from jobs, not the total income of someone in the occupation, i.e., from other jobs or investments and the like. Thus, our question is more about equality of pay than equality of total earnings.

The question in the United States and in Japan was about income before taxes. The tax systems in those two nations produce relatively little redistribution, making it feasible to ask the much simpler question of pre-tax income.[12] In Sweden, however, since the tax and transfer system is highly redistributive, we asked about income both before and after taxes

Figure 1. Income question: United States version

Some occupations are listed below. In the first column, please indicate what you think the average annual earnings are for someone in that occupation before taxes. In the second column, please indicate what you think someone in that occupation should earn, again before taxes. (Most people do not have precise information on salaries in other occupations, but we would like your best estimate.)

	Average annual salary is	Fair annual salary would be
A grade school teacher with five years' experience in a midwest school.	$----------	$----------
President of one of the top hundred corporations.	$----------	$----------
A semi-skilled worker in an auto assembly plant.	$----------	$----------
Star center, NBA basketball team.	$----------	$----------
A bank teller.	$----------	$----------
U.S. Cabinet member (Secretary of Commerce, Labor, HEW, etc.)	$----------	$----------
An elevator operator.	$----------	$----------
A policeman in a midwest city with five years' experience.	$----------	$----------
An aeronautical engineer.	$----------	$----------
A college professor.	$----------	$----------
A doctor in general practice in a large city.	$----------	$----------
Someone at your level in your own occupation.	$----------	$----------
A plumber.	$----------	$----------

and transfers. In this essay, the income data for Sweden refer to income after taxes and government transfers.

Our approach to influence equality parallels our approach to income. We were interested in the "is" and "ought" of influence. We asked the leaders to rate the relative influence of various actors in the political process and to indicate how much influence they thought these actors should have. As with the measurement of perceived and desired income, we had to decide what an appropriate measure of influence was and whose influence we wished to compare. And as with our income measures, our approach was simple. Although it clearly oversimplifies one of the most complex concepts in social analysis, it provides useful data for comparison.

Our respondents were asked to compare a series of "target" groups in terms of their relative influence over life in their country (Figure 2). They did so by placing each group on a scale ranging from "very influential" at the top to "very little influence" at the bottom. The scale comprised seven points—an arbitrary and perhaps restrictive number, but one that allowed adequate differentiation. The target groups to be compared were presented to the respondents at the same time. The resulting comparative nature of the ratings provided a basis for measuring influence, not in absolute but in relative terms. The leaders were able to make distinctions among the target groups; the task was not difficult and few respondents refused to undertake it.

For income, we asked respondents to rate particular occupations, which seemed appropriate units. For comparisons of influence, it seemed more appropriate to ask about significant groups in society. Where possible, we included among the target groups the same leadership groups who were part of our sample. This allowed us to see how sets of leaders rated the influence of their own group in comparison with that of others.

The data obtained from these leadership survey questions deal with differences between political and economic competition only indirectly. A full account would require close analyses of specific conflict situations. However, the data have some unique advantages. They represent the views of significant actors in the economic and political struggles in which we are interested. They allow a systematic comparison between perceptions of reality and ideals. And they allow a systematic comparison between beliefs

Figure 2. Influence question: United States version

We would like to know how much influence you think various groups *actually have* over American life, and how much influence you *think* they *should have*. Here is a scale in which "1" represents "very influential" and "7" represents "very little influence."

				Actual influence	Influence they should have
Very Influential	—	1			
		2	Labor Unions	----	----
			Farm Organizations	----	----
		3	Business Leaders	----	----
In Between	—	4	Media	----	----
			Intellectuals	----	----
		5	Banks	----	----
Very Little Influence		6	Consumer Groups	----	----
			Feminist Groups	----	----
	—	7	Black Leaders	----	----
			The Political Parties	----	----
No Opinion	—	9			

in the political and the economic domains. Admittedly, our scale of political influence is relatively crude and does not go very far toward solving the problem of measuring influence. Still, it does permit a comparison between ideals and perceptions of reality in the political domain using a constant metric. And that comparison, when juxtaposed with a similar comparison in the economic sphere, reveals much about the differences between economics and politics.

Specific hypotheses

Within each of the three nations, the leadership groups differ substantially in their attitudes on equality. And there are significant differences among similar groups across the nations. These differences will be dealt with in subsequent publications based on these data. In this analysis, we are interested in similarities across the nations and among the leadership groups in each nation—in particular, similarities in the way in which attitudes on income differ from those on influence. If similarities can be found in the pattern of attitudes in three nations with such heterogeneous cultures and among such a wide range of groups within each nation, the validity of the above distinctions about political and economic conflict will be strengthened.

Our principal expectations are:

1. If the conflict over influence approximates a constant-sum game, leaders will want to see their own influence changed so that it exceeds that of the groups they perceive to be more influential. In so doing, they will reverse the influence hierarchy. On income, more of a variable-sum game, they will prefer a narrowing of the gap between those at the top of the earnings hierarchy and themselves, but not necessarily a reversal of the hierarchy.
2. The same distinction between income and influence applies to the relationship between those perceived to be at the top of the hierarchy and those perceived to be at the bottom. The leaders may want to narrow the gap between the top and bottom, but they will not want to flatten or reverse the hierarchy. (The extent to which leaders want a narrowing should vary from group to group.) As for influence, it is more likely that groups will want to see the hierarchy radically flattened or perhaps reversed. This will, of course, be partially contingent on where each group perceives itself to be.
3. Disagreement across groups within each nation in their views on income inequality is likely to be greater on the issue of what the income distribution ought to be than on what the income distribution is. Since there is no comparable metric for influence, disagreement is likely to be at least as great on the "is" of influence distribution as on the "ought."

4. The constant-sum nature of influence conflict coupled with the disagreement over the facts of the influence distribution will make for
greater polarization of group positions in relation to influence than
in relation to income.

The "top dog" versus one's self

Since conflict over influence has a constant-sum quality, relative position is everything; income, on the other hand, is less intensely competitive.
One would therefore expect leaders to be willing to tolerate a wide gap
between their own income and that of the top earners, but to be less tolerant
of a similar disparity in influence between themselves and those they perceive
to be most influential. That this is the case for each group in each nation
is seen in Figures 3 and 4. In Figure 3 we compare how each leadership
group views its own income and the income of the occupation it perceives
to earn the most—business executives in the majority of cases
—in terms of what it thinks is the case and what it would consider fair.
The data come from answers to the questions: what does "someone at your
level in your own occupation" earn and what should he or she earn, and
what does a top business executive (or other highly paid individual) earn
and what should that person earn?[13] Each arrow at the bottom of each graph
refers to the respondent's own group. It begins at the income that a group,
on average, reports for itself. The point of the arrowhead marks the income
the group thinks would be fair for its income. The dashed arrows at the
top of the graphs refer to the income of top earners, what it is perceived to
be and what each group thinks it ought to be. In other words, the arrows
go from "is" to "ought." Each leadership group thinks its own earnings
ought to be more, but not very much more. In contrast, most groups would
reduce top earner income more substantially. It is significant, however, that
in each case the increase in income that a group thinks it deserves, combined
with the much larger decrease it wants for top earners, still does not remove
the gap between the two.

Figure 4 uses the same format to indicate where each group thinks it
currently stands within the influence hierarchy and where it would like to
be. We also place within the influence hierarchy each group's perception of
the group it considers most influential as well as the influence it thinks that
group should have. The scales of income and influence are, of course,
different, and cannot be compared directly. However, we compare income
and influence indirectly by seeing how the "is" and "ought" scales (for self
and top-dog) relate to each other within each domain, then observe how
that relationship differs between the political and economic spheres. This
indirect comparison reveals much about the leaders' attitudes toward the
shape of the influence and income hierarchies.

The bottom set of arrows shows each group's view of its own influence.
All groups—with the notable exception of the media in each country—

Figure 3. Perceived and fair income of self and executive[a]

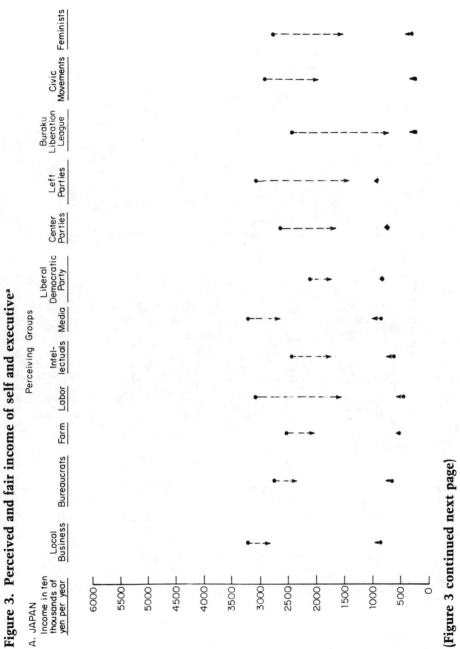

(Figure 3 continued next page)

Figure 3 *(Continued)*

B. SWEDEN

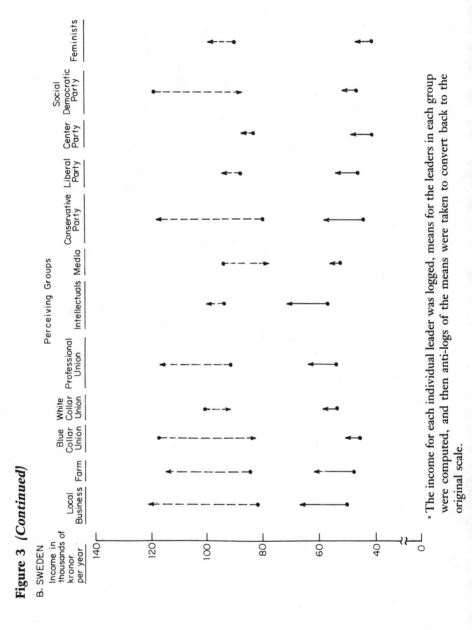

ªThe income for each individual leader was logged, means for the leaders in each group were computed, and then anti-logs of the means were taken to convert back to the original scale.

Figure 3 *(Continued)*

C. UNITED STATES

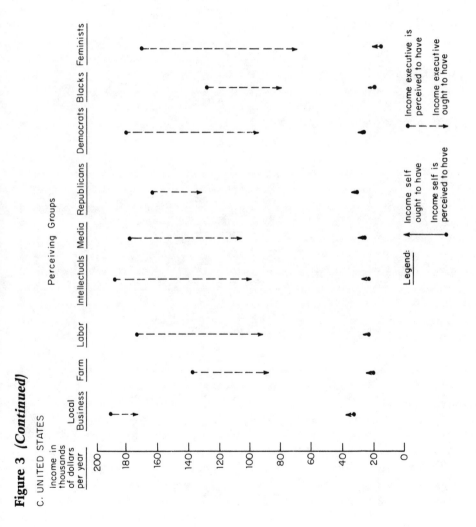

Figure 4. Perceived and fair influence of self and most influential group

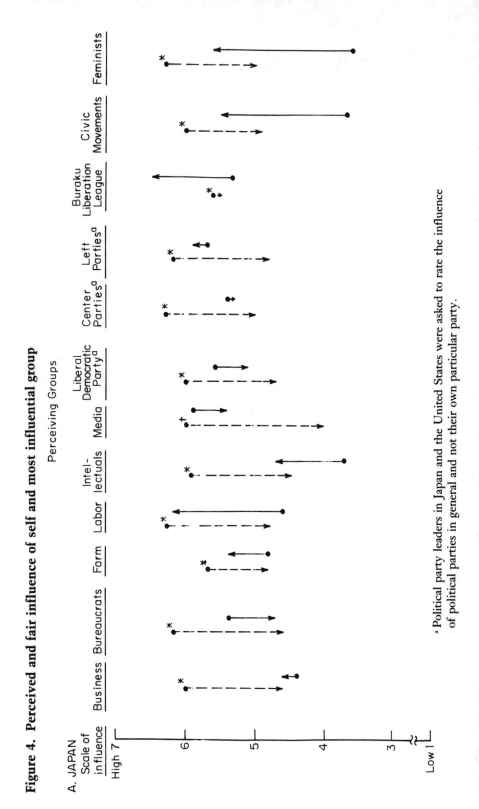

ªPolitical party leaders in Japan and the United States were asked to rate the influence of political parties in general and not their own particular party.

Figure 4 (Continued)

B. SWEDEN

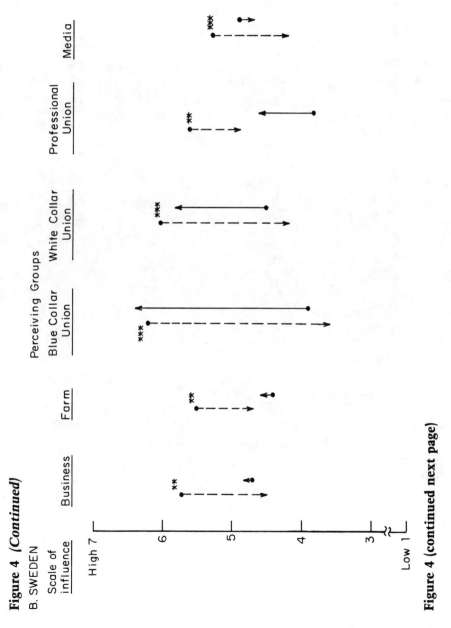

Figure 4 (continued next page)

Figure 4 *(Continued)*

C. UNITED STATES

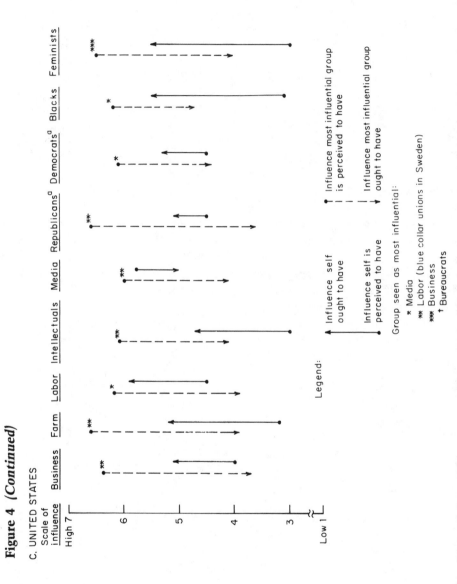

want to move themselves up.[14] The positions of the arrows for the most influential groups indicate where the groups place the "top dogs" relative to themselves. The upward movement of each group relative to the top group is much more substantial in relation to influence than in relation to income. Each wants to raise itself so that it winds up with more influence than the group it considers most influential.[15]

American, Swedish, and Japanese leaders would leave the income hierarchy intact. Each group in each nation accepts an income gap between itself and the top earners. The desire for an increase in income in no way challenges the fact that some should earn more. Yet when they consider the influence hierarchy, they want considerable rearrangement. The difference between Figures 3 and 4 is consistent with the extent to which income and influence each approximates a constant-sum game. That each group moves itself to the top (or very close to the top) of the influence hierarchy is what one would expect in a constant-sum conflict. It is not enough to do better than one is currently doing. One has to do better than others are doing. The cross-national similarity in the income/influence difference—especially across so many varied groups within three nations—is compelling.

How to treat those better off

We can consider more generally the way in which the leaders would treat the income and influence hierarchies by examining how they would deal with those at the top and the bottom of the hierarchy. If our suppositions about the similarities and differences between political and economic equality are correct, we should find that leaders want to cut the income and the influence of those at the top of each hierarchy. The higher a group is on each hierarchy, the greater the cut that will be desired. But since political conflict tends to be more constant-sum, the equalizing effect should be greater in that domain than in the domain of income. In other words, for both income and influence we should see an equalizing tendency, but the result should be a more radical equalization in relation to influence.

For both income and influence, the higher a group's perceived position, the more drastically the leaders want to reduce it. Figure 5 plots the relationship between the average income (on a log scale) that our leaders perceive an occupation to earn and the average change in income that they desire for that occupation. Each point on the graph represents an occupation. It is clear that the leaders would raise the income of those at the bottom of the hierarchy and cut the income of those at the top. The proportional changes are greater as one moves to the top or bottom of the scale. (In Sweden the relationship is curvilinear, with cuts for the top and a raise for the bottom, but little change for those in the middle range.) Figure 6 plots the parallel relationship between the average influence a target group is perceived to have and the average change in influence that the leaders desire for that group. Each point on the graph represents a target group. The same treat-

Figure 5. Perceived income and desired change in income for occupations[a]

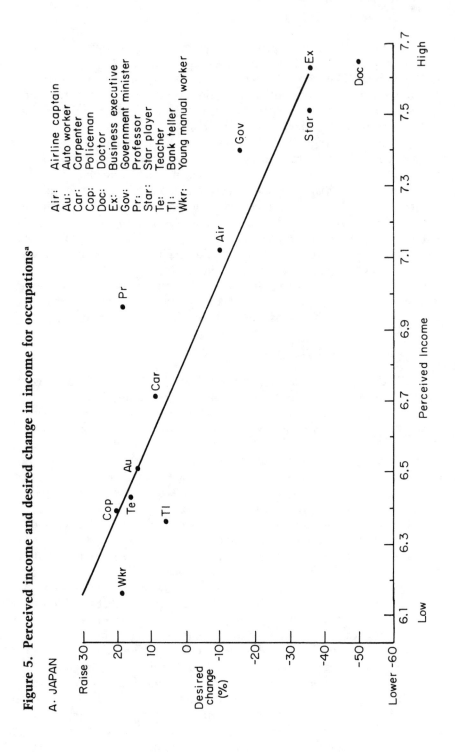

Figure 5 *(Continued)*

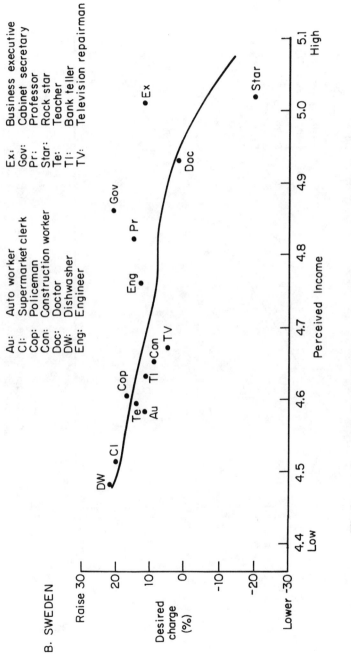

B. SWEDEN

Au: Auto worker   Ex: Business executive
Cl: Supermarket clerk   Gov: Cabinet secretary
Cop: Policeman   Pr: Professor
Con: Construction worker   Star: Rock star
Doc: Doctor   Te: Teacher
DW: Dishwasher   Tl: Bank teller
Eng: Engineer   TV: Television repairman

[a] The income for each individual leader was logged, means for the leaders in each group were computed, and then anti-logs of the means were taken to convert back to the original scale.

(Figure 5 continued next page)

99

Figure 5 *(Continued)*

C. UNITED STATES

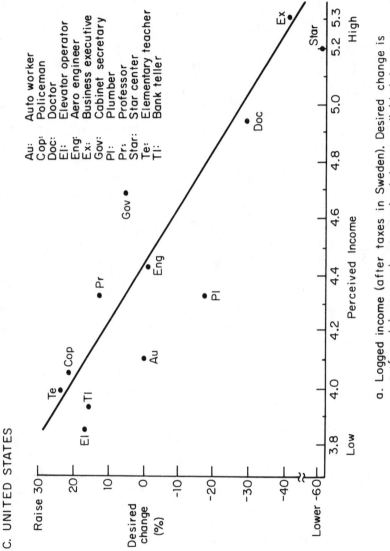

a. Logged income (after taxes in Sweden). Desired change is preferred income minus perceived income divided by perceived income.

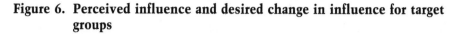

Figure 6. Perceived influence and desired change in influence for target groups

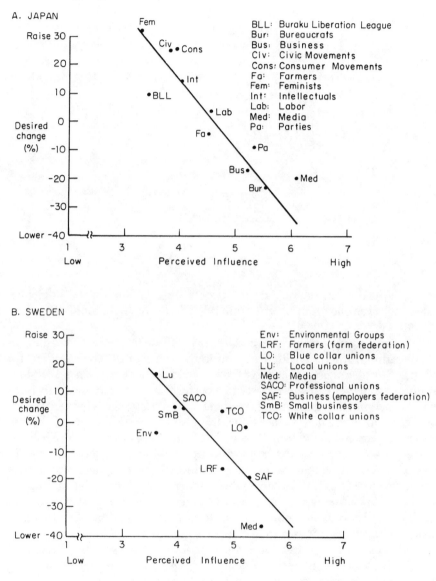

(Figure 6 continued next page)

Figure 6 *(Continued)*

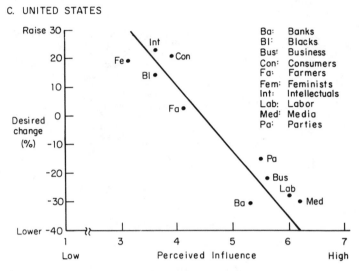

ment accorded to income is accorded those high or low on the influence scale: the lower one group is, the more it is raised; the higher it is, the more it is cut.

Figures 5 and 6 refer to averages across all of the leaders, which can be misleading if there is wide variation in the views of different leadership groups. But a similar tendency is found when we look at each leadership group separately. Table 1 reports the correlation between the perceived level of income and the percentage change desired, as well as the parallel correlation for influence for individual leadership groups. In virtually every case, the relationship is strongly negative. The more each group perceives an occupation to earn or the more influence it perceives a target group to have, the more it would like to lower its income or influence. The single exception to this is in Sweden where the more conservative groups—business, the Conservative Party, and farm leaders—think that income redistribution has gone far enough, if not too far, in their country and do not favor cutting the earnings of higher paid occupations.

The data in Figures 5 and 6 and Table 1 suggest little difference between income and influence. The more of either a group is seen to have, the larger the proportional cut that the leaders want to make. However, although we would not expect the leaders to seek to rearrange the income hierarchy, we would expect them to propose a substantial reordering of the influence hierarchy. This suggests that, though respondents would take proportionally more away from those well endowed in either influence or income, the degree to which they would do this should be much greater for influence than for income.

The data confirm this. In Figures 5 and 6 we looked at the relationship between how much an occupation or target group is perceived to have and how much respondents think the present amount of income and influence should be changed. In Figures 7 and 8 we consider the relationship between how much a target group is perceived to have and how much the leaders

Table 1. Correlations between perceived position and desired change for the income of occupations and for the influence of target groups

	Income	*Influence*
Leadership group	*Correlation of perceived income with desired change in income*[a]	*Correlation of perceived influence with desired change in influence*[b]
JAPAN		
Business	-.45	-.85
Bureaucrats	-.58	-.89
Farm	-.72	-.74
Labor	-.97	-.85
Intellectuals	-.85	-.93
Media	-.69	-.83
Liberal Democratic Party	-.61	-.82
Center Parties	-.90	-.74
Left Parties	-.97	-.91
Buraku Liberation League	-.97	-.64
Civic Movements	-.94	-.91
Feminists	-.94	-.89
SWEDEN		
Business	.58	-.87
Farm	.07	-.82
Blue Collar Union	-.94	-.92
White Collar Union	-.78	-.72
Professional Union	-.14	-.76
Intellectuals	-.49	-.91
Media	-.91	-.67
Social Democratic Party	-.96	-.90
Center Party	-.64	-.89
Liberal Party	-.63	-.90
Conservative Party	.45	-.93
Feminists	-.79	-.92

(Table 1 continued next page)

Table 1 *(Continued)*

Leadership group	Income Correlation of perceived income with desired change in income[a]	Influence Correlation of perceived influence with desired change in influence[b]
UNITED STATES		
Business	-.42	-.71
Farm	-.76	-.76
Labor	-.92	-.69
Intellectuals	-.80	-.90
Media	-.80	-.80
Republicans	-.70	-.67
Democrats	-.80	-.87
Blacks	-.86	-.93
Feminists	-.88	-.97

[a] Correlation between the (mean) income that members of a group believe each occupation has and the change in income desired for each occupation.
[b] Correlation between the (mean) influence that members of a group believe each target group has and the change in influence desired for each target group.

Figure 7. Perceived income and fair income for occupations[a]

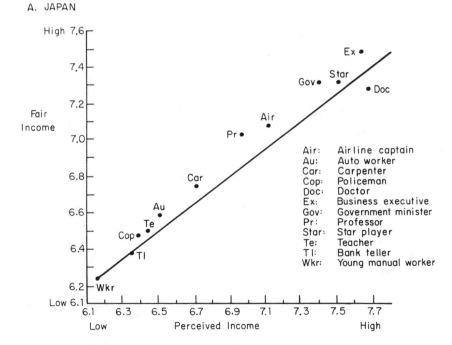

A. JAPAN

Air: Airline captain
Au: Auto worker
Car: Carpenter
Cop: Policeman
Doc: Doctor
Ex: Business executive
Gov: Government minister
Pr: Professor
Star: Star player
Te: Teacher
Tl: Bank teller
Wkr: Young manual worker

Figure 7 *(Continued)*

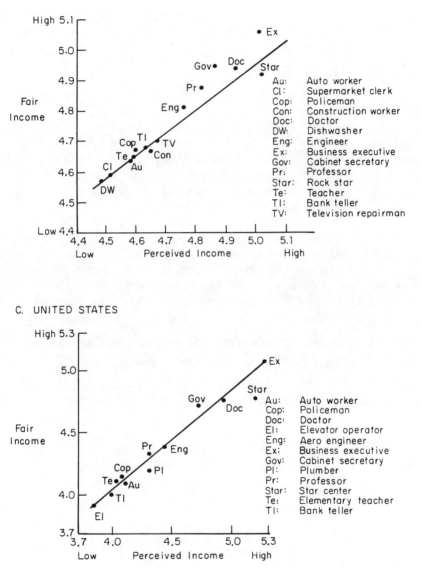

B. SWEDEN

Au: Auto worker
Cl: Supermarket clerk
Cop: Policeman
Con: Construction worker
Doc: Doctor
DW: Dishwasher
Eng: Engineer
Ex: Business executive
Gov: Cabinet secretary
Pr: Professor
Star: Rock star
Te: Teacher
Tl: Bank teller
TV: Television repairman

C. UNITED STATES

Au: Auto worker
Cop: Policeman
Doc: Doctor
El: Elevator operator
Eng: Aero engineer
Ex: Business executive
Gov: Cabinet secretary
Pl: Plumber
Pr: Professor
Star: Star center
Te: Elementary teacher
Tl: Bank teller

a. Logged income (after taxes in Sweden)

[a] The income for each individual leader was logged, means for the leaders in each group were computed, and then anti-logs of the means were taken to convert back to the original scale.

think it ought to have. The income relation (Figure 7) is clear. The more an occupation is seen to earn, the more the leaders feel it ought to earn. This figure contrasts sharply with Figure 5, which indicates that the more an occupation is seen to earn, the more our respondents feel earnings ought to be cut. Nonetheless, the two figures do not contradict each other. Executives are thought to earn more than the other occupations. The leaders would decrease these executive incomes.[16] Nevertheless, they want executives to remain at the top of the income hierarchy. The cut reduces the distance between top and bottom earning occupations, but leaves the hierarchy, or ranking, intact.

Figure 8 contrasts sharply with Figure 7. When we plot the influence that target groups are perceived to have against the influence the leaders think they should have, we discover no relationship. The sharp cut in the influence of those at the top—reflected in the data in Figure 6—results in the flattening of the influence hierarchy seen in Figure 8.

The contrast between the leaders' views on income and influence may be likened to the difference between a progressive and a confiscatory tax. The leaders apply a progressive tax to income. A higher proportion of income is taken from those near the top of the scale. The tax is, in fact, progressive in both a positive and a negative direction. Those who are perceived to have low earnings are given an income boost—the lower the perceived income the bigger the boost. But the progressive tax does not upset the income

Figure 8. Perceived influence and fair influence for target groups

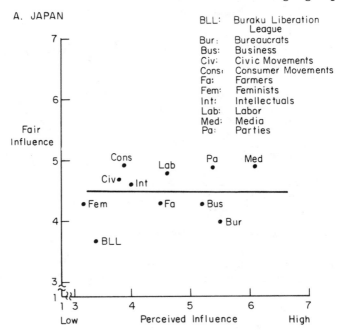

Figure 8 *(Continued)*

B. SWEDEN

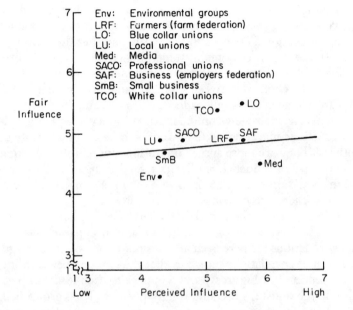

Env:	Environmental groups
LRF:	Farmers (farm federation)
LO:	Blue collar unions
LU:	Local unions
Med:	Media
SACO:	Professional unions
SAF:	Business (employers federation)
SmB:	Small business
TCO:	White collar unions

C. UNITED STATES

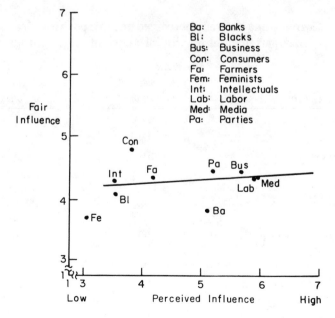

Ba:	Banks
Bl:	Blacks
Bus:	Business
Con:	Consumers
Fa:	Farmers
Fem:	Feminists
Int:	Intellectuals
Lab:	Labor
Med:	Media
Pa:	Parties

hierarchy. It leaves the top earners with substantially higher earnings than those below them. When it comes to influence, however, the leaders apply a confiscatory tax to those they perceive to have higher influence and a countervailing negative tax to those seen as very low in influence. The difference between the two domains is striking. In the economic domain, they propose marginal changes in the status quo, but the income hierarchy remains. In the influence domain, something closer to full equality of result is desired, with each group ending up with similar influence.

Again, the contrast between Figures 7 and 8 could be misleading since the data are averaged across all leadership groups, and these groups are quite heterogeneous in their views on income and influence equality. They differ on how much income equality they want—some are much more egalitarian than others. They are more agreed on the amount of influence equality they want—equality of influence is seen as a good thing. But they vary widely on whom they want to be high or low on the influence scale. The leadership groups must therefore be considered separately.

Table 2 presents the correlations within each leadership group of the perceived and desired income of the various occupations as well as the parallel correlations for perceived and desired influence of the target groups. The pattern of correlations indicates that the contrast between income and influence reflected in Figures 7 and 8 applies to each leadership group. For income the relationships are all strongly positive. Each group believes that the target groups that earn more ought to earn more (even if they have received substantial cuts). The point deserves underlining. The groups range

Table 2. Correlations between perceived and fair positions for the income of occupations and for the influence of target groups

Leadership Group	Correlation of perceived income with fair income[a]	Correlation of perceived influence with fair influence[b]
JAPAN		
Business	.98	.67
Bureaucrats	.97	.57
Farm	.98	.67
Labor	.97	-.18
Intellectuals	.98	-.06
Media	.97	.45
Liberal Democratic Party	.99	.61
Center Parties	.92	-.04
Left Parties	.76	-.49
Buraku Liberation League	.96	-.46
Civic Movements	.97	-.08
Feminists	.99	-.42

Table 2 *(Continued)*

Leadership Group	Correlation of perceived income with fair income[a]	Correlation of perceived influence with fair influence[b]
SWEDEN		
Business	.97	.30
Farm	.95	.38
Blue Collar Union	.96	-.37
White Collar Union	.95	.25
Professional Union	.94	.68
Intellectuals	.93	.33
Media	.92	.35
Social Democratic Party	.95	-.55
Center Party	.96	-.07
Liberal Party	.96	.65
Conservative Party	.95	.05
Feminists	.93	.37
UNITED STATES		
Business	.92	.20
Farm	.93	.11
Labor	.97	.15
Intellectuals	.93	.40
Media	.93	.10
Republicans	.90	.37
Democrats	.95	.17
Blacks	.98	-.01
Feminists	.91	-.68

[a] Correlation between the mean of the income that members of a leadership group believe each occupation has and the mean of the income it ought to have.
[b] Correlation between the mean of the influence that members of a leadership group believe each target group has and the mean of the influence it ought to have.

from leaders of business and conservative parties to groups that take more egalitarian positions, such as leaders of liberal parties, union leaders, and feminist organizations. Across all these groups, including the more egalitarian, the strong positive correlations indicate general satisfaction with the ordering of the income hierarchy. No group wants to change it.[17]

For influence, the pattern is quite varied. For some groups the correlation is positive, though by no means as positive as are the parallel correlations between income perceptions and income values. These groups are generally satisfied with the influence hierarchy as they perceive it. Those most satisfied with the influence hierarchy tend to be more conservative with good access to government: business, farm leaders and leaders of the Liberal Democratic Party in Japan, business and farm groups in Sweden as well as leaders of the professional workers union, Republicans more than Democrats in the United States. There are other groups whose degree of satisfaction with influence is less. For example, for intellectuals in Japan and most of the major economic groups in the United States, the correlation hovers around zero. There is no relationship between what they perceive and what they would like. And for some groups such as feminists in the United States, leaders of the Buraku Liberation League in Japan, and leaders of the major Swedish blue-collar union and the Social Democratic Party (the survey was conducted in Sweden shortly after the Socialists' loss of power after forty years in office), the correlation is strongly negative. These groups would reverse the influence hierarchy they perceive to exist. They appear to levy more than a confiscatory tax on high levels of influence; they levy a penalty tax, and a negative penalty tax to subsidize those low in influence.

To recapitulate, attitudes toward influence approximate what we would expect in a constant-sum contest more than attitudes on income do. Relative position appears to be what counts in relation to influence. Whereas each group of leaders is satisfied with the current income ranking of occupations, their views on influence rankings are more contingent on how they perceive the hierarchy. Some groups would adjust the hierarchy somewhat, others want to flatten the hierarchy, and still others would reverse it. Almost all would put themselves on top.

Perception versus values

Another component of our distinction between influence and income has to do with the relative importance of disagreements in perception and in values. We have suggested that conflict among groups over income would be conflict over what ought to be, not over what is. The groups would agree more on what various occupations actually earn than on what is a fair disparity among them. When it comes to influence, however, both norms and perceptions would be in dispute—perhaps the latter even more than the former. Though a normative consensus in favor of influence equality is tempered by a self-protective desire to be on top, there should remain some agreement across groups on the norm of equal political influence. Thus, we may expect no more consensus across groups on what is than on what should be. Unlike income, influence tends to generate dispute over the ideal and the reality.

This difference between income and influence can be tested with the "is" and "ought" questions in each domain. For income we take several pairs of occupations, each pair consisting of a better- and a worse-paid occupation. We calculate an "is" and an "ought" ratio for each pair; that is, how wide each individual perceives the income gap to be and how wide he or she wants that gap to be. We also calculate such "is" and "ought" ratios for the influence of pairs of groups, where each pair contains a more and a less influential group. We then have four types of ratios: "is" and "ought" for income; "is" and "ought" for influence. Our hypothesis is that the variation across our leadership groups on the "ought" of income is greater than the variation on the "is" of income; and the variation on the "is" of influence is as great or greater than the variation on the "ought" of influence.

These ratios are calculated for each individual leader and then averaged for each leadership group. The measure of consensus is the coefficient of variation of these mean ratios across groups. The larger the coefficient of variation, the greater the disagreement among the groups on that particular ratio. The results of these comparisons are reported in Table 3. In the United States and Sweden, the data clearly support our hypothesis. For

Table 3. **Variations among groups in perceived and desired income and influence ratios.**

	Income Is	Income Ought		Influence Is	Influence Ought
JAPAN					
Executive/ Auto Worker	.26	.33	Business/ Labor	.11	.18
Executive/Young Manual Laborer	.11	.40	Business/ Feminists	.16	.21
			Business/Buraku Liberation League	.22	.26
SWEDEN					
Executive/ Auto Worker	.16	.35	Business/ Blue-collar Unions	.51	.28
Executive/ Dishwasher	.17	.24	Business/ Environmentalists	.21	.14
			Small Business/ Blue-collar Unions	.44	.28
UNITED STATES					
Executive/ Auto Worker	.12	.33	Business/Labor	.29	.16
Executive/ Elevator Operator	.12	.40	Business/Feminists	.23	.19
			Business/Civil Rights Groups	.30	.18

income, there is more consensus across groups on the "is" than on the "ought." The coefficients of variation are substantially larger in relation to desired income than to perceived income. Groups agree more with each other on the actual income situation than on the desired income situation. The pattern for influence is the reverse. The coefficients of variation are higher for the perceived ratios than for the desired ratios. This indicates more consensus on how things ought to be than on how things are. In Japan, the income comparisons are consistent with our hypothesis. They show somewhat more variation in ideal income than in the perception of current income. However, the influence comparisons are less consistent with expectations. The difference between perceptions and values is relatively small in the domain of influence. This is especially true for the widest influence gap: between business and the Buraku Liberation League. On the whole, the data are generally consistent with our point that influence is less precisely measurable than income, the result being that the former is the more likely subject of political debate.

Differences in the perception of the political hierarchy are what one would expect given the difficulty of obtaining objective measures of political influence and given the constant-sum nature of political conflict which colors perceptions. It is not surprising that conflict over political position is generally more intense than that over economics. Disagreements about the reality of the influence distribution exacerbate political conflict and impede the attainment of greater political equality. There may be general agreement on a norm of political equality. But the constant-sum nature of political equality and the ambiguity of political reality prevent that norm from leading to more equality. Each group thinks that it is deprived in terms of influence and that its adversaries have an advantage.

The result, of course, is that the general normative consensus has little equalizing potential. If one of the contending groups were in a position to do so, it might try to equalize the distribution of influence. But if it did so according to its own perceptions of reality, it would only make the situation more unequal from the perspective of other contending groups. Indeed, consensus on the norm of political equality heats conflict because the differing perceptions of reality lead each side to think that the other is violating that norm.

Consider, for example, the views of labor and business. Figure 9 shows for each of the three nations the mutual perceptions that business and labor have of each other's influence. In the eyes of business, labor is more powerful. Labor sees the opposite. The reversal of positions illustrated in Figure 9 is of substantive importance. It is not merely that there is disagreement about the facts of influence, but that the disagreement is systematic. Groups underestimate their own influence and overestimate that of their adversaries.

Suppose we relate these differing perceptions to what the groups would consider to be a fair system of influence. Figure 10 illustrates how business

Figure 9. How labor and business perceive each other's influence

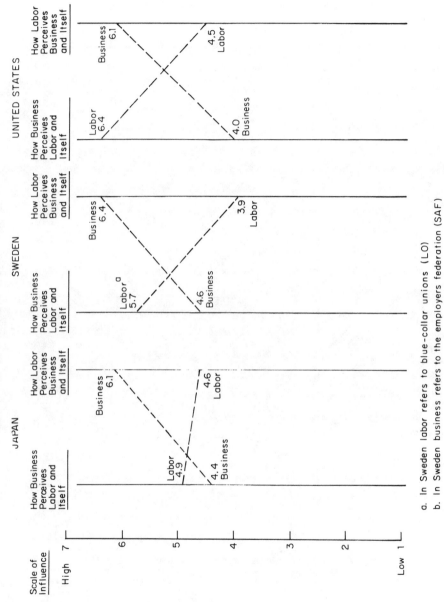

a. In Sweden labor refers to blue-collar unions (LO)
b. In Sweden business refers to the employers federation (SAF)

113

Figure 10. Labor's preference for changing the influence hierarchy from the perspective of labor and business

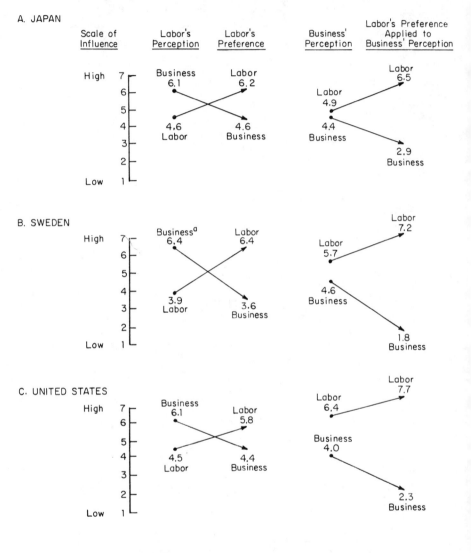

a. In Sweden business refers to the employers federation (SAF)
b. In Sweden labor refers to blue-collar unions (LO)

perceives the threat posed to it by labor. The left side of Figure 10 shows, for each country, how labor perceives the world (business has more influence) and how labor would like the world to be (labor would have more influence than business). This part of the figure aptly reveals how groups would overturn the influence hierarchy as they see it.

The position of labor presented in Figure 10 is rather threatening to business. But it becomes even more threatening given the way business perceives the world, which is quite different from the way labor sees it. This is illustrated on the right-hand side of Figure 10, which shows business's perception of the world as well as what the world would look like if

Figure 11. Business's preference for changing the influence hierarchy from the perspective of business and labor

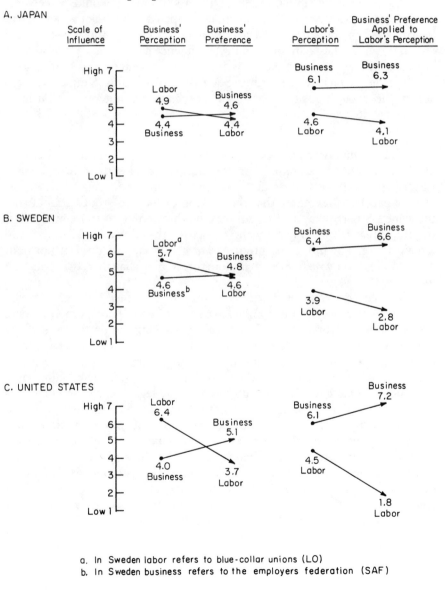

a. In Sweden labor refers to blue-collar unions (LO)
b. In Sweden business refers to the employers federation (SAF)

labor's preferences for change were applied to business's perception of reality. Business perceives labor to be more influential than itself. If one were to change the world as business sees it in the direction that labor wants, one would find an already disadvantaged business community undergoing further deprivation. The result is shown to the far right of Figure 10: business and labor are separated by almost the entire range of the influence scale, with labor at the top. Surely business would consider this illegitimate.

Figure 11 turns the tables and presents the situation as labor would see it. The result is similar. Labor faces a situation it would perceive as going from bad to worse. The outcome in Japan and Sweden is not as bad for labor as it is for business, largely because business in those two nations does not want as large an increase in its influence as labor does (the surveys in each country were conducted with business-oriented conservative governments in power). In the United States, the situation is symmetrical: the outcome for labor if business has its way is as bad as the outcome for business if labor has its way.

The conflict over influence may be more intense than the conflict over income, despite the seemingly greater normative consensus on influence. Leaders in three very different countries dispute the proper size of the income gap but they agree that the ranking of income groups should stay the same. A narrowing of the gap may be threatening to those at the top, but the threat is moderated by the consensus that those at the top should remain there. For influence, groups want a complete reversal of position. To turn a hierarchy upside down is more threatening than merely to constrict its range.[18]

The conflict associated with changing the influence hierarchy is even more severe because the antagonists have such different perceptions of where they and their adversaries are. Each group, viewing the preferences of the other in terms of its own perceptions of influence, sees itself as starting from a deprived position and winding up even more deprived. It also sees its opponent, already at the top of the influence hierarchy, as demanding more influence. Such a conflict calls into question the legitimacy of the demands of the other group. The groups generally agree as to a fair distribution of influence: it is a relatively equal distribution in which no group dominates the others. But groups do not agree on what changes would produce such a fair influence distribution. The evidence from the United States, Japan, and Sweden lends support to our original contention: although equality may be more of a normative ideal in politics than in economics, incongruent perceptions and the constant-sum nature of politics make the attainment of equality as unlikely in political as in economic affairs.

NOTES

1. In most political analyses, income and influence are seen as mutually dependent: either can be used to gain the other. But influence is usually thought of as the instrumental goal and income as the terminal goal. The affluent use income to gain influence and thus to protect or improve their economic position. However, influence itself may be thought of as the terminal goal. For instance, in a critique of those who would redistribute income, Irving Kristol has argued that the real goal of the redistributionists is to place not money in the hands of the poor but power in the hands of the liberals: "the public treasury, where liberals will have much to say about how it should be spent. That is the 'dirty little secret'—the hidden agenda—behind the current chatter about the need for 'redistribution.' The talk is about equality, the substance is about power." Irving Kristol, "Poverty, Taxes, and Equality," *The Public Interest* 37 (Fall 1974), p. 27.
2. The following discussion of the difference between politics and economics draws on the more extensive argument in Sidney Verba and Gary R. Orren, *Equality in America: The View from the Top* (Cambridge: Harvard University Press, 1985), chapter 10. Also see chapters 1, 8, and 9.
3. Talcott Parsons in his review of C. Wright Mills' *The Power Elite*, stressed that power and influence can be thought of as resources than can expand to the benefit of all society. See Parsons, "The Distribution of Power in American Society," in *Structure and Process in Modern Societies* (Glencoe, Ill.: The Free Press, 1960), pp. 199–225. Arnold Tannenbaum makes a similar point in relation to organizations: the amount of influence in an organization can vary. In some industries, more influence is exerted over the behavior of the participants than in others—exerted not necessarily by management but by all participants [See Tannenbaum *et al.*, *Hierarchy in Organizations* (San Francisco: Jossey-Bass, 1974), p. 220]. For the contrary position—that influence is a fixed quantity—see Ralf Dahrendorf, *Class and Class Conflict in Industrial Societies* (Stanford: Stanford University Press, 1968). However, everything depends on the issue over which political influence will be applied. For Catholics of Northern Ireland, an increase in Protestant influence will be seen as negative.
4. James Tobin, "On Limiting the Domain of Equality," *Journal of Law and Economics* 13 (1970), p. 454.
5. Although people need not spend money on themselves and could spend it on friends, they generally do not since they are not obliged to do so. But since governments are often precluded from giving special benefits to individuals, allies sometimes have little choice but to use their influence to acquire decisions and favors for the general benefit of all those who share their interests. Furthermore, people usually only need their own money to buy what they want, given the typical range of prices and incomes. They do not need to pool income with allies. However, few groups have so much influence that they need not worry about the support of their friends. One generally does not need an ally's money to get by, but one often needs its vote.
6. Lester C. Thurow, *The Zero-Sum Society* (New York: Basic Books, 1980).
7. Richard Easterlin, "Does Money Buy Happiness," *The Public Interest* 30 (Winter 1973) and Thurow, *The Zero-Sum Society*, p. 18. Also see Lee Rainwater, *What Money Buys* (New York: Basic Books, 1974), ch. 3.
8. Samuel P. Huntington, *American Politics: The Promise of Disharmony* (Cambridge: Harvard University Press, 1981).
9. For a comparison of economic equality in several democracies see Malcolm Sawyer, "Income Distribution in OECD Countries," OECD Economic Outlook, *Occasional Papers* (Paris: OECD, 1976), p. 19.
10. More complete analysis of these data, dealing with many of the differences within and among the nations, will appear in Sidney Verba *et al.*, *Equality: A Comparative Analysis* (tentative title), in progress.

11. In the United States interviewing was conducted from March to May of 1976. The data collection was a joint project of *The Washington Post* and the Harvard University Center for International Affairs, and was partially funded by a grant from the Ford Foundation. The interviewing in Sweden took place between September 1978 and January 1979 and was supported by a grant from the Bank of Sweden Tercentenary Fund. The Japanese interviews were conducted between March and May of 1980, with support from the Toyota Foundation.

12. Joseph A. Pechman and Benjamin A. Okner, *Who Bears the Tax Burden?* (Washington, D.C.: The Brookings Institution, 1974), p. 61. The authors make several estimates based on different assumptions about the incidence of various taxes in the United States. Under most sets of assumptions, the overall tax bite is about the same across all income categories. Only for the set of assumptions stipulating that taxes would have the most progressive incidence do they find effective rates that differ substantially across categories; and these differences tend to appear at the top and bottom of the income scale. This allows us to locate the worst distortion that our choice of pre-tax estimates could produce: a comparison between the top and the bottom earning occupations under the most progressive assumptions. The occupation that our respondents perceive as highest in earnings is the top corporate executive; they place the elevator operator at the bottom. The former is, on average, perceived by our leaders to earn $206,000, the latter $7,200 before taxes. The ratio of their incomes is 28.6 to 1. If we use Pechman and Okner's most progressive assumptions, the ratio becomes 21.5 to 1. If we use their least progressive assumptions, the after-tax ratio would be 26.9 to 1; not appreciably different from the pre-tax ratio. (See *Who Bears the Tax Burden?*, pp. 48–50. The tax rates we have used are in Table 4–3, p. 49.) Greater disparity between incomes before and after governmental intervention is found if one takes into account not only taxes but also government transfers. Okner and Rivlin find that taxes do not change income shares much in the United States, but a combination of taxes and transfers does. Before taxes and transfers, the lowest quintile of earners receives 1.7 percent of income; after taxes and transfers they receive 6.3 percent. The parallel figures for the top quintile are 53.1 percent and 47.1 percent respectively. However, much of this change comes from transfers to the aged, who do not figure in our analysis of occupations. If we take just those under the age of sixty-five, the figures for the bottom quintile are 1.0 percent and 2.4 percent respectively, and for the top quintile 50.1 percent and 44.0 percent. See Benjamin Okner and Alice M. Rivlin, "Income Distribution Policy in the United States," in *Education, Equality, and Life Chances* (Paris: OECD, 1975), Vol. 2, pp. 191–193. And if the comparison were between a pair of occupations other than the top-bottom comparison we have illustrated, the pre- and post-tax income gaps would be more similar than in this "worst" case. The choice of pre-tax earnings may introduce some distortion (though only under one set of assumptions about tax incidence, not under another equally plausible set), but not so much as to undercut the analysis that follows. For all the reasons cited, pre-tax income seemed the best choice.

Similar analyses of the before- and after-tax distribution in Japan show a parallel result. See Keizai Kikakucho Economic Planning Agency, *Shotoku Shisanbumpu no Jiitai to Mondaiten* (*Status and Problems of Income and Wealth Distribution*) (Tokyo: Okurasho Insatsukyoku (The Government Printing Office), 1975), pp. 316–17. We are grateful to Professor Ikuo Kabashima for this reference.

The impact of government programs on real income is much more substantial in Sweden. Therefore, in Sweden we asked respondents about the amount of income various occupations earned before taxes and social transfer payments and after taxes and social transfers, and what they ought to earn after taxes and social transfers. Since we are interested in comparing perceptions of earnings with views as to what occupations ought to earn, we shall compare the after-tax and after-transfers estimates in Sweden. Though the comparison will be between estimates based on before-tax income in the United States and Japan and after-tax income in Sweden, this should not substantially affect the results. Our ultimate goal is to see what people believe actual earnings are and should be. In the United States and Japan, since the distribution of earnings before and after taxes is not very different, the question on before-tax earnings should be adequate. In Sweden, we tap the subject more directly by asking about after-tax earnings.

For data on the degree of income equality before and after taxes in the three nations, data that show little redistribution in the United States and Japan and significant redistribution in Sweden, see Malcolm Sawyer, "Income Distribution in OECD Countries," *op. cit.*

13. The income data reported in Figure 3 and the following tables and figures are logged. Logged income measures eliminate extremes that can distort a simple arithmetic mean, which is especially important since our study asked about the incomes of occupations with very high salaries, such as top executives and sports stars. Also, logged measures are symmetric. If half the leaders want to double the executive's salary and the others want to cut it in half, a summary measure based on logarithms will appropriately show the "average" person favoring no change. Logged measures can be consistently applied to simple income, desired change from present income levels to the ideal, the difference in earnings between high- and low-paying occupations, or the desired amount of change in the spread between particular occupations. Finally, the logged measure corresponds to the way that people actually think about income, namely in ratio, not absolute, terms. An increase in income from $10,000 to $20,000 is closer in meaning to an increase of $100,000 to $200,000 than it is to an increase from $100,00 to $110,000.

To compute income estimates, therefore, we first log the income for each individual leader, compute the mean for the leaders within a particular group, and then take the anti-log of the mean to convert back to the original income scale. For ratio comparisons, we first compute the ratios for individuals, log them, compute the group means, and take the anti-log.

14. The exceptions are the media in each country and bureaucrats in Japan. See Verba, *et al., Equality: A Comparative Perspective* (in progress).

15. Even those few groups who would lower their own influence reduce the top group so much more as to reverse their relative positions.

16. The sharpness of the cut is obscured on the graph because of the log scale used, but it is apparent on close inspection.

17. There are, of course, differences among these groups which would be revealed by regression slopes rather than correlations. The slopes would all be positive but the steepness would vary since they differ in how steep an income hierarchy they desire. For our purposes, however, the order of the hierarchy is what counts.

18. See Dan Usher, *The Economic Prerequisite to Democracy* (New York: Columbia University Press, 1981), pp. 28–31, for an interesting discussion of the greater conflict associated with the change of rankings in a hierarchy compared with a change in the distribution of rewards that maintain current positions.

Appendix

Description of groups in the leadership study

Japan

Business
Members of the Federation of Economic Organizations and leaders of local "Chambers of Commerce" from a sample of Japanese cities.

Bureaucrats
A random sample of civil service personnel (section chiefs or higher) and executives from the departments of local governments.

Farm
The national officers of the Federation of Agricultural Cooperative Associations and officers of local agricultural cooperatives.

Labor
Officers and members of the executive committees of 100 national unions plus the officers from local unions in the sample of cities.

Intellectuals
A random sample of teachers at Japanese colleges and universities and artists (writers, painters, musicians, etc.).

Media
A random sample of the news staffs of national and local newspapers, news agencies, and broadcast organizations.

Liberal Democratic Party
Members of the LDP in parliament and in municipal assemblies from the city sample.

Center Parties
Members of parliament and municipal assemblies representing the Clean Government Party, Independent Party, and Democratic Socialist Party.

Left Parties
Members of parliament and municipal assemblies representing the Social Democratic Union, the Japan Socialist Party, and the Japan Communist Party.

120

Civic movements	Executive officers listed in the directories of consumer and citizen organizations.
Buraku Liberation League	Officers of the local chapters of the Buraku Liberation League.
Feminists	Executive officers listed in directories of feminist organizations.

Sweden

Business	Elected officials and professional staff of the national employers federation (SAF), affiliated employers groups, the national trade association (IF), affiliated trade associations, and the federation of small businessmen (SHIO); the CEOs of the 200 largest corporations and all commercial and savings banks.
Farm	National and provincial elected officials and professional staff of the national farm interest group (LRF) and the national farmers' cooperatives.
Blue-collar unions	Elected officials and professional staff of the national federation of blue-collar unions (LO) and affiliated unions.
White-collar unions	Elected officials and professional staff of the national federation of white-collar unions (TCO) and affiliated unions.
Professional unions	Elected officials and professional staff of the national federation of professional unions (SACO) and affiliated unions.
Intellectuals	All full professors except for those on medical faculties.
Media	All the professional employees of the news and public affairs departments of Swedish national radio and television.
Conservative Party ***Liberal Party*** ***Center Party*** ***Social Democratic Party***	For each party all members of parliament, editors of party newspapers, members of party regional boards, and members of the national and regional boards of party women's federations.
Feminists	National and provincial boards of the major feminist organization (the Fredrika Bremer Federation).

United States

Business   The chairmen of the board or presidents of a sample of the largest non-banking corporations in the *Fortune* 500 and the chairmen of the board or presidents of a sample of the 200 largest banks in the country; the president of the largest local bank and the chief executive officer of the local Chamber of Commerce in a random sample of cities.

Farm   The national officers of the three largest farm membership organizations and the presidents of major commodity associations plus the local presidents of the farm membership organizations in the city sample.

Labor   The top three or four officers of the largest international labor unions and the presidents of two local unions from each city in the city sample.

Intellectuals   A random sample drawn from *Who's Who*-type directories for the natural sciences, humanities, social sciences, and arts.

Media   A sample of the press and radio-TV galleries of Congress; the managing editor of the largest circulation local newspaper and news director of the highest-rated local TV station in each sampled city.

Republicans   A sample of the members of the Republican National Committee; the local city and/or county Republican chairmen in the selected cities.

Democrats   A sample of the members of the Democratic National Committee; the local city and/or county Democratic chairmen in the selected cities.

Blacks   In the city sample, the highest local elected black official and the local president of the NAACP and/or Urban League; a random sample of other black elected officials (including members of the Congressional Black Caucus).

Feminists   Local officers of the National Organization for Women, the National Women's Political Caucus, the Coalition of Labor Union Women, the Women's Equity Action League, Federally Employed Women, and the State Commissions on the Status of Women.

6

Macroeconomic performance, macroeconomic policy, and electoral politics in industrial democracies

DOUGLAS A. HIBBS, JR.

Professor of Government, Harvard University

"All political history shows that the standing of the Government and its ability to hold the confidence of the electorate at a General Election depend on the success of its economic policy."

Prime Minister Harold Wilson, March 1968

"The wage level (price level) in the modern society is indeterminate because in the final analysis the monetary authorities must—for political reasons— provide a money supply adequate to ratify any given level of money wages, no matter how it was reached, in order to avoid excessive unemployment."

Richard Cooper, 1976

Macroeconomics and electoral politics is a broad topic, and here I shall discuss only a relatively narrow slice of the field.[1] Specifically I shall summarize my recent work on the response of governments' mass political support to macroeconomic performance in the liberal capitalist democracies, and also discuss the implications of this work for electorally motivated macroeconomic policy cycles.

The paper proceeds as follows. Section 1 outlines the broad theoretical framework underlying my research. Section 2 presents some public opinion data on the relative salience of macroeconomic issues to the mass publics of the industrial democracies during the postwar era. Section 3 describes a model for the response of mass political support to economic outcomes, and reports some illustrative empirical results for a selection of industrial democracies. Finally, in Section 4, the concluding section, I suggest how constrained optimization techniques can be used to investigate empirically the impact of electoral pressures on macroeconomic policy behavior in industrial democracies.

1. An interdisciplinary framework for the analysis of the macropolitical economy of industrial democracies

The theoretical framework underlying my empirical work emphasizes that macroeconomic policies affecting economic outcomes are responsive to and constrained by the electorate's reactions to salient economic problems. In other words, in a democratic society macroeconomic policies and outcomes reflect the intersection of both economic and political forces. This interdependence is usefully conceived in terms of a political–economic system of the *demand for* and *supply of* economic outcomes.[2] The principal features of this framework are illustrated in Figure 1.

As Figure 1 suggests, mass political support for the incumbent political party and chief executive—which is measured by votes on election day and poll ratings during interelection periods—depends, among other things, on current and past (and, perhaps, anticipated future) economic performance. The response of mass political support to economic conditions reveals information about the electorate's economic priorities and relative preferences (as between, say, higher inflation and higher unemployment) and constitutes the voters' *demand* for economic outcomes. Because objective (distributional) consequences and public perceptions of macroeconomic outcomes vary systematically across electoral groups (for example, working class voters and partisans of "left" parties typically are relatively more sensitive to unemployment and less sensitive to inflation than white-collar voters and partisans of "right" parties), economic preferences and demands are not homogeneous across voters.

Political administrations attempt to maintain a comfortable level of mass political support, and also pursue ideological and distributional goals that are reflected by the distinctive preferences of their core electoral constituencies. The economic policy reactions of political administrations to voters' economic priorities (demands) determine the electorally induced *supply* of economic outcomes. The impact of political and electoral forces on the formulation and implementation of macroeconomic policies, of course, is subject to institutional arrangements which include such factors as the degree of autonomy of monetary authorities from elected political officials, executive–legislative relations, federalism, and so on. Furthermore, the impact of the conventional policy instruments—notably the supply of money and credit, and government expenditure and taxation—on macroeconomic conditions is constrained by the structure of economic relations (for example, short-run Phillips curves, the institutional setting of wage bargaining) and by international economic influences (for example, OPEC oil supply shocks, the exchange rate regime). Politics and policy, therefore, influence importantly, but do not shape completely, macroeconomic outcomes.

As I indicated above, the macroeconomic policies pursued by political authorities in response to voters' economic priorities or demands, subject to

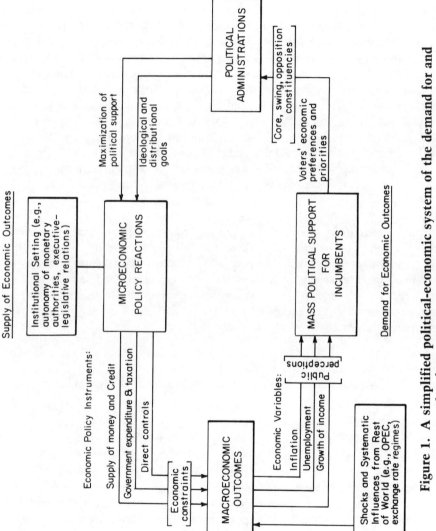

Supply of Economic Outcomes

Institutional Setting (e.g., autonomy of monetary authorities, executive–legislative relations)

MICROECONOMIC POLICY REACTIONS

POLITICAL ADMINISTRATIONS

Maximization of political support

Ideological and distributional goals

Core, swing, opposition constituencies

Voters' economic preferences and priorities

MASS POLITICAL SUPPORT FOR INCUMBENTS

Demand for Economic Outcomes

Economic Policy Instruments:

Supply of money and Credit

Government expenditure & taxation

Direct controls

Economic constraints

Public perceptions

Economic Variables:

Inflation

Unemployment

Growth of income

MACROECONOMIC OUTCOMES

Shocks and Systematic Influences from Rest of World (e.g., OPEC, exchange rate regimes)

Figure 1. A simplified political-economic system of the demand for and supply of macroeconomic outcomes

125

relevant economic and institutional constraints, define the intended electorally induced supply of economic outcomes. Confronted with shifts in
market demand, shocks in market supply, trade union cost push, and other
inflationary pressures, policy authorities are continually forced to make
short-run choices between (i) accommodating such pressures by expanding
government expenditures and the supply of money and credit, thereby
relinquishing control over the price level in order to preserve effective demand and employment, and (ii) leaning against such pressures, by tightening
spending and the money supply, thereby reducing the effective demand and
employment but putting downward pressure on the inflation rate. These
choices have important macroeconomic and distributional consequences profoundly affecting the relative and absolute economic well-being of social
groups, as well as important political consequences affecting the electoral
well-being of incumbent parties and chief executives.

Accounting for variations over time, across political administrations,
and across political systems in fiscal and monetary "discipline," that is, in
the inclination of policy makers to supply inflation, unemployment, and
associated distributional outcomes, poses important questions for analysts
of the contemporary political economies of industrial democracies. The next
two sections of this paper speak to the "demand" side of this issue by
investigating comparatively the response of mass political support for governments to fluctuations in macroeconomic performance. The final section
outlines procedures for investigating the "supply" side of this issue in the
context of my ongoing research on electorally and distributionally motivated
macroeconomic policy cycles.

2. The salience of the economy as a political issue

Not since the Great Depression of the 1930s and the immediate post-
World War II reconversion scare have economic issues occupied a more
salient place on the public agendas of the industrial democracies. This observation, no doubt obvious to even the most casual observer of the political–
economic scene in the West, is amply confirmed by public opinion surveys
of the electorates in a wide range of industrial democracies.

For example, time-series opinion survey data in Figure 2(a) from Britain's Gallup poll on "the most important problem facing the country today"
show that the economy has loomed large among the British public's concerns
since the early 1960s, and virtually has dominated public attention in that
country for more than ten years. Data from the United States Gallup poll
in Figure 2(b) indicate that once the American withdrawal from Vietnam
was completed, the economy outstripped all other issues as a source of
sustained public concern in this nation as well. The Allensbach survey data
for West Germany in Figure 2(c) exhibit a similar pattern. By the early

1970s international issues (reunification of the two Germanys, Berlin, and Cold War tensions) receded into the background and the economy became the most salient public issue.[3] The data for France in Figure 2(d) show that once the Algerian question was finally resolved in 1962, public concern about the economy increased sharply. By the late 1960s, as the long postwar economic expansion was coming to an end, about four out of every ten French voters considered an economic issue to be "the most important problem" facing the country. Following the OPEC supply shock of 1973, the fraction rose to seven out of ten and higher. "Eurobarometer" surveys undertaken every six months since July 1974 by the Commission of the European Communities tell the same story for other western industrial democracies: economic performance, on a consistent basis, has been the most important contemporary political issue.

The economy is of course not the only factor that influences a government's political support in the polls or actual voting outcomes. The Watergate events during the Nixon administration, the crises surrounding the Soviet invasion of Afghanistan and the seizure of American hostages in Tehran during the Carter administration, and the revival of support for

Figure 2a. Aggregate responses to the question "What is the most important problem facing this country today?"[a]—United Kingdom, 1950–1980

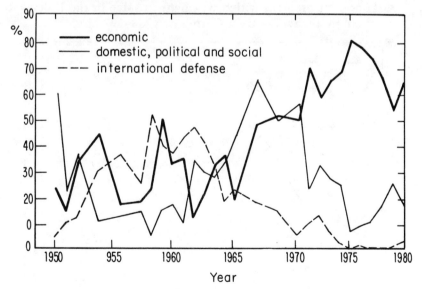

[a] Approximate wording.

Source: Coded from Gallup Opinion Poll data by the author.

Figure 2b. Aggregate responses to the question "What is the most important problem facing this country today?"[a]—United States, 1939–1980

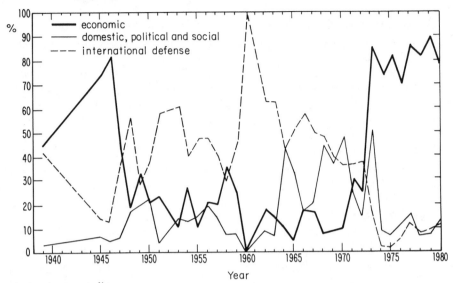

[a] Approximate wording.

Source: George Gallup, 1972 *The Gallup Poll*, Public Opinion: 1935–1971, Vols. I–III (Random House) and American Institute for Public Opinion, *The Gallup Opinion* Index, various issues.

Figure 2c. Aggregate responses to the question "What is the most important problem which we ought to solve in the Federal Republic today?"[a]—West Germany, 1963–1977

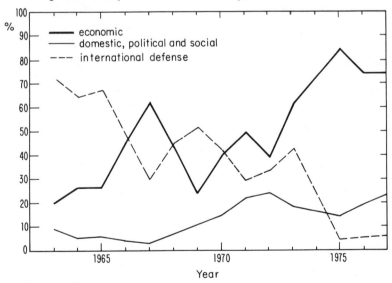

[a] Approximate wording.

Source: Institut fur Demoskopie Allensbach, *Allensbacher Jahrbuch der Domeskopie*, various years, Verlag Fritz Molden (Vienna).

Figure 2d. Aggregate responses to the question "What is the most important problem for France at the present time?"[a]—France, 1957–1978

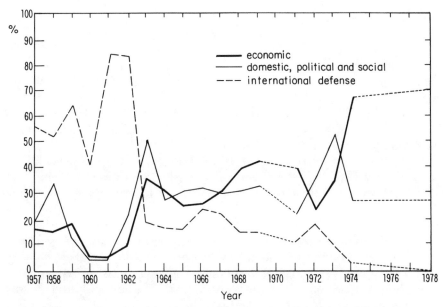

[a] Approximate wording.

Source: George H. Gallup, 1976, *The Gallup International Public Opinion Polls:* France 1939, 1944–1975 and Lafay (forthcoming), Table 1.

Mrs. Thatcher and the Conservatives following the Argentine seizure of the Falklands illustrate how public attention can be diverted from macroeconomic issues. Yet there is little doubt that in a world of supply shocks and continuing macroeconomic instability, economic performance is likely to continue to have great electoral impact. Indeed, this has been convincingly demonstrated by empirical work showing that the economy was decisive in, for example, the center-right's victory over the Social Democrats in Sweden in 1976, the Conservatives' victory over Labour in Britain in 1979, the victory of Reagan and the Republicans over Carter and the Democrats in the United States in 1980, and Mitterand's victory over Giscard d'Estaing in France in 1981.[4]

I turn now to a discussion of how the political effects of economic performance (as well as noneconomic events) in the industrial democracies can be systematically investigated within a well-defined model of political evaluation.

3. Modeling mass political support and electoral outcomes

In order to analyze comparatively the "demand" side of the political–economic system sketched briefly in Section 1, I have assembled quarterly time-series data on popular support for incumbent political parties or chief executives along with quarterly time-series data on unemployment, inflation, per capita personal disposable income, and other relevant economic and noneconomic variables for France, Great Britain, West Germany, Sweden, and the United States. The public's relative aversion to, or "demand" for, various outcomes is then inferred from the coefficients of econometric models used to estimate the response of mass political support to movements in economic (and noneconomic) conditions.

Empirical results reported in my published papers[5] are based on quarterly observations from the late 1950s or early 1960s through 1978. The variables used to measure political support in each country were:

> *United States:* The percentage of the public responding "approve" to the Gallup poll question, "Do you approve or disapprove of the way (the incumbent) is handling his job as President?"
>
> *France:* The percentage of the public responding "satisfied" when asked the question, "Are you satisfied or dissatisfied with (the incumbent) as President of the Republic?"
>
> *Great Britain:* The percentage of the public supporting the principal incumbent party (Labour or Conservative) when asked the question, "If there were a General Election tomorrow, which party would you support?"
>
> *West Germany:* The percentage of the public supporting the principal incumbent party (SPD or CDU/CSU) when asked the question, "If there were an election next Sunday, could you please tell me which party you would vote for?"
>
> *Sweden:* The percentage of the public supporting the incumbent party or bloc when asked the question, "Which party do you consider voting for at the next election?"

Concerning the political support model proper, let me describe briefly three important features of the theoretical structure:

> 1. Voters evaluate an administration's performance *relatively* rather than *absolutely*. In particular, the model expresses voters' support for incumbents as a weighted average of two relative performance comparisons: (a) the cumulative performance of the current incumbent party/bloc in relation to the cumulative past performance of the present opposition parties/blocs, and (b) the cumulative per-

formance of the current administration relative to the cumulative past performance of all previous administrations, regardless of partisan composition.

2. Although past as well as current performance influences voters' contemporaneous political judgments, the present relevance of information conveyed by past performance decays over time. Therefore, the importance attached to past performance outcomes (Z_{t-k}) in the model is discounted backward in time at rate g^k, where g is a decay rate parameter lying between zero and one.

3. Political opinion surveys typically force people to make discrete, qualitative responses. However, in principle, voters' support for the government is not a discrete "yes" or "no" phenomenon but a matter of degree, falling on an underlying continuum ranging from strongly positive to strongly negative. Therefore, following the standard theory of qualitative choice, the dependent variables in the models are derived from a logistic transformation of the observed political support responses in the opinion surveys.

The political support model is defined by the following equations:*

$$Y_t^* = w\,LR_t^q + (1-w)SR_t^q + a_q + u_t \qquad (1)$$

where:

Y* is the political support index (based on a logistic transformation of the political survey responses),

LR^q are interparty comparisons during the qth administration,

SR^q are interadministration comparisons of the qth administration with previous administrations;

a_q are administration-specific constants, and

$0 \leqslant w \leqslant 1$.

$$LR^q = b \cdot D_t \sum_{k=0}^{\infty} g_1^k Z_{t-k} D_{t-k}, \qquad (2)$$

where:

Z denotes a vector of economic (and noneconomic) performance variables (specified ahead) with associated coefficients b,

g_1 is the rate of decay of the lag weights, $0 \leqslant g_1 \leqslant 1$, and

$D_{t(t-k)} = \begin{cases} +1 \text{ if party/bloc A is in power at time } t(t-k), \\ -1 \text{ if party/bloc B is in power at time } t(t-k). \end{cases}$

---

*Equations (1) through (4) are unlikely to interest the general reader and may be passed over.

$$SR_t^q = \sum_{q=1}^{Q} A_{qt}\, b \cdot \sum_{k=0}^{\infty} g_2^k\, Z_{t-k}\, D_{q,t-k}^*, \tag{3}$$

where

$$A_{qt} = \begin{array}{l} +1 \text{ during the } q^{th} \text{ political administration,} \\ 0 \text{ otherwise, and} \end{array}$$

$$D_{qt}^* = \begin{array}{l} +1 \text{ during the tenure of the } q^{th} \text{ political administration,} \\ -1 \text{ otherwise.} \end{array}$$

Substituting (2) and (3) into (1) yields the estimating equation

$$Y_t^* = w\, [b \cdot D_t \sum_{k=0}^{t-2} g_1^k\, Z_{t-k}\, D_{t-k} + R^{LR}] \tag{4}$$

$$+ (1-w)\, [\, \sum_{q=1}^{Q} A_{qt}\, b \cdot \sum_{k=0}^{t-2} g_2^k\, Z_{t-k}\, D_{q,t-k}^* + R^{SR}] + a_q + v_t$$

where
   the truncation remainders $R^{LR} = g^{t-1} LR_{j1}^q\, (D_t/D_1)$, and $R^{SR} = g^{t-1}(SR_{j1}^q - 2b_j \cdot Z_1)$
are safely dropped for estimation purposes.

Fluctuations in political support for various incumbent political parties and chief executives are modelled, as equations (1) through (4) indicate, by dynamic nonlinear equations that include economic as well as noneconomic terms. However, I will not dwell on the theoretical and technical features of the equations here, which are of interest only to academic specialists. Instead, attention will be confined to a discussion of the relative effects of various economic variables on political support implied by empirical estimates of models in the form of equation (4).

Table 1 reports the estimated long-run (or "steady-state") response of the percentage of the public supporting incumbent parties or chief executives to a *sustained* increase of two percentage points in the rate of unemployment, the rate of inflation, and the rate of growth of real per capita disposable personal income. The responses shown in Table 1 represent, then, the political/electoral consequences of sustained changes in economic performance after all adjustment lags have worked their way through the underlying dynamic equations.[6]

The estimates in Table 1 suggests that political support in the United States, the United Kingdom, West Germany, France, and Sweden is quite sensitive to performance in the real side of the economy, that is, to movements in the unemployment and/or real income growth rates. Political support among the mass publics of all the countries, except Sweden, responds

Table 1. Approximate responses of political support percentages to a
sustained increase of two percentage points in the rate of
unemployment, inflation, and real income growth rates[a]
(evaluated at 50% political support level)

	United States	United Kingdom	West Germany	France	Sweden[c]
	(1961:1– 1978:4)	(1959:4– 1978:4)	(1957:4– 1978:4)	(1969:4– 1978:4)	(1967:1– 1978:3)
Per Capita Real Disposable[b] Income Growth Rate, R	+5.4%	+2.8%	+2.1%	+3.8%	—
Unemployment Rate, U	−4.5%	−6.4%	−2.5%	?(−2%, −3%)	−11.5%
Consumer Prices Inflation Rate[b], P	−6.2%	—	−1.7	—	−0.5%
Change in Inflation Rate (sustained 4 quarters), (P-P-1)	—	−2.6%	—	—	—

[a] Based on analyses of quarterly data. See Hibbs, "On the Demand for Economic Outcomes," and Hibbs and Madsen, "The Impact of Economic Performance on Electoral
Support in Sweden, 1967–1978," *Scandinavian Political Studies* 4(1), 1981, and Hibbs
with Vasilatos, "Economics and Politics in France: Economic Performance and Mass
Political Support for Presidents Pompidou and Giscard d'Estaing," *European Journal of
Political Research* 9, 1981.
[b] In the United States and the United Kingdom, this variable was adjusted for adverse
effects of shifts in the terms of trade following the OPEC supply shock. See Hibbs, "On
the Demand for European Outcomes" (refer to footnote a for full reference) for details.
[c] Based on equation (8) of Hibbs and Madsen, *op. cit.*

to the real disposable income growth rate, with the magnitudes of the responses to a two-percentage-point increase ranging between 2.1 and 5.4
percentage points of political support. Since elections often hinge on margins
of only a few percentage points of the vote, these results are not merely of
academic interest. Macroeconomic management and performance obviously
can have pivotal impact on electoral changes.

In each country, increases in the unemployment rate yield declines in
the political support, although in the case of France, measurement problems
with the unemployment data make it difficult to estimate unambiguously
the quantitative political effects. The expected response of mass political
support to a two-percentage-point increase in unemployment in Sweden is
particularly large. This undoubtedly reflects the preeminence in postwar

Swedish political life of the full-employment issue. Low unemployment has been the most important theme of the Swedish Social Democrats' electoral mobilization strategy since the early 1930s. And it proved successful: the Social Democrats governed continuously in Sweden for forty-four years, from the early 1930s until their narrow defeat by the Bourgeois bloc coalition in 1976.

Mass political support for British governments also exhibits great sensitivity to unemployment fluctuations, especially when evaluated relative to the political response to nominal inflation–economic outcomes. Again, this probably reflects the Labour Party's emphasis on low unemployment in political discourse, which has generated widespread public expectation of sustained high employment in Britain.

Taken together, the political responses to unemployment in Table 1 belie the idea that unemployment no longer has sizable adverse political consequences because unemployment compensation programs and other features of the tax and transfer systems of advanced industrial democracies shelter those affected directly from the full impact of recessions and joblessness. It is of course true that tax-transfer systems do spread the costs of unemployment widely throughout society, and therefore for many people, loss of employment no longer poses an economic disaster. Nonetheless, unemployment represents lost real output and underutilized human and physical resources, and the measurable economic costs can reach staggering proportions. In the United States, for example, each extra percentage point of unemployment is accompanied by a real output decline of at least two percent, which in a three-trillion dollar economy amounts to about $60 billion of unproduced output, or $750 per household. In view of the aggregate economic costs, the corresponding aggregate political costs (in the form of declining political support) of rising unemployment and falling real output and income are hardly surprising. Indeed, to readers not familiar with empirical results in this area of research, they probably seem "small."

The estimates of the responses of political support to inflation shown in Table 1 indicate that the political costs of deteriorating nominal economic performance are less uniform cross-nationally than the analogous political costs of higher unemployment and lower real income growth. In France and Sweden, the decline in political support associated with increased consumer price inflation in the models was negligible. In these countries, adverse political consequences of inflation appear to be transmitted largely through the impact of rising prices on the real income growth stream (price increases running ahead of money income growth rates) or on the unemployment rate (if one believes, contrary to the traditional view, that high or accelerating inflation yields increased unemployment). For Great Britain, the results indicate that the electorate is not averse to inflation *per se*, but that changes in the inflation rate (accelerations and decelerations of prices) have important consequences for mass political support. Since the change (first difference) of the inflation rate is a reasonable (though simple) measure of inflationary surprises, this result is consistent with the view that the pain induced by rising prices is primarily due to unanticipated bursts of inflation.

Only in West Germany and the United States does the simple rate of change of consumer prices—the inflation rate—appear to have statistically and politically significant consequences. Since these results are based on models including the rate of change of real personal disposable income among the explanatory variables, the inflation estimates imply that voters are averse to rising prices *per se*. In other words, even if money incomes keep pace with price rises, governments suffer losses of political support as a result of inflation. A discussion of the tangible economic costs underlying the estimated political costs of inflation is beyond the scope of this paper. However, I have treated this question at some length in other articles.[7]

4. Modeling electoral pressures on macroeconomic policies

The political support models described briefly in previous sections yield information about the electoral consequences of current and past macroeconomic outcomes. Political authorities are of course well aware that their electoral fortunes are influenced by economic conditions and, presumably, take this into account when formulating and implementing macroeconomic policies. In other words, the macroeconomic policies pursued by political administrations operating in a democratic setting typically respond to political/electoral pressures rather than to idealized, apolitical "golden rule" norms. Policy authorities of course face economic constraints that may be represented by econometric models of the macroeconomy which specify the relations among unemployment, inflation, income growth, and so on, that will vary across institutional settings. Such econometric models of the macroeconomy supply the set of feasible macroeconomic outcomes constraining politically optimal policy behavior.

On the assumption that policy authorities operating in democratic settings attempt to maintain a comfortable aggregate level of mass political support, and also attempt to pursue ideological/distributional goals, which can be thought of in terms of the distinctive economic interests and priorities of their core political constituencies, electorally motivated macroeconomic policy behavior can be modeled plausibly as the solution(s) to optimization problem(s) in which a political support model is the objective function and an econometric model of the macroeconomy forms the constraints. If the models for (formal representations of) political support and macroeconomic constraints are reasonably accurate, then dynamic optimization experiments can be devised permitting rigorous empirical investigation of such issues as: (1) the relative weight political authorities have given in the past, and are likely to give in the future (in their macroeconomic policy behavior), to the economic preferences (distributional positions) of their core constituency, the opposition party constituency, and marginal/swing groups in the electorate; (2) the weights macroeconomic policy actions appear to place on political support during interelection periods versus election periods; and (3) the time horizon reflected in policy behavior as between, for example, the current administrative term and future administrative terms.

If comparisons of electorally motivated policy plans with actual policy outcomes yield systematic patterns consistent with sensible hypotheses of the sort embedded in points (1) through (3) above, we could seriously entertain the idea of using macroeconomic policy projections generated by models in which the authorities are *political* optimizers to make predictions of future policy reactions to future economic disturbances. However, before one can make strong statements along these lines, a great deal of research in this framework needs to be done. Unlike the situation with respect to political support models, where reliable and theoretically interesting connections between electoral outcomes and macroeconomic performance are well established, optimization-based characterizations of macroeconomic policy behavior and associated predictions of likely future policy actions are for the most part an unexplored area of research.

NOTES

1. For wider ranging treatments readers might consult the recent volumes by Bruno Frey, 1978, *Modern Political Economy* (Wiley); Douglas A. Hibbs, Jr. and Heino Fassbender (eds.), 1981, *Contemporary Political Economy* (North Holland); and Paul Whiteley (ed.), 1980, *Models of Political Economy* (Sage).

2. Cf. Robert J. Gordon, 1975, "The Demand For and Supply Of Inflation," *Journal of Law and Economics* 18, 807–836, and Bruno Frey, 1978, "Politico-Economic Models and Cycles," *Journal of Public Economics* 9, 203–220.

3. Despite the emergence of the "Greens" and the antinuclear weapons movement in Germany, this remains true for the early 1980s as well. Public opinion data (and professional political judgments), for example, indicate that the decisive issues for the March 6 election of 1983 were economic.

4. An exhaustive list of electoral outcomes induced by economics undoubtedly would be much longer. Seymour Martin Lipset ("No Room for the Ins: Elections around the World," *Public Opinion* 5, October/November, 1982) notes that a simple "misery index"—the sum of the inflation and unemployment rates—is a powerful predictor of recent political outcomes in seventeen electoral democracies. Looking at the period 1975–1982, Lipset notes that when the misery index was less than ten percent, incumbents were reelected; when it was higher, they almost always were defeated. My purpose in this paper is not so much to devise a predictive rule of thumb, as it is to tie the connections between economic performance and electoral support to a rigorous theory of political evaluation and choice. However, I encourage readers with less academic interests and tastes to look at Lipset's engaging analysis.

5. See Hibbs, D., and H. Madsen, 1981, "The Impact of Economic Performance on Electoral Support in Sweden, 1967–1978," *Scandinavian Political Studies* 4(1), 33–50; Hibbs, D., with N. Vasilatos, 1981, "Economics and Politics in France: Economic Performance and Mass Political Support for Presidents Pompidou and Giscard d'Estaing," *European Journal of Political Research* 9, 133–145; Hibbs, D., 1982, "On the Demand for Economic

Outcomes: Macroeconomic Performance and Mass Political Support in the U.S., Great
Britain and Germany," *Journal of Politics* 44(2), 426–462; Hibbs, D., 1982, "The Dynamics of Political Support for American Presidents among Occupational and Partisan
Groups," *American Journal of Political Science* 26(2), 312–332; Hibbs, D., 1982, "Economic Outcomes and Political Support for British Governments among Occupational
Classes: A Dynamic Analysis," *American Political Science Review* 76(2), 259–279.
6. For practical purposes, a sustained change may be taken to mean twenty to twenty-five
quarters, that is, five to six years. Given the decay rates of political memories, however,
most of the political effects are felt sooner—by two years.
7. Hibbs, D., 1982, "Public Concern about Inflation and Unemployment in the United
States: Trends, Correlates and Political Implications," in R. Hall (ed.), *Inflation* (NBER,
University of Chicago Press); and Hibbs, D., 1979, "The Mass Public and Macroeconomic Performance: The Dynamics of Public Opinion toward Unemployment and
Inflation," *American Journal of Political Science* 23 (4), 705–731.

7

Patterns of failure in government megaprojects: economics, politics, and participation in industrial democracies

ELLIOT J. FELDMAN

*Director, University Consortium for Research on North America in
the Center for International Affairs, Harvard University*

Megaprojects, as their name implies, are large-scale complex undertakings. They require the coordination of many actors and interests, and it
therefore is not surprising that they may be prone to failure. However, the
fanfare with which they are introduced and the vigor with which they are
pursued suggest commitments of a scale equal to the projects themselves.
When governments mobilize their resources, skills, personnel, power, and
prestige to concentrate on a specific and often narrowly focused project,
success may be expected. Nevertheless, most such projects do fail.

In this discussion I will restrict the category "megaprojects" to public
works, excluding most private-sector undertakings (unless in the public
domain) and large-scale projects that do not involve construction. Any final
judgment on government performance must depend on comparisons with
the private sector, of course, and there are many non-construction activities
in both the public and private sectors that generally would satisfy a reasonable definition of "megaproject" (e.g., AT&T divestiture).[1] This limited
analysis is unavoidably a product of incomplete research in progress.

There are various competing explanations for megaproject failure. The
most popular fall into five main categories:

1. Projects require precise forecasting in environments of excessive
   uncertainty and risk;
2. The sheer complexity of a task simply exceeds the organizing capability of government;
3. Mixed economies cannot cope effectively with government's need
   to coordinate and control private-sector behavior;
4. During project development new information or technological advances erode the economic or technical logic of original plans;

138

5. Narrow citizen-activist groups can paralyze governments and pervert the public interest.

A sixth explanation, that governments undertake projects that the private sector already has judged likely to fail, unfortunately has not received analytical attention.

There also are observations that projects are more likely to fail in some countries than in others. Most popular in this contrast is the perception of French success and British failure. The differences generally are ascribed to a superior quality of French planning and planners, to a *dirigiste* state apparatus and attitude, a historical and cultural commitment to central control, a greater popular French acceptance of government guidance in the economy, and a greater French rejection of interest groups and citizen activists in favor of allegiance to the broad public good. This particular contrast depends above all on assumptions about cultures and the weight of history, but Canadians share British self-doubt when they compare themselves to Americans, with reasoning quite different from the Anglo–French comparison. With no illusion that the United States is *dirigiste* or committed to central control, some Canadians nevertheless imagine that large-scale projects are more likely to succeed in the United States.

Generalizations about failure depend upon reference to numerous detailed cases, and differences among countries can be explained only through systematic comparison. The quantity of theorizing about megaproject failure exceeds the number of carefully documented cases, and analysts tend to develop cases when they are partial to one or another of the popular explanations. Typically, theory precedes the case work and data are collected to support the original theoretical formulations.

Although each of the popular explanations for megaproject failure seems applicable to almost any given case, all such explanations seem necessary yet even in combination insufficient. The task of this paper, a first summary application of preliminary data from some sixty cases, is to cite a range of examples sufficiently varied in character to permit a high level of generalization, but derived from a set of cases that have been compiled in a sufficiently systematic and comparative way to warrant controlled and more reliable theoretical observations. Do megaproject failures have something in common that knows no national frontier in the advanced industrial world, as much theory now suggests, or are the patterns limited enough to promote different outcomes in different countries?

The majority of well-documented cases are American, perhaps because American social scientists are more inclined to detailed case studies of decision-making. Nevertheless, some detailed case studies are available from Canada, Britain, France, Italy, and West Germany and are utilized here. The political systems of these countries range from federal to unitary and from parliamentary to congressional. The role of the state ranges from inclinations toward central planning, to state enterprise, to guarantees of a free market for private enterprise. Bureaucratic authority ranges from autonomy to tight political control. The populations at large, according to survey research, have priorities ranging from general economic growth to greater redistribution of wealth, and elite attitudes are said to range from protection against monopoly to the establishment of state-controlled monopolies.

Megaprojects invariably involve investments for economic growth, so the great variation in attitude and in the sophistication of state apparatus ought to dictate variety in the objectives, styles, and strategies behind project formulation and execution. Yet, despite such a spectrum of elite and mass attitudes, systemic organization and sophistication, objectives and strategies, the case histories do suggest illustrative patterns. Sources of failure, more political than sociological, are broadly similar, even as outcomes are sufficiently different to warrant closer scrutiny.

Definitions of success and failure

Planners and developers measure success according to the completion of projects. If they plan a highway, or a nuclear power plant, or an airport, or a pipeline, or public housing, or any other large-scale public works, they consider the project successful only when it is built and operational. Failure to them refers simply to the inability to complete construction and operate the facility.

The construction of a project rarely represents the initial goal or responsibility of a planner or political advocate, so achievement of the initial goal often loses salience when success is measured by construction. Construction plans typically originate as objectives, means for the satisfaction of goals: the construction of a highway is the means for relieving traffic congestion or improving the efficiency of transportation links; power plants are built to increase the efficient delivery of electricity; airports are built to satisfy air passenger demand, and so forth. Yet, in many instances traffic congestion may be relieved without a new highway; power or fuel requirements are satisfied without new plants or pipelines; and air traffic demand is met without new airports. Construction projects, the objectives, rarely are exclusive means to the achievement of original goals, but often they replace original goals in the minds of planners and politicians.

The most frequent measurement of success in the literature of public administration and planning for public works is the completion of a construction project.[2] However, goals often are met without any particular policy or concerted effort, and the impact of exogenous forces or accidental developments is of little inspiration to the bureaucratic or political activist.[3] A fuel shortage may dampen demand for power, pipelines, and air and surface travel, but no planner or politician can derive much satisfaction from such a negative development. Because of the natural bureaucratic tendencies to grow and to achieve actively, according to Anthony Downs,[4] the premium placed on tangible achievement is inevitable. There is more glory in adding facilities to accommodate more demand than in reducing or shifting demand. A power company prefers to generate and sell more power to more customers rather than induce customers to shift their use of power off peaks so that a smaller but steadier demand could be met. Hence, success becomes associated with the achievement of narrow and specific objectives, often without reference to feasible alternatives, and original goals become secondary or irrelevant.

Bureaucracies, whether public or private, generate forces that guarantee this distortion in the measurement of success.[5] However, any useful criticism must refocus. In this paper I consider success to be the satisfaction of original goals; the achievement of objectives may contribute and therefore warrant designation as success, but where construction yields excess capacity or inefficient use of resources, only failure seems an appropriate appellation. Furthermore, where equity and social justice have been cashiered, regardless of the achievement of efficiency, I also question any claims of success. Finally, although there are occasional examples of success, even according to these revised criteria, this paper is concerned only with explanations of failure.

Conventional explanations of failure

Forecasting: the opaque ball

The concept of planning depends upon the preparation of a project or program for future development and implementation. Because a plan is designed to meet some future need or preference, it requires a forecast. Theoretically, then, forecasting must precede planning, for it must predict needs and the conditions for their fulfillment.

Many project failures are attributed to forecasting failures, which often are inherent to the forecasting exercise itself. Glenn DeSousa finds forecasting for electricity demand little more than simple extrapolation, and he considers all three models used by the electric utility industry to have "significant weaknesses."[6] Richard Timm accuses the nuclear power industry of neglecting the most basic data in forecasting, and cites Pacific Power and Light Company's inability in a site certificate application to "supply energy price data, service area population and employment, or energy use by customer class."[7] According to a Ford Foundation sponsored study group at Resources for the Future, energy demand is price sensitive, prices are subject to exogenous forces and manipulation, and demand forecasts therefore are unreliable.[8] Energy forecasting, moreover, is not unique. Expert traffic forecasts for highway construction in Portsmouth, England, were exceedingly inconsistent,[9] and forecasts of air traffic in eight cities in five different countries have revealed patterns of gross forecasting error.[10] Forecasts of costs for major conventional civil projects average fifty percent below the final bill.[11]

If project failure follows from poor forecasting, then simple logic recommends improvement in forecasting. A substantial literature has emerged to explain why forecasts in so many fields are unreliable,[12] and a corollary literature proposes modest solutions.[13] Both these bodies of literature assume that forecasting is a central feature of decision-making for megaprojects. However, Feldman and Milch found on close examination that major infrastructure decisions for aviation typically are taken without reference to prior forecasts; planners deploy traffic predictions *post hoc* to legitimize political choices.[14] Unfortunately, other available case studies do not report the sequential relationship between key decisions and the generation of forecasts, relying instead on the mere existence of forecasts and the assumption that officials used them to make decisions.

Within important limitations sketched by Hall,[15] forecasting undoubtedly could be improved. Uncertainty may not be reduced significantly, but awareness of its sources could be heightened and more judicious estimates perhaps could be made.[16] Plainly, cost estimates are determined often by political constraints and such political influence may be mitigated. Yet even if forecasting were improved, there is no reliable evidence that such a change would affect substantially the planning or implementation of megaprojects. To the contrary, what systematic evidence does exist on the specific role of forecasting in the decision process suggests that other factors weigh more heavily.

Making goals out of objectives: the simplification of complexity

The most thoroughly analyzed explanation offered for megaproject failure relies on theories of organizational behavior. These theories are abstract, conceptualized to explain behavior in all organizations, but they are derived primarily from American experience by American social scientists.

Peter Hall, a British planner, has amalgamated various American theories in sociology, social psychology, and economics to explain "great planning disasters."[17] He observes that organizations, according to Cyert and March, adjust their goals to the sub-goals of competing subordinate units, and that according to Downs,[18] "in a large organization no one has full control."[19] Bureaucracies will overproduce unwanted goods or services[20] because satisfaction of competing subordinate goals contributes to a natural expansion of staff size and activity.[21] Bureaucrats shape the policy agenda and they are narrow empire-builders determined to expand their own authority through concrete accomplishments. They always will prefer active solutions, such as the construction of highways, power plants, or airports, to more modest proposals that may modify conditions without major capital investment. Inherently conservative in protecting their own interests, bureaucrats prefer the security of over-construction to the uncertainty of being unable to meet some future demand.

This synthetic critique of organizational behavior, much in the way the iron law of oligarchy seems applicable to all political organizations, may apply to all government agencies and bureaus. It goes a long way toward explaining why bureaucrats everywhere are inclined to solutions of monumentalism, and why they typically are unaware of alternatives and compromises for their projects. The critique, however, fails to indicate why bureaucrats achieve their objectives of construction or development in some cases but not in others. Because bureaucratic theories are designed for equal application to all government agencies, they do not differentiate effectively among organizations. The same patterns of behavior are expected everywhere, and it is not without reason that the clichéd slur on bureaucrats therefore has popular resonance throughout the industrial world. Yet, the underlying ideology of these theories is American pluralism—the conviction that decisions ideally and actually are produced by competition among legitimate interest groups. Bureaucracies may become interest groups themselves, and their competition thus mirrors private-sector pluralism. This ideology is distinctly American in character and neither as ideology nor as description can it be applied easily to non-American experience. If the theory designed as a general statement on the human condition, pertaining to all organizations, applies essentially to the United States, then it is more a recasting of American ideological preference than a "theory" of human behavior.

Peter Hall has formulated his synthesis with the background of seven detailed cases, two of which he characterizes as "near disasters." Among the five "disasters" he includes planning for a third London airport, and it is unclear why this example satisfies his own criteria. The airport, unlike other examples (Concorde, London's motorways, San Francisco's BART, Sydney Opera House), was not built. The original planning goal in the 1950s, to meet air traffic demand in London to 1990, seems not to be in much jeopardy despite failure to build. In general, the various decisions not to build were not taken because planners thought they could meet their goals anyway, but it is important to observe that, whatever the reasons, unnecessary large-scale investment was avoided and thus the outcome in the case was quite different from the other disasters. The curiosity of including this case is compounded by the two "near disasters" because Hall explains them as successes produced by exogenous circumstance, not by any particular planning intelligence. Hence, according to Hall, bureaucracy is a principal source of failure. Planners may be better trained, more astute, and circumspect; organizations may be made more flexible. Nevertheless, there is no explanation for success or the avoidance of disaster, and theories of organizational behavior suggest social, psychological, and economic laws that can be manipulated only at the margins.

The laws governing organizations have a further important consequence invoked by Graham Allison, Herbert Simon, and Cyert and March, among others.[22] Because each bureaucracy is defensive about its own turf, it is reluctant to surrender authority or resources that would enhance co-operation with any other bureaucracy. Cyert and March emphasize that even with a single agency or firm there are competing, defensive subordinate units, and Allison argues that similar conditions obtain among agencies subordinate to the President of the United States in the American foreign policy-making apparatus.

The irrationality of mixed economies

The difficulties faced by the public sector for internal coordination are multiplied when megaprojects require cooperation with the private sector. Stephen Cohen argues that French central planning is handicapped per-manently by the self-imposed limitation by government on the coercive powers necessary to compel private-sector behavior.[23] Many of the more celebrated American megaproject failures, such as Consolidated Edison's Storm King Mountain project in New York (and the "failure" is debatable), have succumbed to a maze of bureaucratic impediments.[24] The Pacific Northwest Power Company faced a similar experience in its attempt to build a dam in Hell's Canyon,[25] as did Dow Chemical when trying to build a plant in Solano County, California.[26]

These private-sector initiatives that fell victim to contradictory public-sector signals complement cases where the private sector undermined public-sector initiatives. Sidney Tarrow finds the steel industry extracting an in-calculable subsidy from the French government for development at Fos-Marseilles;[27] Feldman found the private helicopter manufacturer Agusta S.pa. acquiring state lands at the expense of the public airport authority in Milan;[28] Philip Mathias finds foreign investors overwhelming poorly in-formed Canadian provincial authorities;[29] the United States federal govern-ment has ransomed countless defense projects from private contractors, including the legendary C-5A Transport from Lockheed. Furthermore, where the private sector can move without regulation or control, as in the Franklin Town community development in Philadelphia[30] or Renaissance Center in Detroit,[31] the results are no more satisfactory.

These examples all suggest that planning and building megaprojects efficiently may be impossible in any of three circumstances that involve the active or tacit cooperation of public and private sectors: (1) where the private sector is subject to public-sector approval, regulation, and supervision; (2) where the public sector must rely on private-sector contracts and cooper-ation; (3) where the private sector operates without public-sector controls. In this last condition, the key measurement of failure is related more to justice and equity than to efficiency,[32] and it may be that such a shift in criteria for success and failure, like the Arrow theorem, renders all planning in mixed economies impossible.[33] Nevertheless, in liberal democracies equity inevitably is a consideration in all projects involving significant investment, or involving construction in populated areas, or in projects requiring much land. Even pipelines across remote tundra have encountered equity demands raised by native peoples.

Not all planning fails, even if often there is doubt about the causal relationship between planning and success. Therefore, the catastrophic logic of inherent weakness in mixed economies, ratified by numerous examples and analysts (including Shonfield;[34] Heclo, Heidenheimer and Adams;[35] and Hayward and Watson,[36] all of whom argue that great state control is essential for successful guidance of the economy and achievement of major projects), is deficient for explaining success and failure. In explaining everything, the description of anomalies in mixed economies explains too little.

The existence of bureaucracy—and indeed now of technocracy—is inevitable in advanced industrial states.[37] Furthermore, bureaucracy itself, which constitutes essential planning apparatus, apparently is its own source of weakness in the planning and execution of megaprojects. Finally, all mixed economies inevitably invite tensions and inefficiencies between the public and private sectors. Nevertheless, this analysis leaves little room for success, and no room for outside forces, including technological change and citizen participation.

Deus ex machina

In the literature on forecasting, analysts refer to the unexpected as levels of risk or uncertainty. The two most frequently cited influences are general economic conditions and technological change.

The greatest impact of unanticipated changes in economic conditions perhaps can be found in energy megaprojects. The 1973 energy shock triggered numerous monumental schemes ranging from pipelines to tar sands extractions, from coal conversion and extraction to deep water drilling. Many of these projects were begun in the 1970s and abandoned in the early 1980s because world economic circumstances had adjusted to smaller supplies with reduced demand, and the increase in supply implied by new and expensive projects was not met by a corresponding resurgence of demand. As it became apparently more difficult to predict economic conditions, especially because the easy formulas of extrapolated post-war economic growth no longer proved applicable, it became harder to plan long-term large-scale projects. Projects launched and abandoned obviously are more conspicuous failures than those never started.

Technological change also subverts or enhances projects. The cost escalation of Concorde and the American SST that contributed (although not exclusively) to commercial failure for one and abandonment for the other, is attributable above all to the unanticipated costs of new technology.[38] Conversely, Hall argues that the British National Library plan was saved by an unanticipated technological change that liberated an ideal construction site.[39] Similarly, nuclear power planners are convinced that technological breakthroughs will secure their energy production in the next decade, even as environmental hazards and escalating development costs, also partially attributable to technology, undermined their progress in the last decade— and led them to rely on the state to sustain them.[40]

The "technological imperative" dictates a steady decline in cost for the provision of goods or services,[41] as in the proliferation of gadgetry in the electronics and computer industries. But in megaprojects, each case is too grand to be easily replicated, obviating the eventual comparative advantage of unit cost, and the cost of breakthrough therefore is borne by each project. Grand-scale investment in the 1980s in new weapons systems may be a classic example of this problem and a principal explanation for the runaway American defense budget. Technology in these instances almost always escalates cost and typically will contribute to project failure. Furthermore, the technological imperative implies an inevitable process which dictates that initiated projects must be realized, yet in many large-scale planning examples projects either are not completed or similar projects have different outcomes. Hence, the impulse to build is no more attributable to a technological imperative than is the variety of outcomes typifying megaprojects.

This argument implicitly contradicts Nelson's celebrated moon–ghetto metaphor.[42] The difference lies not in what technology can achieve, but in the purpose it serves. Non-commercial megaprojects, undertaken for national prestige or some other intangible goal, have a much greater chance of conventional success than do projects with an explicit commercial intention. Concorde developers systematically avoided serious commercial calculations and kept the project cloaked in military secrecy until a prototype was flying, probably because they recognized that commercial prospects were too tenuous to justify continuation.[43] Other cases cited here all involve investment for profit, whether in the provision of power or services. Even the construction of highways, which do not turn a direct profit, must be calculated in terms of the automobile and trucking industries. Like Concorde, defense projects or moon shots are more likely to be completed because they are less likely to fall victim to the adverse decisions generated by cost escalation.

Macroeconomic and technological dynamism constitute forces unanticipated and unexplained that can alter dramatically the best-laid plans. However, dependence on them as explanation for megaproject failure (or, as Hall suggests, occasional success), precisely because they are unpredictable, would render all efforts to formulate a general explanation or theory futile.

Passionate minorities[44]

Although bureaucracies are the most studied dimension of planning failure, citizen protest in the 1970s has become the most frequently cited explanation. Douglas Yates complains of chaos in the multiplication of voices that has led to the ungovernable city,[45] and Aaron Wildavsky criticizes new activism as a revolt of the middle and upper-middle classes against mass preferences.[46] Several authors credit citizen protest groups with stopping the third London airport,[47] the American SST,[48] the Riverfront Expressway through the Vieux Carré in New Orleans,[49] the Storm King Mountain project,[50] the Pickering Airport in Toronto,[51] the Eugene, Oregon, nuclear power plant,[52] the Alcovy River project in Georgia,[53] field burning in Willamette Valley,[54] among many examples. Books such as *Citizens Make the Difference* are case chronicles extolling the impact of *ad hoc* protest organizations.[55]

This literature is deceptive. Almost invariably it is written by engaged parties eager to justify their own activities in specific case accounts, or by analysts relying heavily on biased accounts to draw general lessons. There are almost no detailed case studies available that include both an account of citizen activity and a report on the policy process based on interviews with decision-makers. In the case of the third London airport, for example, published accounts are unanimous in citing citizen protest at several stages of the planning process, yet interviews with involved bureaucrats reveal a commitment to contradict citizen protest simply to prove bureaucratic purity.[56] Although outcomes corresponded to the preferences of protestors, the causes were different.

More circumspect conclusions about the impact of citizen protest seem in order. Wolpert, Mumphrey, and Seley concluded in the controversy over a Crosstown Expressway in Philadelphia that "citizen groups were effective . . . only to the extent that external events favored them,"[57] and indeed in almost every case study there are sufficient data to encourage alternative interpretations. The objectives of conservation organizations were sustained in the controversy over a jetport in Dade County, but legal requirements for an environmental impact statement were decisive;[58] Pacific Gas and Electric gave up the Bodega Head nuclear reactor when the Atomic Energy Commission feared the proximity of the San Andreas Fault;[59] the Scenic Hudson Preservation Conference fought long and hard for Storm King Mountain, but the outcome of the case appears to have been influenced primarily by project delays that followed formal legal proceedings and licensing requirements, and ultimately by political changes that replaced a Republican governor's administration supporting the project with a Democratic opponent in the State House.[60] Clearly American citizen protest is more influential than the protest of citizens in other political systems (which will be explained below), but even in the United States there is cause to doubt the conclusion that the proliferation of participation and the multiplication of apparently legitimate voices is a major source of project failure. Pluralism was never a fully accurate analysis of American politics;[61] carrying pluralism to its logical participatory conclusion is no more reliable for assessing causal relations in the demise of large-scale public works.

Explaining patterns of failure

Political analysts who focus on sectors regard pressures and consequences outside the sector as "spillover."[62] Economists refer to such phenomena as "externalities." Of course, any complex project necessarily involves cross-sectoral influences, and sound planning must at least be conscious of the potential of intervention from unanticipated sources or of yielding unexpected consequences.

There are discernible cross-national patterns in the project failures cited here and in the others utilized in this study. They generally take two forms, one related to a change in decision-making personnel, the other a consequence of that change.

The rise of technocrats

Megaprojects may be initiated by or assigned to narrowly focused line agencies, but the problems they engender invariably breach the boundaries of any single agency's mandate. The construction of highways or airports may be delegated to departments of transportation or port authorities catering exclusively to a traveling public or to cargo industries, but the projects inescapably involve air and noise pollution (environmental agencies), and land use (typically requiring expropriation handled by justice departments for land acquisition and compensation). Airports are large employers (50,000 at Heathrow in London) whose personnel need nearby housing, and they require surface transit access. Highways connect to local road systems that often are controlled by different levels of government, often with different priorities (e.g., high-speed access to distant points versus convenient roads to local residences or services). Because most public megaprojects are large land users, such cross-sectoral concerns are omnipresent and inevitable.

The rise of technological complexity and competing technical alternatives (e.g., conventional road construction versus pressed concrete) has increased dependence on experts. So has the problem of managing such complexity. In all the advanced industrial western countries there has been an official desire to increase the numbers and improve the status of highly skilled but often narrowly trained experts. They may be engineers or scientists, but they may also be trained in economics, econometrics, or management science.

The French began this process first, through the *grandes écoles*, but other countries have not lagged far behind. The United States may not be a "scientific state"[63] but academic expertise moves in and out of government more easily and frequently than anywhere else and public debate, from the local hearing to the congressional committee, is characterized by the testimony of experts. A royal commission in Canada counseled the infusion of expertise into the upper echelons of decision-making, and the Trudeau government complied.[64] Even in Italy modest steps have been taken to expand the presence and prominence of experts in government.

To some extent this development contributes to an expansion of government generally, but pyramidal organization guarantees the replacement of prior civil servants with new experts. Senior civil servants in the decade after World War II tended to be generalists trained in the liberal arts.

Experts, however, tend to be less sensitive to general concerns. They rise in political systems precisely because they possess special knowledge on which the mandarins before them became dependent.

The decline of politics

No large-scale project could be executed without a supervisory inter-departmental or interagency committee. When these committees were staffed by generalists, there was strong inclination to compromise on contentious issues that seemed to overlap jurisdictional responsibilities. Mandarins participated with negotiating briefs. Experts, however, participate with watching briefs. Their task is to discover the objectives of other affected agencies so that they may improve their own arguments in defense of their narrow mandates. The grounds for compromise have eroded, adding to the visibility of bureaucratic rivalries of the type described by the organizational theorists. Competition may not be inherent in the organization of bureaucracy, but it does typify interagency relations in the era of the technocrat.

Not only has the technocrat risen within bureaucracies. The technocrat also has received greater visibility and responsibility from defaulting politicians who acknowledge the expertise of their appointed officials. Throughout the advanced industrial world civil servants substitute for politicians at public gatherings to explain and defend public policies. Ministers in parliamentary systems find themselves overburdened: they represent geographic constituencies, participate in party caucuses, and meet the interdepartmental requirements of cabinet government. The more technical a project appears, the more prone such elected officials are to send their appointed experts into the public arena. In the American system, cabinet officers are appointed as much for their political acumen and connections as for their expertise; although they devote full time to their departments, they are sensitive to controversy and astute enough to shift public burdens onto the technocrat whom the layman, in theory at least, is unable to challenge. Thus, the responsibility and the authority of the technocrat have grown as his expertise has been honored.

The pattern of increasing the authority of experts, then, is followed by a pattern of consequences. When sufficient authority resides in a single agency for the execution of a project despite interagency discord, the project may be realized, but it will lack the coherence appropriate to a coordinated effort by all affected interests. When the authority is diffused, the outcome will likely be paralysis, overcome only when elected officials accept final responsibility.

Explaining variations in outcome

Decisions to increase the influence of technocrats may be political and therefore peculiar to different political systems, but to varying degrees such decisions have been taken throughout the advanced industrial world and expose patterns that help to explain megaproject failures. Variations in the degree of implementation of these decisions do not explain, however, national variations in outcome, even though the longest-standing technocracies do achieve apparently higher rates of conventionally defined success.

Theories derived from sociology, social psychology, and economics focus on the individual or the organization as levels of analysis and seek to be applicable universally. They presume to explain the behavior of individuals or organized groups in particular settings according to limited dynamics. Crozier says individual Frenchmen avoid confrontation and in groups therefore raise conflicts to ever higher levels of authority. Their cultural aversions then stalemate the organization and society,[65] and presumably such individual behavior, peculiarly French, would have the same consequences in any other organizational setting. Cyert and March predict stagnation and incrementalism in the firm because individuals will behave conservatively and defensively.[66] Downs predicts that each individual will try to minimize personal risk while maximizing personal advantage, yielding competitive stalemate.[67] Allison predicts that all organizations will defend their interests against other organizations, requiring compromise.[68] Derived from theories about the condition of man, these predictions logically are applicable to all societies, cultures, and political systems, with variation attributable exclusively to exogenous intervention or, following Crozier, cultural differences.

Although the explanation of outcomes in most case studies relates to one of the factors described above (forecasting, complexity, technology, participation), case descriptions typically invite alternative interpretations. Wolpert, Mumphrey, and Seley report the crucial timing of an election in the Philadelphia Expressway case,[69] much as Feldman and Milch found in the case of Pickering Airport in Toronto.[70] Delays of more than a decade involving citizen protests in the Storm King Mountain project and the Reserve Mining Company case on Lake Superior,[71] in the Trans-Alaska Oil Pipeline project[72] and the Seabrook nuclear power plant,[73] the Dade County Airport and the Oklawaha River in Florida,[74] and countless other American cases, resulted from access to the judicial system enjoyed by individuals and small groups. In those cases where projects were abandoned, delays translated into exorbitant costs. Hence, the combination of delay and revised economic calculation was decisive, not the protest itself or the strength of protestors' arguments. Decision-makers were no more responsive to the high-profile claims of democracy in the United States than they were to less vocal community resistance to certain projects in other countries, but they were susceptible to the influence of the American judiciary that has no foreign counterpart.

There are three decisive elements dictating outcomes in megaprojects that are not specified in the theoretical literature on forecasting, bureaucratic behavior, or citizen participation, yet surface in the descriptions of every case: (1) adequacy of financing; (2) concentration of authority over all aspects of the project; (3) accessibility of the political system for contending interests.

Megaprojects are built when decisions are controlled, financing is assured, and protest or participation systematically is minimized. Economic conditions for a given project need not be favorable provided governments will guarantee financing through grants and preferred-rate loans.

Why do these elements so frequently escape the analyst's eye? The most important reason is that they are all political in character. The availability of adequate financing depends upon the capacity of government to make and sustain commitments; the concentration of authority varies according to the degrees of fragmentation in the structure of power; accessibility for contending interests depends upon the range of institutionalized democratic mechanisms. None of these elements derives specifically from a technique, such as forecasting, or from individual or group behavior. Hence, dependence on traditional bureaucratic theory establishes an apolitical level of analysis.

A second reason these elements often are described but remain analytically undetected may be found in methodology. Cases selected according to a common theme ("planning disaster," "citizen action," "environmental protection") presuppose explanations. Planning disasters may involve many actors (and Hall, for example, elaborates well the influence of citizens and politicians), but the objective—to focus on planners and bureaucrats—is obvious in the case selection itself. It does not matter from what countries or political systems the cases are drawn, although passing reference ("We need to reinterpret the theory in terms of different formal political structures"[75]) does acknowledge a fundamental weakness. "Environmental" cases are mostly American, and indeed are designed to highlight the influence citizens may have. Yet, when such cases are European and are studied for no such democratic purpose, idiosyncratic political explanations do emerge.[76] Unfortunately, these cases tend to be country-specific.

Part of the difficulty in recognizing the independence of the political variable may be detected in the reasoning that permitted Hall to include the third London airport among his disasters. He was concerned less with outcome than process, and more with the abstraction of organizational behavior than with the impact of political structure. Case selection was random both according to country and according to technology. Because he could not compare reliably motorways with an opera house, he attempted to analyze more abstractly.[77]

The political explanation

Forecasting, bureaucratic behavior, complexity, and citizen participation may all contribute to failures, but the relative impact of these variables depends upon political structure and political choice. If a pending election could determine the construction of an expressway in Philadelphia or an airport in Toronto, the political systems in those cases had to be structured so that opponents might influence an important electoral outcome. There are no case examples available that reveal such potential in France or Italy, although controversy over the Frankfurt airport affected German elections, and the elections then affected the outcome of the controversy.

Although there are no available examples of citizen activists involved in a major case successfully threatening an electoral outcome in the United Kingdom (at least beyond the local level), there are examples of British electoral change that altered case outcomes. Jerry Webman emphasizes the impact of electoral change on urban renewal in Birmingham,[78] and John Grant found political change the single most important factor in determining highway construction in Portsmouth, Southampton, and Nottingham.[79] Feldman, in an independent assessment of the third London airport, found that electoral changes produced transfers of portfolio responsibilities, resulting in different personnel with different responsibilities and criteria reviewing the same project. New decisions were consistent with new mandates, and it is not surprising that aviation specialists reach different conclusions from trade economists.[80] Thus, elections influence megaprojects in the United Kingdom, but not in the same way as in Canada, Germany, or the United States.

Although decision makers do not necessarily change their views or choices because of protest, in the United States the political system guarantees sufficiently affluent groups or individuals the clout to cause substantial delay in project implementation. In some instances, such delay permits a planner to discover alternatives, or to appreciate modification in the economic environment, and to adjust a project accordingly. In other instances, such delay can bring on a cost escalation that forces eventual project abandonment. Access to the system and the capacity to delay does not mean that "opponents prevail,"[81] but it does mean that they have greater opportunity to be heard through their own organizational efforts than in any other advanced industrial state.

Canada and Britain also value citizen participation, but they treat the concept differently and provide more limited institutional mechanisms. Citizens cannot produce court delays similar to the judicial impact in the United States. Instead, elaborate public hearings legitimize government decisions by offering a forum for citizen protest; there is no mechanism to give substance in decisions to contrary opinion. The participatory mechanisms are more restrictive than in the United States, and project delays tend therefore to be more attributable to political change and choice and to the structure of bureaucratic arrangements.

Gross systemic differences are important in determining outcomes. Peters has begun the work of exposing such differences with specific reference to bureaucracies.[82] Feldman and Milch have observed that in parliamentary systems where the prime minister does not take an express interest in the competition on any particular issue among subordinate agencies, nondecision will be the typical result.[83] Conversely, where the prime minister personally is committed, execution of the project is certain. Comparing like conflicts in different provinces in Canada, Feldman and Milch found the prime minister committed personally in Quebec and uninterested in British Columbia; the outcomes ultimately corresponded to this difference.[84] The French president was committed to Concorde and to the construction of a new Paris airport; both were built. However, a succession of British prime ministers focused on Concorde and ultimately committed themselves, thereby guaranteeing development, yet no similar commitment was made by a British prime minister for a third London international airport, and none was built. Such examples strongly suggest that in the explanation of outcomes, the bureaucratic problem is subordinate to the organizational structure of political systems.

Different political systems grant access to decisions on government megaprojects to different actors at different stages in the planning and decision process. Access to the decision process, and hence the institutional structure for the process, is the single most important factor in determining outcomes in highly similar cases that proceed simultaneously through different political structures.[85] These differences, moreover, refer more to the fragmentation or concentration of central authority, contrasting for example Italy with France, than to gross differences, as between congressional or parliamentary systems. Italian international airport development foundered in the chaos of competing agencies in Rome and in controversy between Rome and Milan; French airport construction proceeded because of the magisterial authority of a single central agency.

The French ability to get things done thus is not traceable to superior planners or planning. Rather, the French have concentrated authority over specific projects, insulated from political influence once a political decision has been taken. The key to this authority does not reside in the strength or coherence of rational planning; rather, whatever techniques or choices an agency uses or makes will be protected from competition among equal agencies in the institutional hierarchy.

Here is the explanation of an earlier paradox. The French may see more projects to completion, but not because rational planning assures this outcome. Indeed, a notable incoherence reigns over many projects because whatever limitations the agency may face cannot be overcome through cooperation when autonomy simultaneously is to be preserved. Aéroport de Paris may enjoy all the power necessary to build an airport (including land expropriation, construction, cheap loan claims, fee setting for revenue maximization), but the preservation of such autonomy necessarily implies similar autonomy for the Société Nationale des Chemins de Fer and for the Ministry for Equipment. The latter therefore could refuse to build certain roads designed to service the airport, and the former could build a rail line with a station in the new airport that discourages rail use. Provision of access to an airport is more a political than a technical issue, and the political structure that guarantees bureaucratic autonomy and promotes rational planning as a reinforcement for the preferences of specific departments or agencies must expect each governmental component to operate in like fashion. Rational planning thus assures irrational outcomes. In some institutional arrangements rational planning will produce paralysis, but not where sufficient authority is conferred upon a single agency to execute the main (but rarely all of the) project features. By conventional definition France is likely to be more successful in megaprojects than other industrial states, but not for the reasons normally given or with the outcomes commonly supposed. Rational planning thus may have common implications for advanced industrial states without producing the same outcomes to cope with common problems.

Structures also can determine behavior. Ezra Suleiman rejects Crozier's cultural explanation for French bureaucratic behavior by arguing persuasively that bureaucrats interpret rationally the structure of power and authority and behave accordingly.[86] Although behavior may conform broadly to the rules of organizational theory, the French adaptation functions according to overall institutional arrangements.

The French propensity for white elephants (Fos-Marseilles, Concorde, Charles de Gaulle Airport) is no greater than in other advanced industrial states, but the organization of French government makes their construction more likely. Precisely because the products are white elephants, the conventional notion of success is suspect. The British may permit public hearings and cross-departmental government reviews to delay projects, but most considerations and concerns eventually are aired and it is at least possible, ultimately, to make informed decisions. By contrast, the systematic French ability to exclude contrary opinions guarantees that many decisions will be based on poor information and will be limited in their potential success because they cannot bring about any of the cooperation vital for comprehensive implementation.

Democratic consequences

A dilemma of democratic participation underwrites all these considerations, as does a dilemma for the functional organization of government. Yates and Wildavsky may be correct to some extent that *ad hoc* participation is class-bound and subverts the public interest. However, confinement of decisions to a technocratic elite is no greater guarantee that the public interest will prevail, and when that elite is insulated from competing elites it is even more doubtful that the public is being served. When politicians expect technocrats to defend policies in political and public forums, it is not surprising that the public is inclined to lobby technocrats instead of politicians. When elected officials are bypassed by the public on crucial issues of public policy, a decline in democratic legitimacy appears inevitable. The task, which extends beyond the scope of the present paper, is to discover how institutions may be organized for the adequate presentation of relevant information and citizen concern without paralyzing the decision-making process. Megaprojects must be understood comprehensively, including the full range of their ramifications, and so must be undertaken by teams whose mandates extend beyond the narrowness of the immediate objectives. Yet, these teams cannot be composed exclusively of specialists who reject lay competence and consequently all lay participation, nor can politicians, however busy or technically ignorant, escape their responsibilities to make political decisions. The patterns of megaproject failure may suggest more profound democratic failure whose own cost may be as incalculable as the costs of megaprojects have been unpredictable.

NOTES

The author wishes to thank Ben Dickinson for research assistance, Jerry Milch for sharing data and insight, and Richard Zeckhauser for useful criticism.

1. The Major Projects Association was established in 1982 at the Oxford Centre for Management Studies to "enhance the ability of its members [government, project owners, consultants, contractors, bankers, and insurers] to initiate, assess, secure and accomplish major projects." The Association, which extracts membership fees in excess of $4000/annum and does not make its findings or discussions available to the public or the academy, defines a "major project" as "any collaborative capital project which requires knowledge, skills or resources that exceed what is readily or conventionally available to the key participants." The author is grateful to Professor Uwe Kitzinger, Chairman of the Association, for this information.
2. The logic for this conclusion is developed well by Peter Hall, *Great Planning Disasters* (Berkeley: University of California Press, 1980), pp. 214–222.
3. Bureaucrats need to control their environment and point to their own accomplishments; see Richard M. Cyert and James March, *A Behavioral Theory of the Firm* (Englewood Cliffs: Prentice-Hall, 1963).
4. Anthony Downs, *Inside Bureaucracy* (Boston: Little Brown, 1967).
5. *Ibid.*, and also Anthony Downs, *An Economic Theory of Democracy* (New York: Harper & Brothers, 1957); James G. March and Herbert Simon, *Organizations* (New York: Wiley, 1958); and Cyert and March, *op. cit.*
6. Glenn R. DeSousa, *Energy Policy and Forecasting* (Lexington: D. C. Heath, 1981), p. 26.
7. Richard J. Timm, "Role of the State in Energy Forecasting," in Robert Lawrence, ed., *New Dimensions to Energy Policy* (Lexington: D. C. Heath, 1979), p. 28.
8. Hans H. Landsberg *et al.*, *Energy: The Next Twenty Years* (Cambridge: Ballinger, 1979), p. 94.
9. John Grant, *The Politics of Urban Transport Planning: An Analysis of Transportation Policy Formulation in Three UK County Boroughs between 1947 and 1974* (London: Earth Resources Research Ltd., 1977), p. 74.
10. Elliot J. Feldman and Jerome Milch, *Technocracy versus Democracy: The Comparative Politics of International Airports* (Boston: Auburn House, 1981), chapter 3.
11. Hall, *op. cit.*, p. 220.
12. See especially J. K. Friend and W. N. Jessop, *Local Government and Strategic Choice* (London: Tavistock Publications, 1969); Tom Whiston, ed., *The Uses and Abuses of Forecasting* (London: Macmillan, 1979).
13. Among others, William Ascher, *Forecasting: An Appraisal for Policy-Makers and Planners* (Baltimore: Johns Hopkins Press, 1978); various essays in Whiston, *op. cit.*; Dennis Gabor, *Inventing the Future* (London: Secker and Warburg, 1963); George P. Howard and Johannes G. Augustinus, "Market Research and Forecasting for the Airport Market," and Robert W. Pulling and Herbert J. Guth, "Forecasting Traffic for Airport Development," in George P. Howard, ed., *Airport Economic Planning* (Cambridge: MIT Press, 1974).

14. Feldman and Milch, *Technocracy, op. cit.*, pp. 92–94.

15. Hall, *op. cit.*, pp. 251–253.

16. *Ibid.*, with reference particularly to Amitai Etzioni's "mixed scanning" and Fritz Zwicky's morphological analysis.

17. Hall, *op. cit.*

18. Particularly in Downs, *Inside Bureaucracy, op. cit.*

19. Hall, *op. cit.*, p. 212.

20. W. A. Niskansen, *Bureaucracy and Representative Government* (Chicago: Aldine-Atherton, 1971).

21. Downs, *Inside Bureaucracy, op. cit.*

22. Herbert Simon, *Administrative Behavior* (New York: Macmillan, 1947); March and Simon, *op. cit.*; Cyert and March, *op. cit.*; Graham Allison, *Essence of Decision: Explaining the Cuban Missile Crisis* (Boston: Little Brown, 1971).

23. Stephen S. Cohen, *Modern Capitalist Planning: The French Model* (Cambridge: Harvard University Press, 1969).

24. See the detailed case account, L. K. Caldwell, L. R. Hayes and I. M. McWhirter, eds., *Citizens and the Environment: Case Studies in Popular Action* (Bloomington: Indiana University Press, 1976); a more up-to-date account (1979) has been prepared in the Harvard Business School case study series, although the conclusion was not reached until December 1980, when a compromise did permit Consolidated Edison partial development in exchange for the donation of 500 acres for a park and an $18 million investment to reduce fish kills. *The New York Times*, December 20, 1980.

25. The proposal for a dam on the Oregon–Idaho border was hung up in the Federal Power Commission and the Department of the Interior. The case is reported in Caldwell *et al.*, *op. cit.*, and in a separate Harvard Business School study.

26. Christopher J. Duerksen, *Dow versus California: A Turning Point in the Envirobusiness Struggle* (Washington: The Conservation Foundation, 1982), chapter 10.

27. Sidney Tarrow, "Regional Policy, Ideology, and Peripheral Defense: The Case of Fossur-Mer" in Sidney Tarrow, Peter Katzenstein, and Luigi Graziano, eds., *Territorial Politics in Industrial Nations* (New York: Praeger, 1978).

28. Elliot J. Feldman, *Airport Siting as a Problem of Policy and Participation in Technological Societies: The Case of Milano–Malpensa* (Cambridge and Torino: Harvard University Center for International Affairs and Fondazione Luigi Einaudi, 1978).

29. Philip Mathias, *Forced Growth: Five Studies of Government Involvement in the Development of Canada* (Toronto: James Lorimer & Company, 1971).

30. J. Wolpert, A. Mumphrey, and J. Seley, *Metropolitan Neighborhoods: Participation and Conflict over Change* (Washington: Association of American Geographers Resource Paper #16, 1972), p. 30. The authors objected to such a large development ($400 million on 50 acres of downtown land) because it did not include plans for low-income housing.

31. See G. Bruce Knecht, "Renaissance Center: Ford's Costly and Failing Bid to Revive Detroit," *The New York Times*, July 3, 1983. The Center may even be harmful by driving down rents.

32. See Feldman and Milch, *Technocracy, op. cit.*, chapter 9 for a discussion of this trade-off.

33. Kenneth Arrow, *Social Choice and Individual Values* (New York: John Wiley, 1951); the theorem sets out irreconcilable conditions for the achievement of social welfare; see also Downs' discussion in *An Economic Theory, op. cit.*, pp. 60–63.

34. Andrew Shonfield, *Modern Capitalism: The Changing Balance of Public and Private Power* (New York: Oxford University Press, 1965).

35. Arnold J. Heidenheimer, Hugh Heclo, and Carolyn Teich Adams, *Comparative Public Policy: The Politics of Social Choice in Europe and America* (New York: St. Martin's Press, 1975).

36. Jack Hayward and Michael Watson, eds., *Planning, Politics and Public Policy: The British, French and Italian Experience* (Cambridge: Cambridge University Press, 1975).

37. Max Weber, "Bureaucracy" in H. H. Gerth and C. Wright Mills, *From Max Weber* (New York: Oxford University Press, 1946).

38. For the saga of the American SST, see Mel Horwitch, *Clipped Wings: The American SST Conflict* (Cambridge: MIT Press, 1982); on Concorde, see Hall's summary of secondary literature, *Great Planning Disasters, op. cit.*, chapter 4, and Elliot J. Feldman, *Concorde and Dissent: Explaining High Technology Project Failures in Great Britain and France* (New York: Cambridge University Press, 1985).

39. Hall, *op. cit.*, pp. 170–184.

40. Otto Keck, *Policymaking in a Nuclear Program: The Case of the West German Fast Breeder Reactor* (Lexington: Lexington Books, 1981); also, the Washington Public Power Supply System's financial catastrophe reported on *60 Minutes*, Volume XVI, Number 8, CBS Television Network, Sunday, November 6, 1983, "WHOOPS," produced by Ira Rosen.

41. For definitions and discussion see Langdon Winner, *Autonomous Technology: Technics-Out-of-Control as a Theme in Political Thought* (Cambridge: MIT Press, 1977).

42. Richard Nelson, *The Moon and the Ghetto* (New York: W. W. Norton, 1977).

43. Feldman, *Concorde, op. cit.*

44. Anthony Downs, *An Economic Theory, op. cit.*, described the conditions under which minorities are able to govern, and the circumstances under which, no matter how impassioned their view, they are unable to achieve their political objectives.

45. Douglas Yates, *The Ungovernable City: The Politics of Urban Problems and Policy Making* (Cambridge: MIT Press, 1977).

46. Aaron Wildavsky, *The Revolt Against the Masses and Other Essays on Politics and Public Policy* (New York: Basic Books, 1971).

47. David McKie, *A Sadly Mismanaged Affair: A Political History of the Third London Airport* (London: Croom Helm, 1973); Peter Bromhead, *The Great White Elephant of Maplin Sands* (London: Paul Elek, 1973); David Perman, *Cublington: A Blueprint for Resistance* (London: The Bodley Head, 1973); Olive Cook, *The Stansted Affair: A Case for the People* (London: Pan Books Ltd., 1967).

48. Richard Wiggs, *Concorde: The Case Against Supersonic Transport* (London: Ballantine Books, 1971); William A. Shurcliff, *SST and Sonic Boom Handbook* (New York: Ballantine Books, 1968); Horwitch, *op. cit.*, also gives credit to protestors, but more cautiously.

49. Wolpert, Mumphrey, and Seley, *op. cit.*

50. Caldwell, Hayes, and McWhirter, *op. cit.*

51. Sandra Budden and Joseph Ernst, *The Movable Airport* (Toronto: Hakkert, 1973); Hector Massey and Charles Godfrey, *People or Planes* (Toronto: Copp Clark, 1972); Sandford Borins, "The Economics of Airport Planning: The Case of Toronto," unpublished Ph.D. dissertation, Harvard University, 1976.

52. Caldwell, Hayes, and McWhirter, *op. cit.*

53. Citizen's Advisory Committee on Environmental Action, *Citizens Make the Difference* (Washington: Citizen's Advisory Committee on Environmental Quality, 1973).

54. Harvard Business School Case Study, *Field Burning in Willamette Valley, Oregon.*

55. Citizen's Advisory Committee, *op. cit.*

56. Feldman, *Concorde, op. cit.*

57. Wolpert, Mumphrey, and Seley, *op. cit.*, p. 27.

58. Caldwell, Hayes, and McWhirter, *op. cit.*

59. *Ibid.*

60. *The New York Times*, February 18, 1979.

61. Theodore J. Lowi, *The End of Liberalism: Ideology, Policy, and the Crisis of Public Authority* (New York: W. W. Norton, 1968); Grant McConnell, *Private Power and American Democracy* (New York: Alfred Knopf, 1966).

62. Elliot J. Feldman, "Comparative Public Policy: Field or Method?" in *Comparative Politics* (January 1978).

63. Robert Gilpin, *France in the Age of the Scientific State* (Princeton: Princeton University Press, 1968).

64. See Elliot J. Feldman and Jerome Milch, *The Politics of Canadian Airport Development: Lessons for Federalism* (Durham: Duke University Press, 1983), pp. 34–41; Richard French, *How Ottawa Decides: Planning and Industrial Policy-Making, 1968–1980* (Toronto: Lorimer, 1980); Colin Campbell and George J. Szablowski, *The Super-Bureaucrats: Structure and Behavior in Central Agencies* (Toronto: Macmillan, 1978).

65. Michel Crozier, *The Bureaucratic Phenomenon* (Chicago: University of Chicago Press, 1964); Michel Crozier, *The Stalled Society* (New York: Viking, 1973).

66. Cyert and March, *op. cit.*

67. Downs, *Inside Bureaucracy, op. cit.*

68. Allison, *op. cit.*

69. Wolpert, Mumphrey, and Seley, *op. cit.*

70. Feldman and Milch, *The Politics of Canadian Airport Development, op. cit.*

71. Caldwell, Hayes, and McWhirter, *op. cit.*

72. Harvard Business School Case Study, *The Trans-Alaska Oil Pipeline Project.*

73. Harvard Business School Case Study, *Public Service Company of New Hampshire.*

74. Caldwell, Hayes, and McWhirter, *op. cit.*

75. Hall, *op. cit.* p. 198.

76. Keck, *op. cit.*; Dorothy Nelkin and Michael Pollack, "The Politics of Participation and the Nuclear Debate in Sweden, The Netherlands and Austria," 25 *Public Policy* (Summer 1977), pp. 335–357.

77. This criticism is not meant to single out Hall's work, for it is an exceptionally careful attempt to generalize from complex case materials. It is in this respect perhaps the best of recent literature seeking to explain patterns of failure. But its own failure to appreciate fully the influence of political structure in each case follows inevitably from dependence on secondary accounts (hence the sometimes unwarranted significance given citizen groups), the random country selection, and the disaster theme without technological case controls.

78. Jerry Webman, *Reviving the Industrial City: The Politics of Urban Renewal in Lyon and Birmingham* (New Brunswick: Rutgers University Press, 1982).

79. Grant, *op. cit.*

80. Feldman, *Concorde, op. cit.*

81. Wolpert, Mumphrey, and Seley, *op. cit.*, p. 29.

82. B. Guy Peters, *The Politics of Bureaucracy: A Comparative Analysis* (New York: Longman, 1978).

83. Feldman and Milch, *Technocracy, op. cit.*

84. Feldman and Milch, *The Politics of Canadian Airport Development, op. cit.*

85. Feldman and Milch, *Technocracy, op. cit.*

86. Ezra Suleiman, *Power, Politics and Bureaucracy in France* (Princeton: Princeton University Press, 1974).

IV

Regional politics: Latin America and the Middle East

JORGE I. DOMÍNGUEZ
The foreign policies of Latin American states in the 1980s: retreat or refocus?

HERBERT KELMAN
Overcoming the psychological barrier: an analysis of the Egyptian-Israeli peace process

8

The foreign policies of Latin American states in the 1980s: retreat or refocus?

Jorge I. Domínguez

Professor of Government, Harvard University

The foreign policies of the major Latin American states[1] changed from the late 1960s to the early 1980s. Some changes are reflected in several major reports. In August 1969, Governor Nelson Rockefeller transmitted his report on the Americas to the President of the United States; the first chapter noted that "The United States has allowed the special relationship it has historically maintained with the other nations of the Western Hemisphere to deteriorate badly." That report focused on a self-contained hemisphere, where the foreign policies of Latin American states did not look too far beyond the oceans.[2]

Five years later, the subtitle of one of the decade's major books on the same topic was: *Latin America Takes Charge of Its Future*. The sights of the major Latin American states had clearly moved beyond the hemisphere.[3] And the report issued by a commission led by Sol Linowitz emphasized that Latin American countries were taking "a more active role in global politics," that they would exercise leadership increasingly in international arenas, and that the old assumption of mutuality of interests in a special relationship between the United States and Latin America was no longer valid. Latin American countries still mattered to the United States not because of their Latin American "specialness" but because of their new, general importance in world affairs.[4]

In 1983, yet another group co-chaired by Sol Linowitz asserted in a report that "The Western Hemisphere today faces challenges more serious than any since World War II, or perhaps even the Great Depression."[5] And yet, the 1983 report featured some changes. It was the first to be co-chaired by a Latin American, Galo Plaza, former President of Ecuador and former Secretary General of the Organization of American States (OAS). It was also the first to have been designed as an "inter-American dialogue," where Latin America was not just an object of conversation among Yankees; citizens of Latin American countries had become the equals of their U.S. interlocutors. Change had, indeed, occurred.

What was this change in Latin American foreign policies? Did a noble experiment in international activism and diversification collapse, leading to a retreat to a more parochial era? Or did a permanent shift occur which is partly obscured by the financial crisis of the early 1980s but which is likely to endure? This essay cannot explain all that happened in the foreign policies of Latin American states. It will focus, instead, on a narrower question: how to explain the origins and later demise of Latin America's globalist activism, and how to understand the main content of those foreign policies. The success or efficacy of those policies still needs to be studied.

Latin American foreign policies had been rather passive and parochial before 1970. To be sure, Perón's Argentina attempted to project a somewhat more active foreign policy beyond southern South America in the late 1940s and early 1950s; Brazil featured its so-called "independent" foreign policy from 1960 to 1964. Neither case was characterized by a sustained effort; neither endured. Only revolutionary Cuba had developed a very active foreign policy to defend itself against the United States since the early 1960s.

Around 1970, most major Latin American states changed their foreign policies. They believed that they had to become actively involved in global affairs, for the first time ever, to protect their interests. Latin America's new activism since the early 1970s had a very high economic policy content. Thus explanations must address the emergence of activist foreign economic policies. Such activism embodied three features: a change in the country's own foreign economic policy, an effort to get other countries to change their economic policies to support or to accommodate these changes, and an effort to change the international economic order accordingly.

By the late 1970s, however, military and territorial foreign policy issues also became important. Thus a full explanation needs to account as well for the change in the content of policy activism. Latin American countries, of course, had had many such conflicts in the 19th century, but these had, in general, been resolved or contained. The extant territorial disputes had lain dormant. The reactivation of these old concerns by the late 1970s, and the persistence of a still generally activist, though more focused, foreign economic policy, was an unprecedented combination in the history of the Americas.

Three general answers will be given. They are not mutually exclusive; each addresses a part of the problem. The first answer suggests an ideological change. Top political leaders apply their ideological predispositions to the making of internal and international policies especially in moments of transition. When leaders change, ideologies and policies may change. There is also a correspondence between the rise of state intervention in the internal economy in the early 1970s and the increase in foreign policy statist activism designed to reorder the international economy. By the late 1970s and early 1980s, the shift toward market policies in the home economy also corresponded with a deemphasis of foreign policy statist activism.

A second answer suggests a rational-actor behavior. States respond to the constraints and opportunities of short-run variations in the international system. They emphasize the structure and distribution of power and resources, and they calculate their possibilities accordingly.

A third answer is that elites learn about the capacities of the states they lead. The growth of state capacity and of elite learning about it explain the gradual refocusing of the foreign policies of the major Latin American states. Latin American foreign policies had not collapsed in the early 1980s; instead, they had refocused on issues of more clearly identifiable interest to their countries than their previous foreign policy agendas had emphasized.

The context of foreign policy change in the early 1970s

An era had seemed to have ended in the early 1970s. The Bretton Woods international monetary system broke down, the final blow delivered by President Richard Nixon in August 1971 through his unilateral devaluation of the dollar, suspending its gold convertibility and seeking to coerce other governments to make concessions to the United States by imposing a tariff surcharge on their exports to the United States until they yielded. About two years later, the world price of oil skyrocketed in the aftermath of the fourth Arab–Israeli war. The non-oil-exporting world, including the United States, appeared helpless. These changes had profound consequences for Latin American countries. Oil-exporting countries, such as Venezuela and Ecuador, experienced unprecedented economic booms. Most other Latin American countries, especially the largest oil importer, Brazil, were hurt deeply by the increase in the prices of imports and, to a lesser extent, by the sharp industrial world recession of 1974–1975.[6] By mid-decade, the fall of Saigon and Vietnam's reunification under Hanoi's control were seen as defeats for the United States. In economics and in military affairs, the global role of the United States was thought to have declined sharply. The United States–Soviet détente, evolving through the 1960s but crystallizing during the Nixon and Ford presidencies, appeared to open also a new political space for other governments to pursue their more independent foreign policies.[7]

These international system changes had consequences for the internal policies of Latin American governments. They were jolted by President Nixon's August 1971 decision; their appeals to an historic "special relationship" to protect them from the tariff surcharge were of no avail. As a result, President Luis Echeverría of Mexico arrived at the view, for this and other reasons, that his country needed to fashion a new foreign policy strategy,[8] and President Carlos Andrés Pérez of Venezuela felt that the time had come to invest in a new, more activist foreign policy thanks to the new oil revenues.

Some changes had been occurring in the major Latin American countries that preceded, and were somewhat independent of, these international changes. A military coup brought the armed forces to power in Peru in 1968 under the leadership of General Juan Velasco Alvarado. Over a few years, that government expropriated the International Petroleum Company (a subsidiary of Standard Oil of New Jersey) as well as subsidiaries of International Telephone and Telegraph, Cerro de Pasco Copper Corporation, W. R. Grace's sugar plantations, and many other foreign and nationally owned firms.[9] In 1970, Salvador Allende was elected President of Chile, heading a coalition of the Socialist, Communist, and other smaller parties of the left, the first popular-front government elected to power in Latin America since the late 1940s. In Argentina, the military regime that had come to power in 1966 had been weakening since 1969, primarily for internal reasons. It eventually held elections which the Peronista party won, and in 1973 after some complex maneuvering, Juan Domingo Perón, the man the armed forces had overthrown in 1955, returned to the Presidency.

Changes in revolutionary Cuba allowed its partial reintegration in Latin American international relations. Cuba's support for revolutionary movements in Latin America, most evident in the 1960s, came to a virtual end in the early 1970s (even though Cuba continued to support revolutionary movements in Africa and Asia). Cuba was also hurt by the rise in petroleum prices—though the blow was softened temporarily by the simultaneous rise of sugar prices. Learning from the failure of its unorthodox experiments of the 1960s, Cuba adopted more conventional policies at home and toward Latin American countries, with a renewed emphasis on foreign economic diplomacy.[10]

One consequence of these international and internal changes was the development of unusually active foreign policies of worldwide scope by several major Latin American states early in the 1970s. Chile, Cuba, Mexico, Peru, Venezuela, and, to some degree, Argentina changed their international relations during the first half of the 1970s to project a new global international activism, especially over economic issues. Brazil's foreign policy changed less abruptly, but it also evolved toward more activism. Of the major Latin American states, only Colombia and, to a lesser degree, Brazil retained in the early 1970s the more traditional, cautious, relatively passive foreign policies that had been the region's norm.

By the early 1980s, foreign policies had changed again. Of those countries which had become globally activist in the early 1970s, only Cuba had remained on the same course so that it was even more globally active a decade later. In contrast, Argentina, Chile, Mexico, Peru, and Venezuela had reduced their global engagement while Brazil continued to become much more internationally active and Colombia perked up although only after President Belisario Betancur's election in 1982. Can both sets of changes be explained simultaneously?

The ideological sources of foreign policy change

There may be a *correspondence* between the internal and the international behavior of these governments. Relative, comparative judgments are summarized in Table 1. States that become more assertive in their internal

Table 1. Ideological preferences and foreign economic policy trends

Early 1970s	
Market preferences, passive overseas	*Statist preferences, activist overseas*
Brazil[a]	Argentina[a]
Colombia	Cuba
	Chile
	Mexico
	Peru
	Venezuela

Early 1980s			
Market preferences, passive overseas	*Less statist,[b] less activist overseas*	*More statist,[b] more activist overseas*	*Statist preferences, activist overseas*
Argentina[c]	Peru	Brazil	Cuba
Chile	Mexico[d]		
Colombia	Venezuela		

[a] Marginal placement.
[b] Compared to 1970.
[c] Except for 1982 war. See text.
[d] Except for 1982 state takeover of the banks.

economic policies are also more likely to seek more influence over international economic issues. Government decision makers who believe that they should and can intervene effectively in markets at home are more likely to believe that it is possible and necessary to shape the international economic environment in which their countries find themselves. State intervention in the home economy has often also created state enterprises that act internationally, linking internal and international policy explicitly.

Several key policy makers in Latin American countries in the early 1970s believed that markets had failed to deliver on the promise of prosperity for all. Markets had failed at home to provide quick enough and fair enough gains for all; this insufficiency required increased state intervention in the economy. And markets had failed abroad, as the collapse of the Bretton Woods monetary system, the energy crisis, and the appearance of inflation and recession demonstrated. Added to the persistent view that the old economic order had benefited the industrialized countries more than the developing ones, the stage was set for major changes in state international activity. A corollary of this argument is that states that experienced fewer sharp internal economic policy changes were less likely to change their foreign policy behavior.

Equally important is the correspondence between the decline of statism in internal economic policy and a decline in foreign economic policy activism. As decision makers become less economically assertive at home, they also become less assertive in foreign economic policy. These decision makers have less confidence in the efficacy of the state's intervention in markets, internal or international. They often seek to limit the growth of state enterprises or to sell off such concerns to private entrepreneurs. The belief in the efficacy and desirability of market allocation means that foreign direct investment and foreign borrowing are not to be obstructed and may even be stimulated. That belief leads governments to shy away from United Nations-related institutions that favor regulation of international markets by treaty. Beliefs in markets may, other things being equal, facilitate relations with the United States whereas statist preferences may increase conflicts with the United States.

This argument emphasizes the cognitive map or the ideology of decision makers.[11] It underlines the importance of beliefs about the role of the state and markets and about the role of political and governmental leaders. The replacement of leaders proclaiming one set of ideologies by leaders with different ideologies explains much policy change. The argument also suggests that this ideology (or worldview or mindset) is not compartmentalized. The ideology is a package of principles, perspectives, and prescriptions that apply to internal and international affairs across a wide array of issues. The principles, or core values, shape the perspectives that help leaders make sense of their world, and from these flow policy prescriptions that remain somewhat independent of empirical data. The argument is strongly voluntaristic, with decision makers acting upon these beliefs. This argument also emphasizes the primacy of economic considerations as decision makers shift in their approach between laissez-faire and statist policies in economic issue areas. The hypothesis does not shed much light, however, on politico-military activism. The connection between views of the market and politico-military activism is probably nonexistent.

This argument has some preliminary appeal. For example, Table 2 presents central government expenditures in seven countries as a percentage of gross domestic product (GDP). The evidence is remarkably consistent with the argument just sketched. From 1970 to 1975, the impact of the central government on the economy grew considerably by increased government spending in all but Brazil and Colombia. In Cuba, of course, the impact of the government on the economy was already very large. The states that intervened more in the home economy by increases in government expenditures also became the most assertive in their foreign policies.

The data in Table 2 are also consistent with the flip side of the argument

Table 2. Total expenditures by central governments as percentage
of gross domestic product (GDP)

	1970	1975	1980	1982	Trend shifts 1970–75	1975–80	1980–82
Argentina	9.2	13.1	15.4	16.0	+ 3.9	+ 2.3	+ 0.6
Brazil	9.5	9.0	9.2	8.7	− 0.5	+ 0.2	− 0.5
Chile	20.6	24.5	21.0	24.1	+ 3.9	− 3.5	+ 3.1
Colombia	10.2	9.5	10.3	11.2	− 0.7	+ 0.8	+ 0.9
Mexico	10.8	17.3	18.8	26.5	+ 6.5	+ 1.5	+ 7.7
Peru	15.8	21.3	23.4	19.9	+ 5.5	+ 2.1	− 3.5
Venezuela	19.3	33.8	24.7	27.6	+ 14.5	− 9.1	+ 2.9

Source: Inter-American Development Bank, *Economic and Social Progress in Latin America*,
1983 (Washington, D.C.), p. 356.

for the later 1970s, though the pattern is less clear. There was retrenchment
in the impact of the central government on the economy in Chile and
Venezuela, and there was a deceleration in the growth of state intervention
in Argentina, Mexico, and Peru. There was a modest growth of state activism in Brazil and Colombia. In the foreign policy area, this corresponds
to less globally activist foreign policies, especially in Argentina, Chile, and
Venezuela. From 1980 to 1982, deceleration in the growth of statism continued in Argentina and Peru; and deceleration resumed in Brazil. The
Colombian pattern remained unchanged. However, the increases in the
growth rate of statism in Chile and Venezuela are inconsistent with the
correspondence hypothesis. The increase of the state's economic impact in
Mexico coincided with Mexico's heightened assertiveness in foreign policy
from 1979 to 1982. We now proceed to illustrate this hypothesis.

Peru

The military government that came to power in Peru in 1968 was the
first to believe explicitly in a correspondence between internal and international policies and to opt for statism in both.[12] The first Manifesto of the
Revolutionary Government of the Armed Forces to the people of Peru
(October 2, 1968), in its second paragraph, linked the "powerful national
and international economic forces" that acted against Peru's national interest.
The first four matters of immediate concern listed in that government's
"plan," published on the following day, were: petroleum, planning, foreign
policy, and agrarian reform.

The plan noted that foreigners virtually controlled the entire petroleum
industry; especially unacceptable was the role of the International Petroleum
Company. The goal was that all stages of petroleum activity would be the
exclusive prerogative of the state. "Permanent and comprehensive" planning
would have to be emphasized. Foreign policy had been "timid and depen-

dent, especially on the u.s.a." International relations had been limited to capitalist countries, and there was little awareness of Peru's appropriate role among Third World countries. Foreign economic relations served mostly foreign interests. There was no policy toward border territories. In contrast, the new government proposed a "nationalist and independent foreign policy." Finally, one of the "bad" conditions in the agrarian sector was foreign ownership; a land reform would end that and other ills.[13]

The Peruvian government's foreign policy in the early 1970s, as Peruvian Ambassador Ricardo Luna has written, emphasized

> . . .the idea of an interdependence between economic development and external security . . . without real economic progress and effective social integration, the external security of the country could not be ensured. Similarly, without enhancing the international context, without applying a dynamic foreign policy that would preserve Peru's international security, the process of economic development within the nation would be compromised.

The link between the internal and the international policies was explicit; the means were comparable. At home, the Peruvian government increased its control over the economy, expropriating much of the private sector. It created many large powerful state enterprises, involving the state in economic life well beyond the significance of the central budget alone. The government increased regulatory activity over the residual private business sector. In foreign policy, Peru defended its right to expropriate private property. It also became very active in the United Nations family of organizations and a major supporter of proposals for a New International Economic Order. Peru supported producers' cartels in copper and sugar, and generally showed a strong preference for statist rather than market instruments. It was ideologically consistent within and beyond its borders.[14]

In 1975, President Luis Velasco Alvarado was overthrown in a bloodless coup by General Francisco Morales Bermúdez, who launched what he called the "Second Phase" of the Peruvian revolution. Within months, the new President was defending his government against charges that it had swung to the right, that it was too gradualist and reformist, not revolutionary, and too supportive of guarantees for private investment.[15] Peru was hard hit by an economic crisis in the late 1970s, partly of its doing but also resulting from factors beyond its control. As Peru sought to cope with near-default on its international debt obligations, it became necessary to adopt more market-oriented policies at home and to strengthen again the links with the United States.[16] With Fernando Belaúnde Terry's election in 1980, an even more market-oriented policy was adopted as Peru reduced its activist involvement in global affairs. In the early 1980s, statism was preferred neither for the world nor for itself.[17]

Chile

Chile exemplifies an even more dramatic shift stemming from the military coup of September 1973 that overthrew President Salvador Allende and brought to power a military junta led by General Augusto Pinochet. Chilean internal policies had been based on a consensus on the appropriately high role of the state in the economy; for example, central government expenditures as a percentage of GDP were already the highest of the large Latin American countries in 1970 before Allende's rise to the presidency (Table 2). Chilean foreign policy had also been based on a consensus on the need for governmental intervention in international markets.[18] A consensus had also developed in the mining sector that culminated with the state's takeover of the large foreign-owned copper firms in 1971.[19]

The Christian Democratic government of President Eduardo Frei (1964–1970) had increased the Chilean government's regulation and ownership share of the foreign-owned copper mines. It promoted treaties on regional economic integration; it was a founder of the Andean Pact. The Frei government was also a founder of the Intergovernmental Committee of the Copper Exporting Countries (CIPEC) designed to coordinate the policies of such countries. The Frei government hosted the Latin American Consensus at Viña del Mar in 1969; its conclusions on collective Latin American economic needs and demands were presented by Chilean Foreign Minister Gabriel Valdés to President Richard Nixon on behalf of the hemisphere's governments.

The Allende government's heightened activism built upon this record. Chile vigorously pursued a Third World foreign policy style, symbolized by its hosting of the Third United Nations Conference on Trade and Development (UNCTAD). Partly to protect itself from growing U.S. hostility, Chile sought to diversify its international economic relations with Communist countries, the smaller European countries, especially in Scandinavia, and Third World countries. Allende's views about the international system were explicit:

> . . . the toil and the resources of the poorer nations subsidize the prosperity of the affluent peoples . . . Over the last twenty years, the ebb and flow of foreign capital into and out of the Third World has meant a net loss for us of many hundreds of millions of dollars . . . this economic, financial and trade order, so prejudicial to the Third World precisely because it is so advantageous to the affluent countries, is defended by most of these with bulldog tenacity . . .

Allende's Chile joined the Nonaligned Movement and it intensified its commitment to CIPEC. Allende implemented the takeover of the larger foreign-owned copper mines; in addition, he deducted past "excess profits," making it virtually impossible to compensate the affected firms.[20]

The Pinochet government's foreign policy broke radically with Chile's past. Chile withdrew from the Andean Pact because it considered the Pact's policies too statist; especially unacceptable were its strong regulations over direct private foreign investment. Foreign economic policy moved away sharply from Third World orientations to emphasize free trade and foreign investment. The shift from statism toward a market-oriented economy has endured although the Chilean economic strategy entered a profound crisis in the early 1980s,[21] along with the internal policy correction evident in Table 2.

As Chile's Minister of Economy and Finance summarized the decade:

> Starting in 1973 . . . private property once more became the base of the economic system, although a few state-owned enterprises were retained where there was social justification for doing so. In addition, freedom of prices and interest rates was restored; the economy opened to international trade and to the flow of external capital and credit; the role of the state was circumscribed as far as was possible or advisable . . .

The Pinochet government sought to destatize at home and to rely on market forces abroad. With some modest adjustments that provided more government protection for the home economy, the basic policy continued even in the midst of severe economic crises. As the Economy and Finance Minister asserted in 1982, "at this time we cannot afford to listen to the eternal illusion mongers who believe only in the magic of state intervention." The Minister was realistic to note that "the behavior of external factors . . . will always be determinant of our rate of recovery." But as befits a market-conforming foreign policy, he also said that the behavior of such external factors "is not in our power to control." He should have added that it was his government's policy not even to try.[22]

Chilean foreign economic policy remained consistent with the Pinochet government's preference for market forces; a certain lack of correspondence appeared in the early 1980s, however, because the slightly greater state intervention in internal markets was not matched by a corresponding foreign policy change.

Venezuela

Venezuela had been moving toward greater government control of the foreign-owned petroleum industry since the establishment of its democratic political system in 1958, culminating in the state's takeover of the oil industry on January 1, 1976. The quadrupling of oil prices in 1973–74 gave Venezuela the funds to pay for what it had expropriated. The roots of this action are found in Venezuelan domestic politics. Venezuelanization had broad political support.[23] The weight of the state was not limited to the central government's direct expenditures; many state enterprises (oil, steel, aluminum, and other sectors) commanded vast resources. This regulative and entrepreneurial state substituted for internal market forces in major ways.

Venezuelan international involvement also grew. A founder of the Organization of Petroleum Exporting Countries (OPEC), Venezuela became more active internationally under President Carlos Andrés Pérez (1974–79). His administration established state control over oil and other natural-resource industries; it launched huge development projects that the private sector was judged incapable of undertaking; it became a major spokesman for a new international economic order. The oil industry, it argued, should be in state hands at home and in OPEC hands internationally. Other markets, at home and abroad, should also be regulated by state action. Venezuela's leadership was recognized by its election as co-chairman of the Paris Conference on International Economic Cooperation (CIEC), where global negotiations between the industrialized capitalist "north" and the underdeveloped "south" were to occur, and where the "south's" demands were strongly statist. Venezuela was a co-founder with Mexico of the Latin American Economic System (SELA), which included Cuba but excluded the United States; SELA was to promote the integration and coordination of development projects. Venezuela launched a foreign aid program to Central American and Caribbean countries to offset in part the sharp increases in oil prices. Relative to Venezuela's resources, this aid program represented a greater effort than that made by the majority of industrialized countries.[24]

The Christian Democratic (COPEI) administration of President Luis Herrera Campins (1979–84) curtailed many of the projects initiated by President Pérez. It cooled down the economy to such an extent that Venezuela had no real economic growth after 1979, well before the debt crisis hit.[25] By the early 1980s, Venezuelan foreign policy had not abandoned its concern with the international economic order, but the extent of its involvement had been scaled back. Instead, Venezuela developed a diplomacy to "project" its influence primarily among its smaller Caribbean and Central American neighbors. The international debt crisis struck Venezuela in 1983.

Whereas ideas changed in the cases of Chile and Peru—away from reliance on the market in the early 1970s and toward more reliance on it a decade later—Venezuela experienced the first shift, but less so the second. Table 2 shows a substantial drop in Venezuelan central government expenditures as a percentage of GDP by 1980 (though remaining Latin America's highest ratio), but there was a modest rise by 1982. The impact of state enterprises in Venezuela has remained considerable. Venezuela did not experience the substantial sell-off of state enterprises which occurred in Chile or the more moderate reprivatization which took place in Peru. The consolidated public sector in Venezuela increased dramatically, consistent with this argument, from about 14% of GDP in 1973 to about 40.5% in 1979, and continued to rise (though more slowly) to about 42.3% in 1981.[26] Thus the Venezuelan case may be described only as merely a modification of the rate of growth of statism, which remained substantial in the early 1980s. This occurred in part from the contradictory government efforts to cool off an overheated economy while not permitting a drop in GDP. Venezuela responded to the debt crisis by promising its creditors that it would curtail the growth of the public sector, but it was reluctant to cut its net size.[27] Faith in the efficacy of the state had crumbled, but faith in the market had not reappeared outside the business community. Ideological factors matter in Venezuela's post-1979 changes but less decisively than in Chile or Peru.

Colombia

Colombian foreign policy was the least activist of the large countries, though not the least effective. General works about Colombia often omit discussions of its foreign policy. Bibliographies on the international relations of Latin American states record little about it; a bibliography of articles dealing with the international relations of Latin America and the Caribbean (1975–1982) has fewer items on Colombia than on any other country under study.[28] Miguel Urrutia has argued:

> Colombian policymakers dedicate little time and effort to international relations. For example, in the period from 1974 to 1977, international relations, other than those pertaining to Andean Group negotiations, were never discussed by the Council of Ministers or the Council on Economic and Social Policy (CONPES) (the two executive councils chaired by the President and which meet regularly).[29]

These were the peak years of international discussion of a New International Economic Order and global North/South negotiations.

And yet, Colombian foreign policy has served its national interests. From the mid-1960s to the mid-1970s, Colombian exports as a percentage of GDP grew steadily. They represented about 7% of GDP in 1966 and 10.9% in 1975 on the eve of a coffee price export boom. Apart from Venezuela's earlier oil-led boom, none of the other countries had increased the role of exports in their economies to such a degree; only Brazil's share of exports within its GDP had increased at all during that decade (from 6% to 6.5%). Exports as a share of GDP fell in Argentina, Chile, Mexico, and Peru from 1966 to 1975.[30] Colombia increased fourfold its manufactured exports to the United States in the early 1970s.[31]

Colombian exports to Andean Pact countries also grew. Among the Pact countries, the Colombian government was the least supportive of state regulations controlling the economy, including foreign investment. Colombia used banking regulation loopholes inserted at its request in Decision 24 that governed foreign investment in all Pact countries; Colombian regulations in 1974 removed most restrictions on foreign banks that might have been imposed if the main intent of Decision 24 had been carried out. Colombian public and private elites favored direct foreign investment in the early 1970s—more so than those in Venezuela or Mexico did, for example.[32]

The Pact's governing Junta interpreted its charter, the *Acuerdo de Cartagena*, to postulate that "to the state there corresponds a decisive role in the general conduct of the process of development, a role more important than that traditionally recognized. This role is to be expressed through planning and direct investment in some strategic sectors." Urrutia has argued convincingly that there was only mild and declining support in Colombia for this position in the 1960s and 1970s. Colombia supported the Pact's trade liberalization decisions in the 1970s but it opposed increased protection through changes in the common tariff and it opposed the ambitious industrial programs coordinated for the entire Andean region.[33] It was skeptical about statist policies for the internal or for the international markets, leaving room for market forces.

Colombia's was not a laissez-faire economy, but the role of state intervention in the economy was less marked than in the other countries. As Berry has summarized Colombia's economic experience from the late 1950s to the mid-1970s, the goal was economic growth with enough reform as needed only to reduce violence and maintain social peace. Agrarian reform policies—drastic in Peru or Chile in the early 1970s and significant in earlier years in Venezuela and Mexico—had modest goals and results in Colombia. Colombia had pursued, as had all Latin American countries, an import substitution industrialization strategy that required considerable economic intervention on the part of government. Nevertheless, Colombia shifted earlier than other countries to an export promotion strategy that curtailed some of the problems of the earlier strategy. While the state's capacity was strengthened under President Carlos Lleras Restrepo (1966–70), other policies simply held state power constant as it regulated the economy. Berry has noted that Colombian governments were "conducive to legitimization of technical as opposed to 'political' policies."[34] There was a preference for market-conforming rather than statist government policies. Colombia's economic growth proceeded at a steady rate from 1960 to 1980 exceeded only by that of Mexico and Brazil. The Colombian growth rate of real GDP held constant at 5–6% per year, avoiding the busts that characterized the economic affairs of Argentina, Chile, Cuba, Mexico, Peru, and Venezuela.[35]

Colombia's unheroic foreign policy did not receive universal praise, however much it may have contributed to economic development. Conservative party intellectuals plausibly criticized the political passivity of Liberal party administrations from 1974 to 1982 (the Conservative party government of Belisario Bentancur attained office in 1982). Conservatives disapproved of Colombia's nonparticipation in discussions about aid and other policies toward the Caribbean and Central America; of the "surrender" of Colombian canal rights to Panama when the treaties were renegotiated with the United States; of the politicization of the Andean Pact for non-economic purposes; of Colombia's "subservience" to the United States in the United Nations and other fora, even siding with the United States against Argentina at the time of the Falklands/Malvinas war; and of the mishandling of border disputes with Venezuela.[36]

Colombia, in short, had been comparatively nonstatist in its international and in its internal policies. Its elites had believed that prosperity was possible at home and abroad through market-conforming policies that required some state actions but fewer than were taken in other Latin American countries. Its government had been criticized for its political passivity but not recognized for its successes in foreign economic policy.

Peru, Chile, Venezuela, and Colombia exemplify most clearly the correspondence between internal and international trends, especially in the early 1970s. In Colombia, this correspondence held steady for years, with greater activism beginning only after 1982. In Peru, Chile, and Venezuela, the coming to power of new leaders (1968–74) made way for new ideologies. The greatest state economic intervention at home coincided with the greatest international activism seeking to reshape international markets. As internal state economic intervention stopped increasing or declined, thanks in most cases to change in leadership, international activism also decreased. The correspondence in the latter shift was most marked (though increasingly imperfect) for Chile, most gradual for Peru, and most ambiguous for Venezuela. For the next four countries, the correspondence hypothesis remains pertinent but its application is even more difficult.

Argentina

"Argentina has been almost invisible on the international scene more recently," wrote John Finan in the mid-1970s, "because of her severe internal political disunity."[37] Argentina's recent experience has been terrifying: defeat in war by the United Kingdom; massive arbitrary repression and killings by the armed forces to crush a terrorist wave that almost overwhelmed its society; repeated military coups and stalemated politics; astonishingly high rates of inflation and dramatic economic collapse. These events have occurred with dizzying speed since the early 1970s. Argentine foreign policy was cautious during these years as the Foreign Ministry attempted to protect the country's international position despite these events. Foreign policy underwent some changes during these years but, on the whole, it was surprisingly steady. For example, trade relations with the Soviet Union, Cuba, and other Communist countries inaugurated in the early 1970s under Peronist governments endured and prospered under military governments later in the 1970s and early in the 1980s.[38] In other words, the near-chaos of internal Argentine politics does not correspond to the stability of its foreign policy.

Nevertheless, there is some correspondence. Juan Carlos Puig has argued persuasively that Argentina's international posture was relatively open to the international system until the first government of Juan Domingo Perón, when Argentina developed a more activist foreign policy oriented toward the Third World. There was a retreat, Puig suggests, from that activism beginning with the fall of Perón in 1955 until the return of Peronismo to power in 1973. In fact, the new assertiveness and Third World orientation of Argentine foreign policy began earlier in the 1970s under military rule.[39]

In the early 1970s, military and Peronist governments (primarily the latter) sought to regulate Argentina's markets internally and internationally; Argentina joined the Nonaligned Movement and established trade and joint investment relationships with Communist countries. There was support for restructuring the international economic order. After the overthrow of the Peronista regime in 1976, a major effort was made to reduce the state's economic power and to sell off state enterprises to private business. Trade liberalization was instituted and had some positive results, but it was carried through to an extent that threatened Argentine industry with massive bankruptcy. Internationally, Argentina did not change all of its foreign policy, but it became less activist.[40] Argentina did not leave the Nonaligned Movement, but its foreign economic policies assumed a more laissez-faire character. The country dissociated itself from internationally statist efforts.[41] The massive and severe violations of human rights that had occured in the antiterrorist campaign contributed to Argentina's international isolation.[42] Argentina's decision to occupy the South Atlantic islands in 1982, however, makes it difficult to characterize the foreign policy of its free-market governments as "passive." Clearly other factors beyond the correspondence argument explain the continuity and the changes in Argentine foreign policy. In general, there was too much stability in foreign policy and too little in internal affairs to fully support a correspondence argument.

Cuba

Cuban foreign policy's high profile at first seems consistent with the correspondence hypothesis. The Cuban government has a very strong preference for state rather than market allocation of resources. Its strong foreign policy activism emphasizes the role of states. Cuba has been a steadfast supporter of the political reorganization of international markets.

However, there has been little direct relationship between trends in internal and in international Cuban affairs. Cuba has committed troops overseas at the end of years of economic growth (war in Angola, 1975) and after two years of recession (war in the Horn of Africa, 1977). Cuba has supported revolutionary movements overseas during an economic recovery (1959, 1978) and during an economic collapse (early and late 1960s or 1979–1980). Cuba has had excellent diplomatic and economic relations with ideologically distant regimes (Franco's Spain, Argentina under military rule 1976–83) and rather poor relations with ideologically closer regimes (the People's Republic of China).[43] Cuba has remained ideologically statist, but it has granted greater autonomy to market forces since 1970, decriminalizing penalties for some private transactions in farmers' markets and for private arrangements of professional services. Profitability has been used more often to assess the performance of state enterprises, and these have received more decision-making autonomy.[44] If the correspondence hypothesis were accurate, there should have been a decline in Cuban international activism from the early 1970s to the early 1980s. That has not happened.

Cuba thus resembles Argentina because of the greater consistency in the formulation and implementation of its foreign policy than in its internal policies. Cuba, of course, has been much more stable than Argentina in the latter respect as well. But, in both cases, the hypothesis that stresses the correspondence of ideas provides at most a partial explanation for foreign policy trends.

Mexico

Upon Luis Echevarría's accession to the presidency of Mexico in December 1970, "both the internal and the external situation pushed the government to search for solutions at home and abroad. Foreign policy would have to adjust to the changes in internal policy." Mario Ojeda's description of President Echevarría's initial political problem confirms the correspondence hypothesis: Many believed that Mexico's model of internal economic development had to change to sustain growth and improve distributional equity. Echevarría was shocked into a highly personal and activist diplomacy in the aftermath of President Nixon's decision to devalue the u.s. dollar in August of 1971. Mexico appeared weak and vulnerable in the face of u.s. government actions and of an international market that seemed increasingly unreliable. It became a champion of the New International Economic Order and, with Venezuela, a co-founder of the Latin American Economic System (SELA). It also increased its foreign indebtedness, in part as a means to counteract the difficulties of raising tax revenues at home.[45]

Mexican foreign policy gave a new image to its government at home, reincorporating the political left within the government coalition, although at the cost of alienating parts of the business community. Echevarría's foreign policy corresponded to the increase in government regulation of the economy, including more regulation of foreign direct investment. The number and importance of state enterprises increased. Decisions made at home had important consequences for Mexican international economic relations, often weakening, albeit unintentionally, the material bases required to conduct foreign policy. The real value of Mexican agricultural and manufacturing exports leveled off, or dropped, partly as a result of a deepening internal crisis.[46]

At the beginning of the José López Portillo presidency, the Mexican government became less activist internationally, less willing to support calls for a new international economic order, and more willing to collaborate with the United States. At home, the López Portillo administration, partly as a result of its agreement with the International Monetary Fund, curtailed the state's economic role. There appeared to be a correspondence between internal and international circumstances, and between the ideas about the relative efficacy of state control versus market forces in the allocation of resources at home and abroad.[47]

Alone of the eight countries under study, Mexico swung again in 1979 toward a more activist foreign policy, having recovered from the internal recession and with new confidence about its clout stemming from petroleum resources. It linked oil sales to trade and investment agreements with other governments; it refused to join the General Agreement on Tariffs and Trade (GATT) in 1980. The effect of these two decisions was to opt for a statist rather than a market-conforming activist trade strategy. Mexico rediscovered its interest in global North/South negotiations; it hosted the Cancún conference in 1981. But Mexican Third Worldism in the late López Portillo administration was more restrained than Echevarría's in the early 1970s. Mexico sought to bridge North and South, not just act on behalf of the South. Mexico continued to refuse to join OPEC, though it fell in line informally with major OPEC decisions. However, Mexico remained more aloof from the full array of Third World issues while it paid closer attention to Central American issues.[48]

Consistent with the correspondence hypothesis, Mexican central government expenditures also rose as a percentage of GDP (Table 2) in the second half of the López Portillo administration. The non-oil economy weakened; Mexico came to rely more on the strength of PEMEX, the state-owned oil firm. By late 1981 the basis for the conduct of Mexican international affairs had weakened despite the discovery of hydrocarbons, and in part because of the use of the fruits of that discovery in Mexico's economy and politics.[49] The López Portillo presidency ended with a quantum jump in the state's economic intervention when the President seized the private national banking system as the country faced an international debt crisis, a panicky devaluation of the peso, and the prospects for recession and further human misery at home.

President López Portillo's turn to international activism after 1979 seemed to rest on the belief that Mexico could use oil power to increase its benefits from international markets. However, the President's own decisions to delay the devaluation of the Mexican peso against the u.s. dollar hurt Mexico deeply and cast serious doubt on the ability of political leaders acting alone to calculate accurately the country's international economic interests.

Mexico differs, therefore, from all the other countries under discussion because it has experienced several foreign policy swings over a period of only a few years. From the late 1960s to the early 1980s, Mexican foreign policy underwent two full cycles of passivity and activism, perhaps reentering yet a third cycle of reduced activism in 1983. Mexico also responded to the oil price increases in 1979–80 differently from Venezuela. By 1979, Venezuela had lost some of its confidence in the blessings of state action; its internal economy remained close to zero real growth, while Mexico was newly confident that its oil was an instrument for the advancement of its international interests. In short, the Mexican experience emphasizes the rapidity of foreign policy changes even under the same president, in contrast to the more "permanent" shifts observable in the first four countries studied or the greater continuity of foreign policy in Argentina and Cuba.

Brazil

Brazilian policy shows a different pattern in the relationship between internal and international affairs. The military coup of 1964 which inaugurated the present regime in Brazil was supposed to enhance the private sector's role, repudiating the policies that had held back business activity. Thomas Skidmore has written,

> Interestingly enough, none of the major state corporations was dismantled. Instead, they were reorganized, thereby increasing both their production and productivity. The result was a pro-free-enterprise government that helped make the state sector—largely begun during the Estado Novo during the 1930s—more effective, while at the same time creating conditions in which efficient private business could prosper.[50]

Brazil hedged its choice between statist and market policies. The growth of its state enterprises was not designed to occur at the expense of private business. This approach distinguished Brazilian policy from that of Peru, Chile, or Mexico in the early 1970s, where "zero-sum" perceptions and experiences were more common, or even from Argentina and Venezuela, where "zero-sum" perceptions were less marked though state enterprises grew rapidly (in Argentina, as a result in part of private business bankruptcies). Brazil's economic structure featured a strong state and a strong market.[51] Therefore, in Brazil's case a correspondence argument that hinges on the antinomy of state versus market is misplaced.

Brazilian foreign policy underwent one sharp shift at the time of the 1964 coup and subsequently turned to gradual evolution. In 1964, Brazil departed from the previous, short-lived foreign policy "independent" of u.s. policies. Instead, it cooperated with u.s. foreign policy, even dispatching Brazilian troops in 1965 to the Dominican Republic to contribute to the "inter-Americanization" (under the auspices of the Organization of American States) of what had been a unilateral u.s. intervention there.[52]

As the Brazilian economy grew rapidly, its international trade also grew and diversified in both product profile and trade partners. Trade developed with countries the world over, depending less on the United States. Exports as a percentage of Brazilian GDP grew from about 5% in 1970 to about 8% in 1980. About one-third of Brazilian exports were shipped to the United States in 1965 but only about one-sixth went there in 1975. Brazil's share of world exports had fallen steadily through the 1950s and most of the 1960s, to rise through the 1970s into the early 1980s.[53] Brazil has become an internationally competitive exporter of manufactured goods and of many primary products.

This internationalization and diversification of the Brazilian economy was accompanied by an increasingly independent foreign policy during the later 1970s which, however, did not encompass the overt statist preferences of Mexico, Venezuela, Peru, Chile, or Cuba. Brazil gave only cautious support to new schemes for a new international economic order. As a major petroleum importer, it was skeptical of the policies of oil producers designed to legitimize indefinitely the jump in oil prices. Brazil gave only lukewarm support to the Mexican and Venezuelan initiatives to found a new Latin American Economic System (SELA). However, Brazil also discovered its policy differences with the United States over Brazilian plans for the development of nuclear energy. The 1973–74 energy crisis propelled Brazil's state-owned oil enterprise (PETROBRAS) to search for oil supplies the world over. Brazilian relations with oil-producing Arab countries improved (Brazil endorsed the U.N. resolution branding Zionism as racism). After the collapse of the Portuguese empire, Brazil was the first nonsocialist government to recognize the new MPLA government of Angola—placing Brazil far closer to the Cuban than to the U.S. position. Brazil was diplomatically active among other Portuguese successor states. It also developed a more active foreign policy toward its South American neighbors to enhance its influence,[54] successfully gaining for a Brazilian diplomat the post of Secretary General of the Organization of American States in 1984.

Brazil's new activism of the late 1970s and early 1980s contrasted with its rather passive policies of the late 1960s but also with the less activist policies of other Latin American states. Its recent foreign policy activism cannot be traced to a change toward statism within Brazil in the late 1970s; on the contrary, there are some efforts in Brazil, as elsewhere, to limit the continued growth of state economic power. Brazilian foreign policy in the early 1980s is concerned about the need for concerted action by governments and banks to avert international financial ruin (and its own ruin), but Brazilian pronouncements on debt issues are well within the norms of discourse in the industrial world and major international financial organizations.[55]

In short, the logic of Brazilian foreign policy change responds to factors other than the ideological correspondence between beliefs in the efficacy of internal markets and beliefs in the efficacy of international markets. Beliefs about markets, or about the nature and propriety of state intervention, changed rather little under the military presidents after 1964, and yet Brazilian foreign policy changed a good deal more.

This "tour" of the eight countries illustrates the striking changes in the foreign policies of most Latin American governments, first in the early 1970s and then again by the end of that decade or the beginning of the 1980s, approximately along the lines summarized in Table 1. There is some substantial support for the hypothesis that state activism in the regulations of the internal economy corresponds to foreign policy activism to seek to restructure any given country's international environment; conversely, a low level or a decline of internal state activism corresponds to a comparable low level or decline in foreign policy activism. These changes result (though not exclusively) from changes in leadership. The correspondence hypothesis focuses on a cognitive or ideological link; it is clearest in evidence in the early 1970s in Peru, Chile, Venezuela and, as an example of opposite patterns, in Colombia. Mexico also showed some substantial degree of correspondence between beliefs and actions in internal and international affairs, but with many more frequent changes even under the same presidents over a short period of time, suggesting that other short-run factors may have been more important. Finally, Argentina, Brazil, and Cuba adopted foreign policies that provided less support for the correspondence hypothesis. Argentine foreign policies were too stable to correspond to the considerable internal upheavals; in the Cuban case, the correspondence hypothesis would have forecast greater passivity by the late 1970s and early 1980s, which clearly did not happen; and Brazilian elite ideology about markets and state intervention changed little while foreign policy changed more.

The correspondence hypothesis does not explain politico-military activism over territorial disputes. It, therefore, provides the student of Latin American affairs with a first approximation to foreign policy changes in these countries; that is, it is a necessary tool to understand what has occurred but it is not sufficient to explain the reasons for the developments under consideration.

The international system as a source of foreign policy changes

A second approach to understand foreign policy change emphasizes that these states respond to constraints and opportunities in the international system. Rational, pragmatic, nonideological actors, analyzing the distribution of power and resources and conscious of their own strengths and weaknesses formulate a realistic design for each government's foreign policy. This process will be called the *calculating hypothesis*. It presumes that comparably situated elites will draw comparable inferences about the nature of the same international system. Leaders have the capacity to choose, but structural constraints are important. Economic, political, and military issues matter. These states are not confronted by any issues that require absolute priority. Whereas for the United States military issues are of top priority, war has been sufficiently infrequent and limited in Latin America that foreign economic policy often receives a priority comparable to military issues. There may be many short-run opportunities. Longer-range structural changes are less frequent but may have great impact when they occur, as in the early 1970s. Issues are global. Much information on the eight countries has already been provided; this and the next sections will only supplement it as needed.

The calculating hypothesis has much to recommend it. Venezuela's international activism after 1973 rested on its new strength derived from the international quadrupling of oil prices. Similarly, the Mexican government's renewed activism in 1979 reflected its increasing self-confidence, flushed with the discovery of new resources from hydrocarbons and blessed by another oil price jump in 1979. Brazilian foreign policy's increased activism since the early 1970s was a response, first, to its international weaknesses (e.g. relations had to improve with Arab countries to ensure a steady oil supply) and, later, to its growing economic strength compared to its immediate neighbors and to the international economic system. Cuban activism from the mid-1970s onward responded to specific opportunities (wars in Angola and the Horn of Africa and revolution in Central America) under circumstances when U.S. intervention against Cuba, directly or in the theater of operations, seemed highly unlikely.

These eight governments experienced the large-scale changes underway in the international system: the relative decline of U.S. power; the growth of economic relations with industrial countries in Western Europe, Canada, and Japan; and the evolution of East–West détente, making Latin American relations with the Soviet Union, Eastern European governments, and the People's Republic of China more feasible.

The calculating hypothesis, however, is less persuasive than these observations suggest. The curtailment of Venezuelan foreign policy activity in 1979–80, at the very moment that Mexico increased its international activism riding the second wave of sharply increased petroleum prices, suggests that other factors were at work. In Venezuela, the Luis Herrera administration believed that the previous administration had "overheated" the Venezuelan economy, being too assertive and intervening too much internally and internationally; it was appropriate to cool things off. Thus the correspondence hypothesis is required to distinguish between Venezuelan and Mexican foreign policy behaviors at the same moment in time. Ideological changes in both countries help to explain these differences in their responses to the oil price jumps.

The calculations made by the Brazilian and Peruvian armed forces about each country's role in the international system in the 1960s were also very different. The Brazilians moved closer to, while the Peruvians moved away from, the United States. The same international situation did not lead to the same foreign policy by these military regimes. The reasons are rooted in the internal circumstances and ideologies of the coming to power of each military regime.

The bureaucratic-authoritarian military governments that came to power in Argentina and in Chile in the 1970s differed in their foreign policy behavior. Argentina retained excellent economic relations with the Soviet Union and other Communist countries; Chile did not. Argentina remained a participant in Third World fora, though a more quiet one, and would eventually reactivate those links seeking support against the United Kingdom in the 1982 South Atlantic war. Chile put much greater distance between itself and the Third World. It withdrew from the Andean Pact for explicitly ideological reasons (the Pact regulated foreign investment too much). Chilean foreign policy under President Augusto Pinochet adhered much more closely to the correspondence hypothesis, while Argentine foreign policy could afford to show more continuity over time because its government's calculation about the international system mitigated the impact of ideology.

A calculating hypothesis does not explain the relative passivity of Colombian foreign policy. Such a hypothesis might predict that Colombia "should have been" at least as active and influential as Peru. These two countries are fairly similar in size and in resources, although the Colombian GDP grew far more rapidly than Peru's from 1960 to 1980 and Colombia was more involved in international trade than Peru was.[56] While Colombia did not have the surplus resources that propelled Venezuela and later Mexico into international activism, it did benefit from a coffee price boom in the mid-1970s that might have enabled it to pursue a more vigorous foreign policy. Gerhard Drekonja has shown that Colombia had a marginally more active policy coincident with the economic bonanza during the presidency of Alfonso López Michelsen, but even that policy was a far cry from what other governments of the region were undertaking. Drekonja attributes Colombia's inability to calculate its interests more effectively, and to implement appropriate policies, to the fragmentation of the decision-making process.[57] While his argument about Colombia is persuasive, Colombia's foreign policy making process is not that much more fragmented than is the case elsewhere. An argument based on ideological correspondence—relative laissez-faire at home and abroad—appears to be required to explain Colombian foreign policy.

The calculating hypothesis would also forecast a shift in foreign policy as changes occur in the international system. The severe financial difficulties in which most Latin American countries found themselves by the early 1980s—rapidly rising debt levels (see Table 3), high real interest rates, and

Table 3. Gross disbursed external
debt at year end

(Millions of dollars, current prices)

	1977	1983[a]
Argentina	8,210	42,000
Brazil	32,758	83,000
Chile	4,899	17,600
Colombia	3,892	10,300
Mexico	26,583	85,000
Peru	6,260	10,600
Venezuela	10,812	30,000

[a] Preliminary
Source: United Nations, Economic Commission
        for Latin America, Preliminary Overview
        of the Latin American Economy during 1983,
        E/CEPAL/G.1279 (1983), p. 36.

international recession—called for a curtailment of foreign policy activism. Decision makers, in fact, did focus more on internal problems. Negotiations with the u.s. government and with public and private international financial institutions required the countries involved to attend to the problems associated with the external debt, rather than disperse their international resources across several issue areas. The debt problem also reduced the capacity of these governments to negotiate on an international level and thus lessened their ability to launch activist initiatives.

The swing away from activism summarized in Table 1 is consistent with this aspect of the calculating hypothesis. Latin American governments are less globally engaged when their internal and their international positions are weaker; then calculations of their ability to act internationally counsel caution and retrenchment. The recrudescence of the East–West conflict has also increased the marginal costs of independent foreign policies for governments that depend, in part, on the u.s. government's goodwill to address their short-run and medium-run economic problems. There are also some instances when the relative deactivation of the foreign policy of a particular government appears to be related to a severe international debt problem: Peru's foreign policy moderated in the late 1970s as it signed an agreement with the International Monetary Fund.[58]

However, the calculating hypothesis does not hold up too well as an explanation of foreign policy trends in the early 1980s. One of the world's major debtors, Brazil, has retained a moderately activist and pragmatic foreign policy. It has not mitigated it; on the contrary, it uses it now as part of the strategy to address its international financial difficulties. Moreover, Latin America's most internationally activist government, Cuba's, has also faced a major international debt rescheduling problem. These severe economic problems have not curtailed Cuban activism.[59]

Argentina's decision to go to war against the United Kingdom in 1982 over the South Atlantic islands has often been presented either as a reaffirmation of Argentine sovereignty over the disputed territories or as an effort by the military government to divert attention from internal difficulties. The second alternative contains some elements of calculation, but it is different from that suggested by the hypothesis under consideration in that it is unrelated to the international system. The "patriotic" view of the decision is closer to an ideological explanation than to an emphasis on prudence weighing foreign policy ends and means.

The international debt crisis had little effect on the deactivation of Chilean foreign policy in the 1970s that preceded the debt crisis. While Chile's severe internal recession in the mid-1970s might have led prudent statesmen to retreat internationally, the Chilean economic recovery in the late 1970s did not bring about much change in Chilean foreign policy to provide substantial support for this view. Even in Peru, the Morales Bermúdez government began moving away from the policies of its predecessor and from its erstwhile friends of the Nonaligned Movement by 1976—well before the financial crisis brought Peru to agree with the imf.[60]

The shift in Venezuela's foreign policy early in the Herrera presidency also occurred in advance of the international debt crisis. The subsequent debt crisis "should have led" Venezuela and Mexico to cancel the San José Agreement, in which they had agreed to subsidize petroleum sales to nine Central American and Caribbean countries. This cancellation would have been warranted as early as 1981 when oil prices began to fall, or when Mexico had its first devaluation early in 1982 or the more severe one in August 1982, or when Venezuela devalued in early 1983. Even though the funds available in the San José Agreement have been curtailed, it is remarkable that Venezuela and Mexico have remained committed to this activist aspect of their foreign policy despite its cost amidst a debt crisis.[61]

In conclusion, a calculating hypothesis helps to explain why several Latin American governments became more internationally engaged in the early 1970s. Many recognized the slow but persistent major changes in the structure of the international system. The calculating hypothesis forecasts the lowering of sights in the foreign policies of Latin American states by the late 1970s. However, the hypothesis does not handle well the timing of foreign policy change or, more importantly, the causes of the new trends, nor does it explain why similarly situated governments draw such different conclusions about the same international system.

State capacity and learning as a source of foreign policy change

A third attack on the problem of understanding foreign-policy change combines aspects of the earlier approaches. It looks at the capacity of the state to act in international affairs and at how the elite learns about and evaluates these capacities and the international system. Ideas also matter because they change. Structure also matters because it changes. For these countries, their internal capacity is of greater impact than the international system; only the internal capacity enables a state to act. Economic growth is both a means and an end, but new political and military objectives have appeared in foreign policy. Paradoxically, a more capable state with a better-focused foreign policy may choose to be less active internationally because it has learned more about ends and means. State elites learn also that their capacity to act is greatest in international subsystems such as their relations with neighbors. Foreign policy is shaped and changed close to home by internal capacity and by elite learning, focusing on the international subsystem and on those few global issues which have direct impact on the given society.

This explanation must prove that state economic, military, and cognitive capacities have grown, and that these changes are related to important foreign policy changes. It must show the "fine tuning" of policies by leaders responding to an analysis of less successful previous policies or an analysis of new challenges or opportunities.

To understand the foreign policy changes of the early 1970s, it remains important to look at international system changes and how these were incorporated in the calculations the elites made about them. To comprehend why Peruvian and Brazilian military governments arrived at different conclusions concerning international affairs in the 1960s, or why Chilean foreign policy turned passive after 1973, the internal ideological roots of foreign policy must be understood. These first two explanations, however, can handle only the largest, the gross changes; they say less about more subtle foreign policy changes. Moreover, at times these two grand explanations are in error.

Most major Latin American states have taken a new look at their policies as their capacities have changed. From 1960 to 1980, the real GDP per capita of Latin American countries increased by an average of 89% in 1980 constant dollars. The GDP (in constant prices) of Argentina, Chile, and Peru doubled from 1960 to 1980; it tripled for Colombia, Mexico, and Venezuela; and it quadrupled for Brazil. From 1960 to 1980, life expectancy at birth increased by 5 to 8 years in Argentina and Brazil, by about 10 years in Colombia, Chile, Cuba, Peru, and Venezuela, and by about 13 years in Mexico. In 1980, life expectancy at birth was over 63 years in all above-mentioned countries but Peru.[62] State intervention in the society and the economy grew in most of them. The states' repressive capacity also increased, so that by the mid-1970s southern South America was dominated by bureaucratic-authoritarian regimes.[63] Even those regimes that sought to return many state enterprises to the private sector (as in Argentina and Chile in the mid and late 1970s) retained impressive powers of economic control (especially over labor) and production.

Military capabilities also increased. By 1970, Colombia, Cuba, Venezuela, and Peru had defeated moderate to major insurgencies. Varying degrees of insurgency were crushed in Argentina, Brazil, and Chile in the 1970s. (The most serious threat to state power was in Argentina.) Mexico never had to face a major insurgency, but it defeated a number of minor ones. All the armed forces could boast confidently of some counterinsurgency successes; all complained of unilateral u.s. decisions to limit arms shipments to them. Since the 1960s these armed forces began to diversify their military equipment suppliers. Military industries grew in Argentina and especially in Brazil. Latin American military budgets remain modest by world standards; as a percentage of GDP the numbers are small and virtually constant over time. But the actual cash available for military purposes has grown as the economies have grown. Economic growth made military modernization possible.[64]

The newly professional and modernized armed forces, victorious over their internal enemies, came to believe that "security" required their involvement in, and supervision of, large areas of the economy and society. This held true for all the varieties of bureaucratic-authoritarian regimes in Argentina, Brazil, and Chile, but also for the different regimes in Cuba and Peru.[65] The Colombian and Venezuelan military became also more involved in social and economic issues, but less so than in the other countries.

The growing capacities also led states to attempt to round out their boundaries by occupying undeveloped borderlands, and to lay claim to disputed areas. An international "accident," negotiations concerning the law of the seas, and the evolution of policies on the governance of the oceans, helped to intensify or reopen dormant boundary disputes. Maritime jurisdiction in the 200-mile economic zones had to be delimited, especially where yet another "accident"—the discovery and implementation of cost-effective offshore hydrocarbon exploitation technologies—heightened the stakes for the disputing states.[66] Among the more serious is the dispute between Venezuela and Colombia. The development of new state capacities at the borders was not all bad. It often led to binational development projects, such as the huge Brazil-Paraguay Itaipú hydroelectric complex. New transportation and communications facilities stimulated intraregional trade.[67] But this progress, in turn, raised the importance of relations with neighbors which have advanced well beyond romantic symbols of continental solidarity, to focus on trade, investment, resources, territory, and migration.

State capacity grew also in terms of human capabilities. New generations of technically trained and skillful government officials began to occupy leading positions. Opinions may differ about the wisdom or importance of their advice, but the technocratic presence in the bureaucracy spread dramatically. It was now possible to learn cumulatively, to identify choices and constraints, and to follow through on policy decisions.[68]

Latin American governments learned about the changes in the international system in the early 1970s. They learned also that they were most effective if they focused on their own geographic international subsystem and on a few issues. Where state elites have been autonomous and strong, as in Cuba and Brazil, growing state capacity furthered international engagement, relatively unconstrained by internal pressures but adjusting to changing international circumstances. Where the professional foreign service corps has been weak or only recently established, as in Venezuela or Peru, learning has been less institutionalized and enduring; the rhythm of foreign policy has been imparted principally by presidential preferences responding to ideology and short-term tactics. Where the professional foreign service corps has been able and has enjoyed continuity but the political leadership has been subject to upheavals, as in Argentina, there has been a surprisingly high ability to steer a stable foreign policy, except that the Argentine diplomats lacked the power to prevent the South Atlantic war. Mexico has combined a professional foreign service of some standing and a comparatively strong state activism, but its foreign service had not been used for an assertive foreign policy until the 1970s; the influence of presidential power on foreign-policy formulation has been very marked. For these reasons, Mexico showed the most frequent changes in foreign policy, despite evidence of learning.

Can an emphasis on state capacity and learning focused on a few issues and on international subsystems explain some anomalies left unexplained by hypotheses concerned with ideology and systemic calculations? Colombian foreign policy does not lend itself to an explanation that focuses on changes in the international system. The correspondence hypothesis helps explain much about Colombian foreign policy but it suggests (mistakenly) that it is invariant. Colombian foreign policy has fostered the country's economic growth. There have also been some modest bursts of foreign policy activism during the presidencies of Carlos Lleras Restrepo and Alfonso López Michelsen and, most recently, Belisario Betancur. Colombian foreign policy has changed more than the correspondence hypothesis suggests. There has been foreign policy learning.

A severe dispute with the International Monetary Fund (IMF) led Colombia to a crawling peg exchange rate policy in 1967. Although President Carlos Lleras Restrepo had resisted the IMF's policy suggestions, Colombia's crawling peg worked well; it became a foundation for the country's subsequent export boom. Although there are doubts about the Andean Pact's importance for Colombian economic growth, Colombia has learned under several presidential administrations to protect its interests within the Pact effectively. By the mid-1970s, Colombia also rediscovered the importance of other relations with neighbors. The López Michelsen presidency delimited maritime jurisdiction with Panama, Costa Rica, Haiti, the Dominican Republic, and Ecuador. It worked to protect Colombian interests during the Panama Canal negotiations (although not to the satisfaction of its political opposition). It reestablished diplomatic relations with Cuba to protect Colombia from possible Cuban support for revolutionary forces within its borders. Colombia focused also on the more serious maritime boundary dispute with Venezuela. Many of these policies continued during the presidency of Julio César Turbay Ayala, including an important, though ultimately unsuccessful, effort to settle the dispute with Venezuela and an attempt to use the Andean Pact for collective political initiatives in the Andean region and in Central America.[69]

There is little globalism in this foreign policy evolution and little about it is overtly ideological. Colombian policy has been focused on allowing its trade to grow—supported by market-conforming exchange rate policies— and on designing policies with regard to Colombia's immediate neighbors that are remote from the general questions of international system structure. As with Colombia's relatively laissez-faire international economic policies, the country's subsystemic foreign policy has served it well, if without drama.

In general, as Latin American governments have become more capable and better able to understand and act on their own interests, they have moved away from the vague discussions of a new international economic order or global North-South negotiations, although they did not abandon such concepts. They worry less about East–West relations. They have identified priority matters more clearly, especially international debt and trade questions as well as their relations with neighbors in an international subsystem. For Colombia this approach suggests a focusing of its foreign policy for the first time; for the other countries it suggests that a refocusing is underway. Latin America's foreign policies did not collapse by the early 1980s but they now concentrate on matters of more clearly identifiable importance to the countries involved. This development is somewhat independent of ideological issues and of the larger trends in the international system.

Venezuelan foreign policy, for example, was certainly less activist on a global scale under the Herrera than under the Pérez presidency—in part for ideological reasons. But Herrera's foreign policy can be better described as an effort to refocus Venezuelan policy on items of identifiable national importance where Venezuela could make a difference. That refocused policy created its own problems, of course, but the changed emphasis was itself prudent and reasonable. Economically, Venezuela focused on the petroleum market and, during the later years of the Herrera presidency, on the rescheduling of its international debts. The Herrera government also attended to relations with its neighbors. There was an effort (unsuccessful) to settle the boundary dispute with Colombia in 1980 and to contain the boundary dispute problems with Guyana. In the Caribbean and Central America, the Herrera government continued the economic assistance policies of its predecessor and it succeeded in enlisting Mexico to share the cost. The Herrera government tried to curb the resurgent Cuban interest in the international subsystem and to promote the type of pluralist democracy that has characterized Venezuela's own politics. The Andean Pact was used not only for economic integration but also as a political alliance.[70]

The Herrera government's policies are open to criticism. For this essay's purposes, however, these policies were an effort to learn from the previous experience, to understand the capacities of the Venezuelan government in the international arena, and to conserve and to focus resources on those areas judged to be most important. The Herrera government, though it tried to be less activist than the Pérez government, may still have attempted too much. But its refocused foreign policy was not passive. Petroleum was to be used not as a general strategy to seek influence and advantage everywhere—a lesson Mexico had yet to learn—but to promote the country's internal development and international subsystemic influence.

Venezuela's refocused foreign policy was not a result of its economic recession (begun at the end of the 1970s) or of the international debt crisis the country faced in 1983. Surprisingly perhaps, the new foreign policy continued to commit resources to Central America and the Caribbean even in the midst of the international debt crisis. Furthermore, the Herrera government's policies were not a result of an ideological correspondence between internal and international policies, for it was slowing down the growth of the state at home but expanding its power abroad.

In short, while the correspondence and the calculating hypotheses seem necessary and sufficient to explain the origins of Venezuelan activism in the early 1970s, the more appropriate explanation for the evolution of Venezuelan policies by the early 1980s is that they were refocused upon learning about the state's capacity in foreign-policy matters and choosing priorities accordingly.

All South American governments paid more attention to territorial issues with neighbors by the late 1970s and early 1980s—an international subsystemic focus with a vengeance.[71] The earlier correspondence hypothesis sheds no light on why this happened. Most serious were the wars between Ecuador and Peru in 1981 and between Argentina and the United Kingdom in 1982. These regrettable conflicts are evidence of a new foreign policy focus on close-to-home national interests. Argentina and Chile also came to the edge of warfare over the Beagle Channel islands and related issues of maritime jurisdiction; and Chile, Peru, and Bolivia also approached the outbreak of hostilities in the mid- to late 1970s. Mention has already been made of the Venezuela–Colombia dispute.

War, or its greater likelihood, forced governments to reassess foreign-policy priorities and to reallocate and conserve resources. This meant less time, less personnel, and less money expended on a global foreign policy. This process has relatively little to do with the correspondence hypothesis, although the retrenchment from global concerns was facilitated in several countries by the ideological shift in their government policies. The new foreign policy is more responsive than in the past to an analysis of each country's place in the international subsystem; there are specific calculations about relations with neighbors and about each state's capacities at the border. This has little to do with global systemic changes concerning East–West relations or the international debt.

This refocused policy can be illustrated further with reference to Cuba, Brazil, and Mexico, which did not have severe territorial disputes. The Cuban government has not abandoned its globalist foreign policy. It committed troops to fight on Ethiopia's side (along with the Soviet Union and East Germany) against Somalia in 1977–1978. It became chairman of the Nonaligned Movement in late 1979. But the most important initiatives of the Cuban government since the late 1970s have been focused on its neighbors. Cuba rediscovered a revolutionary situation in Central America and reactivated its long-standing interest in its closest international subsystem. It has supported its insurgent friends in northern Central America (though its support was not the main cause of those insurgencies) and, since July 1979, it has also given assistance to the revolutionary government of Nicaragua. Cuba also supported the revolutionary government of Grenada, from its March 1979 victory to its demise in October 1983. Cuba competed vigorously—though unsuccessfully—with the United States for influence elsewhere in the English-speaking Caribbean. And Cuba found itself embroiled in new, serious disputes with the Bahamas, Jamaica, Venezuela, Colombia, and most Central American governments.

Cuba's refocusing on the western hemisphere reflected its long-standing priority concerning relations with neighbors, but the new policy also showed evidence of learning compared to Cuba's unsuccessful support for revolution in the 1960s. Cuba sought to bring about unity of the left in each country instead of picking a revolutionary "champion" to support to the exclusion of others and at the cost of splitting the left. Cuba sought to cooperate closely with the Soviet Union and other Eastern European governments to assist revolutionary Nicaragua. And Cuba worked to build broad-based international coalitions to support the insurgencies against Somoza in Nicaragua and against El Salvador's government. By the early 1980s Cuba's new capacity enabled it to send its personnel to assist Nicaragua's revolutionary government in tasks ranging from international defense and internal security to a literacy campaign and road construction.[72]

Mexico's activism during the second half of the López Portillo presidency may be criticized but it was not an irrational foreign policy. It responded to a refined analysis of Mexico's capacity and of its national interests. It recognized a new revolutionary situation in several Central American countries; Mexican security and other interests were at stake in this international subsystem. Mexico's neighbors came to receive much of its attention; Mexican concerns for the rest of the Third World did not vanish but were assigned lower priorities. Mexico's Central American policy looked for political negotiations rather than the use of force. Mexico also supported left-wing governments and movements since it thought them most likely to win and most important, therefore, to the region's long-range stability. Mexico implicitly put forth its own experience as an alternative to what Cuba and the United States might recommend to Central American countries: a dominant political party, some important internal reforms, an independent foreign policy, and a mixed economy with ample room for private business. Mexico joined with Venezuela in 1980 to subsidize the petroleum purchases of all the Central American and three Caribbean countries.[73]

Beyond Central America, Mexico believed that its petroleum and natural gas might be used to bargain for the larger goals of Mexican development. It did not abandon the promotion of a new international economic order (some fine speeches were given on its behalf) but the main policy sought to advance more specific Mexican interests.[74] Mexico's bilateral agreements with other governments guaranteed an oil supply in exchange for trade and investment benefits to Mexico. This vigorous "oil weapon" bilateralism was the alternative chosen by President López Portillo when he rejected in 1980 the recommendation of some advisors that Mexico adhere to the General Agreement on Tariffs and Trade (GATT). This bilateralist policy unraveled when the real price of petroleum fell in 1981. Regardless of its inherent merits, the strategy of diverting Mexican foreign economic policy from diffuse international goals and focusing it on the advancement of specific trade and investment objectives did show that the López Portillo government had learned from past Mexican policies and had arrived at a more accurate assessment of the country's priorities.[75]

When Mexico's economy faltered seriously in 1982–83, the management of its large international debt took priority. Even then Mexico retained an activist policy vis-à-vis Central America. President Miguel de la Madrid retained the joint commitment with Venezuela to a scaled-back version of the San José oil subsidy agreement, and authorized Foreign Minister Bernardo Sepúlveda to play a leading role in the Contadora group of governments seeking a peaceful end to Central America's troubles.

The trends in Brazilian foreign policy are different from those of the countries discussed so far. Unlike Mexico, Peru, or Venezuela, Brazil did not develop a high-profile rhetorical foreign policy in the early 1970s; consequently, Brazilian foreign policy has not experienced the wilder swings that marked the policies of some of the other countries. Brazil learned about what the country can and should do in foreign affairs as its internal capacity grew. Its exports have been rising since the late 1960s, although policies adopted in response to the 1973–74 oil shock slowed down the rate of growth of exports. Nonetheless, export growth over time has been remarkably successful. Brazil also chose to maintain a high economic growth rate by borrowing in the international capital markets in the 1970s. Its indebtedness is not just an example of failure. In the 1970s at long last international private banks had judged Brazil skillful, developmentalist, and credit-worthy enough to get into debt.[76]

Brazil also became more closely engaged with its neighbors. Since the late 1960s, Brazil expanded its economic relations and its political influence vis-à-vis Uruguay, Paraguay, and Bolivia. The huge Itaipú hydroelectric dam was built at the border, jointly owned with Paraguay, though serving above all Brazil's development. Brazil's territorial policy was conciliatory, yielding disputed areas to Paraguay and Venezuela in order to improve other aspects of bilateral relations. Brazil compromised with Argentina, reducing the height and capabilities of the Itaipú dam in order not to impair an Argentine dam's capacities farther downstream. The two governments also agreed to exchange nuclear energy information and certain resources, cooling off the dangers of nuclear competition.

Brazilian military planners determined that the United States was not a reliable weapons supplier, given the vagaries of rapidly changing policies in Washington. A national arms industry has been developed; Brazil has become one of the new breed of exporters of some military equipment and weapons to other Third World countries. Brazilian economic security also required a guaranteed petroleum supply. The state oil enterprise, PETRO-BRAS, pursued a vigorous exploration and commercial strategy; Brazil's relations with Iraq, Libya, Nigeria, and Angola serve also this specific national security interest.[77]

Brazilian foreign policy, in short, is now diverse and far-flung, more than that of any other Latin American country but Cuba; its capacity is the greatest among the Latin American countries. The goals of Brazilian foreign policy are specific; they are clearly identifiable and achievable national goals. Its foreign policy responds neither to rigid ideological preconceptions about markets nor to the logic of East–West relations or North–South global international relations. It responds, instead, to an understanding of the country itself, learning through the years about how to pragmatically advance its interests in its international subsystem and in specific global economic issues.

Conclusions

Latin American foreign policies have changed since the late 1960s. Some of these states were important diplomatic actors of the 1970s. But some of their foreign policies changed again at the beginning of the 1980s. This essay has taken three approaches to the study of this foreign policy change.

The first emphasizes *the role of ideology* as an organizing concept for the policies of state leaders. Ideologies shape the actions of leaders in corresponding ways in internal and international policy. The replacement of leaders promoting one set of ideologies by leaders with different ideologies is at the heart of policy change. It was further hypothesized that ideologies that expect states to regulate markets at home were also likely to call for state intervention to regulate international markets; ideologies that expect markets to be "free" at home would also expect states to be less activist internationally.

The second approach emphasizes *the distribution of power and resources* of the international system. Rational, pragmatic, nonideological actors design a foreign policy based on *calculation*. Comparably situated elites would draw comparable inferences about the international system for their own countries. Issues and concerns tend to be global. Concerns may be economic, political, or military, but the choices to be made relate to the global system.

The third approach emphasizes *the capacity of the state* to act in international affairs, the ability of state elites to learn about that capacity, and a consequent focus on the international subsystem (relations with neighbors) and, at most, on a few global issues of great concern for the further development of the state capacity.

The hypotheses about ideological correspondence or about calculations concerning the international system were important to explain the change in foreign policies in the early 1970s which saw a fundamental break with the characteristic passivity of past years. But these two "macro-hypotheses" do not explain well, or "mis-predict," trends in foreign policy evolution in the later 1970s or early 1980s. For this latter purpose, the third hypothesis, emphasizing *learning about state capacities*, is more useful.

The ideological correspondence hypothesis cannot explain well the resurgence of concerns about territorial disputes with neighbors, for example. The international calculation hypothesis, in turn, would have predicted an across-the-board collapse of the foreign policies of Latin American states in the early 1980s. This has not occurred.

By the early 1980s, Latin American foreign policies had refocused. These states were no longer attempting to reshape the entire international system. But there was a much clearer identification of national priorities and a more prudent assessment of the relationship between foreign policy goals and means. This refocused foreign policy was more closely related to the real capacities of the states; it reflected elite learning over the previous decade.

To put it differently, the activism of a number of these states in the early 1970s may have reflected weakness rather than strength—an emphasis on rhetoric in international organizations and conferences as a substitute for a real foreign policy. These states contributed to the erosion of previous international economic norms, but the main explanation for the change in such norms reaches well beyond the actions or effectiveness of the Latin American states. Velasco's Peru, Allende's Chile, or Echeverría's Mexico had an ideology—but little real power.

The activism of the Latin American states depended in part on the temporary increase of the power of commodity producers in the early to mid-1970s. This phase was short-lived, and so was the power of the Latin American states which thought that they might derive greater influence from a purely transitory phenomenon. An international system explanation accounts well for this change, unmasking the policies of the early 1970s. But an international system explanation does not provide a satisfactory explanation of the persisting high activism of Latin American states, refocused once again on the western hemisphere in the early 1980s.

The new foreign policies of Latin American states respond to the logic of statecraft and of its political, military, and economic needs. Foreign policy was not cut back. Only its globalist dimensions were. Latin American foreign policies in the early 1970s had focused on international public goods— the New International Economic Order—in part because they lacked the policy instruments to do much else. This foreign policy of weakness was also global in scope. A decade later, a foreign policy based on limited, but not insubstantial, state capacities was possible. It had been learned. It brought governments to focus on the international subsystem in which they joined their neighbors and to attend to only a few global issues of greatest relevance to their countries. They had to save themselves before they saved the world. These refocused relations have made war "thinkable" again. Governments have put economic policy at the service of political objectives (Brazil, Venezuela, and Mexico with regard to their smaller neighbors). And they have pursued international indebtedness as an instrument of national policy, with troubling results for them and the international financial system. Learning in foreign policy has, indeed, occurred, but not enough learning yet to make for sound policies to serve these states even better.

NOTES

I am very grateful to Peter Katzenstein, David Mares, Theodore Moran, Eric Nordlinger, John Odell, and Carlos Rico for comments on an earlier draft.
  1. Argentina, Brazil, Colombia, Chile, Cuba, Mexico, Peru, and Venezuela.

2. *The New York Times*, ed., *The Rockefeller Report on the Americas* (Chicago: Quadrangle Books, 1969), p. 21 and passim.

3. Luigi Einaudi, *Beyond Cuba: Latin America Takes Charge of Its Future* (New York: Crane, Russak, 1974).

4. Commission on United States–Latin American Relations, *The Americas in a Changing World* (New York: Quadrangle Books, 1975), especially pp. 20–21.

5. Report on the Inter-American Dialogue, *The Americas at a Crossroads* (Washington: The Wilson Center, Smithsonian Institution, 1983), p.5.

6. Bela Belassa, "Policy Responses to External Shocks in Selected Latin American Countries," in Werner Baer and Malcolm Gillis, eds., *Export Diversification and the New Protectionism* (Urbana, IL: National Bureau of Economic Research and the Bureau of Economic Research of the University of Illinois, 1981).

7. Robert Keohane and Joseph Nye, *Power and Interdependence* (Boston: Little, Brown, 1977), and Stanley Hoffmann, *Primacy or World Order?* (New York: McGraw Hill, 1979).

8. Yoram Shapira, "Mexico's Foreign Policy under Echevarría: A Retrospect," *Inter-American Economic Affairs* 31 no. 4 (Spring 1978), pp. 34–38.

9. Shane Hunt, "Direct Foreign Investment in Peru: New Rules for an Old Game," in Abraham Lowenthal, ed., *The Peruvian Experiment* (Princeton: Princeton University Press, 1975).

10. Carmelo Mesa-Lago, *Cuba in the 1970s* (Albuquerque: University of New Mexico Press, 1974), pp. 107–137.

11. For a general discussion, see John S. Odell, *U.S. International Monetary Policy: Markets, Power and Ideas as Sources of Change* (Princeton: Princeton University Press, 1982), pp. 58–75.

12. For overviews of the Peruvian process, see Lowenthal, ed., *The Peruvian Experiment*; and Alfred Stepan, *The State and Society : Peru in Comparative Perspective* (Princeton: Princeton University press, 1978).

13. Comité de Asesoramiento de la Presidencia de la República, *La revolución nacional peruana: manifiesto, estatuto, plan del Gobierno Revolucionario de la Fuerza Armada* (Lima: Editorial Universo, 1974).

14. Ricardo Luna, "Peruvian Diplomacy: The Nuance of Interdependence," Cambridge: Center for International Affairs, Harvard University, 1981, unpublished; Robert H. Swansbrough, "Peru's Diplomatic Offensive: Solidarity for Latin American Independence," in Ronald G. Hellman and H. Jon Rosenbaum, *Latin America: The Search for a New International Role* (New York: Wiley, 1975); and earlier references to Peru.

15. See the following speeches of President General Francisco Morales Bermúdez in the series *La revolución peruana: segunda fase*: "Consideraciones políticas y económicas del momento actual," no. 3 (March 31, 1976), pp. 24–26; "Mensaje a la nación," no. 5 (May 13, 1976), pp. 10–13; "Discursos pronunciados en la ciudad de Huaral," no. 8 (June 24, 1976), pp. 19–22.

16. Stephen M. Gorman, "Peruvian Foreign Economic Policy since 1975: External Political and Economic Initiatives," in Elizabeth G. Ferris and Jennie K. Lincoln, *Latin American Foreign Policies* (Boulder: Westview Press, 1981).

17. John P. Jurecky, "The Political Economy of Contemporary Peru: How Fragile the New Model?" (Cambridge: Center for International Affairs, Harvard University, 1982).

18. For a history, see Frederick B. Pike, *Chile and the United States, 1880–1962* (South Bend, IN: University of Notre Dame Press, 1963).

19. Theodore H. Moran, *Multinational Corporations and the Politics of Dependence* (Princeton: Princeton University Press, 1974) is a now classic account.

20. Carlos Fortín, "Principled Pragmatism in the Face of External Pressure: The Foreign

Policy of the Allende Government," in Hellman and Rosenbaum, eds., *Latin America*. See pp. 218–219 for the quotation. For the complete reference, see Note 14.

21. Manfred Wilhelmy, "Hacia un análisis de la política exterior chilena contemporánea," *Serie Documental de Trabajo*, no. 1 (Valparaíso: Universidad Católica de Valparaíso, 1979).

22. Rolf Luders, *Towards Economic Recovery in Chile* (Santiago: Imprenta INE, 1982), pp. 3, 17.

23. Franklin Tugwell, *The Politics of Oil in Venezuela* (Stanford: Stanford University Press, 1975); and Gustavo Coronel, *The Nationalization Process of the Venezuelan Petroleum Industry: From Technocratic Success to Political Failure* (Lexington, MA: Lexington Books, 1983).

24. Robert Bond, ed., *Contemporary Venezuela and Its Role in International Affairs* (New York: New York University Press, 1977), especially Chapter 7 by Bond. On SELA, see his "Regionalism in Latin America: Prospects for the Latin American Economic System (SELA)," *International Organization* 32 no. 2 (Spring 1978), pp. 401–423.

25. For differences among Venezuelan scholars about the New International Economic Order, compare Oscar García, "El Nuevo Orden Económico Internacional (con referencia a Venezuela)," *Politeia*, 7 (1978), pp. 443–477; and Aníbal Romero, *Venezuelan Foreign Policy, United States Foreign Policy and the North-South Dialogue* (Caracas: Universidad Simón Bolívar, Decanato de Investigaciones, 1980).

26. Banco Mercantil y Agrícola, *Venezuela in Figures* (Caracas: 1982).

27. Republic of Venezuela, *Venezuela: Recent Economic Developments and Medium-Term Prospects* (Caracas: March 30, 1983), pp. 25–26.

28. Robert H. Dix, *Colombia: The Political Dimensions of Change* (New Haven: Yale University Press, 1967); R. Albert Berry, Ronald G. Hellman, and Mauricio Solaún, eds., *Politics of Compromise; Coalition Government in Colombia* (New Brunswick: Transaction Books, 1980); Dolores Moyano Martin, ed., *Handbook of Latin American Studies: Social Sciences*, no. 41 (Austin: University of Texas Press, 1979); Organization of American States, Secretaría General, Departamento de Asuntos Culturales, *Bibliografía de artículos sobre las relaciones internacionales de América Latina y el Caribe 1975–1982* (Washington: mimeograph, 1982).

29. Miguel Urrutia, "Colombia and the Andean Group: Economic and Political Determinants of Regional Integration Policy" in Baer and Gillis, eds., *Export Diversification*, p. 182. For the complete reference, see Note 6.

30. International Monetary Fund, *International Financial Statistics: Supplement on Trade Statistics*, Supplement Series no. 4 (Washington: 1982), pp. 52, 54.

31. John Odell, "Latin American Industrial Exports and Trade Negotiations with the United States," in Jorge I. Domínguez, ed., *Economic Issues and Political Conflict: U.S.– Latin American Relations* (London: Butterworth, 1982), p. 163.

32. Jorge I. Domínguez, "Business Nationalism: Latin American National Business Attitudes and Behavior toward Multinational Enterprises," in Domínguez, ed., *Economic Issues*, pp. 38–40. For the complete reference, see Note 31.

33. Urrutia, "Colombia and the Andean Group," pp. 189, 193. For the complete reference, see Note 29.

34. R. Albert Berry, "The National Front and Colombia's Economic Development," in Berry, Hellman, and Solaún, eds., *Politics of Compromise*, pp. 289, 297–306, quotation from p. 314. For the complete reference, see Note 28.

35. Inter-American Development Bank, *Economic and Social Progress in Latin America, 1983* (Washington) p. 116.

36. Alberto Venegas Tamayo, "Futuro y destino internacional de Colombia," *Revista Centro de Estudios Colombianos*, no. 35 (1982) pp. 77–97.

37. John J. Finan, "Argentina," in Harold E. Davis and Larman C. Wilson, eds., *Latin American Foreign Policies* (Baltimore: The Johns Hopkins University Press, 1975).

38. Argentine exports to the Soviet Union increased from 9.7% of total Argentine exports

in 1975 to 20.1% in 1980 and 21.9% in 1981. In all three years, they were more important than Argentine exports to the United States. International Monetary Fund, *Direction of Trade Statistics: Yearbook 1982* (Washington), pp. 66–67.

39. Juan Carlos Puig, "Política internacional Argentina," paper presented at the Seminar
on Comparative Foreign Policies of Latin America at the Fourth meeting of Centers
affiliated with RIAL, Caracas, October 1982.

40. Ricardo Zinn, "The Evolution and Structure of the Argentine Economy," and José
Manuel Saravia, "The Government of Argentina," in *Argentine-American Forum* (St.
Michael's, Maryland, 1979); and Edward S. Milenky, "Problems, Perspectives, and
Modes of Analysis: Understanding Latin American Approaches to World Affairs," in
Hellman and Rosenbaum, eds., *Latin America*, pp. 96–97. For the complete reference,
see Note 14.

41. For an explanation and defense of the policies instituted by the Minister of Economy,
José Martínez de Hoz, and carried out during his four plus years in office, see "An-
nouncement of a New Stage in the Application of the Economic Programme," in *Bole-
tín semanal del Ministerio de Economía*, no. 357 (September 29, 1980), Appendix. For a
critique of those same policies, see Aldo Ferrer, "El monetarismo en Argentina y
Chile, Parte I," *Comercio exterior* 31 no. 1 (January 1981), pp. 3–13, and "Parte II,"
Comercio exterior 31 no. 2 (February 1981), pp. 176–192.

42. Organization of American States, Inter-American Commission on Human Rights, *Report on the Situation of Human Rights in Argentina*, OEA/Ser.L/II.49 doc.19 corr.1 (Washington: General Secretariat, 1980); and Organization of American States, General
Assembly, *Observations and Criticisms Made by the Government of Argentina with Regard to
the Report of the Inter-American Commission on Human Rights on the Situation of Human
Rights in Argentina*, OEA/Ser.PAG/CP/doc.256/80 (Washington: General Secretariat, 1980).

43. Jorge I. Domínguez, "Political and Military Limitations and Consequences of Cuban
Policies in Africa," in Carmelo Mesa-Lago and June Belkin, eds., *Cuba in Africa*, Latin
American Monograph and Document Series, no. 3 (Pittsburgh: Center for Latin Amer-
ican Studies, University of Pittsburgh, 1982); Jorge I. Domínguez and Juan Lindau,
"The Primacy of Politics: Comparing the Foreign Policies of Cuba and Mexico," *Inter-
national Political Science Review* 5 no. 1 (1984), pp. 75–101.

44. Carmelo Mesa-Lago, *The Economy of Socialist Cuba: A Two-Decade Appraisal* (Albuquerque: University of New Mexico Press, 1981).

45. Mario Ojeda, *Alcances y límites de la política exterior de México* (Mexico: El Colegio de
México, 1976), quotation p. 176; see also pp. 164–169, 176–204.

46. Jorge I. Domínguez, "International Reverberations of a Dynamic Political Economy,"
in Jorge I. Domínguez, ed., *Mexico's Political Economy: Challenges at Home and Abroad*
(Beverly Hills: Sage Publications, 1982).

47. Guadalupe González, "Incertidumbres de una potencia media regional: las nuevas di-
mensiones de la política exterior mexicana," in Olga Pellicer, ed., *La política exterior de
México: desafíos en los ochenta* (Mexico: CIDE, 1983), especially pp. 59–67.

48. Op. cit., pp. 67–80; also chapters by Olga Pellicer, "La 'buena vecindad' en los mo-
mentos difíciles: México y Estados Unidos en 1982," and Rosario Green, "La diplomacia multilateral mexicana y el diálogo norte-sur."

49. Domínguez, "International Reverberations," pp. 221–226. For the full reference, see
Note 46.

50. Thomas E. Skidmore, "Politics and Economic Policy Making in Authoritarian Brazil,
1937–1971," in Alfred Stepan, ed., *Authoritarian Brazil* (New Haven: Yale University
Press, 1973), p. 41.

51. Sylvia Ann Hewlett, "The State and Brazilian Economic Development: The Contemporary Reality and Prospects for the Future," in William H. Overholt, ed., *The Future
of Brazil* (Boulder: Westview Press, 1978).

52. Carlos Estevam Martins, "Brazil and the United States from the 1960s to the 1970s,"

in Julio Cotler and Richard R. Fagen, eds., *Latin America and the United States* (Stanford: Stanford University Press, 1974).

53. Computed from International Monetary Fund, *Direction of Trade*, Annual 1964–1968, pp. 347–349, and *Annual* 1970–1974, p. 293; also from its *Yearbook 1982*, p. 95; and from International Monetary Fund, *International Financial Statistics: Supplement on Trade Statistics*, Supplement Series, no. 4 (1982), pp. 54, 118–120.

54. William Perry, *Contemporary Brazilian Foreign Policy: The International Strategy of an Emerging Power*, Foreign Policy papers, 2 no. 6 (Beverly Hills: Sage Publications, 1976); and Ronald M. Schneider, *Brazil: Foreign Policy of a Future World Power* (Boulder: Westview Press, 1976), Chs. 1 and 2.

55. See the speech by President João Baptista Figueiredo to the xxxvii Session of the General Assembly of the United Nations, September 27, 1982.

56. Inter-American Development Bank, *Economic and Social Progress in Latin America, 1983*, pp. 340, 345, 370.

57. Gerhard Drekonja Kornat, "Colombia: en búsqueda de una política exterior," *Occasional Papers Series*, no. 3 (1982) (Latin American and Caribbean Center, Florida International University).

58. Gorman, "Peruvian Foreign Policy since 1975," pp. 120–121. For the complete reference, see Note 16.

59. Banco Nacional de Cuba, *Economic Report, 1982* (Havana).

60. Gorman, "Peruvian Foreign Policy since 1975," p. 120. For the complete reference, see Note 16.

61. Domínguez and Lindau, "The Primacy of Politics." For the complete reference, see Note 43.

62. Computed from Inter-American Development Bank, *Economic and Social Progress in Latin America, 1983*, p. 345; *World Development Report, 1982* (New York: Oxford University Press), pp. 150–151.

63. David Collier, ed., *The New Authoritarianism in Latin America* (Princeton: Princeton University Press, 1979).

64. Caesar D. Sereseres, "The Acquisition of Arms and Western Hemisphere Relations," in Viron P. Vaky, ed., *Governance in the Western Hemisphere: Background Papers* (New York: Praeger, 1983); and John Child, *Unequal Alliance: The Inter-American Military System, 1938–1978* (Boulder: Westview Press, 1980), Chs. 5 and 6.

65. Stepan, *The State and Society: Peru*, Ch. 4 (for the complete reference, see Note 12); Jorge I. Domínguez, *Cuba: Order and Revolution* (Cambridge: Harvard University Press, 1978), Ch. 9.

66. A preliminary statement appears in Jorge I. Domínguez, "Ghosts from the Past: War, Territorial and Boundary Disputes in Mainland Central and South America since 1960" (Cambridge: Center for the International Affairs, Harvard University, unpublished).

67. See the relevant chapters in the various annual issues of the Inter-American Development Bank's *Economic and Social Progress in Latin America*.

68. Guillermo O'Donnell, *Modernization and Bureaucratic-Authoritarianism*, Politics of Modernization Series, no. 9 (Berkeley: Institute of International Studies, University of California, 1973), pp. 41–52.

69. Drekonja, "Colombia," pp. 10–16; (for the complete reference, see Note 57); Urrutia, "Colombia and the Andean Group (for the complete reference, see Note 6); Richard L. Maullin, "The Colombia-IMF Disagreement of November-December 1966: An Interpretation of its Place in Colombian Politics," in Yale H. Ferguson, ed., *Contemporary Inter-American Relations* (New York: Prentice-Hall, 1972).

70. Carlos A. Romero, "La diplomacia de proyección y el caso cubano en el contexto nacional y regional: las relaciones entre Venezuela y Cuba, 1979–1981," *Fragmentos*, no. 11 (Caracas: Centro de Estudios Latinoamericanos "Rómulo Gallegos").

71. Augusto Varas, "Las relaciones militares internacionales de América Latina: evolución y perspectivas," in Gustavo Lagos Matus, ed., *Las relaciones entre América Latina, Estados Unidos y Europa Occidental* (Santiago de Chile: Editorial Universitaria, 1979); Alberto Sepúlveda, "La dinámica del equilibrio de poder en Sudamérica y sus proyecciones en las políticas exteriores de la región," and Gloria Echeverría, María Teresa Infante, and Walter Sánchez, "Chile y Bolivia: conflicto y negociación en la subregión," in Walter Sánchez, ed., *Las relaciones entre los países de América Latina* (Santiago de Chile: Editorial Universitaria, 1980).

72. Jorge I. Domínguez, "Cuba's Relations with Caribbean and Central American Countries," in Alan Adelman and Reid Reading, eds., *Confrontation in the Caribbean Basin*, Latin American Series, no. 8 (Pittsburgh: Center for Latin American Studies, University of Pittsburgh, 1984).

73. Gabriel Rosenzweig, "La cooperación económica de México con centroamérica a partir de 1979. Perspectivas para los próximos años," in Pellicer, ed., *La política exterior de Mexico* (for the complete reference, see Note 47); and René Herrera and Mario Ojeda, "The Policy of Mexico in the Caribbean Basin," in Adelman and Reading, eds., *Confrontation in the Caribbean Basin* (for the complete reference, see Note 72).

74. Rosario Green, "La diplomacia multilateral mexicana y el diálogo norte-sur." For the complete reference, see Note 48.

75. Dale Story, "Trade Politics in the Third World: A Case Study of the Mexican GATT Decision," *International Organization* 36 no. 4 (Autumn 1982), pp. 767–794; Marcela Serrato, "Las dificultades financieras de México y la política petrolera hacia el exterior," in Pellicer, ed., *La política exterior de México* (for the complete reference, see Note 47); and David Ronfeldt, Richard Nehring and Arturo Gándara, *Mexico's Petroleum and U.S. Policy: Implications for the 1980s:*, R-2510-DOE (Santa Monica: The Rand Corporation, 1980).

76. William G. Tyler, "Changing Perspectives on Brazil's International Economic Relations," in Center for Hemispheric Studies, *Changing Dynamics of the Brazilian Economy: Occasional Papers Series*, no. 5, Howard Wiarda and Janine Perfit, eds. (Washington: American Enterprise Institute, 1983); Millard F. Long, "External Debt and the Trade Imperative in Latin America," in Baer and Gillis, eds., *Export Diversification* (for the complete reference, see Note 29).

77. For overviews, see Wayne A. Selcher, "Brazil in the World: Multipolarity as Seen by a Peripheral ADC Middle Power," in Ferris and Lincoln, eds., *Latin American Foreign Policies* (for the complete reference, see Note 16); Riordan Roett, "Brazilian Foreign Policy: Options in the 1980s," in Thomas C. Bruneau and Philippe Faucher, *Authoritarian Capitalism: Brazil's Contemporary Economic and Political Development* (Boulder: Westview Press, 1981). See also William Ascher's more speculative "Brazil's Future Foreign Relations," in Overholt, ed., *The Future of Brazil* (for the complete reference, see Note 51). For a historical reflection, see Alexandre de S.C. Barros, "The Formulation and Conduct of Brazilian Diplomacy," paper presented at the Meeting of the Latin American Studies Association, Washington, March 1982; and Gabriel Millán, "La política exterior del Brasil: su dimensión interna y su impacto en el nuevo equilibrio regional," in Sánchez, ed., *Las relaciones entre los países de América Latina* (for the complete reference, see Note 71). On territorial issues, see Domínguez, "Ghosts from the Past" (for the complete reference, see Note 66). On nuclear energy and nonproliferation, see John Redick, "Nuclear Trends in Latin America," in Viron P. Vaky, ed., *Governance in the Western Hemisphere* (for the complete reference, see Note 64).

9

Overcoming the psychological barrier: an analysis of the Egyptian–Israeli peace process

HERBERT C. KELMAN

Richard Clarke Cabot Professor of Social Ethics, Harvard University

The Egyptian–Israeli peace process, which started with President Sadat's trip to Jerusalem in November 1977, represents a major turning point in the Arab–Israeli conflict. A psychological threshold has been crossed in the history of that conflict, moving the idea of recognition and peace between the adversaries into the domain of the possible, the thinkable, the imaginable. I shall argue that the conditions allowing such a breakthrough to occur were provided by Sadat's dramatic initiative.

A strategy of unilateral reward, as used by Sadat, has the potential of overcoming profound psychological barriers and producing a major transformation of a protracted conflict relationship. The very magnitude of these effects, however, also makes such a strategy extremely risky. Large changes often bring into play equally large resistances and may thus set the stage for a major setback. The negative consequences of such a setback may be further amplified in view of the high expectations that the dramatic initiative has created. Thus, the features of the strategy that give it its potential strength may also be the source of some of its recurring difficulties.

This paper examines Sadat's initiative as a dramatic use of a strategy of unilateral reward, with the capacity of reversing widely held views of what is possible and thinkable. After describing Sadat's use of this strategy, it will explore where the strategy succeeded and where it failed and try to account for these successes and failures. Such an exploration might not only contribute to an understanding of the Egyptian–Israeli peace process, but also help us assess the potentialities and limitations of the use of unilateral rewards as a general influence strategy in international relations.

The impact of the Egyptian–Israeli peace process

Before turning to Sadat's strategy, let me explain why I see the process that started with the Sadat initiative as a major turning point in the Arab–

Israeli conflict. It is by no means certain that the Egyptian–Israeli peace agreement will lead to a stable, comprehensive peace in the region, or even that the Egyptian–Israeli relationship itself will endure. Yet, the process represents a turning point because it put to rest an assumption that had been unshakable up to that time: the assumption that no Arab state would ever recognize Israel and make peace with it. For Israelis, this was an assumption about empirical reality, which had taken on the character of ideological dogma; for Arabs, it was an ideological principle, which had taken on the character of a political imperative. Sadat's initiative and the ensuing peace process have demonstrated that the impossible is in fact possible and the unthinkable is thinkable. The fact that the Egyptian–Israeli peace—with all of its weaknesses and limitations—has survived the assassination of Sadat and the war in Lebanon has underscored the significance of this change.

The old dogmas have not been universally and fully abandoned. In Israel, there are still some who insist that peace with the Arabs (including Egypt) is impossible; others differentiate between Egypt and other Arab states and believe that a comprehensive Arab–Israeli peace is unattainable; still others can envisage only a peace based on superior Israeli power. In the Arab world, including the Palestinian community, there are still significant elements who consider the recognition of Israel as unthinkable; others, though ready to think the unthinkable, partly in response to the Egyptian–Israeli agreement, vigorously reject that agreement, thus diluting the impact of the change that has actually taken place. Nevertheless, the Egyptian–Israeli peace initiated by Sadat's move has at least broken the consensus on both sides about the validity of the old dogmas and reduced the certainty with which they are maintained.

The assault on these old assumptions has had a major impact on both communities, manifested, for example, in the emergence of new peace groups in Israel (such as Peace Now), which are predicated on the conviction that Arab–Israeli peace has now become possible and that serious exploration of new alternatives has therefore become necessary; in the adoption of the Fez proposals in 1982, in which—in a significant shift from earlier policy—the Arab states (with the sole exception of Libya) accept a political solution to the Arab–Israeli conflict that visualizes the continuing secure existence of Israel; and in the PLO's support for the Fez proposals and increasing readiness to pursue other options for political accommodation based on a two-state solution. Though these changes are not entirely attributable to the Egyptian–Israeli peace process (they have been accelerated, for example, by Israeli policies on the West Bank, by the war in Lebanon, and by the Reagan Plan), they reflect the growing assumption that Arab recognition of Israel and an Arab–Israeli peace agreement are realistic possibilities—within the range of what is empirically and ideologically imaginable.

It cannot be said that a new consensus around this assumption has taken shape in Israel, in the Palestinian community, or in the Arab world.

There is intense internal debate within each community, sometimes expressed in violent form. But this debate itself represents a major change in the psychological atmosphere resulting from the rupture in the old consensus. Even a total collapse of the Egyptian–Israeli relationship—though it would clearly reconfirm many in the view that the prospects for peace are indeed dismal—would probably not lead to a complete resurrection of the psychological *status quo ante*. Both parties have crossed a psychological threshold and come to conceive of Arab–Israeli recognition and peace as an outcome within the realm of what is historically possible.

Strategy of unilateral reward

The Sadat initiative and the ensuing peace treaty could not have occurred unless Egypt and Israel perceived a political settlement as congruent with their respective national interests. But it was by no means inevitable that the convergence of interests would in fact produce an agreement. It was Sadat's unique strategy—his ability to conceive, carry out, and follow through on an initiative that transcended the prevailing assumptions and broke the prevailing rules—which made this achievement possible.

In speaking of "Sadat's initiative," I do not mean to suggest that Sadat's trip to Jerusalem was a disembodied act, an entirely personal and spontaneous creation of Sadat's mind. It is undoubtedly true that Sadat's idiosyncratic characteristics, his worldview and self-concept, and his decision-making style contributed to his ability to take a daring, innovative step that other leaders would have eschewed under similar circumstances. This step, however, must be understood in the context of domestic and regional developments.[1] Starting with the 1967 war, and particularly after the 1973 war, Israel's permanent status in the region had become increasingly accepted as a reality within the Arab world (although explicit acknowledgment of that conclusion remained taboo). Within Egypt, there were signs of interest in an accommodation with Israel even during the Nasser regime, but these became more pronounced in the Sadat era. For Sadat, accommodation with Israel was closely linked to two major policy orientations: domestically, his open door policy (*infitah*), which increased the role of private investment in lieu of government involvement in economic development; and internationally, his alignment with the West, and especially the United States.[2] After the 1973 war, the interest in accommodation found concrete expression in the disengagement agreements between Egypt and Israel, as well as Syria and Israel, in 1974, and the second Sinai disengagement in 1975.

Thus, Sadat's trip to Jerusalem, though qualitatively different from earlier steps, can be seen as part of the evolution of Arab thinking and Egyptian policy. It is, moreover, not surprising that an Egyptian President was the first Arab leader to break the taboo against recognizing Israel. In an interesting analysis, Adeed Dawisha points out that "the Egyptians' spiritual links . . . with their own past and their own cultural heritage . . .

are so powerful that they have given Egypt a measure of independence from accepted Arab norms of political behavior."[3]

It must also be pointed out that, whether or not the specific idea of going to Jerusalem was Sadat's own or suggested by someone else, other actors certainly played a role in his search for new initiatives. Some of the impetus came from President Jimmy Carter (and, indeed, Sadat's gesture was directed as much to the United States as to Israel). Encouragement came from other political figures, in touch with both parties, such as Romanian President Nicolae Ceausescu. And there was indirect and at least some direct communication between Egypt and Israel about possible peace moves in the months preceding Sadat's initiative.[4]

Whatever the historical context that made Sadat's initiative possible and the various factors that contributed to it, the fact remains that his trip to Jerusalem was the decisive, visible step that changed the political landscape and set powerful new forces into motion. The strategy informing this step and Sadat's subsequent steps can be described as a strategy of unilateral reward. I use the term "reward" broadly to include positive incentives, following Louis Kriesberg's definition of rewards as "positive sanctions, offers or grants to the adversary of something it values, and made in anticipation of a reciprocating concession."[5] Sadat's offers, concessions, and conciliatory gestures represented unilateral initiatives, but they were not unconditional. There was a definite expectation of reciprocal acts and indeed some prior assurance that these would be forthcoming.

Sadat's unilateral initiative differed from those called for by Charles Osgood's GRIT strategy (graduated and reciprocated initiatives in tension reduction),[6] which starts with small concessions and gradually builds on these. Rather, he made a massive, fundamental concession by accepting the basic principles of Israel's position: its legitimacy, its security needs, and its definition of peace. He dramatically conceded Israel's legitimacy by paying a state visit to Jerusalem. He made explicit his understanding that any settlement would have to take account of Israel's security needs. He accepted the view, long propounded by Israel, that peace means normal relations, not just the end of belligerency. In accepting these fundamental Israeli principles Sadat was, in a sense, starting at the end in the anticipation that negotiations would fill in the intervening steps.

Sadat's initiative constituted an irreversible step, even though he made no specific commitments when he took that step. The mere fact that the leader of the largest Arab state came to Jerusalem and acknowledged Israel's legitimacy—and the broadcasting of that fact in a gripping drama, presented on a worldwide stage—created a new reality that from that point on could not be totally ignored or undone by any party. It was clear that, whatever else might happen, Sadat's initiative was in itself a fundamental concession that he could no longer withdraw. By offering himself as a hostage, as it were, he was giving substance to the strategy of unilateral reward. Sadat believed that such a step would break through the psychological barrier, offer Israel reassurances against its fears and suspicions, and create an atmosphere of mutual trust conducive to a peace agreement.

Sadat's concession was never unconditional; in effect, he offered it "on credit." He was clearly creating an obligation of reciprocal concessions on Israel's part. What he expected, in return for his acceptance of Israel's fundamental principles for a settlement, was Israeli acceptance of fundamental Arab principles, including territorial integrity and Palestinian national rights. He was explicit about that from the beginning, as evidenced by his address to the Knesset (the Israeli parliament). He made it very clear that his goal was a comprehensive peace, stressing in his Knesset speech that he had not come to Jerusalem to sign a separate agreement between Egypt and Israel.

It should be noted that Sadat never abandoned—at least at the level of policy pronouncements—his insistence on Palestinian rights. The Camp David accords incorporated a commitment to the legitimate rights of the Palestinian people and held out the possibility of an independent Palestinian state at the end of the transitional period of autonomy. It can be argued that the Camp David agreements did not sufficiently link the Egyptian–Israeli provisions to settlement of the Palestinian problem, and that the Egyptian–Israeli peace treaty that finally emerged was, for all intents and purposes, a bilateral agreement. But this outcome was not inherent in Sadat's strategy. In fact, I am inclined to view it as a deviation from his original strategy of making fundamental concessions to Israeli principles in return for parallel Israeli concessions at the level of Arab principles—a deviation probably due to a combination of Israeli bargaining tactics, u.s. pressures, and Arab rejection of Sadat's initiative.

One can only speculate about what would have happened if Sadat had adhered to his original strategy and insisted on linkage between an Egyptian–Israeli agreement and an agreement on the Palestinian issue. It is often assumed that, under those conditions, the Camp David accords and the Egyptian–Israeli peace treaty would never have been concluded. It is also possible, however, that such a stand by Sadat would have induced other Arabs, including Palestinians, to support him and thus created a wholly new dynamic conducive to a comprehensive settlement. Thus, there is some ambiguity as to whether the "deviation" in the strategy accounts for its success in achieving an Egyptian–Israeli agreement, or its failure to achieve a comprehensive agreement, or both.

Throughout the uneven course of Egypt's negotiations with Israel in the years following his 1977 initiative, Sadat remained committed to his strategy of unilateral rewards. On the whole, he took a conciliatory posture; he carried out the steps agreed upon at the proper time or even ahead of schedule (as did the Israelis); he introduced certain goodwill gestures (such as offering Nile waters to Israel for its development needs); he insisted on proceeding with agreed-upon elements of normalization, despite objections from his advisors. His explicit purpose in this approach was to reinforce his original effort at overcoming the psychological barriers in Israel, to reassure the Israelis, to avoid the resurgence of old suspicions, to build further confidence, to maintain momentum. Despite various ambiguities and inconsistencies, Sadat seemed to be pursuing a novel strategy, based on the use of positive incentives. How effective was this strategy?

Impact of the strategy on the adversary

In any assessment of the effectiveness of an influence strategy in international relations, the most obvious—though certainly not the only— question to be raised is what impact it has on the target of the influence. A social-psychological analysis suggests five possible mechanisms through which the use of rewards might influence an adversary to move in the direction of accommodation and conciliatory action.

1) Rewards may serve as *reinforcements*, in the technical psychological sense of strengthening the behavior that preceded them. Thus, if the reward is timed so as to follow some conciliatory gesture or signal of willingness to compromise on the part of the adversary, then it should increase the probability of further conciliatory or accommodative acts. Of course, the effect depends on precisely how the adversary perceives the behavior that is being reinforced, i.e., on the nature of that behavior from the target's own perspective.

2) Rewards may create *incentives* for conciliatory behavior on the part of the adversary by enhancing both the attractiveness of a peaceful settlement of the conflict and the perceived probability that such a settlement could be achieved. The rewards, in other words, may encourage a conciliatory response by signaling that accommodation has a high probability of producing an attractive outcome.

3) Rewards may produce a *change in the image* that the adversary holds of the party initiating the gesture. They may provide new information about the other's interests, intentions, and credibility. The new image may be conducive to accommodation by suggesting that the other has the will and capacity to seek a settlement and by engendering a greater degree of trust in the other's sincerity.

4) Rewards may contribute to a *reduction in tension*, by creating an atmosphere of goodwill, of optimism, and of positive expectations. Such an atmosphere, coupled with changing images, is conducive to the development of mutual trust and the exploration of common interests and possibilities for compromise.

5) Probably the most important effect of rewards is that they may set off an *obligation to reciprocate* on the part of the adversary. The strength of this obligation depends on the degree to which the adversaries are co-members of a community and thus subject to a shared norm of reciprocity. In the absence of this condition, third parties play an important role in inducing adversaries to live up to the normatively prescribed requirement of reciprocating positive gestures.

Although the combination of these mechanisms makes it likely that unilateral rewards will be reciprocated by conciliatory behaviors on the part of the adversary, one can also postulate reasons why or conditions under which a strategy of unilateral reward might be ineffective or even counter-productive. For example, significant elements in the adversary's camp may not be interested in the positive gestures that are offered because they prefer (for whatever reason) to continue the conflict or because they are not pre-pared to pay the price (by way of reciprocal concessions) entailed by the other's offer. It is also possible that the conciliatory gestures may not be sufficiently powerful to overcome strongly held attitudes of hostility and distrust. They may therefore be reinterpreted—usually with the active help of those elements who prefer the *status quo* to a compromise solution—as tactical maneuvers, as attempts to deceive and psychologically disarm your side, or as insincere posturing designed to gain a public-relations ad-vantage. Finally, a strategy of unilateral rewards may be read by the ad-versary not as a sign of conciliation and readiness to compromise, but as a sign of weakness. The adversary may respond, therefore, by pocketing the first party's concessions and proceeding to take advantage of its exposed position, rather than by offering reciprocal concessions. The last possibility is usually cited by those who oppose a strategy based on positive incentives.

While some such negative effects may have cropped up in the Israeli reaction to the Sadat initiative, they were decisively outweighed, at least in the initial stages, by the initiative's positive effects. Each of the five mech-anisms described above seemed to play a role in moving Israel toward reciprocation of Sadat's conciliatory gestures. The Sadat initiative—by clearly disproving the strongly held expectation that no Arab leader would ever accept Israel's legitimacy and make peace with it—produced significant changes in Israeli images of Egypt. Although it was widely assumed that Sadat was motivated by the pressing needs of Egyptian society (including the country's economic problems), his initiative was seen as a sign of strength rather than weakness. Israelis came to perceive Egypt (whose image had been undergoing gradual change even prior to Sadat's initiative) as having a clear national interest in peaceful resolution of the conflict and as sincerely seeking a settlement based on compromise. The trust in Egypt's intentions implicit in this changing atmosphere was enhanced by the dramatic reduc-tion in tension between the two countries occasioned by Sadat's visit to

Jerusalem. Many of Sadat's actions in the course of his trip, such as the round of handshakes on his arrival at the airport, his visit to Yad va-Shem (the Holocaust memorial), and his statements about Israel's security requirements, conveyed a sensitivity to Israeli needs that further contributed to the development of trust.

Perhaps the most significant positive effect of the Sadat initiative was that it created powerful incentives among Israelis for entering into a process of serious negotiation and bringing it to a successful completion. The Sadat visit broke through the profound pessimism that had pervaded Israeli thinking. By persuading Israelis that acceptance and peace were indeed possible, it gave birth to an exciting vision of the future that they had not dared to entertain before. The desire to hold on to this vision and to fulfill it provided a major incentive for Israelis to reciprocate Sadat's initiative and to pursue a conciliatory course. The expectations of the Israeli public and of the world at large created an obligation to reciprocate that the Israeli leadership could not ignore, even if it had been inclined to do so. Furthermore, the immediate positive response by the Israeli government to Sadat's initial offer to come to Jerusalem provided the conditions for reinforcement of conciliatory behavior: Israeli accommodation was followed by the actual delivery of the very significant reward that Sadat had offered. This initial experience set the stage for an Israeli policy of reciprocation, which helped to set the Egyptian–Israeli peace process into motion.

The strategy of unilateral reward was thus effective in inducing the desired reciprocal response in the adversary and in setting into motion a process that culminated in the Egyptian–Israeli peace treaty (although that culmination point was reached only with great difficulty and after many reversals, and thanks to very active American intervention). Despite some dissenting voices, this treaty is generally regarded as serving the national interest within each of the countries. At the same time, there is wide agreement that the Egyptian–Israeli peace process did not wholly fulfill itself, that it did not produce the kind and amount of change that many had hoped for, either at the level of attitudes or at the level of policy. Some analysts, particularly on the Arab side, go even further and argue that Camp David and the ensuing Egyptian–Israeli treaty have retarded rather than advanced the prospects for peace in the Middle East. Let me first describe and then try to explain the limited success of Sadat's strategy in achieving Egyptian and Israeli goals and in creating movement toward comprehensive peace.

Limited success of the strategy

In describing the course of attitude change, social psychologists have distinguished three steps: *unfreezing*, which refers to the processes involved in overcoming resistance to change and loosening up the personal and social forces that tend to stabilize existing attitudes; *changing*, which refers to the processes whereby new attitudes are induced; and *refreezing*, which refers to the ways in which these new attitudes are integrated into cognitive and social structures and thus, to a degree, stabilized.[7] In terms of this framework, it can be said that the Sadat initiative and the ensuing events have succeeded in unfreezing the old attitudes—in Israel as well as in the Arab world—but it can hardly be said that new attitudes have fully developed and certainly not that these have become "refrozen" or integrated.

In part, of course, this limited progress can be attributed to time: Given the protracted and intense character of the conflict, it would be unrealistic to expect new attitudes to take shape and to become integrated overnight. But, apart from time, it would appear that certain systematic barriers to change are operating, since there are many indications in Israel and in Egypt that the attitude change process is moving backward rather than forward. For example, many of the old suspicions have reemerged on both sides and a mood of pessimism seems once again to pervade the atmosphere.[8] In my view, the unfreezing effect of the Sadat initiative has not been reversed; it manifests itself in the breakdown of the old assumption, or at least of the consensus around the old assumption, that the recognition of Israel and Arab–Israeli peace are impossible. But attitude change at the official or mass level has not moved far beyond this first step in the process.

The limited progress at the level of attitudes is paralleled by limited progress at the level of national policy and national action. The failures at the policy level have clearly slowed down the process of attitude change, and the limited progress in the restructuring of attitudes has probably contributed, in turn, to the policy failures. The Sadat initiative did succeed in setting into motion a process that culminated in the Egyptian–Israeli peace treaty. The most visible achievement of this treaty from Israel's point of view was the establishment of diplomatic relations with Egypt; the most visible achievement from Egypt's point of view was Israel's withdrawal from the Sinai. In both countries there is the widespread feeling that the end of military confrontation between them serves the national interest (although for many Egyptians guilt and shame, in the wake of the Lebanon war, have created some ambivalence in this regard).

Whether—beyond Israel's and Egypt's perceived interests—the Egyptian–Israeli treaty contributes to a just and comprehensive peace in the Middle East is a matter of judgment. In my own view, it does, despite its limited and bilateral nature, just as the mere unfreezing of old attitudes does. It demonstrates the possibility of a peaceful resolution of the Arab–Israeli conflict, it strengthens internal and external forces acting on Israel to pursue a broader peace (in part by maintaining within Israel the vision of the future and the incentive for compromise generated by Sadat's initiative), and it strengthens the incentive for peaceful resolution of the conflict in the Arab world.

Whatever our evaluation of the Egyptian–Israeli peace treaty, we can agree that it fell short of the goals that many had hoped would be achieved by the Sadat initiative. The process set into motion by this initiative has not so far shown any progress toward the comprehensive agreement desired by Sadat and proclaimed in the Camp David accords. In fact, it has been argued that the Egyptian–Israeli peace treaty made it easier for the Israeli government to pursue aggressive policies in the occupied territories and in Lebanon, thus undermining potential progress toward a comprehensive peace. Nor has there been much progress toward the normalization of relations between Egypt and Israel—a major goal from the Israeli perspective. The lack of movement toward a comprehensive peace (and particularly toward a solution of the Palestinian problem) has been one—though by no means the only—factor contributing to slowing down the normalization process; the war in Lebanon has brought it to a virtual halt. Thus, the process started by the Sadat initiative has failed to produce movement on the Palestinian problem and normalization, the two acid tests of genuine, long-term change for Egypt and Israel, respectively.

In sum, the evidence suggests that the Sadat strategy did have the expected initial impact on Israeli society. The impact was sufficiently powerful to unfreeze old attitudes on both sides, making the successful conclusion of the Egyptian–Israeli peace agreement possible. Nevertheless, this powerful psychological impact has proved insufficient so far to produce a more thorough restructuring of attitudes or to move the peace process forward to the comprehensive agreement and the normalization of relations that the parties had hoped to achieve. To understand this relative failure (or incomplete success) of the strategy, it is necessary to look beyond the dramatic, global influence that Sadat's initiative had on attitudes in the two societies, and to explore its differential effects on the different domains of attitude and different segments of society, as well as the more subtle effects that the resulting peace process has had on attitudes within each society and on the interaction between the two. Such an exploration should reveal some of the shortcomings and some of the unintended side effects of Sadat's strategy, which together put limits on the possibilities of change.

More specifically, I shall propose that the single most important factor that has interfered with the process has been a fundamental difference in the perceived interests of the two parties. Although they have shared throughout an interest in achieving peace between their two countries, a central goal of Egyptian policy has been that this peace go beyond a separate Egyptian–Israeli arrangement, whereas a central goal of Israeli policy has been to restrict it to a bilateral process. These contrasting views are the outcome of divisions *within* each society about the peace process as a whole. In launching his strategy, Sadat failed to address himself to the divisions in the Arab world and within Egypt itself, and to take adequate account of the divisions within Israel. As a result, the reward he offered to Israel was not sufficiently credible and attractive to important segments of Israeli society to bridge the gap in perceived interests between the two parties. This shortcoming may be characteristic of a strategy of unilateral reward, because—by starting at the end, as it were, and jumping over intervening steps—such a strategy is less capable of building consensus at home and testing reactions abroad than a more gradual approach to negotiation. The differences and divisions, apart from interfering with the positive evolution of the peace process and limiting attitude change, led to actions by each party that rearoused mistrust and confirmed old attitudes. These trends were further intensified by indirect effects of the strategy of unilateral reward that contributed to sharpening the preexisting divisions within each party and differences between them.

Separate versus comprehensive peace

President Sadat and Prime Minister Begin, along with large majorities of their respective societies, had a common interest in achieving an Egyptian–Israeli peace agreement. It has become increasingly clear, however, that there were fundamental differences between them in the meaning they attached to such an agreement.

For Sadat, the ultimate goal was a comprehensive peace and he saw an Egyptian–Israeli understanding as a first step in that direction (and clearly this view underlies Egyptian policy today, under President Mubarak). Under American pressure, and in the absence of Arab support, Sadat ultimately accepted a bilateral agreement at Camp David. But he always saw a comprehensive peace as essential to Egyptian interests and he undertook his initiative on the assumption that, by overcoming the psychological barrier, he would elicit Israeli commitment to such a peace which, in turn, would bring the other Arab actors into the process. Within Egypt itself, Sadat could count on a consensus in favor of a comprehensive peace, but not in favor of a separate peace.

By contrast, Begin could count on an Israeli consensus in favor of a separate peace, but not in favor of a comprehensive peace. Whereas in Egypt (and, even more so, elsewhere in the Arab world) nothing less than a comprehensive peace could gain widespread support, in Israel nothing more than a separate peace could be assured of general approval. To be sure, Sadat's initiative aroused a strong (though far from universal) interest in a comprehensive peace within Israel. This vision captured not only large segments of the Israeli public, but also key members of the first Begin administration. Ezer Weizman and Moshe Dayan were responsive to Sadat's efforts to broaden the peace because of their commitment to keeping the Egyptian–Israeli process on track. It is possible that Begin himself was initially captured by the vision of a comprehensive peace, although many analysts now propose that his strategy from the beginning was to exchange the Sinai for the West Bank—that he saw generous Israeli concessions to Egypt as a way of consolidating the Israeli position in the other occupied territories. In any event, by the time of the Camp David meetings, Begin's interest was clearly in a separate peace, and this remained the interest of the Shamir government.

Sadat was undoubtedly aware that Israel's primary interest was in a separate peace, but he believed that his dramatic and generous gesture could bridge the gap and induce Israel toward a comprehensive peace. He made the further assumption that significant Arab—including Palestinian—elements would follow his lead in accommodation with Israel. It soon became apparent that he was caught in a vicious circle: Without Arab and Palestinian support, it was difficult to attract Israel to the concept of a comprehensive peace; but without Israeli commitment to that concept, it was impossible to entice Arab actors into joining the process.

Sadat clearly overestimated the Arab support that he would receive for his unilateral action. The widespread rejection of his initiative and accusations of treason against him in the Arab world, which escalated even further after the signing of the Camp David accords, also contributed to an erosion of his domestic support. Many Egyptian elites were skeptical about Sadat's initiative from the beginning, primarily because of their concern over Egypt's separation from the rest of the Arab world. As it became more apparent that a bilateral agreement was in the making, these domestic critics distanced themselves from the process as much as they could. The lack of Arab support and the half-hearted domestic support for Sadat's policy had their impact on Israeli attitudes. For present purposes, the relevant effect is that Arab rejection of Sadat's initiative made his call for comprehensive peace considerably less credible in Israeli eyes. Clearly, Sadat was not in a position to deliver rewards—in the form of recognition and the promise of normal relations—on behalf of other Arab actors. Hence, he was also unable to induce in Israelis the changed images, the enhanced trust, and the obligation to reciprocate, that would have encouraged them to make the concessions necessary to broadening the peace process.

Sadat's failure to pay adequate attention to the impact of his initiative on Arab and domestic Egyptian constituencies limited the effectiveness of his strategy by reducing the credibility of the rewards he was offering, particularly as inducements for Israel to embrace the concept of a comprehensive peace. It must be kept in mind, however, that this relative disregard of his Arab and domestic constituencies helped to make his initiative possible in the first place. Had he been concerned about consensus, he would have been much less likely to take the daring, taboo-breaking step of flying to Jerusalem. Thus, the partial failure of the strategy is made of the same cloth as its dramatic, if partial, success: The same attributes that made it possible for Sadat to initiate the peace process also made it difficult for him to expand it.

Sadat made another miscalculation in underestimating the resistances within Israel to the kinds of concessions—on the West Bank and Gaza Strip, on Jerusalem, and on the Golan Heights—required for a comprehensive peace agreement. Many Israelis were then and are now prepared to entertain significant concessions on these fronts, particularly in response to the sense of opportunity engendered by Sadat's initiative. But Israeli society is deeply divided on this issue. For many Israelis, the reward offered by Sadat was not sufficiently attractive to compensate for the costs of withdrawing from these territories—the less so in that the reward was recognition by and normalization with Egypt in return for concessions to be made to Syria, Jordan, and the Palestinians. Sadat's reward, despite its powerful impact, was incapable of overcoming this particular psychological barrier and generating an Israeli consensus in favor of a comprehensive peace. At best, he was able to create or reinforce the incentive for broadening the peace among those segments of Israeli society that were inclined toward compromise on the Palestinian issue and/or on the Syrian and Jordanian front.

With respect to these non-Egyptian issues, Begin was not the appropriate partner for Sadat's initiative. Begin was probably the Israeli leader most ideally suited to starting the process in response to Sadat's initiative: Like Sadat, he was given to grand gestures; he was not as worried, as Labor Party leaders might have been, about criticisms from his right; and he was probably convinced that he would know how to contain the process and avoid yielding on those issues that were ideologically central to him. By the same token, however, Begin was not the Israeli leader suited to expanding the process. However much he may have been moved toward a comprehensive peace in the beginning (a point on which observers differ), he was bound to be constrained by his own long-time ideological commitments, as well as by his core constituency. He was particularly sensitive to any criticism that he was endangering the territorial integrity of the Land of Israel and therefore intent on demonstrating that the disposition of the Sinai would not serve as a precedent for the West Bank. Thus, for Begin, as much as for Sadat, it can be said that the same attributes that enabled him to initiate the peace process also made it difficult for him to expand it.

Sadat's overestimation of the Arab and Egyptian support that his initiative would elicit and underestimation of Israeli resistances to the comprehensive peace he called for can be attributed in part to his idiosyncratic characteristics. It may well be, however, that a strategy of unilateral reward, at least as practiced by Sadat, with the crucial elements of drama and surprise, is particularly vulnerable to this kind of miscalculation. This strategy, as I have proposed, starts at the end, in the anticipation that negotiations would fill in the intervening steps. This may well mean skipping over such critical steps as building consensus at home, garnering the support of important allies, exploring the elements of flexibility and resistance in the adversary's camp, and testing the reactions of relevant parties to various possible moves. These are the kinds of steps that are typically pursued as part of a more gradual prenegotiating and negotiating process. In principle, such preparatory activities can be undertaken in conjunction with a strategy of unilateral reward, but they are not entirely compatible with the elements of spontaneity and surprise that enhance the impact of dramatic gestures.

In any event, it soon became apparent that Sadat's gesture was sufficiently credible and attractive to Israel to elicit a reciprocal response to

Egypt, but not enough to draw Israel into a commitment to a comprehensive peace. The resulting gap between the two parties in their perceived goals of the peace process made it very difficult for them to reach an agreement and, time and again, negotiations were on the verge of breaking off. Only the active intervention of President Carter ensured the signing of the Camp David accords in 1978 and the peace treaty in 1979. These difficulties and disappointments in the interaction between the two parties—and the increasing awareness of their fundamental policy differences—soured the relationship. As a result, old stereotypes were resurrectd, old suspicions were rearoused, and the development of new attitudes was severely inhibited. Each party tended to conclude that the other was not sincerely interested in peace—in peace, of course, according to each party's own definition.[9]

Their different conceptions of the peace process, moreover, led each party to engage in actions that reconfirmed the other's earlier attitudes. When Israel accelerated its settlement process in the West Bank, annexed Jerusalem and the Golan, bombed the Iraqi nuclear reactor and Beirut targets, and, above all, invaded Lebanon in 1982, Egyptians were shocked and embarrassed. They felt that the Israeli government was undermining them and was violating the spirit, if not the letter, of the peace process. From the Israeli point of view, these actions against other Arab parties were not precluded by what they saw as a separate peace process with Egypt. In engaging in this process, they were not accepting any constraints vis-à-vis other Arab parties, who were not involved in the negotiations. From the Egyptian point of view, however, these actions—clearly inconsistent with their idea of comprehensive peace—demonstrated that Israel was not committed to peace and was taking advantage of the Egyptian–Israeli peace process to pursue its aggressive policies. They thus found in these actions confirmation of their earlier attitudes about Israel's aggressiveness, expansionism, and untrustworthiness.

Both the Egyptian government and various elites within Egyptian society often responded to Israeli actions that they found embarrassing by slowing down or reversing the normalization process. One of the more recent and dramatic of these gestures was the recall of the Egyptian Ambassador from Israel after the massacres at Sabra and Shatila. Slowing down normalization is one of the few sanctions Egyptians can apply to Israel without going back on the peace treaty. It is also a way of dissociating themselves from Israeli actions against Arab parties and denying complicity in them. Although Egypt's "cold peace" policy has become more pronounced since the Lebanon war, Egyptians at official and unofficial levels have been holding back on normalization from the beginning. They have consistently limited the number and variety of exchanges, joint projects, and cooperative economic activities with Israel in which they have involved themselves. From their point of view, full normalization must await achievement of, or at least steady movement toward, a comprehensive peace. Thus, their reluctance to normalize relationships with Israel is not inconsistent with the peace process as they perceive it. From the Israeli point of view, however, Egyptians' unwillingness to extend the normalization process is inconsistent with the peace treaty. It indicates that Egyptians are insincere, that they are not fully committed to peace with Israel, and that now that they have regained the Sinai, they are going back on their part of the bargain. As a result, Israeli mistrust of Egypt has again been aroused and earlier attitudes have been revived.

Similar reactions have been engendered in Israel by Egyptian expressions of support for the PLO and efforts at rapprochement with the Arab world, both of which have been accelerated during the Mubarak administration. From the Egyptian point of view, these actions are not inconsistent with the peace treaty, since Egyptians do not regard their agreement with Israel as a separate peace, but as an opening toward a comprehensive peace. Improving their relations with the Arab world, they would assert, can only help to bring such a comprehensive peace closer to realization. From the Israeli point of view, however, any move toward the PLO and other Arab elements which are still at war with Israel is a move away from Israel. It raises questions in their minds about Egyptian sincerity, trustworthiness, and long-term commitment to peace.

So far I have proposed that Sadat was confronted with a fundamental difference in perceived interests between Egypt and Israel, which was magnified by divisions within each society. His initiative did not succeed in bridging this difference, in moving Israel from its interest in a separate peace with Egypt toward the Egyptian concept of a comprehensive peace. The different meanings assigned to the peace process by each party made it difficult for them to reach agreement and also led each party to engage in actions that the other found inconsistent with its own view of the process. As a result, old suspicions were rearoused, earlier attitudes were reconfirmed, and the possibilities for change were severely limited. Thus, the failure of the initiative to address adequately important differences between the parties and divisions within each party set limits on the kinds of changes at the policy level and at the level of attitudes that the ensuing peace process was able to achieve. It is also possible, however, that the strategy itself may have had an indirect effect of intensifying preexisting divisions and differences and thus further setting limits on the possibilities of change. Specifically, I shall suggest two types of effects of the strategy that may have made attitude change less likely to occur: It sharpened some of the internal conflicts within each society, which made certain kinds of change more controversial and more costly; and it created unrealistic expectations about the other, which were frustrated and therefore led to a resurgence of old attitudes.

Effects of ambivalence and polarization

The Egyptian–Israeli peace process, following the Sadat initiative, made the possibility of ending the conflict more real, more palpable, than it had ever been before. This created a sense of opportunity, hope, and excitement, which strengthened the motivation to move the process forward. Psychologists speak of this phenomenon as the "goal gradient": Evidence suggests that the motivation to achieve a goal increases the closer the individual comes to that goal. But the goal gradient effect operates not only on approach tendencies, but also on avoidance tendencies. If the endpoint toward which we are moving is unknown, frightening, or noxious, then our level of anxiety and our desire to pull back will increase the closer we come to that point. When a particular goal is both desirable and anxiety-producing, we speak of an approach-avoidance conflict, which is characterized by a high degree of vacillation. How such a conflict is resolved depends on the relative steepness of the approach and avoidance gradients.

The peace process, in addition to arousing strong positive incentives on each side, also created doubts, anxieties, and various kinds of objections— ideological as well as pragmatic. As the possibility of a settlement became more palpable following the Sadat initiative (and particularly once the initial excitement abated), these avoidance tendencies were heightened. On both sides there was an increased awareness of the risks, as well as the potential benefits, of a peace agreement. It is not unlikely that the avoidance gradient rose more steeply than the approach gradient as such an agreement became closer, since there is a general tendency in intense conflicts to give greater weight to the risks of underestimating the enemy's hostility than to the risks of underestimating the enemy's readiness to make peace.

Serious doubts were raised, on both sides, about the implications of a peace agreement: Will it really work? Are we leaving ourselves defenseless? Will the contact have a corrupting effect on our values and way of life? Some Israelis objected on ideological grounds to the return of any territory or the dismantlement of any settlement. Most Israelis were worried that return of the Sinai would weaken Israel's security. Furthermore, there was concern about the precise endpoint of the process. There was fear that the return of territory to Egypt would set a precedent for the return of the West Bank and Gaza, to which many Israelis objected on security grounds, some on ideological grounds. Many Egyptians, in turn, had ideological objections to the recognition of Israel. Some elements of the Egyptian intelligentsia, in particular, had great emotional and cognitive difficulties in adjusting to the idea of a Jewish state ensconced in the Middle East. There was great concern that the process would end as a separate peace, further alienating Egypt from the rest of the Arab world. This alienation was feared by many for both ideological and pragmatic reasons. Finally, many Egyptians were concerned that a peace agreement would constitute a betrayal of the Palestinians—or be seen as such.

For these various reasons, most Israelis and Egyptians were ambivalent about the peace process. Even those who were enthusiastic about it had some lingering doubts and anxieties, which were heightened as the prospect of a settlement became more real. But the strength of the approach and avoidance tendencies differed among different individuals and groups within each society. For some, the approach tendencies predominated. A good example are the members of the Peace Now movement in Israel, whose main concern was to ensure that the opportunity created by the Egyptian–Israeli peace process would not be missed. For others, avoidance tendencies predominated, which led to organized opposition either to the Egyptian–Israeli peace process itself or, more commonly, to a particular interpretation of the impending peace agreement. In Egypt, objections focused on the fear that the process would produce *merely* a separate Egyptian–Israeli agreement, whereas in Israel objections focused on the fear that it would produce *more than* a separate agreement.

Thus, the ambivalence at the individual level was accompanied by conflict at the societal level, a conflict that predated Sadat's initiative, but was sharpened by the sense that a settlement had suddenly become a realistic, early possibility. In Israel, the societal division led to a polarization between those who saw the Egyptian–Israeli peace as opening opportunities for a comprehensive peace and were prepared to make significant concessions to the Palestinians to that end, and those who saw the Egyptian–Israeli peace as an opportunity to crush the PLO and impose their own solution on the West Bank and Gaza. This polarization has persisted and, in fact, has become even sharper since the Lebanon war. In Egypt, the internal division reflected the polarization of the Arab world caused by the Sadat initiative and the ensuing peace process. Egyptian critics of Sadat's policy were not opposed to the search for a political settlement as such, but to what they saw as Sadat's readiness to accept a settlement that would damage the Palestinian cause and undermine Egypt's Arab relations.

The elements in each society for whom avoidance tendencies predominated, i.e., who were most impressed by the dangers of the process and were bent on containing it, gained political and psychological strength from the ambivalence that marked the reactions of even the enthusiastic proponents of the process. Since the process was risky and its final outcome unknown, since it required trust in a historical enemy and faith in the dynamics of the process itself, it was relatively easy to generate doubt, anxiety, and even guilt in the proponents. The proponents of the process were psychologically and politically vulnerable to the critics' charges that they were endangering the survival of the nation, contributing to disunity, or betraying the national cause. Even if they felt certain about their positions, they had to worry about becoming politically irrelevant or even worse. In terms of the goal gradient hypothesis, the social pressures applied by the opponents can be said to have affected the slope of the avoidance gradient, causing it to be steeper than the approach gradient, even among moderates.

As a result of these dynamics, the critics—the "avoidance" elements, for want of a better term—were able to dictate the terms of the debate within each society. Even proponents of the peace process felt it necessary to dissociate themselves from the most controversial aspects of the process. In Egypt, this meant dissociation from any activities that could be perceived as part of normalization, since such activities represented a symbolic re-enactment of the larger process of accommodation between Egypt and Israel at the expense of the Palestinians. Egyptians concerned about their status in the Arab world were particularly averse to be seen (and to see themselves) as personally benefiting from a "sell-out." In Israel, most of the proponents of the peace process were careful to dissociate themselves from views that explicitly favored Palestinian self-determination, a Palestinian state, or dealing with the PLO. Ironically, as larger segments of the society—those captured by the vision generated by the Sadat initiative—came to see the central importance of satisfying Palestinian rights in order to achieve a comprehensive settlement, the Sheli Party, which explicitly favored a Palestinian state and communication with the PLO, became isolated and politically irrelevant.

Thus, the conflicts generated by the peace process in the form of ambivalence at the individual level and polarization at the societal level had the consequence of containing the process. The internal dynamics of the two societies severely limited the interactions between them. In view of the steepness of the avoidance gradient, Israelis and Egyptians avoided precisely those activities that could have contributed most to reassuring the other, to building confidence, to heightening the other's sense of opportunity, to maintaining the other's vision of peace—the Egyptians' vision of a comprehensive peace, rather than a peace that isolates Egypt from the Arab world, and the Israelis' vision of a peace based on normal relations, rather than a peace that continues their pariah status in the Middle East. It is not surprising, therefore, that both parties were disappointed and felt a sense of betrayal and that old attitudes of distrust and suspicion reemerged.

Effects of frustrated expectations

Disappointment and distrust were heightened by another indirect consequence of Sadat's strategy. The dramatic commitment to peace by Egypt and Israel in response to Sadat's initiative created, on each side, some rather idealized notions about the change that the other had undergone and therefore certain unrealistic expectations about the other's actions and reactions. Each side seemed to assume that the other had turned around and been converted to its views of the conflict, of the nature of the adversaries, and of the requirements and goals of the peace process. They were not sufficiently cognizant of the fact that the other party, though sincere about the peace process, was not thereby abandoning its own perspective, its own interests, its own view of history. The internal divisions within each party and the narrowing of the peace process, discussed above, soon revealed that the initial high expectations were unwarranted and that fundamental differences between the two sides still prevailed. In keeping with the social-psychological concept of relative deprivation, these differences were experienced as more acutely disturbing relative to the higher level of expectation that the peace process had produced. Moreover, as it became clear to each party that the other did not conform to its expectations, both began to feel that they had been deceived and exploited, that the other was insincere, and that perhaps their old suspicions and pessimism were justified. Three major areas of misunderstanding and conflict that have cropped up in Egyptian–Israeli relations since the Sadat initiative can help illustrate the dynamics of frustrated expectations leading to the reemergence of old suspicions.

1) Differences in what is viewed as proper reciprocation. The Egyptians—and the rest of the Arab world—saw Sadat's visit to Jerusalem and his acceptance of Israel's legitimacy as major concessions at the level of fundamental principles. Egyptians expected Israel to reciprocate at the same level by explicitly accepting fundamental Arab principles for a settlement. From their perspective, Israel simply pocketed these concessions and then proceeded to haggle about details. They reacted with bitterness, resentment, and indignation to what they saw as Israel's failure to distinguish between an offer of a new relationship based on friendship and conciliation, and a transaction at a bazaar. An appropriate response, from their point of view, would have shown sensitivity to Egypt's Arab identity, its position in the Arab world, and its concern about the Palestinian issue, just as Sadat showed sensitivity to Israel's concerns about legitimacy and security. Even though Israel clearly made very major concessions, particularly in agreeing to withdraw from the whole of the Sinai, a common Egyptian view was that it did not reciprocate Sadat's initiative at all. They seemed to focus more on the process than on the substance of the Israeli response. As a result, they were reconfirmed in their old view that Israelis cannot be trusted, that they are likely to take advantage of your friendship, and that it is impossible to enter into a reciprocal relationship with them.

Israelis, for their part, felt that they had more than reciprocated Egyptian concessions. They did not see Sadat's initiative as a concession, but as an acknowledgment of what they had always considered to be true and self-evident—that Israel had a legitimate right to secure existence in the Middle East. They deeply appreciated this acknowledgment as demonstrated in their warm reaction to Sadat, but they did not see that it called for any response other than gratitude and a readiness to sit down and negotiate. After all, they had always acknowledged Egypt's legitimate right to secure existence in the Middle East and Sadat's initiative simply provided the basis for Egypt and Israel to enter into negotiation on equal terms. For Israelis, Egyptian insistence on statements of principles suggested a reluctance to tackle concrete issues and hence a failure to bargain in good faith. Israelis were also resentful and suspicious about Egyptian accusations that they were not reciprocating their concessions, since they felt that in fact their concessions were more substantial than the Egyptians'. They were giving up tangibles—land, air fields, strategic depth, oil wells, settlements—in return for Egyptian words. The experience raised doubts in Israeli minds about Egyptian sincerity and trustworthiness.

The differences in perception here reflect, in part, cultural differences in the meaning attached to conciliatory gestures and in negotiating styles. But they also reflect differences in perspectives, as well as in interests. For the Egyptians, Israeli gestures indicating a shift in ideology and acceptance of Arab principles were of great importance, because they would have demonstrated that the Sadat initiative had in fact produced a visible return from the Palestinian and Arab point of view. Begin, on the other hand, had an interest in saying as little as possible about general principles, particularly with respect to Palestinian rights, since he was in fact not prepared to make major concessions on that front. In focusing on bargaining details, he was pursuing his interest in working out the visible manifestations of Egyptian–Israeli peace (e.g., diplomatic relations, trade arrangements, tourism), while avoiding any pressure to go beyond bilateral issues. Thus, the apparent misunderstanding about the proper form of reciprocation reflected an important difference in perceived interests, which was amplified by the heightened expectations in the wake of Sadat's initiative.

2) Differences between own and other's definition of each party's national identity. The Sadat initiative and the Israeli response to it created the expectation of mutual acceptance of each other's identity. However, Egyptian–Israeli interactions at the political and personal level have revealed to each party that the other does not fully accept the first party's own definition of its collective identity.

Egyptians accept the reality of the state of Israel and they often express friendly sentiments toward Jews as a religious group that has lived in the Arab world for generations. They find it difficult, however, to conceive of Jews as a nation with a right to a state of its own. Now that this religious group has—inappropriately, in their view—managed to acquire a state, they are prepared to come to terms with it, but they do not regard it as a realization of historically based Jewish national rights. Thus, they do not accept the Zionist foundation of the state and their image of Israel's eventual integration in the region implies a dezionized Israel.[10]

Israelis, for their part, have not fully accepted the Arab part of Egypt's identity. They have tended to interpret Egypt's rapprochement with Israel as a decision on the part of the Egyptians to resolve their conflict between Egyptian and Arab identity by opting for the former. Thus, they have emphasized and indeed tried to encourage Egypt's separation from the Arab world and have often structured situations so as to confront Egypt with the necessity to choose between its Arab and its Israeli connection. They clearly preferred and expected to deal with a dearabized Egypt, just as the Egyptians preferred and expected to deal with a dezionized Israel.

Israelis and Egyptians both have perceived such reactions as profoundly threatening to their group identity and insensitive to their needs. The discovery that Egyptians did not really accept the validity of Jewish nationhood cast doubt in Israeli minds about their sincerity in the peace process and about their ultimate intentions. The Egyptians' apparent image of Israel's future integration in the region (which, from the Egyptian point of view, was an indication of their readiness to welcome Israel in their midst) was perceived by Israelis as a threat to the Jewish identity of the state and an attempt to strip it gradually of its unique character.[11]

The Egyptians, in turn, saw Israel's attempt to separate Egypt from the other Arabs as threatening to their Arab identity (however ambivalent they themselves may feel about that identity) and to their status in the Arab world. They felt that, in making them choose between Israel and the Arabs (e.g., by pressuring them to abandon the Palestinian cause), the Israelis were displaying insensitivity to Egypt's needs, were embarrassing Egypt, and were undermining Egyptians' ability to pursue their broad range of activities embedded in the Arab context. They saw the Israeli attitude as an indication that Israel was seeking domination over Egypt, rather than a comprehensive peace.

Furthermore, the failure of each side to conform to the identity that the other was ascribing to it became another source of renewed distrust. When the Egyptians affirmed their Arab identity and sought to reintegrate themselves in the Arab world, Israelis tended to perceive this as a threat and an indication of Egypt's low commitment to peace with Israel. When the Israelis affirmed the Zionist identity of their state, Egyptians tended to perceive this as a sign of Israel's unwillingness to become integrated in the region and to live in peace and on a basis of equality with its neighbors.

3) Differences in the perceived goal of the peace process. I have already discussed in detail what I see as perhaps the fundamental problem in Egyptian–Israeli relations: the increasing realization by both parties that they have been pursuing contradictory goals in the peace process. The Egyptian quest for a comprehensive peace and the Israeli quest for a separate peace have created conflicts in their negotiations and have caused each party to engage in actions—consistent with their own respective definitions of the process—that the other has found threatening, insensitive, and indicative of a lack of commitment to peace. These experiences have thus provided new information confirming the old images the two parties have held of each other. The impediments to attitude change created by these experiences were further aggravated by the dynamics of frustrated expectations.

Initially, each side made the assumption that the other shared its own perception of the process and thus expected the other to act accordingly. The Egyptians, conceiving the process as one designed to achieve a comprehensive peace, expected Israel to act in ways that would help them draw Palestinians and other Arab actors into the process. Thus, they saw military actions by Israel against Arab targets or any Israeli actions that closed off possibilities for compromise (such as the expansion of West Bank settlements and the annexation of Jerusalem and the Golan) or that contributed to isolating Egypt from the Arab world as clearly contradictory to the peace process. The Israelis, on the other hand, conceiving the process as one designed to achieve a bilateral agreement, expected Egypt to distance itself from the Arab world and, in effect, enter into a new alliance with Israel. Thus, they saw Egyptian reluctance about normalization, its gradual return to the Arab fold, its advocacy of a Palestinian state, and its increasing support of the PLO as clearly contradictory to the peace process. These deviations from the two parties' divergent expectations and the growing realization that they do not really have a common vision and a shared agenda have led to disillusionment and a sense of betrayal. Their mutual accusations of undermining the peace process have only served to confirm each party's view of the other's bad faith, since neither sees its own actions as inconsistent with the process.

Each party's disappointment at the other's failure to live up to its expectations and to act in accordance with its view of the peace process has greatly contributed to the resurgence of old suspicions and despair. These are not the ideal conditions for the restructuring of mutual attitudes to occur.

Conclusion

The analysis of the Sadat initiative and its effects suggests certain generalizations about the strengths and weaknesses of a strategy of unilateral reward. Perhaps the greatest strength of the strategy is its capacity to un-freeze attitudes, which is particularly significant in a conflict in which the parties are locked into rigid assumptions about the impossibility of a peaceful and just solution. The strategy in and of itself, however, is not capable of producing new attitudes, reflecting a transformation of the relationship be-tween the former enemies. Stable attitude change can only come about through a process of constructive interaction between the parties, which almost invariably must be accompanied by vigorous internal debates within the two societies as they move toward a new relationship.

The question is whether a strategy of unilateral reward increases the likelihood that interactions and internal debates conducive to attitude change will occur. On the one hand, by helping to unfreeze old attitudes, it provides one of the essential conditions for attitude change. On the other hand, however, it contains a serious risk of setbacks, which may lead to reconfir-mation and even intensification of hostile and suspicious attitudes. To be effective in the long run, the strategy must offer rewards that remain credible and attractive after the initial euphoria has died down. This means that it must be generally supported by the initiator's own constituencies and that it must be appealing to a broad consensus within the recipient party. There is a danger that these conditions will not be met if the strategy relies on the elements of surprise and drama to the extent of precluding some of the needed preparatory efforts at exploring and building consensus on both sides. Furthermore, the strategy itself may produce side effects that impede attitude change by sharpening internal divisions within each society, thus making change more controversial and more costly, and by creating unrealistic expectations, thus giving rise to disillusionment and a sense of betrayal.

The Sadat initiative, as I have tried to show, illustrates both the strengths and weaknesses of a strategy of unilateral reward. It constituted a turning point in the Middle East conflict by breaking down old assumptions about the impossibility of Arab recognition of Israel and of Arab–Israeli peace. The process set into motion by the unfreezing of old attitudes did lead to an Egyptian–Israeli peace agreement, which seems to be holding despite its serious limitations. So far, however, it has not led to a comprehensive peace or to full normalization of relations, which have been central goals for Egypt and Israel, respectively. As a result, we have not witnessed the kind of transformation of the Egyptian–Israeli relationship that is conducive to attitude change. I have attributed this state of affairs to the failure of Sadat's initiative to bridge the gap between the two parties' goals for the peace process, a gap based on Israel's perceived interest in a separate peace and Egypt's in a comprehensive peace. The effects of this fundamental difference have been amplified by the sharpening of internal divisions on each side and the frustration of expectations in the wake of the Sadat initiative. Despite these failures, a psychological threshold has been crossed in the history of the conflict. The new psychological situation in which Arabs and Israelis find themselves is concretized by the Egyptian–Israeli peace agreement. This agreement, notwithstanding the "cold peace" by which it is expressed, represents a new starting point for all further efforts at resolving the Arab–Israeli conflict.

In evaluating the Sadat initiative, we have to distinguish between the outcomes that it has produced so far and the potential that it may have created (or failed to create) for movement toward a comprehensive peace. How one measures the outcome so far depends, of course, on one's vantage point. For Egypt and Israel, the peace agreement has provided some tangible benefits, and there is general consensus in both societies that it is in their interest to adhere to the basic terms of the treaty. To be sure, there are skeptics and critics of the Egyptian–Israeli peace process in both countries, particularly in Egypt, where criticism has accelerated since the Lebanon war,[12] but there has been no significant demand to reverse the process. On the other hand, among Palestinians and elsewhere in the Arab world, the visible products of Sadat's initiative—the Camp David agreements and the peace treaty—are seen as obstacles to peace and are blamed for creating the conditions that made the Lebanon war possible.[13] There is no way of determining, of course, whether the failure to reach an Egyptian–Israeli agreement would have prevented the Lebanon war—or would have led to an even larger, multiparty war in the Middle East. But even if the agreement bears some of the blame for this tragic war, one cannot conclude that it has lost all of its potential for contributing to a just and lasting comprehensive peace. Indeed, some of the lessons from this war may provide the impetus for new efforts to complete the process that Sadat initiated.

It is my assessment that the Sadat initiative and the ensuing peace process have in fact created an opening for a genuine resolution of the Arab–Israeli conflict by shaking up the old assumptions that made such a resolution unthinkable. More and more Israelis, still captured by the new sense of opportunity that the Egyptian–Israeli peace has created but discouraged by the Lebanon war, the events on the West Bank, and Israel's deteriorating relations with Egypt, have come to the realization that there can be no improvement in the quality of the Egyptian–Israeli peace—no fulfillment of their vision of normal relations between Israel and its neighbors—without a solution of the Palestinian problem. It should be possible to draw on this sentiment within Israel, as well as on the increasing readiness for accommodation shown on the Palestinian and Arab side, in order to develop a shared commitment to a comprehensive peace. To this end, it is necessary to start the slow process of mutual exploration, particularly between Israelis and Palestinians, which will allow each party to develop fuller insight into the other's perspectives and constraints; and to continue the internal debate within each society, from which the consensual willingness to take risks for peace must emerge. For these efforts to succeed, we will have to find ways of strengthening the approach tendencies and weakening the avoidance tendencies on each side, of raising hopes and lowering fears, of heightening the sense of opportunity and reducing the sense of danger that the peace process brings to the fore. The Egyptian–Israeli peace represents a foundation on which such efforts can be built. It will then fulfill its potential of serving, not as the final step in a bilateral agreement, but as the first step toward a comprehensive peace.

NOTES

This paper was originally presented at the 25th Anniversary Conference of the Harvard Center for International Affairs, on June 10, 1983. I have greatly benefited from the reactions of several colleagues to the first draft of the paper. I particularly want to thank Adnan Abu-Odeh, who served as commentator on the paper at the Anniversary Conference; and to Jeffrey Rubin, who made many helpful editorial and substantive suggestions. I am also indebted to the Ford Foundation, which has supported my work on the Arab–Israeli conflict.

1. See Bahgat Korany, "The Cold Peace, the Fifth Arab–Israeli War, and Egypt's Public," *International Journal* 35 (Autumn 1983), pp. 652–673.
2. Ibid. See also Saad Eddin Ibrahim, *The New Arab Social Order: A Study of the Social Impact of Oil Wealth* (Boulder, Colorado: Westview Press, 1982), pp. 66–68.
3. Adeed Dawisha, "Comprehensive Peace in the Middle East and the Comprehension of Arab Politics," *Middle East Journal* 37 (Winter 1983), p. 46.
4. See Moshe Dayan, *Breakthrough: A Personal Account of the Egypt–Israel Peace Negotiations* (New York: Knopf, 1981), for an account of Dayan's meeting with Egyptian Deputy Premier Hassan Tuhami in Morocco, in September 1977.
5. This definition is taken from an unpublished paper by Louis Kriesberg. For a discussion of his views on noncoercive inducements (including persuasion and positive sanctions), see his "Social Theory and the Deescalation of International Conflict," *Sociological Review* (August 1984).

6. Charles E. Osgood, *An Alternative to War or Surrender* (Urbana: University of Illinois Press, 1962).

7. The distinction was first introduced by Kurt Lewin, one of the great pioneers of social psychology. See his *Field Theory in Social Science* (New York: Harper, 1951), pp. 228–229. For elaboration of the three stages, see Warren G. Bennis, Edgar H. Schein, David E. Berlew, and Fred I. Steele, *Interpersonal Dynamics: Essays and Readings on Human Interaction* (Homewood, Illinois: Dorsey Press, 1964), pp. 357–394; and Edgar H. Schein, "The Mechanisms of Change," in Warren G. Bennis, Kenneth D. Benne, and Robert Chin, eds., *The Planning of Change*, 2nd ed. (New York: Holt, Rinehart and Winston, 1969), pp. 98–107.

8. For a discussion of Egyptian attitudes, particularly in the wake of the Lebanon war, see Bahgat Korany, "The Cold Peace." (For the complete reference, see Note 1.) For a view of evolving Israeli attitudes at an earlier stage in the process, see *The Peace Treaty with Egypt: Achievements and Setbacks*, which summarizes a colloquium jointly sponsored by the Shiloah Center for Middle Eastern and African Studies and the Research Project on Peace, both of Tel-Aviv University, in March 1981.

9. For an insightful analysis of the return to "the traditional social order" after the "peace ritual" initiated by Sadat's trip to Jerusalem, see Arnold Lewis, "The Peace Ritual and Israeli Images of Social Order," *Journal of Conflict Resolution* 23 (December 1979), pp. 685–703. Lewis argues that, though the enthusiasm of the peace ritual was short-lived, the process led to a significant shift in Israeli attitudes about Israeli–Egyptian relations.

10. These observations derive from an analysis by Shimon Shamir in a seminar on "Egyptian–Israeli Relations: Perceptions, Issues, Prospects," which he presented at the Harvard Center for International Affairs on April 11, 1982. See also the summary of the Tel-Aviv University colloquium, *The Peace Treaty with Egypt*.

11. Stephen P. Cohen and Edward E. Azar, "From War to Peace: The Transition between Egypt and Israel," *Journal of Conflict Resolution* 25 (March 1981), pp. 87–114.

12. See Bahgat Korany, "The Cold Peace." (For the complete reference, see Note 1.)

13. See, for example, Bassam Tibi, "Ägypten und seine arabische Umwelt," *Beiträge zur Konfliktforschung*, 12 (4/1982), pp. 33–60.

V

The prospects for prosperity, freedom, and stability

RAYMOND VERNON

Old rules and new players: GATT in the world trading system

SAMUEL P. HUNTINGTON

Will more countries become democratic?

STANLEY HOFFMANN

The future of the international political system: a sketch

10

Old rules and new players: GATT in the world trading system

RAYMOND VERNON

Clarence Dillon Professor of International Affairs Emeritus, Harvard University

Military planners, according to a time-worn cliché, are usually found preparing for the last war. Policymakers in the field of international economic relations can sometimes be accused of a similar bias. Today, the world's principal trading and investing nations are wrestling with the problem of how to maintain the benefits and minimize the costs that are associated with international trade. A critical question is how well the basic assumptions that underlay United States thinking in the formulation of the General Agreement on Tariffs and Trade apply today; and to the extent that new factors have appeared, what they may suggest about revising the terms of the existing trade regime.

The GATT's founding

The United States role

The end of World War II marked a new era in international economic relations. The war had helped push the u.s. economy into a position of unchallenged dominance in the international system. The country's economic weight and its position as the leader of a political and military alliance briefly endowed it with an extraordinary measure of influence over the rules and institutions that were established at the war's end. To be sure, other countries in the western coalition strongly supported one aspect or another in the package of newly created rules and institutions. But with hindsight, it is clear that the views of the United States on the nature of an ideal international economic regime were measurably different from those that typically prevailed in Europe and Japan, and sharply at variance with the views of most developing countries.

Perhaps the most pervasive factor that has distinguished the United States position from those of most other countries has been the deeply rooted preference of Americans for limiting the direct transactional role of government in international economic affairs. Tightly linked to that preference is the u.s. predilection for letting the market determine the direction of international transactions. This set of preferences has been embedded in a system of governance that persistently limits the discretionary (hence to some extent arbitrary) power of its agencies, partly by requiring that each bureaucratic decision should be tested for its validity against some specified general rule.

The trade policy that the United States government adopted after World War II reflected all of these concepts. But the circumstances that led to its adoption at that particular time were in some respects quite unique. By 1948, Democratic administrations had been in power for sixteen years. As a result, a small group of antiquarian congressmen from the southern states had come to dominate many of the key committees of the Congress.[1] From those positions, this small group could express the historical preference of the south's cotton, tobacco, and apple exporters against high industrial tariffs and in favor of the promotion of exports. The influence of the southerners was bolstered by some distinguished survivors of the Wilsonian crusade at the end of World War I; centered mainly in the industrial and financial centers of the northeast, this group still firmly believed in the link between world trade and world peace. Finally, there were America's professional economists, projected by the New Deal and the special conditions of World War II into key planning positions in the u.s. government; this group, still smarting from its failed effort to block the passage of the Smoot–Hawley Tariff Act in 1930, was strongly committed to the neoclassical preference for open markets and nondiscrimination.[2]

Historical forces also explain the respective roles of the two political parties in the formulation of the postwar trade regime. In those years, as today, the Republicans were identified as the party of American business. Until World War II that identification usually carried the Hamiltonian connotation, a commitment to protect America's infant industries against European competitors. The Democrats, then as now, were a more diverse coalition, composed at the time of organized labor, southern agricultural interests, and northern internationalists. Where international trade policy was concerned, labor's attachment to the Democratic party was an anomaly, inasmuch as labor had traditionally been almost as protectionist as the industrialists. But labor's attachment to the Democratic party served to blunt its hostility to an open international trading system. Labor's ambivalence could be detected in 1934, when the first Trade Agreements Act was passed as part of a package of measures to fight the Great Depression, as well as in 1948, when the leaders of the AFL–CIO were closely identified with the nation's efforts to rebuild a destroyed Europe through the Marshall plan.

That was the background against which the u.s. planners after World War II attempted to frame a set of institutions and rules for governing international trade. Given their ideology and their outlook, their early plans placed heavy emphasis on a number of basic objectives: to outlaw inter-national cartels; to bring down tariff rates; to phase out national licensing requirements that limited foreign trade; and to curb discrimination in the administration of trade regulations. These objectives—albeit much qualified and diluted—found expression in 1948 in a draft charter for an International Trade Organization, one of whose chapters would provide the basis for the General Agreement on Tariffs and Trade. The GATT, as numerous com-mentators have observed, was originally perceived as a stop-gap organiza-tion; the agreement was expected to do no more than provide the framework for international trade liberalization efforts during the period in which the ITO charter was being ratified. As it turned out, the charter never was ratified by any of the fifty-two countries that participated in its drafting. Other countries, viewing it largely as a U.S.-inspired document reflecting a U.S.-inspired ideology, saw no reason to take the lead in the ratification process.

Meanwhile, however, various groups in the United States were be-ginning to balk at some of the alien ideas that had been introduced in the charter's draft in the course of the negotiations.[3] These included various qualifications and demurrers regarding the rights of foreign investors, elab-orate provisions for the negotiation of international commodity agreements, an approach to the restrictive business practices of state-owned enterprises that was more lenient than the approach applied to private enterprises, and a special tolerance for trade restrictions that were intended to promote economic development. By 1950, it became clear that the draft ITO charter did not represent a workable consensus. Besides, by that time, the U.S. foreign policy agenda was crowded with other more urgent issues, including the administration of the Marshall plan, the building of NATO, and the prosecution of the Korean war.

The death of the ITO left the much less ambitious provisions of the GATT to fill part of the breach. Enough of the U.S. ideology had been retained in its complex clauses covering the conduct of international trade so that U.S. policymakers could live with those provisions in reasonable comfort. The ideas of reducing trade barriers, avoiding dicrimination, and settling disputes by discussion were still the paramount propositions of the agree-ment. And in the one major area in which U.S. domestic politics demanded import restrictions and export subsidies, that of agricultural commodities, the U.S. negotiators had tried strenuously to carve out the requisite excep-tions to their own general principles, so that direct conflict between the GATT provisions and U.S. law could be held to a minimum.

The Congress, therefore, felt no strong need to block U.S. participation in the GATT. Indeed, in the years that followed, individual congressmen occasionally used the provisions of the GATT as an argument for modifying or abandoning some conflicting action that the Congress had under consid-eration. On the other hand, the GATT never acquired the legitimacy that would have been accorded to an agreement that had been explicitly approved by the Congress or to a treaty ratified by the Senate. Instead, the Congress tolerated the participation of the executive branch in the GATT, while occasionally ignoring and violating the agreement's provisions when they seemed to stand in the way.

GATT in operation

United States policies

Despite the equivocal character of United States official support for the GATT, the organization proved to be a pivotal instrument in the shaping and execution of U.S. trade policy during the three decades following its founding. In that respect, as we shall presently see, the United States was almost unique. In most other countries, the differences between the general approach embodied in the GATT and the national trade policies that they actually employed were much larger.

Not that other countries were necessarily in formal violation of the GATT. In addition to the U.S.-inspired exceptions applicable to agricultural commodities, the agreement's numerous escape clauses were sufficient to tolerate a considerable amount of deviation from its underlying concepts. Countries in balance-of-payment difficulties, for instance, could do very much as they liked to restrict imports and to discriminate among their trading partners. Countries that claimed developing-country status could use numerous provisions of the agreement to justify deviant measures.

At first, when European recovery occupied U.S. policymakers, the centrality of the GATT for U.S. trade policy was not very obvious. As long as the European recovery objective prevailed, the U.S. government devoted its energies mainly to helping the European participants in the Marshall plan shape a preferential system of trade relations among them, a system that discriminated systematically against the United States and other outsiders in the interests of promoting easier trade relations among the Europeans themselves.

Indeed, in those early days, GATT's main role was to organize and preside over a series of exercises that at the time seemed to border on a charade. The President from time to time requested and received limited powers from the Congress to reduce U.S. tariffs in order to carry out trade agreements undertaken with other countries. According to the norms of the negotiation that followed, all countries were expected to reduce their tariffs in roughly equal degree. In the late 1940s, however, practically all countries other than the United States and Canada were controlling their trade primarily by means of foreign exchange licenses rather than by tariffs; a reduction in tariffs, therefore, did not necessarily reduce the barriers to U.S. exports. Moreover, the question whether the various countries had reduced their tariffs in equal degree could never be resolved in terms that were theoretically defensible. The negotiators nevertheless devised various measures of each country's reductions, to be paraded before the United States

Congress as proof of "reciprocity." Congress itself was content to take note of the outcome of those negotiations, expressing neither approval nor disapproval of the results.

The actions of the United States in those early days of the GATT rested on certain views among Americans that would soon be altered. One of these was the view—widely shared at the time by leaders in business, labor, and government circles—that the United States should play a role appropriate to the head of a worldwide coalition. Like any leader of a coalition, the u.s. government was prepared to overlook some of the peccadillos of its junior allies if this would promote the collective arrangement. A second view, reenforcing the first, was that the u.s. economy itself was practically invulnerable, at least from economic forces that were external to the country; that widely held view made it much easier to overlook the unbalanced character of the trade agreements.

As it turned out, these early acts of leadership paid off handsomely. By the middle 1950s, most European countries were in a position to abandon their discriminatory import licensing systems and to rely on tariffs for their trade protection. To be sure, the Europeans were not long in putting another system in place that discriminated against dollar goods, this time in the form of a customs union embedded in the provisions of the European Economic Community. The effect of that agreement was to eliminate tariffs in trade between the member countries and to establish a common external tariff, to be applied by the members to imports from nonmember countries including the United States. But the tariffs that were applied to u.s. goods by the Community's original six members reflected rates that had been drastically reduced as a result of the GATT-sponsored tariff negotiations.

The sense of the u.s. leadership that the country stood at the head of a world coalition remained strong through much of the 1960s. But the country's sense of economic invulnerability evaporated more quickly. Indeed, as early as 1956, the u.s. government was already belaboring Japan for its growing exports of cotton textiles to u.s. markets, and was already finding ways of restricting imports of oil and ores from other sources. And by the 1960s, American leaders were worrying over the steady decline in the country's gold holdings and over the competitive position of the u.s. economy as a whole.

As long as the United States saw itself in a leadership role, however, it was in no position to entertain seriously any general move to restrict its imports. The u.s. response to problems of increasing competition, therefore, mainly took the form of greater efforts to open up the markets of its trading partners, especially of the formidable European community. This was the chief impetus that produced the extensive tariff negotiations of the 19͜os, the so-called Kennedy round; and it continued to provide enough momentum into the 1970s to produce still another round of tariff reductions, sometimes dubbed the Tokyo round. Piled on top of the tariff negotiations of the late 1940s and 1950s, these reductions cut the tariffs of the world's principal trading countries from levels that had characteristically run on the order of 20% or 30% to levels that were typically in the neighborhood of 5%. That reduction was an extraordinary achievement, quite unparalleled in the history of the world's trade relations.

From the u.s. viewpoint, however, GATT's achievements were largely submerged during the 1970s by a growing sense of dissatisfaction with the system. Increasingly, Americans chafed under what they perceived to be the asymmetrical impact of the GATT's provisions. That asymmetry could perhaps be tolerated as long as the United States saw itself steering the world toward a trading system that was compatible with its interests. But by the 1970s, the u.s. government no longer saw itself as the unchallenged leader of a new world trading system, nor would many other countries have acknowledged any such claim to leadership. One notable change was the slippage of the u.s. position in world trade; whereas u.s. merchandise exports in 1953 accounted for 29% of such exports from the industrialized countries as a whole, the analogous figure in 1970 had fallen to 19%.[4]

There was another element in the u.s. reaction, however. The United States saw itself as using the tariff as the principal instrument of trade control; other countries, however, were thought to be using various other means to control their trade, means that came to be known as nontariff barriers or simply NTBS. The GATT had operated effectively enough in reducing high tariffs; but its effectiveness in dealing with these so-called NTBS had yet to be tested. And there was considerable skepticism everywhere whether GATT could measure up to the test.

Accordingly, when in 1974 Congress gave the President fresh authority to negotiate for the reduction of trade barriers, it included a series of new emphases in the enabling legislation. The reduction of the offending nontariff barriers was stressed as an objective. More significantly, the President was instructed and authorized to take restrictive measures against countries that maintained "unjustifiable or unreasonable" import restrictions against the United States.[5]

The negotiations that the United States conducted under authority of the 1974 Act demonstrated that some fundamental shifts were taking place in u.s. policy. Some of the practices to which the u.s. government particularly objected, such as governmental subsidies and discriminatory procurement practices, were singled out for special negotiations whose results were embodied in separate codes. In ratifying the results, the u.s. Congress stipulated that rights under those codes would be extended by the United States only to those foreign governments that adhered to the codes rather than to all GATT members, a provision that the administration accepted. The inference was clear: The United States was prepared to accept major deviations from the nondiscrimination principle if necessary to make progress on these impediments to trade.

Since 1979, the sense that the United States was being unfairly treated in international trade has been prominent both in congressional deliberations and in executive pronouncements. The u.s. position has been that it confronts a world that bristles with nontariff barriers. With that conviction as a backdrop, the u.s. government has found it less difficult than in the past to square its ideological preferences for nondiscrimination and open markets with various *ad hoc* measures of trade restriction, including some measures that breached the principle of nondiscrimination. By 1980, according to one estimate, the u.s. industries that benefited from special measures of protection—from so-called voluntary export restraints, trigger price devices, and the like—accounted for about 30% of the country's industrial output.[6]

Yet it would be a gross mistake to infer from such evidence that the United States had reverted to a simple protectionist position. On the contrary; although the American public at large was expressing protectionist sentiments, there was ample evidence that leadership opinion in the United States remained strongly wedded to open international markets.[7] By the 1980s, practically every major u.s. industrial enterprise and banking institution was organized on a multinational basis, with subsidiaries and affiliates all over the world. As a result, the common interest that management and labor once had shared in repelling foreign competition when it threatened home markets had disappeared. In the United States as well as other advanced industrialized countries, many managers and technicians were associating their well-being with the worldwide performance of multinational enterprises by which they are employed; labor, on the other hand, continued to see its interests in protecting the home market. More generally, those groups in the advanced industrialized countries from whom civic leaders are typically drawn—businessmen, bankers, academics, lawyers, and the like—came to identify their interests more strongly with open international borders than the population at large, creating a special set of problems for political decisionmakers.

European policies

To the extent that the United States succeeded in bringing down tariff barriers through the instrumentality of the GATT during the decades after World War II, its principal partners in the operation were the major countries of Europe operating either in their separate capacities or as members of the European Economic Community. Yet, as mentioned earlier, the main trade policies of the Europeans were preferential from the very beginning. The discriminatory trade liberalization schemes of the Marshall plan years were followed by the more enduring preferential arrangements associated with the European Economic Community. In addition to establishing a customs union among its members, the Community also developed a network of preferential arrangements with nonmembers. Free trade agreements were negotiated with each of the main nonmember countries in Europe, thereby eliminating tariffs on industrial products in trade with those countries. Bilateral trade agreements also were negotiated with various countries in North Africa and southern Europe bordering on the Mediterranean, providing for special trade treatment of their exports. Blanket five-year conventions were negotiated with several scores of poor countries located in Africa, the Caribbean, and the Pacific, former colonies of the EEC's members; these agreements also included wide-ranging preferences extended to the selected countries, along with various measures of aid.

The EEC's various preferential schemes were significant in at least two important respects. All told, they constituted a major departure from the nondiscriminatory world that the United States had been trying to promote through the GATT's key provisions. But they also provided a relatively rare example of a liberal trading system that had been created largely by discriminatory measures of trade liberalization. As a rule, discriminatory import regimes have usually proved to be highly restrictive of trade. In the case of the EEC countries, however, total imports rose from 12% of the EEC countries' gross domestic product in 1953 to 24% in 1980; and the relative increase in imports were due not only to a relative rise in trade within the customs union itself but also to a relative rise in imports from outsiders.[8]

To be sure, the EEC's liberalization policies did not extend to all products; even more than in the U.S. case, agricultural products were protected by a special set of import restrictions and export subsidies. Nor was the EEC prepared to entertain preferential trade-liberalizing arrangements with all countries; an arrangement with Japan, for instance, would have been unthinkable. Still, the EEC's markets, measured by any historical or comparative standard, were opened wide to foreign goods.

The challenge to GATT concepts that the Community members have posed, therefore, has not been a challenge to open markets so much as it has been a challenge to nondiscrimination. But there has been another challenge as well. Governments in most European countries have been quite prepared to deal with problems of industrial development, economic adjustment, and export promotion by various *ad hoc* means: for instance, by creating state-owned enterprises and endowing them with capital and operating funds,[9] or by providing subsidies and extending preferences in various forms to their national producers.[10] In this respect, most Europeans reflected a political outlook and a historical tradition that were measurably different from those of the United States and that revealed the tenuous and incomplete character of the consensus underlying the GATT.

Japanese policies

Japan's participation in the GATT has served to emphasize even more strongly the limited nature of the GATT consensus.[11] As noted earlier, already by 1956 Japan's success as an exporter was testing the strength of the U.S. commitment to a nondiscriminatory trading system; *in extremis* the United States itself proved unprepared to follow the nondiscrimination principle to the letter. To be sure, the United States went to some lengths to avoid an overt violation of the GATT's strictures against discrimination; to achieve its purpose, the United States compelled Japan "voluntarily" to restrict its exports to the U.S. market. That disingenuous measure, it should be noted, may have weakened the GATT more than an overtly discriminatory import restriction would have done, because it seemed to legitimate the *de facto* avoidance of a basic GATT rule by a blatant subterfuge.

But Japan's participation in the GATT provided a second major lesson as well, a lesson already suggested by the reaction of the Europeans. GATT has been structured on the basis of assumptions that were largely consistent with the conditions of the U.S. economy—conditions in which the direct transactional role of government was limited, governmental institutions had little to do with the promotion or adaptation of business enterprises, and cooperative behavior by national enterprises was sharply limited through the operation of antitrust laws. The case of Japan illustrated how atypical the United States economy was in these respects. Although the numerous studies that scholars have recently produced of the Japanese economy differ in many details, almost all agree on a number of points that emphasize the differences from the United States.

For several decades before World War II, the Japanese government had had a major hand in stimulating, supporting, and coordinating the growth of private enterprise.[12] After World War II, the close ties between business and government continued. The institutions responsible for maintaining those ties included a ministry, MITI, that was charged with defining the country's development targets; a series of government-supported financial intermediaries that doled out credit on preferential terms to favored enterprises; and an extensive network of business organizations that interacted with the government to shape the required goals and produce the needed responses at the enterprise level. Apart from the United States, practically all other countries of the world also had developed some of the institutional features of the Japanese economy. But in the United States, such arrangements have been uncommon, except for a few exceptional cases mainly encountered in wartime. It is not surprising, therefore, that the GATT has largely failed to address the trade problems created by such institutions.

The Japanese case, of course, also has included some rather distinctive features of its own. Inside the country, Japanese enterprise has tended to organize itself in a number of clusters of interrelated firms. Until World War II, six or eight such clusters—the so-called zaibatsu—made up most of Japan's modern industry. After World War II, Japanese firms continued to be linked in a large number of clusters of a looser sort—the so-called keiretsu. One consequence of that structure was that most Japanese firms which were users of intermediate materials were linked to Japanese suppliers by vertical ties. In many cases, the intermediate materials were produced under conditions that generated substantial increasing returns to scale. As a result, Japan's aluminum fabricators normally acquired their metal from related aluminum smelters at home, Japan's automobile plants from related Japanese parts manufacturers, and so on. A study of the Japanese semiconductor industry suggests that returns to scale also have been a factor that explains the practices of Japanese firms of swapping specialty items with one another.[13] The Japanese case has driven home with particular force the fact that the structure of corporate relationships could significantly affect the propensity of a nation to import or export, a possibility that the GATT's founders did not address and the GATT itself did not consider.

The considerable gap between the U.S. perception of a GATT-inspired trading world and the Japanese perception of GATT's requirements explains in part the acute frustrations of the two countries in their quarrels over Japanese trade practices. From the U.S. viewpoint, Japan's record is commonly seen as one of extensive evasion; from the Japanese viewpoint, its record is one that compares quite favorably with that of other industrialized countries.[14] The size of that gap reflects in part the extent of the omissions, exceptions, and ambiguities of the GATT itself when measured against the U.S.-inspired conception of an open trading world.

Developing countries and socialist economies

The qualified nature of the developing countries' adherence to the GATT needs only a few words of elaboration.

Most members of the GATT claim developing status. Members in that category normally feel free to take any measures they think appropriate in their national interests. These measures have included widespread resort to import licensing, subsidies, and discriminatory trade regimes.

The size of the gap between pristine GATT concepts and developing country practices has been due to a number of factors. One of these has been the extent to which the GATT itself has provided for such deviations. Apart from the provisions applicable to all countries in balance-of-payment difficulties, a number of exceptional provisions have been fashioned especially to relieve developing countries from GATT obligations. Perhaps as important has been the fact that the institutions, practices, and values that typically prevailed in these countries with regard to the role of government have borne a closer resemblance to the Japanese model than to the American: Government-supported financial intermediaries have been extensive; industrial groups of the zaibatsu or keiretsu type, with local variations, have been ubiquitous;[15] government sponsorship of and participation in industrial development have been nearly universal. As a result, the actual practices of developing countries in the conduct of their international trade have had little in common with the system that the U.S. government had hoped to promote through the GATT.

The size of the gap between U.S. views and developing country views over the meaning and intent of the GATT has been underlined by efforts to have some of the newly industrializing countries, such as Brazil and Korea, accept some of the restraints that are embodied in the GATT's general rules, including restraints on the use of subsidies and on discriminatory trade practices.[16] Those efforts have now been going on for about a decade. One cannot say for certain that the efforts have been wholly fruitless; some of the newly industrializing countries have taken measures from time to time in the direction of trade liberalization. But the hostility generated by U.S. pressures has been monumental as compared with the meager results.

The participation of socialist economies in the GATT has been even more equivocal than that of the developing countries with mixed economies. The membership of several east European countries, the prospective membership of the People's Republic of China, and the Soviet Union's interest in obtaining observer status in the GATT have served mainly to highlight the irrelevance of the agreement's provisions for the conditions of a centrally directed economy. The provisions of the GATT that apply explicitly to the enterprises of socialist economies are in fact quite quixotic; their aim is to have enterprises in such countries behave as if they were independent entities responding to "commercial considerations," so that they are expected to buy from the cheapest foreign source and sell to the highest foreign bidder.[17] The fact that the enterprises are state-owned is acknowledged in only one important particular: The mark-ups of state-owned enterprises that import foreign goods for resale in the home market are analogized to a tariff and are therefore made subject to negotiation with other GATT members.

In actual practice, to be sure, the GATT signatories have exhibited a greater degree of eclecticism in dealing with centrally directed economies than the GATT's rules might suggest. They have largely ignored those provisions and have demanded other commitments of various kinds, such as commitments on the part of such countries to expand their foreign trade by some agreed amounts. But these commitments have only served to underline the fundamental point, that the United States-inspired provisions of the GATT cannot usefully be applied in trade agreements with centrally directed economies.

Trade and traders

During the sixty years or so since the United States adopted the principle of unconditional most-favored-nation treatment in tariff matters, the conditions of international trade have undergone revolutionary changes. Some of those changes, such as the dramatic improvements in the means of international transport and communication, have facilitated movement toward the United States concept; but other changes, including the structure and ownership of industrial firms, have had more complex implications.

Cartels and multinationals

The fact that industrial structure can substantially influence trade behavior became sharply apparent in the decades before World War II. During those decades, the leading firms that dominated their respective national markets in various capital-intensive industries found themselves from time to time in costly rivalrous contact with one another in international markets.

This was an era in which each national market in the new capital-intensive industries was characteristically dominated by only a firm or two, which accounted for the bulk of the country's foreign trade in the products of those industries.[18] In chemicals, DuPont, Imperial Chemicals, and I. G. Farben were overwhelmingly dominant in their respective markets. In electrical equipment, the leaders were only a little more numerous, including General Electric, Westinghouse, Thomson-Houston, Tokyo Shibaura, and Allgemeine Electrizitäts Gesellschaft. In aluminum, ALCOA, Pechiney, and later ALCAN dominated the world market. In copper, the international market was largely in the hands of America's Big Three plus Union Minière; and in oil, an equally small number was in control of the international side of the industry.

The new industries typically enjoyed substantial economies of scale; and because the leading firms commonly saw their positions in foreign markets as relatively insecure and transitory, they often dumped their products in the markets of rivals at prices that did not recapture their full costs. Soon, however, the leaders recognized the destructive consequences of such practices; and with that recognition came an era of cartel agreements, marked by the division of markets on national lines and by rules on the pricing of products that were sold across national borders. The power of these agreements during the 1930s was bolstered by high tariffs, by the extensive use of import licensing, and by the use of bilateral clearing arrangements with favored trading partners.[19]

After World War II, the international cartels that had been so ubiquitous in earlier years almost disappeared. To be sure, evidence occasionally surfaced after World War II that the institution of the cartel was not quite dead. In uranium, diamonds, and a handful of other products, restrictive trade arrangements still persisted. And the OPEC saga is too well known to require recounting. But these cartels were on nothing like the scale of the period before World War II. Moreover, there is considerable evidence —despite widespread impressions to the contrary—that the degree of industrial concentration in the mature product lines during the decades following World War II typically underwent a considerable decline.[20] With the risks of cartels and monopolies somewhat reduced, the role of tariffs, import licenses, subsidies, and the like took on added importance in shaping international trade. In this one respect, at any rate, the provisions of the GATT became more relevant rather than less. At the same time, however, other developments were reducing GATT's relevance.

One of these developments was the greatly increased role of the multinational enterprise. Although no precise data have been developed on changes in the relative importance of multinational enterprises in the conduct of international trade, it is clear that their role grew considerably in the decades after World War II and came to account for a greatly increased share of the world's trade. In the United States, for instance, 298 enterprises classified as multinational in structure were responsible in 1970 for 62% of all U.S. exports of manufactured products. Between 1966 and 1975 the majority-owned affiliates of U.S. firms located in foreign countries originated about one-third of United States imports.[21]

One reason why the growth of multinational enterprises introduces problems with regard to the relevance of the GATT's rules has to do with the underlying paradigm on which those rules are structured. These implicitly contemplate a world of buyers and sellers operating at arm's length across international borders, bearing costs that are primarily determined by the factor prices within their respective countries, and buying or selling in international markets on the basis of their position in the comparative advantage profile of their countries. In such a world, there is an objectively determined "right" pattern for international trade, which can be specified without regard to the structure of the firm.

In the abstract, the growing importance of multinational enterprises in world trade posed no particular threat to the GATT concept. On the contrary: Because multinational enterprises produced from a number of locations, they appeared to be in a relatively strong position to react more or less swiftly to changes in the cost structures of competing areas, precisely on patterns assumed in the GATT paradigm. In reality, however, various elements in the behavior of multinational enterprises served to demonstrate that the GATT's implicit assumptions regarding the behavior of international traders might be incomplete in various critical respects.

For one thing, the growth of the multinational enterprise appears to have increased the number of countries for which scale economies and learning curves were determining the patterns of international trade. Even before the era of multinational enterprises, governments in developing countries were insisting on their right to establish and protect various industries with large static and dynamic economies of scale, such as steel and chemicals. But the obstacles to acquiring the needed capital, technology, and access to markets and of putting them to work often appeared formidable. Multinational enterprises commonly seemed to offer an attractive way out because they were in a position to provide the required ingredients as a package; sometimes those resources came from within the multinational system, sometimes from foreign markets, and sometimes from within the developing country itself. What the multinational enterprises generally required in return was some expectation that they would be able to shelter their early output, which would be produced at high cost, from the competition of established producers. Developing countries often provided that shelter by import restrictions or by subsidies.

Once a multinational enterprise had established a production capability for any given product in more than one country, the existence of static and dynamic scale economies served to complicate its choices among various locations when expanding or contracting its production. Because the costs of the enterprise in each such facility were typically sensitive to the volume of production in that facility, it was not easy to specify how an enterprise would respond to any given change in comparative advantage. A multinational enterprise that was calculating the prospective benefits of setting up a facility in a new area, for instance, would have to take into account the possibility that one of its existing units in another area might be required as a result to cut back its production, thereby raising the average costs of that facility. Theorists have not yet developed any extensive hypotheses about rational behavior under such conditions on the part of multinational enterprises.[22] On the basis of empirical observation, however, there were suggestions that multinational enterprises have been less sensitive to factor-cost changes than national producers have.[23]

Wherever multinational enterprises dominated in international trade, other factors came into play that were disturbing to the GATT assumptions. The available data demonstrated persuasively, for instance, that multinational enterprises with prior experience in any given area were much more strongly disposed to make added investments in that area than in areas in which they had no prior experience.[24] Moreover, with static and dynamic scale factors much on the minds of their managers, they have been sensitive to the moves of rivals when setting up new production or distribution facilities in major foreign markets. Extensive research on the subject offers strong support for the hypothesis that this sensitivity has led to the follow-the-leader patterns in the investments of multinational enterprises; and that behavior, in turn, could easily produce patterns of trade that were quite different from those generated in a world in which locational decisions depended mainly on factor costs and markets.[25] In general, where static and dynamic economies of scale are important, the theory of international trade is somewhat underdeveloped not only in postulating the optimum behavior of the multinational enterprise but also in postulating the optimum behavior of governments. The theoretical basis for justifying GATT's emphasis on nondiscrimination and on the reduction of trade barriers becomes more uncertain;[26] accordingly, the persuasive power of the comparative advantage paradigm as a justification for lowering trade barriers loses some of its force.

GATT's rules have proved somewhat inadequate for dealing with the multinational enterprise for still another reason. Many governments have used the affiliates of multinational enterprises in their jurisdictions to impose various so-called performance requirements. Commonly, governments have offered special subsidies and tax exemptions to those enterprises they wished to attract and have shut out those unlikely to perform in accordance with governmental requirements. Those requirements, in practice, typically have included provisions for expanding exports and reducing imports.[27]

The influence of government performance requirements on the behavior of multinational enterprises, however, is probably even greater than their formal presence would suggest. Aware of the need to make themselves indispensable to governments, some multinational enterprises have been planning the location of their production facilities in ways that would reduce their vulnerability. Anecdotal evidence suggests that some have tended to develop organic links among their various affiliates in different countries that keep the affiliates dependent on one another for components or for markets. When coupled with performance requirements, that tendency may explain in part why the subsidiaries of multinational enterprises played such a substantial part during the 1970s in the striking expansion of manufactured goods exports from the newly industrializing countries.[28] At the same time, however, performance requirements have created a new impediment for maintaining an open nondiscriminatory trading regime.

State-owned enterprises

Another development that has tended to influence international trade during the past few decades has been the rapid growth in the role of state-owned enterprises. The trend has been especially strong in crude oil, copper, and iron ore, products in which state-owned producers have increased their share of international sales from practically zero in the 1950s to commanding levels in the 1980s.[29] In addition, state-owned enterprises have grown considerably in the import-substituting industries, especially in those industries that require large-scale capital-intensive facilities such as chemicals, metal producing, and metal fabricating plants.[30] Finally, there has been a tendency for governments to take control of the exportation or importation of some products critical for their economies, sometimes in order to exploit what monopoly or monopsony power they could muster, sometimes in order to simplify the administrative problems of taxing or subsidizing their importers or exporters.[31]

To be sure, governments have occasionally shrunk back the scope of their state-owned enterprise sector, rather than enlarge it. Cases of gross mismanagement or back-breaking cost have usually been influential in producing such reversals. But many governments do not see the state-owned enterprise as an exception or aberration in a market economy; instead, they tend to see such enterprises as an acceptable instrument of government, whose use depends more on empirical than on ideological factors.[32] Accordingly, it is doubtful that the occasional reversals foreshadow a countertrend on a large scale. It was observed earlier that the basic concepts of the GATT could not easily be applied to the operations of socialist states. For similar reasons, the application of GATT concepts to state-owned enterprises in market economies proves to be exceedingly difficult. Remember that the basic GATT approach is to insist that state-owned enterprises must behave as if they were making their choices on the basis of commercial considerations alone. The fact is, however, that state-owned enterprises commonly receive their initial capital as a cost-free endowment, which is replenished as necessary when it is impaired by losses. Some shrinkage in the productive capacity of such enterprises may be allowed to occur, as evidenced by the state-owned steel industries of Britain, France, and Italy, but total liquidation is practically unheard of. In addition, it is inevitable that governments will attempt from time to time to use their enterprises for a multiplicity of purposes: to stimulate investment, to stabilize employment, to damp down inflation, to develop backward regimes, to subsidize exports, and so on. Managers of state-owned enterprises, therefore, cannot be expected to behave in ways that approximate those of the profit-maximizing bankruptcy-threatened private manager.

The countertraders

In recent years, a variety of institutions have taken to arranging deals in which specified imports are linked directly to specified exports. Of course, bilateral deals between pairs of countries, balancing imports with exports, have a long history in international trade; and as long as such deals have been between two countries with balance-of-payment difficulties, the exemptive provisions of GATT have left them free to develop such arrangements. Contemporary versions of such deals, however, have not necessarily been justified on balance-of-payment grounds. And they have taken a variety of forms not previously encountered. Sellers of technology and equipment, for instance, agree to accept payment for their goods and services in the form of products from the buyer's economy. Sometimes, the products used in payment are produced in the very plant provided by the equipment seller, as when Levi Strauss received payment from Hungary in the form of blue jeans; sometimes, the products in payment come more broadly from the buying country, as in the case of Rumania's purchase of nuclear turbines from General Electric or Pepsico's swap of soft drinks for vodka with the Soviet Union.[33] When the relationship is for the long term rather than for a single isolated transaction, as in the case of mining or oil projects, prospective importers commonly lend capital to prospective producers on a long-term basis, sometimes at terms more favorable than those available to an arm's length borrower; and such loans often carry a provision that forgives the producer portions of the loan to the extent that the lender has failed to buy specified quantities of the output. In some of these instances, the value of the products involved is determined by world market prices at time of delivery; but in other instances, where the use of world prices is impractical or undesirable, more complicated formulas are preferred.[34]

From the point of view of a GATT world, the difficulties presented by these countertrades can be formidable. One is the fact that no transaction can be judged by its own terms; each transaction is related to an offsetting trade. The price that Pepsico has paid for the vodka it brings to the U.S. market, therefore, cannot be determined without considering the price it receives for its soft drink in the USSR. The problem is exacerbated when long periods of time separate the offsetting transactions—when, for instance, a machinery export is paid for by materials imported many years later. The separation of the two transactions in time means that the marginal cost of the materials to the importers at time of importation may be close to zero. Moreover, in most of the cases in which a substantial period of time separates the offsetting imports from the original exports, the transaction is financed in part with public funds, thereby increasing the difficulties of measuring the transaction by the standards of the open market.

It is hard to estimate the importance of trades of this sort in world commerce. Japan's nine principal trading companies, which account for about 40% of Japan's exports and nearly 50% of the country's imports, make extensive use of countertrade arrangements of various kinds. So too do the western firms that engage in trade with members of the COMECON and the People's Republic of China. In addition, Brazil and Korea among others have been learning how to put together countertrade deals, especially in their transactions with other developing countries; Indonesia is making an effort to move in the same direction. Nevertheless, trade conducted on this basis probably represents only a small proportion of world trade, perhaps less than 10%. Besides, much of that trade probably involves multinational enterprises or state-owned enterprises or both. Accordingly, such trade does not necessarily enlarge the overall dimensions of the problem categories. But it does exacerbate the difficulties of applying GATT standards.

An overall appraisal

A considerable proportion of the world's trade is conducted on a basis that is substantially at variance with the u.s.-inspired concept of a trading world based on GATT principles.[35] Some of that variance is simply due to violations of the GATT, in letter or in spirit, which could conceivably be remedied by more vigorous enforcement of the agreement's provisions; voluntary export agreements, trigger price mechanisms, and various other disingenuous devices fall in this category.

But the problems lie deeper still. As suggested here, the institutions of international trade commonly march to a music that was not written for the GATT script. To be sure, despite all the obstacles, prices and costs continue to be relevant factors in international trade.[36] Moreover, the presumption that trade restrictions and subsidies will prove harmful to global welfare continues to be strong. Accordingly, the imperfect fit between GATT's underlying assumptions and the realities of international trade need not by itself be a sufficient reason for jettisoning the GATT's present approach.

Yet the risks of attempting to cling to the present GATT structure without some major modifications seem substantial. One reason why the risks seem so high is that other countries are no longer so readily prepared to accept the ethnocentric tilt that the United States was once in a position to implant in the GATT rules. The u.s. view that governmental restrictions or subsidies create "distortions" in world trade presupposes a concept of an ideal trading system that is not shared by many other countries and probably never was; and with the declining willingness or capacity of the United States to assert the leadership position, its ability to maintain that ideological tilt can be expected to decline. If maintained in its present form, therefore, the GATT seems destined to continue losing its persuasive power as an instrument for trade policy.

Another reason why revisions are needed is the special political sensitivity that attaches to certain categories of international trade. One such category is the sale of massive capital goods, such as a petrochemicals complex or a new subway system. Transactions such as these, which routinely involve government credit, countertrade, and state-owned enterprises, are often highly visible, being the object of vigorous hauling and pulling between governments; moreover, they commonly involve products with advanced technologies, products that exporting countries are usually especially eager to support.

Still another category of trade that is highly politicized, needless to say, involves the products of declining industries such as steel and textiles. The experience of the past decade suggests that governments are prepared eventually to allow such industries to shrink, possibly because any effort to retain them is so expensive; but governments are usually not prepared to allow them to shrink as rapidly as they might in the face of open world competition.[37]

The critical challenge for the United States therefore is to find a line of policy appropriate to the altered conditions of international trade.

A course of action

Three alternatives

Each of the alternatives available for u.s. policymakers is filled with risk. One alternative—the obvious one to which many u.s. policymakers are attracted—is to cling to the GATT's original principles, in the hope that other governments will eventually see those principles as the only ones that can be made to work in the long run.[38] The risks of that approach are too obvious to require elaboration. The odds are that the approach will fail to persuade other countries. And as that happens, a frustrated United States will be prodded into applying such unilateral measures of protection as its short-term interests seem to require.

The second alternative is no more promising than the first. This is the tit-for-tat approach, embodied in a number of different proposals that are being offered in the Congress and elsewhere under the general rubric of reciprocity. The details of the different proposals vary somewhat. But essentially they call for a unilateral determination by the United States whether a trading partner is providing access to its markets that is sufficient to meet the standard of full reciprocity; and, if the trading partner is found lacking, they provide for the imposition of new trading restrictions by the United States sufficient to restore the balance. This is obviously an approach destined to generate the lowest common level of market access. Moreover, because it entails a series of unilateral moves, it runs the usual risk of generating a downward spiral of restrictive action and restrictive counteraction. It is, in short, an approach that courts disaster.

The challenge is to develop a third alternative, with less risk and more promise than the two just described. It is not easy to define the third alternative in detail; but some elements are fairly evident. For one thing, we dare not proceed on the basis of unilateral action; international bargaining must continue to be central to the U.S. approach. In addition, the content of the bargains must be such as to contribute on balance to the promotion of open markets, not to the piecemeal closing of such markets. To achieve those results, we shall have to be tolerant of bargains that are less universal in country coverage and more eclectic in content than those negotiated under the GATT. One can picture agreements with the EEC and Japan on some trade subjects, agreements with a group of Latin American countries on other problems, and so on. Some of these agreements could cover such complex subjects as performance requirements, the behavior of state-owned enterprises, or trade in services, while others might be limited to more conventional subjects such as tariffs and export duties.

In some respects, an approach of this sort resembles that followed by the EEC, with its maze of multilateral and bilateral agreements formulated among its members and with outside states. In other respects, it is reminiscent of the various codes, such as those on government procurement and subsidies, that were concluded under the GATT's aegis in 1979. Despite these similarities, the approach raises a number of major questions that have to be tackled.

Relating to the GATT

To begin with, any search for a supplement to the GATT undertaken by the United States might be interpreted as a signal that the GATT was being abandoned. For various reasons, that kind of signal could have calamitous effects. The tariff truce that has existed over the decades among the world's principal trading countries could be undermined; and the GATT's role as a unique forum for airing trade quarrels and launching trade initiatives could be lost. Accordingly, we shall have to find ways to avoid destroying the GATT itself before any alternative has been created.

Whatever initiatives the U.S. government might undertake, therefore, must be formally linked to the GATT, even if the nature of the undertaking is quite foreign to the GATT's principles. Some formula must be found, for instance, for accommodating agreements that formally violate the nondiscrimination principle, so long as they contribute to the trade liberalization objective. The precedents for such cases are already numerous, including the various discriminatory trade arrangements of the European Community with nonmember countries, the innumerable discriminatory trade agreements among developing countries, the bilateral and swap arrangements of the centrally directed economies, and so on.

Developing U.S. bargaining power

Another obstacle to pursuing the third alternative is much more formidable, and the means for overcoming the obstacle much more risky. Other countries have to be persuaded that there is something to be gained in discussing problems with the United States such as those posed by counter-trade, state-owned enterprises, performance requirements, trade in services, and so on. In attempting to persuade others to discuss such subjects, the United States no longer can draw support from its leadership position. All that is left as a basis for stimulating serious discussion leading to joint rules of the game is the anxiety of other countries that the United States may decide to join the game—that it may begin to use restrictive or supporting devices purposefully and on a scale that could constitute a threat to others.

To be sure, other countries have felt threatened in the past by u.s. actions outside of the traditional field of tariffs that seemed to restrict imports or promote exports. Long-standing governmental support granted to u.s. agriculture and the spill-over assistance that u.s. military procurement contracts have given to the country's commercial aircraft industry have been repeatedly noted. And the Export–Import Bank has not been slow to match the credit terms extended by other governments to their exporters of capital equipment. As a rule, however, these programs have been designed without foreign bargaining considerations in mind. Administrators of such programs have been obliged to stress transparency, public accountability, and responsiveness to the annual authorization and appropriation process of the Congress; and the President has not had the power, analogous to those he has exercised in the case of tariffs, to alter the provisions of such programs in order to bring them into line with international agreements.

Other countries have come to recognize, therefore, that the instruments which the u.s. government has fashioned for itself for dealing with international trade problems are relatively limited in scope, formalistic in application, and often not under the control of the executive. When protectionist threats arise, they come mainly from actions initiated by private individuals which the u.s. government cannot control from legislation initiated in the Congress, and from the sporadic demands of the u.s. government for so-called voluntary export agreements. From the viewpoint of other governments, therefore, one conclusion seems fairly well indicated: Negotiating on such trade matters with the u.s. executive may be largely a waste of time. Until the u.s. negotiators seem in a position effectively to apply or to withhold measures that affect u.s. trade, it may prove difficult to persuade other governments to come to the bargaining table.

That conclusion carries a disconcerting implication. In order to increase the chances of effective negotiation, it may be necessary first of all to equip the u.s. government with more powers for the control or promotion of foreign trade than it now possesses, and to place the use of those powers more firmly in the hands of the country's negotiators. In effect, that was what the Congress originally did in 1934 when it authorized the President to negotiate internationally on the subject of tariffs. As in the tariff case, any such delegation of power would have to be subject to limitations and standards of various sorts. In that context it might be possible to stipulate that the new powers be used to negotiate in good faith for the expansion of foreign trade and services rather than for their restriction, or by other means to limit the risk of reversion to the tit-for-tat reciprocity approach. But some increased risk is probably inescapable.

Fingers on the trigger

Any effort to equip the u.s. government with powers sufficient to persuade other governments to come to the negotiating table courts all the risks that go with any international policy based on the principles of mutually assured destruction and negotiated limitations. In the case of trade policy, the problem is exacerbated by the fact that the Congress has usually insisted on placing more than one finger on the trigger; under u.s. law, for instance, both the Congress itself and private parties are in a position to force new trade restrictions over the resistance of the executive.[39]

It would be unrealistic to assume that the Congress would relinquish such powers to the executive. In an extraordinary case or two in the past, however, Congress has been willing to share such powers in ways that were consistent with effective negotiation. A hint of how this might be done is offered by the country's experience in negotiating a series of codes under the powers of the 1974 Trade Act. On most of the subjects covered by the codes, other countries were already uneasy about u.s. behavior, past or prospective. Under the rather extraordinary provisions of the Trade Act of 1974, members of the Congress tied their own hands in advance, undertaking to consider expeditiously and without amendment the results of any subsequent negotiation authorized under the Act. In return, selected congressmen took major substantive roles in planning and negotiating the codes. These codes, completed in 1979, covered the use of subsidies, government procurement practices, customs formalities, and a number of other subjects.

If Congress can be drawn into the negotiating process by some such formula as that in the 1974 Trade Act, there will still be the problem of curbing the power of individual firms to force restrictive measures on the u.s. government. In the case of trade policy, the power of the individual firm to compel government action stems from its ability under the law to initiate proceedings on the contention that imports were doing serious injury to the firm, or that a country was engaging in "unfair practices," or that goods were coming into the United States with the help of foreign subsidies or through dumping. Those powers must be curtailed if the u.s. negotiating position is to be strengthened. Yet it seems improbable that any of the required changes in u.s. law and practice will be adopted unless a considerable proportion of u.s. business is persuaded that the changes are desirable.

At the moment, the u.s. industries that see themselves as under the gun of foreign competition are bigger and more important than in the past. At the same time, the overall stake of u.s. business in reducing international barriers is also larger than ever before by a very considerable margin. In the past, u.s. business organizations identified with a specific industry have almost always directed their efforts in the field of trade toward restriction.

Such organizations have done very little to institutionalize their interest in widening access to foreign markets. That lopsided emphasis has been understandable enough. Even though exports may be substantial and getting more so, the u.s. market is even more important for most u.s. firms. Besides, the u.s. government's efforts to liberalize trade in the past have taken place mainly through GATT tariff negotiations; these have been operations on so gargantuan a scale that the influence of individual firms or industries has generally been quite limited. For the most part, therefore, trade associations and Washington representatives have proven their worth to their constituents not by seeking to open foreign markets but by seeking to close the u.s. market.

A critical question is whether trade negotiations that take place among smaller groups of countries, that cover narrower targets and more specific practices, and that are undertaken on a more frequent basis will be seen by u.s. industries as offering a greater opportunity for opening up foreign markets of specific interest to them. The same question could also be asked of u.s. labor unions, albeit with less optimism over the prospects of an affirmative answer. The answer to that question may depend in part on how effective the new agreements promise to be.

Improving enforcement

One of the critical questions in the formulation of international agreements is deciding how firmly to frame the commitments and how strongly to build the machinery for enforcement. In different international settings, the decisions of governments on this score have wandered all over the spectrum, producing agreements from vaguely formulated "codes of conduct" to the treaty provisions of the European Economic Community. When placed on that spectrum, GATT proves to be one of the more ambitious international agreements, relatively specific in some of its commitments and backed up by the threat of authorized retaliation against wrongdoers.

Still, GATT has always been a paper tiger, disappointing in its ability to compel adherence to its provisions. This has been partly because of the equivocal character of the u.s. role in the organization. GATT has been an organization subscribed to by the u.s. executive, not by the u.s. government, so that Congress has not felt bound by its strictures.

There is room for debate whether under any circumstances an international organization can reasonably be expected to exercise sufficient influence to restrain the action of the u.s. Congress on a subject with as much domestic sensitivity as that of import and export trade restrictions.[40] Still, there are various indications that Congress would respect trade commitments that it had had a direct hand in developing. For instance, Congress has rarely if ever altered any tariff rates that the President negotiated under the explicit authority granted to him in trade legislation; but it has readily enacted legislation that violated the GATT's general provisions—provisions that Congress regards as having been negotiated solely by the executive branch. It remains to be seen if Congress will also feel bound to honor the various GATT codes negotiated in 1979, such as those on government procurement and subsidy practices, which were negotiated explicitly with its advice and consent.

In any event, if Congress could be linked more directly to the negotiation of international trade agreements of the sort contemplated here, the possibility of developing a more effective international system of enforcement might be improved. The GATT system of adjudicating international trade disputes has not been wholly without success; but its limitations have been painfully obvious. The ineffectual character of the GATT's efforts has contrasted, for instance, with the respect that members of the EEC accord to the decisions of their own Court of Justice; the difference suggests that where the public good to be nurtured is sufficiently important to the countries concerned, effective international enforcement is not altogether out of the question. In the new network of agreements outlined here, it may be that some segment of the network could be linked to a process of enforcement that offers more hope than the present GATT pattern.

Reprise

It does not take long to realize that the case of the GATT is illustrative of a fundamental problem in the management of international relations which extends far beyond trade policy. Nations are no longer very manageable as economic units. Their external economic links have become vital to their national existence; and those economic links lie beyond their control to manage, except jointly with other nations. The problem is seen just as vividly in monetary and countercyclical economic policies as in trade.

This is a lesson that the United States finds more difficult to assimilate than most other industrialized countries do. One reason is that the external sector of the U.S. economy, until very recently, was of so little importance to the country. But that is hardly a sufficient explanation. Like a few other aberrant countries, including notably Japan, the United States embraces some values and institutions that are especially resistant to the fashioning of strong international regimes.

One such value is the strong American preference for the diffusion of governmental power and the extensive use of checks and balances. That preference means that the U.S. head of state, the President, will ordinarily prove incapable of speaking for the country on matters that greatly involve the domestic economy.

Another value that clashes with the development of effective international regimes is the distinctive U.S. view of the appropriate role of government, a view that balks at the selective intervention of the public sector in the management of the economy. That view is proving to be a formidable restraint on action at this stage. The stresses that are created by the growth of international economic links are highly selective in their effects: They are favoring managers over workers, aircraft over automobiles, agriculture over steel. And it is especially difficult for the United States to contemplate the selective national measures that might ease the adaptation process, whether taken unilaterally or in concert with other countries.

The result is that proposals which offer some slight chance of bridging the economic differences between countries at the present time, such as those suggested here, almost always seem radical in u.s. eyes, perhaps too radical for serious consideration. In the case of trade policy, however, the obvious alternatives are so bleak and so lacking in promise that the u.s. government may feel it has no choice but to seize the nettle.

NOTES

1. Barbara Hinckley, *The Seniority System in Congress* (Bloomington, Ind.: University of Indiana Press, 1977), p. 41.
2. These points are developed in somewhat more detail in Raymond Vernon, "International Trade Policy in the 1980s: Prospects and Problems," *International Studies Quarterly*, vol. 26, no. 4, December 1982, pp. 483–510.
3. William Diebold, Jr., *The End of the i.t.o.*, Essays in International Finance no. 16, October 1952, Princeton University, Princeton, n.j.
4. Bela Balassa, "The United States in the World Economy," in Christian Stoffäes (ed.), *The Political Economy of the United States* (New York: North-Holland Publishing, 1983), p. 448.
5. "Trade Act of 1974," Public Law 93-618, 93rd. Cong., h.r. 10710, Sec. 301.
6. William Cline, *Exports of Manufacturers from Developing Countries: Performance and Prospects for Market Access*, Brookings Institution, Washington, d.c., 1982.
7. See for instance John E. Rielly (ed.), "American Public Opinion and u.s. Foreign Policy 1983," Chicago Council on Foreign Relations, 1983, p. 24; also Council on Foreign Relations, "New Directions in u.s. Foreign Policy," New York, 1981, pp. 6–7.
8. Balassa, "The United States in the World Economy," p. 451.
9. The role of state-owned enterprises in western Europe is described in Raymond Vernon and Yair Aharoni, *State-Owned Enterprise in the Western Economies* (London: Croom Helm, 1981).
10. S.J. Anjaria and others, *Developments in International Trade Policy*, International Monetary Fund Occasional Paper no. 16, November 1982, pp. 14–62.
11. The Japanese and European approaches are summarized in "The Mercantilist Challenge to the Liberal International Trade Order," Joint Economic Committee, 97th Cong., second session, g.p.o., Washington, d.c. 1982, prepared by John Zysman and Stephen S. Cohen.
12. Chalmers Johnson, mit i *and the Japanese Miracle: The Growth of Industrial Policy, 1925–1975* (Stanford, ca: Stanford University Press, 1982), pp. 83–156.
13. Michael Borrus, James Millstein, and John Zysman, *International Competition in Advanced Industrial Sectors: Trade and Development in the Semiconductor Industry*, prepared for Joint Economic Committee, 97th Cong., 2nd. Sess., g.p.o., Washington, d.c. 1982.
14. See for instance *Report of the Japan–United States Economic Relations Group*, January 1981, Washington, d.c. and Tokyo, u.s. Government Printing Office, p.x.
15. Harry W. Strachan, *Family and Other Business Groups in Economic Development* (New York: Praeger Publishers, 1976), pp. 34–39.
16. Isaiah Frank, "The 'Graduation' Issue for ldcs," *Journal of World Trade Law*, vol. 13, 1979, pp. 289–302.

17. General Agreement on Tariffs and Trade, Article XVII. See also Ivan Bernier, "State Trading and the GATT," in M.S. Kostecki (ed.), *State Trading in International Markets* (London: Macmillan Press, 1982), pp. 245–260.
18. For a description of the leading cartels of the period, see Ervin Hexner, *International Cartels* (Chapel Hill: University of North Carolina Press, 1946).
19. For a description of trade restrictions during this period, see W.S. Woytinsky and E.S. Woytinsky, *World Commerce and Governments: Trends and Outlooks* (New York: The Twentieth Century Fund, 1955), pp. 252–264, 267–278, 293–295.
20. The evidence is summarized in Raymond Vernon, *Storm Over the Multinationals* (Cambridge: Harvard University Press, 1977), pp. 73–82.
21. Summarized in G.K. Helleiner, "Intra-Firm Trade and the Developing Countries: An Assessment of the Data," in Robin Murray (ed.), *Multinationals Beyond the Market* (New York: John Wiley and Co., 1981), pp. 31–55. Using a more relaxed definition of "foreign affiliate," according to other data summarized there, the import figure would be much higher, exceeding one half of U.S. imports.
22. A start in that direction is found in Mark Casson, "Multinationals and Intermediate Product Trade: A Computable Model," Discussion Paper no. 70, January 1983, Department of Economics, University of Reading, England. But the most comprehensive survey to date of the economic theory relating to the multinational enterprise, Richard E. Caves, *Multinational Enterprise and Economic Analysis* (Cambridge: Cambridge University Press, 1982), does not mention the subject.
23. David J. Goldsbrough, "International Trade of Multinational Corporations and Its Responsiveness to Changes in Aggregate Demand and Relative Prices," International Monetary Fund, *Staff Papers*, vol. 28, no. 3 (September 1981), pp. 573–599.
24. For strong statistical evidence on the point, see Raymond Vernon and William Davidson, "Foreign Production of Technology-Intensive Products by U.S.-Based Multinational Enterprises," *Report to the National Science Foundation*, no. PB 80 148636, January 1979, pp. 3–5.
25. The supportive evidence on follow-the-leader behavior is summarized in Richard E. Caves, *Multinational Enterprise and Economic Analysis*, pp. 97–99, along with some minor dissents. For an exploration of the effects of this behavior on location and trade, see Raymond Vernon, "The Location of Economic Activity," in John H. Dunning (ed.), *Economic Analysis and the Multinational Enterprise* (London: George Allen and Unwin, 1974), pp. 96–97.
26. Elhanen Helpman, "Increasing Returns, Imperfect Markets, and Trade Theory," Harvard Institute for Economic Research, Discussion Paper 921, October 1982.
27. *Incentives and Performance Requirements for Foreign Direct Investments in Selected Countries*, U.S. Department of Commerce, Industry and Trade Administration, G.P.O., Washington, DC, 1978. See also U.S. Labor–Industry Coalition for International Trade, *Performance Requirements: A Study of the Incidence and Impact of Trade Related Performance Requirements, and an Analysis of International Law*, Washington, D.C., March 1981, pp. 5–7.
28. For data on the growth of exports of manufactured goods in third-world countries during the 1970s see *Development Co-operation: 1980 Review*, Paris, November 1980, p. 77. For evidence of the expanding role of U.S.-owned subsidiaries in such exports see Robert E. Lipsey, "Recent Trends in U.S. Trade and Investment," Working Paper no. 1009, National Bureau of Economic Research, Cambridge, MA, October 1982, p. 36.
29. Raymond Vernon, *Two Hungry Giants* (Cambridge: Harvard University Press, 1983), pp. 32, 39, 55.
30. The data on this subject, though fragmentary, clearly reflect the trend. See, for instance, Leroy P. Jones and Edward S. Mason, "Role of Economic Factors . . ." in Leroy P. Jones (ed.), *Public Enterprises in Less-Developed Countries* (Cambridge: Cambridge University Press, 1982), pp. 17–47; also John R. Freeman, "International Economic Relations and the Politics of Mixed Economies," Working paper, Massachusetts

Institute of Technology, Cambridge, MA, presented at Rio de Janeiro, August 9, 1982, pp. 1–4.

31. See for instance M.M. Kostecki (ed.), *State Trading in International Markets* (London: Macmillan Press, 1982).

32. Leroy P. Jones and Edward S. Mason, "Role of Economic Factors . . .," p. 21.

33. These transactions and others are cited in "Countertrade and Merban Corporation," Harvard Business School Case 0–383–116, 1983, prepared by David B. Yoffie.

34. See *East–West Trade: Recent Developments in Countertrade*, OECD, Paris, October 1981; also *Analysis of Recent Trends in U.S. Countertrade*, USITC Publication 1237, U.S. International Trade Commission, Washington, D.C., 1982.

35. In Samuel Brittan, "A Very Painful World Adjustment," *Foreign Affairs*, vol. 61, no. 3, December 1982, p. 546, reference is made without attribution to an estimate that in 1980, 40% of world trade was "managed."

36. See Morris Goldstein and Mohsin S. Khan, "The Supply and Demand for Exports: A Simultaneous Approach," *The Review of Economics and Statistics*, vol. 60, no. 2 (May 1978), pp. 275–286; Irving B. Kravis and Robert E. Lipsey, "Prices and Market Shares in the International Machinery Trade," *The Review of Economics and Statistics*, vol. 64, no. 1 (February 1982), pp. 110–116; Jacques R. Artus and Susana C. Sosa, "Relative Price Effects on Export Performance: The Case of Nonelectrical Machinery," *Staff Papers*, International Monetary Fund, vol. 25, no. 1 (March 1978), pp. 25–47.

37. For background on the governments' approach to the steel industry problem, see Edward S. Florkoski, "Policy Responses for the World Steel Industry in the 1980s," *Steel in the 80s* (Paris: Organization for Economic Co-operation and Development, 1980), pp. 154–167.

38. A thoughtful set of proposals that in general are based on such an approach is contained in C. Fred Bergsten and William R. Cline, *Trade Policy in the 1980s*, Institute for International Economics, Washington, D.C., November 1982.

39. Such possibilities are especially present in the operation of Secs. 201 and 301 of the Trade Act of 1974. For a proposal to use Sec. 301 in its present form as a means of opening up foreign markets, see Bart S. Fisher and Ralph G. Steinhardt III, "Section 301 of the Trade Act of 1974," *Law and Policy in International Business*, vol. 14, no. 3, 1982, pp. 569–690.

40. See, for instance, Robert O. Keohane, "International Agencies and the Art of the Possible: The Case of the IEA," *Journal of Policy Analysis and Management*, vol. 1, no. 4, Summer 1982, pp. 469–481, who argues for the inherent limitations in the power of international agencies.

11

Will more countries become democratic?

SAMUEL P. HUNTINGTON

Eaton Professor of the Science of Government
Director, Center for International Affairs, Harvard University

What are the prospects for the emergence of more democratic regimes in the world? This question has intellectual and policy relevance for the 1980s. During the 1950s and early 1960s, scholars concerned with this issue were generally optimistic that decolonization and economic development would lead to the multiplication of democratic regimes. The history of the next decade dealt roughly with these expectations, and people became more pessimistically preoccupied with the reasons for the breakdown of demo-cratic systems. By the late 1970s and early 1980s, however, the prospects for democracy seemed to have brightened once again, and social scientists have responded accordingly. "Transitions to democracy" became the new. focus of attention. The optimists of the 1950s were rather naively optimistic; those of the 1980s have been more cautiously optimistic, but the optimism and the hope are still there. Coincidentally, the Reagan administration moved far beyond the Carter administration's more limited concern with human rights and first launched "Project Democracy" and "The Democracy Pro-gram" to promote democratic institutions in other societies, and then per-suaded Congress to create a "National Endowment for Democracy" to pursue this goal on a permanent basis. In the early 1980s, in short, concern with the development of new democratic regimes has been increasing among academics and policymakers. The purpose of this article is to use social science theory and comparative political analysis to see to what extent this new, more cautious optimism may be justified.

This issue is important for at least four reasons. First, the future of democracy is closely associated with the future of freedom in the world. Democracies can and have abused individual rights and liberties, and a well-regulated authoritarian state may provide a high degree of security and order for its citizens. Overall, however, the correlation between the existence of democracy and the existence of individual liberty is extremely high. Indeed, some measure of the latter is an essential component of the former. Con-versely, the long-term effect of the operation of democratic politics is probably to broaden and deepen individual liberty. Liberty is, in a sense, the peculiar virtue of democracy; hence, if one is concerned with liberty as an ultimate social value, one should also be concerned with the fate of democracy.

Second, the future of democracy elsewhere in the world is of importance to the United States. The United States is the world's premier democratic country, and the greater the extent to which democracy prevails elsewhere in the world, the more congenial the world environment will be to American interests generally and the future of democracy in the United States in particular. Michael Doyle has argued quite persuasively that no two liberal societies have ever fought each other.[1] His concept of liberalism differs from the concept of democracy employed in this paper, but the point may well be true of democratic regimes as well as liberal ones. Other things being equal, non-democratic regimes are likely to pose more serious challenges to American interests than democratic regimes.

Third, "a house divided against itself," Abraham Lincoln said, "cannot stand. . . . This government cannot endure permanently half-slave and half-free." At present the world is not a single house, but it is becoming more and more closely integrated. Interdependence is the trend of the times. How long can an increasingly interdependent world survive part-democratic and part-authoritarian and totalitarian? At what point does interdependence become incompatible with coexistence? For the Soviet bloc and the Western world, that point may still be some distance in the future, but tensions arising out of the growing interaction between totally different political systems are almost inevitably bound to increase. At some point, coexistence may require a slowing down or halting of the trends toward interdependence.

Fourth, the extension or decline of democracy has implications for other social values, such as economic growth, socioeconomic equity, political stability, social justice, and national independence. In societies at one level of development, progress toward one or more of these goals may be compatible with a high level of democracy. At another level of socioeconomic development, conflicts may exist. The question of the appropriateness of democracy for poor countries is, in this context, a central issue. But even highly developed societies may achieve their democracy at some sacrifice of other important values, such as national security.

In addition, if it is desirable to extend the scope of democracy in the world, obviously it is necessary to know what conditions favor that in the late twentieth century. Empirical analysis is necessary to answer the question: What policies should governments, private institutions, and individuals espouse to encourage the spread of democracy? To what extent do efforts such as those of the Reagan administration have an impact, positive or negative, on the state of democracy in the world, and at what cost in terms of other social values and national goals?

The first step in evaluating the prospects for democracy is to define the dependent variable with which we are concerned. Definitions of democracy are legion. The term has been applied to areas and institutions far removed from politics. It has also been defined as an ideal impossible of human achievement. For Peter Bachrach, for instance, a democratic system of government has for its paramount objective "maximization of the self-development of every individual." Robert Dahl says a democratic political system is one which is "completely or almost completely responsible to all its citizens."[2] Such definitions may be relevant to normative political theory, but they are not very useful for comparative empirical analysis. First, they are often so vague and general that it is virtually impossible to apply them in practice. How does one judge whether a political system is attempting to maximize the self-development of individuals or is completely responsive to all its citizens? Second, democracy may also be defined in such broad terms as to make it identical with almost all civic virtues, including social justice, equality, liberty, fulfillment, progress, and a variety of other good things. Hence it becomes difficult if not impossible to analyze the relationship between democracy and other social goals.

For comparative analysis a more empirical and institutional definition is desirable, and this paper follows in the traditions of Joseph A. Schumpeter. A political system is defined as democratic to the extent that its most powerful collective decision-makers are selected through periodic elections in which candidates freely compete for votes and in which virtually all the adult population is eligible to vote. So defined, a democracy thus involves the two dimensions—contestation and participation—that Dahl sees as critical to his realistic democracy or polyarchy.[3]

The record of democratic development

The historical emergence of modern democratic regimes falls into four phases. What could reasonably be called a democratic political system at the national level of government first appeared in the United States in the early nineteenth century. During the following century democratic regimes gradually emerged in northern and western Europe, in the British dominions, and in a few countries in Latin America. This trend, which Alexis de Tocqueville had foreseen in 1835 and which James Bryce documented in 1920, appeared to be irreversible if not necessarily universal. Virtually all significant regime changes were from less democracy to more democracy. Writing at the end of this period, Bryce could well speculate as to whether this "trend toward democracy now widely visible, is a natural trend, due to a general law of social progress."[4]

The trend was reversing, however, even as he wrote. The year 1920 was in many aspects the peak of democratic development among the independent nations of the world.[5] During the following two decades, democracy or democratic trends were snuffed out in Germany, Italy, Austria, Poland, the Baltic states, Spain, Portugal, Greece, Argentina, Brazil, and

Japan. The war fought to make the world safe for democracy seemed instead to have brought its progress to an abrupt halt and to have unleashed social movements from the Right and the Left intent on destroying it.

The aftermath of World War II, on the other hand, marked another dramatic, if brief, spurt in the multiplication of democratic regimes. With the support of its allies, the United States imposed democracy on West Germany, Austria, Italy, and Japan (where it took root), and attempted to do so in South Korea (where it did not). Coincidentally, the process of decolonization got underway with newly independent countries usually adopting at first the political forms of the imperial powers. In at least some cases, such as India, Israel, Ceylon, and the Philippines, the forms of democracy were accompanied by the substance also. Other countries, such as Turkey and some Latin American states, moved to emulate the political systems of the victorious Western powers. By the early 1950s, the proportion of democracies among the world's independent states had reached another high.

The fourth period in the evolution of democratic regimes, from the early 1950s to the 1980s, differs from the other three. In each of them, there was an overwhelmingly dominant trend, either toward the extension of democracy (1820–1920 and 1942–1953) or toward its reduction (1920–1942). In each period there were very few, if any, significant regime shifts against the dominant trend. The thirty years from the early 1950s to the early 1980s, however, were not characterized by a strong move in either direction. The trends were mixed. As we have seen, the number of democratic regimes seemed to expand in the 1950s and early 1960s, to shrink in the middle-late 1960s and early 1970s, and then to expand again in the late 1970s and early 1980s. Overall, however, the net record of change in the state of democracy in the world was not very great. It would be difficult to argue that the world was more or less democratic in 1984 than it had been in 1954. Indicative of this relative stability, albeit for a much shorter period of time, are Freedom House's estimates of the proportion of the world's population living in "free" states. In the first such estimate, in January 1973, 32.0 percent of the world's population was found to live in "free" states. In the next year, the percentage increased to 36.0 percent. During the following ten years, except for the two years India was under emergency rule (when it was 19.8 percent and 19.6 percent), the proportion of the world's population living in free states never went above 37.0 percent and never dropped below 35.0 percent. In January 1984 it was 36.0 percent, exactly where it had been ten years earlier.[6]

The overall stability in the extent of democracy does, however, conceal some important developments in both directions. With a few notable exceptions, almost all colonies that achieved independence after World War II shifted from democratic to nondemocratic systems. In contrast, a few countries moved in the opposite direction. These include Spain, Portugal, Colombia, Venezuela, Greece, and the Dominican Republic. Several South

American countries, including two with long-standing democratic systems (Chile, Uruguay) and two with less stable populist systems (Brazil, Argentina), became bureaucratic–authoritarian states, with military governments intent upon fairly sustained rule. By the end of 1983, however, Brazil had made substantial progress back toward a democratic system, and Argentina had a democratically elected government. Many other countries (including Peru, Ecuador, Ghana, Nigeria, and Turkey) seemed to oscillate back and forth between democratic and undemocratic systems, in a pattern traditionally characteristic of praetorian societies. In East Asia: Korea, Singapore, Indonesia, and the Philippines became less democratic; Taiwan remained undemocratic; the Indochinese states succumbed to a ruthless Vietnamese totalitarianism; and Thailand and Malaysia remained partially democratic. Finally, efforts to move Hungary, Czechoslovakia, and Poland toward more democratic politics were halted directly or indirectly by Soviet action.

Any estimate of the future of democracy in the world must be rooted in an explanation of why these mixed trends prevailed between the 1950s and the 1980s, and hence whether the overall stability in the prevalence of democratic regimes in the world will continue. Ancient and modern political analysts have many theories to explain the rise and fall of democratic regimes. To what extent do these various and conflicting theories explain what happened and did not happen after World War II and what could happen in the 1980s?

Thinking about the reasons for the emergence of democratic regimes has typically had two foci. One approach has focused on the preconditions in society that favor democratic development. A second approach has focused on the nature of the political processes by which that development has occurred. Each will be considered in turn.

Preconditions of democratization

In 1970, Dankwart Rustow published a penetrating article on "transitions to democracy," in which he criticized studies that focused on "preconditions" for democratization because they often tended to jump from the correlation between democracy and other factors to the conclusion that those other factors were responsible for democracy. They also tended, he argued, to look for the causes of democracy primarily in economic, social, cultural, and psychological, but not political, factors.[7] Rustow's criticisms were well taken and helped to provide a more balanced view of the complexities of democratization. It would, however, be a mistake to swing entirely to the other extreme and ignore the environmental factors that may affect democratic development. In fact, plausible arguments can be and have been made for a wide variety of factors or preconditions that appear to be associated with the emergence of democratic regimes. To a large extent these factors can be grouped into four broad categories—economic, social, external, and cultural.

Economic wealth and equality

In his critique, Rustow gave special attention to an influential article published by Seymour Martin Lipset a decade earlier. In that piece, Lipset highlighted the seeming correlation between high levels of economic development and the prevalence of democratic political systems among European, English-speaking, and Latin American nations. The "more well-to-do a nation," he postulated, "the greater the chances that it will sustain democracy."[8] His study stimulated a flood of further analyses that criticized, qualified, and refined his argument. Whatever the academic hairsplittings, however, his basic point seemed to make sense. "There is," as another scholar put it in 1960, "a positive correlation between economic development and political competitiveness."[9] A quarter-century later, that correlation still seemed to exist. In 1981, for instance, a comparison of the World Bank's ratings of countries in terms of economic development with Freedom House's ratings of them in terms of liberty showed these results: two of thirty-six low-income countries were classified "free" or democratic, fourteen out of sixty middle-income countries were so classified, and eighteen out of twenty-four countries with industrial economies were so classified.[10] As one moves up the economic ladder, the greater are the chances that a country will be democratic.

The correlation between wealth and democracy is thus fairly strong. How can it be explained? There are three possibilities. First, both democracy and wealth could be caused by a third factor. Protestantism has, for instance, been assigned by some a major role in the origins of capitalism, economic development, and democracy. Second, democracy could give rise to economic wealth. In fact, however, high levels of economic wealth require high rates of economic growth and high rates of economic growth do not correlate with the prevalence of democratic political systems.[11] Hence, it seems unlikely that wealth depends on democracy, and, if a connection exists, democracy must depend on wealth.

The probability of any causal connection running from wealth to democracy is enhanced by the arguments as to why this would be a plausible relationship. A wealthy economy, it is said, makes possible higher levels of literacy, education, and mass media exposure, all of which are conducive to democracy. A wealthy economy also moderates the tensions of political conflict; alternative opportunities are likely to exist for unsuccessful political leaders and greater economic resources generally facilitate accommodation and compromise. In addition, a highly developed, industrialized economy and the complex society it implies cannot be governed efficiently by authoritarian means. Decision-making is necessarily dispersed, and hence power is shared and rule must be based on consent. Finally, in a more highly developed economy, income and possibly wealth also tend to be more equally distributed than in a poorer economy. Since democracy means, in some measure, majority rule, democracy is only possible if the majority is a relatively satisfied middle class, and not an impoverished majority confronting an inordinately wealthy oligarchy. A substantial middle class, in turn, may be the product of the relatively equal distribution of land in agrarian societies that may otherwise be relatively poor, such as the early nineteenth century United States or twentieth century Costa Rica. It may also be the result of a relatively high level of development, which produces greater income equality in industrial as compared to industrializing societies.

If these arguments are correct, economic development in the Communist world and the Third World should facilitate the emergence of democratic regimes. Yet one must be skeptical as to whether such an easy conclusion is warranted. In the first place, there is the quesion as to what level of economic development is required to make possible the transition to democracy. As Jonathan Sunshine has conclusively shown, the countries of Western Europe generally became democratic when their per capita gross domestic products were in the range of $300–$500 (in 1960 dollars). By 1981, perhaps two-thirds of the middle-income developing countries had reached or exceeded that level of development. Most of them, however, had not become democratic. If the economic theory holds, the level of economic development necessary to facilitate the transition to democracy must be higher in the late twentieth century than it was in the century prior to 1950.[12] In addition, different countries may still transit to democracy at widely varying levels of development. Spain, after all, did grow extremely rapidly during the 1950s and 1960s and did become democratic after the death of Francisco Franco in the mid-1970s. Could this have happened without the industrialization, urbanization, and development of the middle class that were central to Spanish economic growth? Quite probably not. Lopez Rodo was at least partially right when he had earlier predicted that Spain would become democratic when its per capita income reached $2,000 per head.[13] But then what about Portugal? It made a simultaneous transition to democracy, without having experienced the massive economic development of Spain and while still at a much lower level of economic well-being.

In addition, what about the experience of the southern cone states of Latin America? They too went through major processes of economic development and yet turned away from democracy, a phenomenon that led Guillermo O'Donnell to develop his theory of bureaucratic authoritarianism that posited just the opposite of the Lipset wealth-democracy theory. Instead, O'Donnell argued that economic development and particularly the strains produced by a heavy emphasis on import substitution led to the emergence of new, stronger, and more lasting forms of authoritarian rule.[14]

There is also the experience of the East Asian newly industrializing countries. In the 1960s and 1970s, these countries not only had the highest economic growth rates in the world, but they also achieved those rates while in most cases maintaining very equitable systems of income distribution. Yet none became more democratic and two of the most notable economic achievers, Korea and Singapore, became less so.

At the same time, the economic theory may still serve a purpose in terms of focusing attention on those countries where transitions to democratic or other types of modern political systems are most likely to occur. As countries develop economically, they can be conceived of moving into a zone of transition or choice, in which traditional forms of rule become increasingly difficult to maintain and new types of political institutions are required to aggregate the demands of an increasingly complex society and to implement public policies in such a society. In the 1981 World Bank ordering of countries by level of economic development, the zone of choice might be conceived as comprising the top one-third of the middle-income countries, that is, those running from Number 77 (the Republic of Korea) up to Number 96 (Spain). To these should be added Taiwan, which in terms of per capita income fits in the middle of this group. Of these twenty-one countries:

> · seven were democracies, including four (Spain, Venezuela, Portugal, Greece) that transited to democracy after World War II, two that became democratic on independence (Israel, Trinidad and Tobago), and one that had sustained democracy for many years (Costa Rica);
> · four were the bureaucratic–authoritarian (B-A) states of the southern cone (Brazil, Chile, Argentina, Uruguay);
> · four were the newly industrializing countries (NICs) of East Asia (the Republic of Korea, Taiwan, Singapore, Hong Kong);
> · two were Communist (Rumania and Yugoslavia);
> · and the remaining four (Algeria, Mexico, Iran, and South Africa) were resource rich, ideologically diverse, and politically undemocratic.

Two years later, this group of countries, now labeled by the World Bank as "upper middle income countries," had been reduced by the graduation of Spain into the category of "industrial market economies," but had been enlarged by the movement upward of Malaysia, Lebanon, and Panama, and by the Bank's transfer into it of Iraq from the category of "high income oil exporters."[15]

If the wealth theory of democracy were valid, one would predict further movement toward democracy among the twenty-odd states in this group, perhaps particularly on the part of the East Asian NICs and the B-A states of South America. Experience suggests, however, that what is predictable for these countries in the transition zone is not the advent of democracy but rather the demise of previously existing political forms. Economic development compels the modification or abandonment of traditional political institutions; it does not determine what political system will replace them. That will be shaped by other factors, such as the underlying culture of the society, the values of the elites, and external influences.

In the late 1950s, for instance, both Cuba and Venezuela were reaching the level of economic development where the traditional sort of military despotism to which each had been subjected for years (Fulgencio y Batista

Zaldivar, Marcos Pérez Jiménez) was no longer adequate for the needs of the society. These military despotisms came to their ends in 1958 and 1959. Batista collapsed in the face of an armed revolutionary movement that rapidly seized and consolidated power, nationalized private property, and installed a pervasive Marxist-Leninist dictatorship. The Pérez Jiménez regime collapsed as a result of the withdrawal of support by virtually all the major groups of Venezuelan society. That collapse was accompanied, however, by the negotiation of a series of pacts among Venezuelan leaders representing the major political and social groups that set the framework for a democratic political system.[16] By the late 1950s, the days of traditional personalistic despotism in Cuba and Venezuela were numbered; what was not fixed was what would replace them. Fidel Castro chose to lead Cuba in one direction; Rómulo Betancourt chose to lead Venezuela in a very different one. Fifteen years later in somewhat comparable circumstances King Juan Carlos and Adolfo Suárez in Spain and António Ramalho Eanes in Portugal made similar choices on behalf of democracy. In another case, by the mid-1970s the rapid economic development of Iran had clearly undermined the basis for the shah's regime. The shah did not attempt to develop a broader, more participatory set of democratic institutions. His inaction, combined with the decision or lack of decision by the military leaders and the political skill of the mullahs, opened Iran to a religious revolution. Different and earlier decisions by Iranian leaders in the 1960s and 1970s might have moved Iran in a more democratic direction.

If the concept of a transition zone is valid, economic development produces a phase in a nation's history where political elites and the prevailing political values can shape choices that decisively determine the nation's future evolution. The range of choice may be limited. In 1981, for instance, all countries with per capita gross national products of $4,220 or more (aside from the small oil-exporting states and Singapore) were either democratic or Communist. Conceivably, transition zone countries could make other choices. Iran is obviously in the fanatic pursuit of a different course; possibly the East Asian NICs and the Latin American B-A regimes may find other alternatives. To date, however, those countries that have come through the transition zone have almost always emerged as either democracies or as Communist dictatorships.

Social structure

A second set of often-discussed preconditions for democracy involves the extent to which there is a widely differentiated and articulated social structure with relatively autonomous social classes, regional groups, occupational groups, and ethnic and religious groups. Such groups, it is argued, provide the basis for the limitation of state power, hence for the control of the state by society, and hence for democratic political institutions as the most effective means of exercising that control. Societies that lack autonomous intermediate groups are, on the other hand, much more likely to be dominated by a centralized power apparatus—an absolute monarchy, an oriental despotism, or an authoritarian or totalitarian dictatorship.[17] This argument can be made on behalf of groups and pluralism in general or on behalf of particular groups or types of pluralistic structure which are singled out as playing a decisive role in making democracy possible.

According to one line of argument, pluralism (even highly stratified pluralism) in traditional society enhances the probability of developing stable democracy in modern society. The caste system may be one reason why India has been able to develop and to maintain stable democratic institutions.[18] More generally, the argument is made that societies with a highly developed feudalism, including an aristocracy capable of limiting the development of state power, are more likely to evolve into democracies than those that lack such social pluralism. The record of Western Europe versus Russia and of Japan versus China suggests that there may well be something to this theory. But the theory fails to account for differences between North America and South America. Tocqueville, Louis Hartz, and others attribute democracy in the former to the absence of feudalism. The failure of democracy in South America has, conversely, often been attributed precisely to its feudal heritage, although the feudalism that existed there was, to be sure, highly centralized.[19]

The theory that emphasizes traditional pluralism is, in a sense, the opposite of the one that emphasizes wealth as a precondition of democracy. The latter makes democracy dependent on how far the processes of economic development and modernization have gone. The traditional pluralism theory, in contrast, puts the emphasis on where the process started, on the nature of traditional society. Was it, in Gaetano Mosca's terms, primarily a "feudal" or a "bureaucratic" society? If pushed to the extreme, of course, this theory implies societal predestination: it is all determined in advance that some societies will become democratic and others will not.

The most significant manifestation of the social structure argument, however, concerns not the existence of a feudal aristocracy, but rather the existence of an autonomous bourgeoisie. Democracy, the Marxists argue, is bourgeois democracy, reflecting the interests of that particular social class. Barrington Moore has restated the proposition succinctly in a more limited formulation: "No bourgeois, no democracy."[20] This argument would seem to have much to commend it. The failure of democracy to develop in Third World countries despite their economic growth can, perhaps, be related to the nature of that growth. The leading roles have been played by the state and by multinational enterprises. As a result, economic development runs ahead of the development of a bourgeoisie. In those circumstances where a bourgeoisie has developed, however, the prospects for democracy have been greater. The move to democracy in Turkey in the 1940s coincided with the move away from the étatisme of Kemalism and the appearance of a group of independent businessmen. More significantly, the ability of a developing country to have an autonomous, indigenous bourgeoisie is likely to be related to its size. Countries with small internal markets are unlikely to be able to sustain such a class, but large ones can. This may be one factor explaining why India (with one short interlude) has sustained a democratic system, and why Brazil, which is also developing a vigorous indigenous bourgeoisie, steadily moved away from bureaucratic authoritarianism in the 1970s and early 1980s. In South Africa, businessmen have been among those most active in attempting to ameliorate apartheid and broaden democracy in that country.

The seemingly important role of an autonomous bourgeoisie for the development of democracy highlights the question of the relation between economic system and political system. Clearly political democracy is compatible with both a substantial role in the economy for state-owned enterprises and a substantial state welfare and social security system. Nonetheless, as Charles Lindblom has pointed out (in a volume that otherwise highlights the conflict between the business corporation and democracy), all political democracies have market-oriented economies, although quite clearly not all market-oriented economies are paired with democratic political systems.[21] Lindblom's message would seem to be like Moore's—a market-oriented economy, like a bourgeoisie, is a necessary but not sufficient condition for the existence of a democratic political system.

Why should this be the case? At least two reasons suggest themselves. Politically, a market economy requires a dispersion of economic power and in practice almost invariably some form of private property. The dispersion of economic power creates alternatives and counters to state power and enables those elites that control economic power to limit state power and to exploit democratic means to make it serve their interests. Economically, a market economy appears more likely to sustain economic growth than a command economy (although the latter may, as the Soviet and East European cases suggest, do so for a short period of time), and hence a market economy is more likely to give rise to the economic wealth and the resulting more equitable distribution of income that provide the infrastructure of democracy.

A third source of autonomous social pressure in a democratic direction may be provided by labor unions. Historically, unions played this role in Western Europe and the United States. In the contemporary world, unions have also had a role in the struggles against the racist oligarchy in South Africa, against military rule in the southern cone, and against the Communist dictatorship in Poland. At the same time, the experience of these cases also suggsts the limits on the extent to which, in the absence of affiliated political parties, labor unions can affect political change.

Under some conditions, communal (that is, ethnic, racial, or religious) pluralism may be conducive to the development of at least limited forms of democracy. In most cases of communal pluralism, democracy can operate only on a consociational rather than a majoritarian basis.[22] And even when it is organized on a consociational basis, it will often break down as a result of social mobilization that undermines the power of elites or as a result of the intrusion of external political and military forces (as in Cyprus or Lebanon). Even in the best of circumstances, consociational democracy can often only remain stable by in effect becoming consociational oligarchy (as in Malaysia), that is, by sacrificing contestation in order to maintain representation.

External environment

External influences may be of decisive importance in influencing whether a society moves in a democratic or non-democratic direction. To the extent that such influences are more important than indigenous factors, democratization is the result of diffusion rather than development. Conceivably, democracy in the world could stem from a single source. Clearly it does not. Yet it would be wrong to ignore the extent to which much of the democracy in the world does have a common origin. In 1984, Freedom House classified fifty-two countries (many of them extremely small) as "free."[23] In thirty-three of those fifty-two countries, the presence of democratic institutions could be ascribed in large part to British and American influence, either through settlement, colonial rule, defeat in war, or fairly direct imposition (such as in the Dominican Republic). Most of the other nineteen "free" countries where democracy had other sources were either in Western Europe or in South America. The extension of democracy into the non-Western world, insofar as that has occurred, has thus been largely the product of Anglo–American efforts.

Ever since the French Revolution, armies have carried political ideologies with them. As we have indicated, where American armies went in World War II, democracy followed (in four cases enduringly, in one case temporarily). Where Soviet armies went, communism followed. Military conquest is clearly one way of extending democracy and other political systems. Historically, however, Western colonialism has been the most important means of diffusing democratic ideas and institutions. The enduring results of such colonialism have, however, been rather limited. As of 1983, no former French, u.s., Dutch, Portuguese, or Belgian colony was rated "free" by Freedom House. Several former British colonies were. Myron Weiner has, indeed, emphasized that *"every single country in the third world that emerged from colonial rule since the second world war with a population of at least one million (and almost all the smaller countries as well) with a continuous democratic experience is a former British colony."*[24] British rule seemingly had a significantly different impact from that of other colonial powers. Only six countries meet Weiner's conditions, however, and a much larger number of former British colonies have *not* sustained democracy. The question then becomes how to distinguish among former British colonies. One possibility is that the duration of democratic institutions after independence is a function of the duration of British rule before independence. The colonies where democratic institutions appear to have taken the firmest root are those such as India, Sri Lanka, and the West Indian Anglophone states, where British rule dates from the eighteenth century. The record of former British colonies in Africa, on the other hand, where British rule dates only from the late nineteenth century, is not all that different from that of the former African colonies of other European powers.

In large measure, the rise and decline of democracy on a global scale is a function of the rise and decline of the most powerful democratic states. The spread of democracy in the nineteenth century went hand in hand with the Pax Britannica. The extension of democracy after World War II reflected the global power of the United States. The decline of democracy in East Asia and Latin America in the 1970s was in part a reflection of the waning of American influence.[25] That influence is felt both directly, as a result of the efforts of the American government to affect political processes in other societies, and also indirectly by providing a powerful and successful model to be followed.

Regional external influences can also have a significant effect on political development within a society. The governments and political parties of the European Community (EC) helped to encourage the emergence of democratic institutions in Spain and Portugal, and the desire of those two countries plus Greece to join the community provided an additional incentive for them to become democratic. Even beyond the confines of the EC, Western Europe has generally become defined as a community of democratic nations, and any significant departure by one nation from the democratic norm would clearly create a major crisis in intra-European relations. In some measure, a similar development may be taking place among the countries of the Andean Pact. The departure from the Pact of Chile and the addition of Venezuela in the mid-1970s, plus the transitions to democracy in Ecuador and Peru, then laid the basis for identifying pact membership with the adherence to democratic government.

In some regions, but most notably in Latin America, regional trends may exist. By and large, Latin American governments moved in a democratic direction in the late 1950s and early 1960s, then in an authoritarian direction in the late 1960s and early 1970s, and then once again in a democratic direction in the late 1970s and early 1980s. The reasons for these regional shifts are not entirely clear. They could be a result of four factors: simultaneous parallel socioeconomic development in Latin American societies; the triggering of a trend by the impact of one "pace-setting" Latin American society on its neighbors; the impact on Latin America of a common external influence (such as the United States); or some combination of these factors.

Cultural context

The political culture of a society has been defined by Sidney Verba as "the system of empirical beliefs, expressive symbols, and values which defines the situation in which political action takes place."[26] Political culture is, presumably, rooted in the broader culture of a society involving those beliefs and values, often religiously based, concerning the nature of humanity and society, the relations among human beings, and the relation of individuals to a transcendent being. Significant differences in their receptivity to democracy appear to exist among societies with different cultural traditions.

Historically, as many scholars have pointed out, a high correlation existed between Protestantism and democracy. In the contemporary world, virtually all countries with a European population and a Protestant majority (except East Germany) have democratic governments.[27] The case of Catholicism, particularly in Latin countries, on the other hand, is more ambivalent. Historically, it was often argued that a natural opposition existed between Catholicism and democracy. By and large, democratic institutions developed later and less surely in European Catholic countries than in Protestant ones. By and large, however, these countries also developed later economically than the Protestant countries, and hence it is difficult to distinguish between the impact of economics and that of religion. Conceivably, the influence of the latter on politics could have been mediated through its impact on economic development and the rise of an entrepreneurial class. With economic development, however, the role of the church changed, and in most Catholic countries now the church is identified with support for democracy.

Islam, on the other hand, has not been hospitable to democracy. Of thirty-six countries with Moslem majorities, Freedom House in 1984 rated twenty-one as "not free," fifteen as "partially free," none as "free." The one Islamic country that sustained even intermittent democracy after World War II was Turkey, which had, under Mustapha Kemal, explicitly rejected its Islamic tradition and defined itself as a secular republic. The one Arab country that sustained democracy, albeit of the consociational variety, for any time was Lebanon, 40 to 50 percent of whose population was Christian and whose democratic institutions collapsed when the Moslem majority asserted itself in the 1970s. Somewhat similarly, both Confucianism and Buddhism have been conducive to authoritarian rule, even in those cases where, as in Korea, Taiwan, and Singapore, economic preconditions for democracy have come into being. In India and Japan, on the other hand, the traditional Hindu and Shinto cultures at the very least did not prevent the development of democratic institutions and may well have encouraged it.

How can these differences be explained? Both doctrinal and structural aspects of the religions could play a role. At the most obvious level, those cultures that are consummatory in character—that is, where intermediate and ultimate ends are closely connected—seem to be less favorable to democracy. In Islam, for instance, no distinction exists between religion and politics or between the spiritual and the secular, and political participation was historically an alien concept.[28] Somewhat similarly, Confucianism in China was generally hostile to social bodies independent of the state, and the culture was conceived as a total entity, no part of which could be changed without threatening the whole. Instrumental cultures, in contrast, are "characterized by a large sector of intermediate ends separate from and independent of ultimate ends" and hence "ultimate ends do not color every concrete act."[29] The Hindu tradition, for example, is relatively tolerant of diversity. S. N. Eisenstadt has written that "the basic religious and cultural orientations, the specific cultural identity of Indian civilization were not necessarily associated with any particular political or imperial framework. . . ."[30]

As a whole, consummatory culture is thus more resistant to change, and when change comes in one significant element of the culture, the entire culture is thrown into question or is displaced and destroyed. In the instrumental culture, on the other hand, change can come gradually and incrementally. Hence, less resistance exists to the adaptation of new political forms, such as democratic institutions, and the process of adaptation can be an extended one that in itself facilitates the development of stable democracy.

With respect to the more narrowly political culture of a society, it seems reasonable to expect that the prevalence of some values and beliefs will be more conducive to the emergence of democracy than others. A political culture that values highly hierarchical relationships and extreme deference to authority presumably is less fertile ground for democracy than one that does not. Similarly, a culture in which there is a high degree of mutual trust among members of the society is likely to be more favorable to democracy than one in which interpersonal relationships are more generally characterized by suspicion, hostility, and distrust. A willingness to tolerate diversity and conflict among groups and to recognize the legitimacy of compromise also should be helpful to democratic development. Societies in which great stress is put on the need to acquire power and little on the need to accommodate others are more likely to have authoritarian or totalitarian regimes. Social scientists have attempted to compare societies along these various dimensions, but the evidence remains fragmented and difficult to systematize.[31] In addition, of course, even if some beliefs and values are found to correlate with the presence of democratic institutions, the question still remains concerning the relationship among these in a developmental sense. To what extent does the development of a pro-democratic political culture have to precede the development of democratic institutions? Or do the two tend to develop more simultaneously with the succesful operation of democratic institutions, possibly created for other reasons, generating adherence to democratic values and beliefs?"[32]

Processes of democratization

The classic model of democratization that has infused much discussion of the subject is that of Britain, with its stately progression from civic rights to political rights to social rights, gradual development of parliamentary supremacy and cabinet government, and incremental expansion of the suffrage over the course of a century. It is basically a linear model. Dankwart A. Rustow's model, based on Swedish experience—national unity, prolonged and inconclusive political struggle, a conscious decision to adopt democratic rules, habituation to the working of those rules—also involves a relatively simple linear progression. These "ingredients," he has argued, "must be assembled one at a time."[33] These linear models primarily reflect European experience during the century ending in 1920 and the experience of some Latin American countries (such as Argentina until 1930 and Chile until 1973).

Two other models have generally been more relevant than the linear model to the experience of Third World countries. One is the cyclical model of alternating despotism and democracy. In this case, key elites normally accept, at least superficially, the legitimacy of democratic forms. Elections are held from time to time, but rarely is there any sustained succession of governments coming to power through the electoral process. Governments are as often the product of military interventions as they are of elections. Such interventions tend to occur either when a radical party wins or appears about to win an election, when the government in power threatens or appears to threaten the prerogatives of the armed forces, or when the government appears incapable of effectively guiding the economy and maintaining public order. Once a military junta takes over, it will normally promise to return power to civilian rule. In due course, it does so, if only to minimize divisiveness within the armed forces and to escape from its own inability to govern effectively. In a praetorian situation like this, neither authoritarian nor democratic institutions are effectively institutionalized. Once countries enter into this cyclical pattern, it appears to be extremely difficult for them to escape from it. In many respects, countries that have had relatively stable authoritarian rule (such as Spain and Portugal) are more likely to evolve into relatively stable democracies than countries that have regularly oscillated between despotism and democracy (such as Peru, Ecuador, Bolivia, Argentina, Ghana, Nigeria). In the latter, neither democratic nor authoritarian norms have deep roots among the relevant political elites, while in the former a broad consensus accepting of authoritarian norms is displaced by a broad consensus on or acceptance of democratic ones. In the one case, the alternation of democracy and despotism *is* the political system; in the other, the shift from a stable despotism to a stable democracy *is a change* in political systems.

A third model is neither linear nor cyclical but rather dialectical. In this case, the development of a middle class leads to increased pressures on the existing authoritarian regimes for expanded participation and contestation. At some point, there is then a sharp break, perhaps in the form of what I have elsewhere called the "urban breakthrough," the overthrow of the existing authoritarian regime, and the installation of a democratic one.[34] This regime, however, finds it difficult or impossible to govern effectively.

A sharp reaction occurs with the overthrow of the democratic system and installation of a (usually right-wing) authoritarian regime. In due course, however, this regime collapses and a transition is made to a more stable, more balanced, and longer-lasting democratic system. This model is roughly applicable to the history of a number of countries, including Germany, Italy, Austria, Greece, and Spain.

Most theories of political development in general and of democratization in particular see these processes as involving a number of different elements. The sequence in which those components appear may have important implications for the overall results of the process. Several theorists have suggested, for instance, that the preferable overall process of development for a country is first to define its national identity, next to develop effective institutions of authority, and then to expand political participation. The "probabilities of a political system's development in a nonviolent, non-authoritarian, and eventually democratically stable manner are maximized," Eric Nordlinger has argued, when this sequence occurs.[35] In somewhat parallel fashion, it has been argued that the development of broad-gauged political institutions for political participation, such as electoral and party systems, must coincide with or precede the expansion of political participation if instability and violence are to be avoided. Similarly, Robert A. Dahl emphasizes the greater probability of success in transitions to democracy (or polyarchy in his terms) if the expansion of contestation precedes the expansion of participation.[36]

All these theories thus emphasize the desirability for the eventual development of stable democracy of the expansion of political participation occurring relatively late in the sequence of change. However, given the widely accepted desirability of political participation (including in totalitarian regimes) and the major increases in social mobilization (such as urbanization, literacy, and media consumption) produced by economic development, the prevailing tendencies in the contemporary world are for participation to expand early in the process of development, and before or concurrently with contestation. This may be one reason why economic development in the Third World has not stimulated the emergence of more stable democratic regimes. At present, the one notable case where contestation has clearly developed in advance of participation is South Africa. Hence, according to the Dahl thesis, the prospects for democratic development should be greater in South Africa than elsewhere in Africa.

It is often assumed that since democracy, to a greater degree than other forms of government, involves rule by the people, the people therefore play a greater role in bringing it into existence than they do with other forms of government. In fact, however, democratic regimes that last have seldom, if ever, been instituted by mass popular action. Almost always, democracy has come as much from the top down as from the bottom up; it is as likely to be the product of oligarchy as of protest against oligarchy. The passionate dissidents from authoritarian rule and the crusaders for democratic principles, the Tom Paines of this world, do not create democratic institutions; that requires James Madisons. Those institutions come into existence through negotiations and compromises among political elites calculating their own interests and desires. They are produced when, as Rustow argued, political leaders decide "to accept the existence of diversity in unity and, to that end, to institutionalize some crucial aspect of democratic procedure." The political leaders may do this because they are convinced of the ethical and political superiority of democracy and hence view democracy as a desirable goal in itself. More likely, however, they will view democracy as a means to other goals, such as prolonging their own rule, achieving international legitimacy, minimizing domestic opposition, and reducing the likelihood of civil violence, from which they will probably suffer. Hence, whatever institutions are agreed on will, in Rustow's words, "seem second-best to all major parties involved."[37] One could paraphrase Reinhold Niebuhr: the ability of elites to compromise makes democracy possible; the inclination of elites to vengeance makes democracy desirable—for the elites.

In the decades after World War II, democratic regimes have usually been introduced in independent countries through one or some combination of two processes. *Replacement* occurs when an authoritarian regime collapses or is overthrown as a result of military defeat, economic disaster, or the withdrawal of support from it by substantial groups in the population. Its leaders are killed, imprisoned, flee the country, or withdraw from politics. The leaders of the now-dominant groups, which had not been actively involved with the authoritarian regime, agree among themselves to institute a democratic system. This agreement may be reached very quickly because of previous experience with democracy and because its inauguration is seen as the "obvious" solution by the relevant political elites, as in Venezuela in 1958 and Greece in 1974. Or it may come about as a result of political struggle among elites with differing views as to the future of their country, out of which the leaders committed to democracy emerge successfully (as in Portugal in 1975–76). This process may involve, as it did in the case of Venezuela, a series of carefully negotiated pacts among the relevant groups that can cover economic policy and the role of institutions (such as the church and the army), as well as the procedures for choosing a government. One critical issue on which the constitutive elites must agree is how to treat those actively involved in the previous authoritarian regime.[38]

The alternative process for inaugurating a democratic regime might be termed *transformation*. In this case, the elites within an authoritarian system conclude that, for some reason or another, that system which they have led and presumably benefited from no longer meets their needs or those of their society. They hence take the lead in modifying the existing political system and transforming it into a democratic one. In this case, while there may well be a variety of internal and external pressures favoring change, the initiative for such change comes from the rulers. Transformation involves, as Juan Linz put it, "change through *reforma* rather than *ruptura*."[39] Notable examples include, of course, Britain in the nineteenth century, and after World War II, Turkey in the 1940s, Spain in the 1970s, and Brazil in the 1970s and 1980s. The leaders of the transformation process typically confront all the problems of the political reformer, having to maneuver skillfully between the stand-patters opposed to any democratization, on the one hand, and the committed dissident and opposition groups demanding the immediate dissolution of the authoritarian system, on the other. Essential to their success is that they be seen as keeping control, acting from a position of strength and not under duress, and dictating the pace of change.

The replacement process requires compromise and agreement among elites who have not been part of the authoritarian regime. The transformation process requires skilled leadership from and agreement among the elites who are part of that regime. In neither case is agreement necessarily required between elites who are within the regime and those opposing the regime. This situation makes replacement and transformation possible, since reaching an agreement between out-groups and in-groups is far more difficult than reaching an agreement among out-groups or among in-groups. Except for Costa Rica in 1948, it is hard to think of a case where a democratic system of any duration was inaugurated by explicit agreement between the leaders of a regime and the leaders of the armed opposition to that regime.

"As long as powerful vested interests oppose changes that lead toward a less oppressive world," Barrington Moore has argued, "no commitment to a free society can dispense with some conception of revolutionary coercion."[40] His thesis is that liberty and democracy can be inaugurated by bloody revolution and that such a course may well impose fewer costs than the alternative of gradual reform. When in world history, however, has violent revolution produced a stable democratic regime in an independent state? "Revolutionary coercion" may bring down an authoritarian regime but, except again for Costa Rica in 1948, guerrilla insurgencies do not inaugurate democratic regimes. All revolutionary opponents of authoritarian regimes claim to be democrats; once they achieve power through violence, almost all turn out to be authoritarian themselves, often imposing an even more repressive regime than the one they overthrew. Most authoritarian regimes are thus replaced by new authoritarian regimes, and a democratic succession usually requires minimum violence. "In the future as in the past," as Dahl concluded his study of this issue, "stable polyarchies and near-polyarchies are more likely to result from rather slow evolutionary processes than from revolutionary overthrow of existing hegemonies."[41]

The prospects for democracy

This brief and informal survey of the preconditions and processes conducive to the emergence of democratic regimes argues for caution in any effort to predict whether more countries will become democratic. It may, however, be useful to attempt to sum up the modest conclusions which seem to emerge from this review.

With respect to preconditions, the emergence of democracy in a society is helped by a number of factors: higher levels of economic well-being; the absence of extreme inequalities in wealth and income; greater social pluralism, including particularly a strong and autonomous bourgeoisie; a more market-oriented economy; greater influence vis-à-vis the society of existing democratic states; and a culture that is less monistic and more tolerant of diversity and compromise. No one of these preconditions is sufficient to lead to democratic development. With the possible exception of a market economy, no single precondition is necessary to produce such development. Some combination of some of these preconditions is required for a democratic regime to emerge, but the nature of that combination can vary greatly from one case to another. It is also necessary, however, to look not only at what preconditions must be present but also at the negative strength of any precondition that may be absent. The powerful absence of one favorable condition, or, conversely, the presence of a powerful negative condition, that overrides the presence of otherwise favorable conditions, may prevent democratic development. In terms of cultural tradition, economic development, and social structure, Czechoslovakia would certainly be a democracy today (and probably Hungary and Poland also) if it were not for the overriding veto of the Soviet presence. In similar fashion, extreme poverty, extreme economic inequalities, or deeply ingrained Islamic and Confucian cultural traditions could have comparable effect in Africa, Central America, or the Middle East and East Asia.

With respect to the processes necessary to bring about democratic development, a central requirement would appear to be that either the established elites within an authoritarian system or the successor elites after an authoritarian system collapses see their interests served by the introduction of democratic institutions. The probability of stable democracy emerging will be enhanced to the extent that the transition can be a gradual one, that the introduction of contestation precedes the expansion of political participation, and that the role of violence in the transition is minimized. The probability of democratization decreases sharply to the extent that political life in a society becomes highly polarized and involves violent conflict between social forces.

Possibility of regime changes

In terms of these generalizations, prospects for democratic development in the 1980s are probably greatest in the bureaucratic-authoritarian states of South America. Cultural traditions, levels of economic development, previous democratic experience, social pluralism (albeit with weak bourgeoisies outside Brazil), and elite desires to emulate European and North American models all favor movement toward democracy in these countries. On the other hand, the polarization and violence that has occurred (particularly in Argentina and Chile) could make such movement difficult. The prospects for a relatively stable democratic system should be greatest in Brazil. Beginning in the early 1970s, the leadership of the Brazilian regime began a process of *distensão*, gradually relaxing the authoritarian controls that had been imposed in the 1960s. By the early 1980s, Brazil had acquired many of the characteristics of a democratic system. The principal deficiency was the absence of popular elections for the chief executive, but those were generally viewed as certain to come sometime in the 1980s. The gradualness of the Brazilian process, the relative low level of violence that accompanied it, and the general recognition among elite groups of the importance of not disrupting it in any way, all seemed to enhance the prospects for democracy.

In Argentina, the economic and military failures of the authoritarian regime led to a much more dramatic and rapid transit to democracy in 1983. The probabilities of this replacement being sustained would seem to depend on three factors: the ability of the Alfonsín government to deal with the economic problems it confronted; the extent to which Peronista, as well as Radical, elites were willing to abide by democratic rules; and the extent to which military leadership was effectively excluded from power or came to identify its interests with the maintenance of a democratic regime. The two other southern cone countries with bureaucratic-authoritarian regimes, Chile and Uruguay, are the two South American countries that did have the strongest democratic traditions. As of 1984, however, in neither country had authoritarian rule lost its legitimacy and effectiveness to the point where it could no longer be maintained and a replacement process could occur (as in Argentina). Nor had the leaders of either regime embarked on a meaningful transformation process to democratize their system (as in Brazil). The Brazilian and Argentine changes, however, cannot fail to have impact on political development in the smaller countries.

The probability of movement in a democratic direction in the East Asian newly industrializing countries is considerably less than it is among the Latin American B-A states. The economic basis for democracy is clearly coming into existence, and if their economic development continues at anything like the rates it did in the 1960s and 1970s, these states will soon constitute an authoritarian anomaly among the wealthier countries of the world. The East Asian countries generally have also had and maintained a relatively equal distribution of income. In addition, the United States, Britain, and Japan are the principal external influences on these societies. All these factors favor democratic development. On the other side, cultural traditions, social structure, and a general weakness of democratic norms among key elites all impede movement in a democratic direction. In some measure, the East Asian states dramatically pose the issue of whether economics or culture has the greater influence on political development. One can also speculate on whether the spread of Christianity in Korea may create a cultural context more favorable to democracy.

Among other less economically developed East Asian societies, the prospects for democracy are undoubtedly highest but still not very high in the Philippines. The Marcos government is not likely to attempt to transform itself, and hence efforts to create a democratic system must await its demise.

At that time, American influence, previous experience with democracy, social pluralism (including the influence of the Catholic Church), and the general agreement among opposition political leaders on the desirability of a return to democracy, should all provide support for movement in that direction. On the other hand, military leaders may not support democratic norms, and the existence of a radical insurgency committed to violence, plus a general proclivity to the use of violence in the society, might make such a transition difficult. Conceivably, Philippine development could follow the lines of the dialectical model referred to earlier, in which (as in Venezuela) an initial experience with democracy is broken by a personalistic authoritarian interlude that then collapses and a new, more stable democratic regime is brought into existence by agreement among political leaders. The Philippine Betancourt, however, may well have been gunned down at the Manila airport.

Among Islamic countries, particularly those in the Middle East, the prospects for democratic development seem low. The Islamic revival, and particularly the rise of Shi'ite fundamentalism, would seem to reduce even further the likelihood of democratic development, particularly since democracy is often identified with the very Western influences the revival strongly opposes. In addition, many of the Islamic states are very poor. Those that are rich, on the other hand, are so because of oil, which is controlled by the state and hence enhances the power of the state in general and of the bureaucracy in particular. Saudi Arabia and some of the smaller Arab oil-rich Gulf countries have from time to time made some modest gestures toward the introduction of democratic institutions, but these have not gone far and have often been reversed.

Most African countries are, by reason of their poverty or the violence of their politics, unlikely to move into a democratic direction. Those African and Latin American countries that have adhered to the cyclical pattern of alternating democratic and authoritarian systems in the past are not likely to change this basic pattern, as the example of Nigeria underlines, unless more fundamental changes occur in their economic and social infrastructure. In South Africa, on the other hand, the relatively high level of economic development by African standards, the intense contestation that occurs within the minority permitted to participate in politics, the modest expansion of that minority to include the Coloureds and Asians, and the influence of Western democratic norms, all provide a basis for moving in a more democratic direction. However, that basis is countered on the other side by the inequalities, fears, and hatreds that separate blacks and whites.

In some small countries, democratic institutions may emerge as a result of massive foreign effort. This did happen in the Dominican Republic; in 1984 it was, presumably, happening in Grenada; it could, conceivably, happen at extremely high cost in El Salvador.

The likelihood of democratic development in Eastern Europe is virtually nil. The Soviet presence is a decisive overriding obstacle, no matter how favorable other conditions may be in countries like Czechoslovakia, Hungary, and Poland. Democratization could occur in these societies only if either the Soviet Union were drastically weakened through war, domestic upheaval, or economic collapse (none of which seems likely), or if the Soviet Union came to view Eastern European democratization as not threatening to its interests (which seems equally unlikely).

The issue of Soviet intervention apart, a more general issue concerns the domestic pattern of evolution within Communist states. For almost four decades after World War II, no democratic country, with the dubious possible exception of Czechoslovakia in 1948, became Communist and no Communist country became democratic through internal causes. Authoritarian regimes, on the other hand, were frequently replaced by either democratic or Communist regimes, and democratic regimes were replaced by authoritarian ones. In their early phase, Communist states usually approximated the totalitarian model, with ideology and the party playing central roles and massive efforts being made to indoctrinate and mobilize the population and to extend party control throughout all institutions in the society. Over time, however, Communist regimes also tend to change and often to become less totalitarian and more authoritarian. The importance of ideology and mobilization declines, bureaucratic stagnation replaces ideological fervor, and the party becomes less a dedicated elite and more a mechanism for patronage. In some cases, military influence increases significantly. The question thus arises: Will Communist authoritarian regimes, absent Soviet control, be more susceptible to movement toward democracy than Communist totalitarian regimes?

The answer to that question may well depend on the extent to which Communist authoritarian regimes permit the development of a market-oriented economy. The basic thrust of communism suggests that such a development is unlikely. Communism is not, as Karl Marx argued, a product of capitalist democracy; nor is it simply a "disease of the transition" to capitalist democracy, to use Rostow's phrase.[42] It is instead an alternative to capitalist democracy and one whose guiding principle is the subjection of economic development to political control. Even if it becomes more authoritarian and less totalitarian, the Communist political system is likely to ensure that economic development neither achieves a level nor assumes a form that will be conducive to democracy.

The United States and global democracy

The ability of the United States to affect the development of democracy elsewhere is limited. There is little that the United States or any other foreign country can do to alter the basic cultural tradition and social structure of another society or to promote compromise among groups of that society that have been killing each other. Within the restricted limits of the possible, however, the United States could contribute to democratic development in other countries in four ways.

First, it can assist the economic development of poor countries and promote a more equitable distribution of income and wealth in those countries. Second, it can encourage developing countries to foster market economies and the development of vigorous bourgeois classes. Third, it can refurbish its own economic, military, and political power so as to be able to exercise greater influence than it has in world affairs. Finally, it can develop a concerted program designed to encourage and to help the elites of countries entering the "transition zone" to move their countries in a more democratic direction.

Efforts such as these could have a modest influence on the development of democracy in other countries. Overall, however, this survey of the preconditions for and processes of democratization leads to the conclusion that, with a few exceptions, the prospects for the extension of democracy to other societies are not great. These prospects would improve significantly only if there were major discontinuities in current trends—such as if, for instance, the economic development of the Third World were to proceed at a much faster rate and to have a far more positive impact on democratic development than it has had so far, or if the United States reestablished a hegemonic position in the world comparable to that which it had in the 1940s and 1950s. In the absence of developments such as these, a significant increase in the number of democratic regimes in the world is unlikely. The substantial power of anti-democratic governments (particularly the Soviet Union), the unreceptivity to democracy of several major cultural traditions, the difficulties of eliminating poverty in large parts of the world, and the prevalence of high levels of polarization and violence in many societies all suggest that, with a few exceptions, the limits of democratic development in the world may well have been reached.

NOTES

1. Michael W. Doyle, "Kant, Liberal Legacies, and Foreign Affairs, Part I," *Philosophy and Public Affairs* 12 (1983); 213ff.

2. Peter Bachrach, *The Theory of Democratic Elitism: A Critique* (Washington, D.C.: University Press of America, 1980), 24, 98ff.; Robert A. Dahl, *Polyarchy: Participation and Opposition* (New Haven: Yale University Press, 1971), 2. For a useful analysis of "rationalist" and "descriptive" concepts of democracy, see Jeane J. Kirkpatrick, "Democratic Elections, Democratic Government, and Democratic Theory," in David Butler, Howard R. Penniman, and Austin Ranney, eds., *Democracy at the Polls* (Washington, D.C.: American Enterprise Institute for Public Policy Research, 1981), 325–48.

3. Dahl, *Polyarchy*, 4–9. See also Joseph A. Schumpeter, *Capitalism, Socialism, and Democracy*, 2nd ed. (New York: Harper and Bros., 1947), 269: "the democratic method is that institutional arrangement for arriving at political decisions in which individuals acquire the power to decide by means of a competitive struggle for the people's vote."

4. James Bryce, *Modern Democracies*, 2 vols. (New York: Macmillan, 1921), 1:24.

5. The proportion of independent states that were democratic was roughly 19 percent in 1902, 34 percent in 1920, 32 percent in 1929–30, and 24 percent in 1960. See G. Bingham Powell, Jr., *Contemporary Democracies* (Cambridge: Harvard University Press, 1982), 238.

6. See "The Comparative Survey of Freedom" compiled annually for Freedom House by Raymond D. Gastil, particularly *Freedom at Issue*, no. 17 (1973):2–3; no. 70 (1983): 4; no. 76 (1984): 5. Freedom House classifies a state as "free" if it rates in first or second place on a seven-place scale for both political rights and civil liberties. The countries so classified all have the minimum features of a democratic political system, at least at the time of classification. While recognizing the importance of institutionalization, the Freedom House survey does not attempt to measure the extent to which democracy has become institutionalized. Thus, its 1984 survey, published at the very beginning of 1984, rated both New Zealand and Nigeria as "free," although the latter had presumably left the category as a result of the coup on New Year's Day.

7. Dankwart A. Rustow, "Transitions to Democracy: Toward a Dynamic Model," *Comparative Politics* 2 (1970):337ff.

8. Seymour Martin Lipset, "Some Social Requisites of Democracy: Economic Development and Political Legitimacy," *American Political Science Review* 53 (1959): 75.

9. James S. Coleman, "Conclusion," in Gabriel A. Almond and James S. Coleman, eds., *The Politics of the Developing Areas* (Princeton, N.J.: Princeton University Press, 1960), 538.

10. World Bank, *World Development Report 1981* (New York: Oxford University Press, 1981), 134–35; and *Freedom at Issue*, no. 64 (1982): 8–9. See also Seymour Martin Lipset's update of his earlier analysis, *Political Man: The Social Bases of Politics*, 2nd ed. (Baltimore: Johns Hopkins University Press, 1981), 469–76.

11. This is not to argue that authoritarian regimes necessarily have higher economic growth rates than democratic ones, although they may. See Robert M. Marsh, "Does Democracy Hinder Economic Development in the Latecomer Developing Nations," *Comparative Social Research* 2 (1979): 215–48; G. William Dick, "Authoritarian Versus Nonauthoritarian Approaches to Economic Development," *Journal of Political Economy* 82 (1974): 817–27; and Erich Weede, "Political Democracy, State Strength and Economic Growth in LDCs: A Cross-National Analysis" (paper presented at the Annual Meeting of the American Political Science Association, Chicago, Ill., September 1983).

12. Jonathan Sunshine, "Economic Causes and Consequences of Democracy: A Study in Historical Statistics" (Ph.D. diss., Columbia University, 1972), 115ff.

13. John F. Coverdale, *The Political Transformation of Spain after Franco* (New York: Praeger Publishers, 1979), 1.

14. Guillermo A. O'Donnell, *Modernization and Bureaucratic-Authoritarianism* (Berkeley: University of California, Institute for International Studies, 1973), 3–15, 113–14. For analysis of this theory, see David Collier, ed., *The New Authoritarianism in Latin America* (Princeton, N.J.: Princeton University Press, 1979).

15. World Bank, *Development Report 1981*, 134–135, and *World Development Report 1983* (New York: Oxford University Press, 1983), 148–49.

16. See Terry Karl, "Petroleum and Political Pacts: The Transition to Democracy in Venezuela" (Latin American Program Working Paper 107, The Wilson Center, 1981).

17. Those who hold a more Rousseauistic conception of democracy will, of course, tend to see intermediate groups as obstacles to the realization of true democracy. For a balanced analysis of these issues, see Robert A. Dahl, *Dilemmas of Pluralist Democracy: Autonomy vs. Control* (New Haven: Yale University Press, 1982). For a general argument for intermediate groups as a bulwark against totalitarianism, see William Kornhauser, *The Politics of Mass Society* (Glencoe, Ill.: Free Press, 1959).

18. See Lloyd I. and Susanne Hoeber Rudolph, *The Modernity of Tradition: Political Development in India* (Chicago: University of Chicago Press, 1967), 15–154.

19. For elaboration of these themes, see among others: Louis Hartz, *The Liberal Tradition in America* (New York: Harcourt Brace, 1955), and idem, ed., *The Founding of New Societies* (New York: Harcourt Brace, 1964), especially Richard M. Morse, "The Heritage of Latin America;" James M. Malloy, ed., *Authoritarianism and Corporatism in Latin America* (Pittsburgh: University of Pittsburgh Press, 1977); Howard J. Wiarda, "Toward a

Framework for the Study of Political Change in the Iberio-Latin Tradition," *World Politics* 25 (1973): 206–35; Claudio Veliz, *The Centralist Tradition of Latin America* (Princeton, N.J.: Princeton University Press, 1979).

20. Barrington Moore, Jr., *Social Origins of Dictatorship and Democracy* (Boston: Beacon Press, 1966), 418

21. Charles E. Lindblom, *Politics and Markets* (New York: Basic Books, 1977), 161–69.

22. See primarily the works of Arend Lijphart, particularly *The Politics of Accommodation: Pluralism and Democracy in the Netherlands*, 2nd ed. (Berkeley: University of California Press, 1975) and *Democracy in Plural Societies: A Comparative Evaluation* (New Haven: Yale University Press, 1977).

23. *Freedom at Issue*, no. 76 (1984): 8–9.

24. Myron Weiner, "Empirical Democratic Theory," in Myron Weiner and Ergun Ozbudun, eds., *Comparative Elections in Developing Countries* (Washington, D.C.: American Enterprise Institute, manuscript, 26 [italics in original]).

25. Samuel P. Huntington, *American Politics: The Promise of Disharmony* (Cambridge: Harvard University Press, 1981), 246–59.

26. Sidney Verba, "Comparative Political Culture," in Lucian W. Pye and Sidney Verba, eds., *Political Culture and Political Development* (Princeton, N.J.: Princeton University Press, 1965), 513.

27. For the statistical correlation between Protestantism and democracy, see Kenneth A. Bollen, "Political Democracy and the Timing of Development," *American Sociological Review* 44 (1979): 572–87.

28. See Daniel Pipes, *In the Path of God: Islam and Political Power* (New York: Basic Books, 983), 48–69, 144–47.

29. David E. Apter, *The Politics of Modernization* (Chicago: University of Chicago Press, 1965), 85.

30. S. N. Eisenstadt, "Transformation of Social, Political, and Cultural Orders in Modernization," *American Sociological Review* 30 (1965): 668. In contrast to the Hindu tradition, Eisenstadt writes, "the identity between political and religious communities represents a very important similarity between the Chinese and Islamic societies" (p. 663).

31. See Pye and Verba, *Political Culture and Political Development*; Dahl, *Polyarchy*, 124–87; Gabriel A. Almond and Sidney Verba, *The Civic Culture* (Princeton, N.J.: Princeton University Press, 1963); David McClelland, *The Achieving Society* (Princeton, N.J.: D. Van Nostrand, 1961).

32. For arguments on the priority of democratic values, see the case Dahl makes on Argentina, *Polyarchy*, 132–40, and Jonathan Tumin's amendment of Barrington Moore in "The Theory of Democratic Development: A Critical Revision," *Theory and Society* 11 (1982): 143–64.

33. Rustow, "Transitions to Democracy," 361.

34. Samuel P. Huntington, *Political Order in Changing Societies* (New Haven: Yale University Press, 1968), 72–78.

35. Eric A. Nordlinger, "Political Development: Time Sequences and Rates of Change," *World Politics* 20 (1968): 494–530; Dankwart A. Rustow, *A World of Nations* (Washington, D.C.: Brookings Institution, 1967), 126ff.; Leonard Binder et al., *Crises and Sequences in Political Development* (Princeton, N.J.: Princeton University Press, 1971), 310–13.

36. Dahl, *Polyarchy*, 33–40; Huntington, *Political Order*, esp. pp. 32–59, 78–92. See also Richard A. Pride, *Origins of Democracy: A Cross-National Study of Mobilization, Party Systems, and Democratic Stability*, Comparative Politics Series, vol. 1 (Beverly Hills: Sage Publications, 1970).

37. Rustow, "Transitions to Democracy," 355–57.

38. John H. Herz, "On Reestablishing Democracy after the Downfall of Authoritarian or Dictatorial Regimes," *Comparative Politics* 10 (1978):559–62.

39. Juan Linz, "Crisis, Breakdown, and Reequilibration," in Juan Linz and Alfred Stepan, eds., *The Breakdown of Democratic Regimes* (Baltimore: Johns Hopkins University Press, 1978), 35.
40. Moore, *Social Origins of Dictatorship*, 508.
41. Dahl, *Polyarchy*, 45.
42. Walt W. Rostow, *The Stages of Economic Growth* (Cambridge: Cambridge University Press, 1960), 162.

The future of the international political system: a sketch

STANLEY HOFFMANN

C. Douglas Dillon Professor of the Civilization of France
Chairman, Center for European Studies, Harvard University

Thoughts on change

This essay will examine, sketchily, the coming evolution of the international political system. This is a risky exercise, for several reasons.

1) In the first place, any effort at discovering the future in a given field is made easier when there exists, for that field, a theory of change: a set of hypotheses and propositions, derived from or confirmed by empirical research, which identify the main factors of continuity and causes of transformation. It so happens that we have no satisfactory theory of change in international relations at all. To be sure, we have several theories of the international system. This is not the occasion to review them in detail, but it is necessary to point out their weaknesses as theories of change.

Let us set aside Immanuel Wallerstein's theory of the world capitalist system,[1] derived from Fernand Braudel's work on the world economy. Here, clearly, change results from the transformations of capitalism, and particularly of the market. But how these changes are reflected in or translated into changes in the relations *among states*, how the evolution of the capitalist system dictates or shapes that of the international polity (whose form—the coexistence and competition of multiple political systems—he declares necessary to the world economy) is nowhere made clear. Indeed, in his second volume, the simplicity of his scheme (the core-periphery distinction) dissolves into an unwieldy mass of specific analyses.

Robert Gilpin's theory of change[2] focuses on the rise, decline, and fall of "hegemons," but it suffers from two weaknesses. It provides a better account of the international economic system than of the international political one; for instance, Britain may well have been the economic hegemon in the 19th century, and thus was able to dictate the terms of the international monetary system and (often) of international trade. But the international political system was quite obviously multipolar; the image of Britain as the "holder" of the balance of power is only partly accurate (and it reflects geography—Britain's distance from the continent—rather than superiority); the so-called holder was not able to prevent the rise of formidable challengers. Moreover, as Robert Keohane has pointed out, Gilpin's theory "does not account well for the rise of the hegemon in the first place, or for the fact that certain contenders emerge rather than others."[3]

If we turn to theories of the international political system itself, we find the ambitious attempt by Kenneth Waltz.[4] I have little to add to what I have written about it earlier and above all to recent criticisms by John Ruggie and Keohane.[5] Waltz's general conception, as Ruggie has shown, puts the problem of change into a "structural" straitjacket: change can come only from a revolution in the ordering principle of the system (such as a switch from anarchy to central rule), or from a transformation in the distribution of capabilities among the actors. But, on the one hand, Waltz seems to consider as a significant change in the latter only a passage from a bipolar to a multipolar structure (or vice versa); and he leaves out as factors of change both what Ruggie calls a missing dimension, the prevailing type of domestic relations between state and society, and what he calls a determinant, the "dynamic density" of relations among states.[6] On the other hand, Waltz's conception of power, which underlines his view of the distribution of capabilities, does not fully take into account either the non-fungibility of power (i.e., the fact that in a given international system there may be different hierarchies and structures, corresponding to different kinds of power) or the essential difference between the availability, the uses, and the effectiveness of power, which makes the mere distribution of capabilities an insufficient indicator of power. As for Waltz's more specific theory of the balance of power, it is "so general that it hardly meets the difficult tests that he himself establishes for theory," and it fails to "state precisely the conditions under which coalitions will change."[7]

All this means that we have neither a complete nor an integrated theory of change. What we have is a number of conclusions derived from history. One is the idea of turbulence in periods of hegemonic decline, turbulence not only in the world economy but also in the international political system, when the loss of economic predominance corresponds to an overall decline in relative power. Another is the existence of two ways in which multipolar systems lead to a general war (and balance of power systems are destroyed): through gradual erosion of the restraints observed by the major actors (an erosion that can result from domestic changes, or from a change in the relations among these actors, or from the interaction between these two levels) or through deliberate destruction of these restraints after a revolutionary change in the polity of one of the major players. Another conclusion still is, literally, the explosiveness of bipolar systems, because of each "pole's" dialectic of commitment, its fear of decisive loss resulting from a client's defection or a neutral's alignment with one's adversary, the dilemma of appearing either provocative or "appeasing."

2) A second difficulty, however, lies in the fact that these "lessons from the past" may not be valid for the present international system, whose original features will be sketched below. Do these features amount to a difference in kind, or merely in degree? Is the simple distinction between bipolarity and multipolarity still significant? What is the relationship today between systemic constraints and domestic determinants?

Let us linger a moment on the latter. It is of course true that "under different systemic conditions states will define their self-interests differently."[8] But, on the one hand, there is little agreement on what the current "systemic conditions" are (to give one example, most observers believe that bipolarity is inherently unstable, and that economic interdependence today is high, but Waltz thinks the opposite). On the other hand, while systemic conditions are obviously an important constraint or a determinant of state behavior, they also provide an opportunity for state action, and indeed a target for efforts at change. Nothing is more pernicious than a view of international relations that exaggerates the power of the system. A simple reflection here is useful. All "realists," pure or modified, tell us that we live in a global order of anarchy (the absence of central power and, I would add, of any consensus on goals and procedures). If this is the case, then attention should be put primarily on the *actors*, not on the system: on the way in which they interpret the latter, define their own interests, constitute their power, and set their goals. There is no *a priori* reason to attach greater importance either to systemic imperatives or to geopolitical necessities than to purely domestic factors, when one wants to understand an actor's behavior. Moreover, in a bipolar system, dominated by two contending "hegemons," it is even more obvious that the decision-making process, the political regime, its relations with society, the belief systems of the leaders, as well as the specific resources and power positions of these two actors, must be given decisive importance, since any bipolar contest is a struggle about the shape and leadership of the international system.

However, putting questions about change where they largely belong, i.e., at the level of the units, does not simplify the task of futurologists. We now have to cope not only with a question to which we need an answer in order to begin to know what the future will be, but which only the future will settle—whether one can apply to the present system notions derived from bygone ones—but also with the multiple possibilities of evolution or revolution in the major actors, and with the uncertain effects of the contest in the international system on the actors' own polities. To look for the roots of systemic change solely at the level of the system, as does Waltz, has the virtue of simplifying one's task (at the cost of providing irrelevant or skimpy answers). To look for those roots wherever they may be has the defect of making the task almost impossible. At a minimum, it suggests that we shall talk not about the future of the international political system, but of possible *futures*.

3) Talking about futures is necessary for another reason as well. Past international systems have succeeded one another through the dark intercession of general wars. But those wars, occurring when they did, were not always inevitable. Like most historical events, they usually resulted from the interplay of the necessary and of the contingent, of fundamental trends (in the system or in the main units) and of accidents; they were "overdetermined." Except when they were deliberately provoked by a revolutionary power, or when they came out of a crisis in which such a power consciously accepted the risk of the general war which it deemed inevitable sooner or later (barring the capitulation of its foes), they were produced at least as much by the particular circumstances of a given crisis as by the deeper reasons for hostility or clashes of interests characteristic of the system, by the momentary configuration at least as much as by the more permanent structure. This has been intelligently shown, in the case of 1914, by Richard Ned Lebow.⁹ To be sure, it is not always easy to know in advance whether one is in the universe of revolutionary thrusts or in the more ordinary world of clashes among conservative and revisionist powers. (Moreover, when does a revisionist state cross the great divide and become a revolutionary challenge, a question raised by the Japanese case of 1931–1941?) But the role of accidents cannot be neglected: at one moment, a crisis may be "managed" intelligently; the same kind of crisis at a later moment, or a different kind of crisis at almost the same one, could lead to disaster for reasons that have far more to do with the circumstances than with the deeper trends. This is relevant to our present condition unless one has already decided that this bipolar system is exactly like past ones, and that, as before, the current struggle between one revolutionary power and one *status quo* actor is doomed to end in global war.

4) A last reason why this exercise is risky is that it will be limited, primarily, to the international political system: a study of the future of the world economy is beyond my reach and competence, and yet it is clear that certain trends and crises in the world economy could have extraordinarily serious effects on the international political order. It is therefore not possible to leave this out altogether; but my primary emphasis will be on what Raymond Aron used to call the strategic-diplomatic game.

The present international political system

1) The future of the international political system can only be discussed if one begins by having a clear picture of the nature of the present one. The main characteristic is its *originality*: it does not approximate any of our models of the past.

It differs from classical bipolar systems. To be sure, in the strategic–diplomatic arena, there are still only two major powers. But nuclear prudence inhibits the actual use of the atomic arsenals of these powers, and it has also, so far, led them to great restraint in their use of conventional forces against each other. This does not amount to an "equalization" of power between them and less mighty states, but it somehow reduces the distance, and above all makes a violent outcome of the great powers' contest less certain. Moreover, classical bipolarity described a system in which the strategic–diplomatic arena was, if not the only one, at least by far the most important one for the states' interactions. Today, there are other important games, and they are not bipolar. Economic interdependence had, in the 19th century, developed in the transnational *society* that coexisted with the interstate *political* system. It now characterizes several of the arenas of *interstate* relations, because of the decisive *political* importance of economic issues in the agendas of most states, i.e., because of the profound changes in state–society relations in an era of managed economies. In these arenas, one of the two superpowers is not a major actor, given the nature of its own polity and ideology (an anticapitalist command economy); and, as I have tried to describe it elsewhere, economic interdependence as a political factor brings as many handicaps as it provides benefits and opportunities to the other superpower.[10]

Thus, what might be called the structural heterogeneity of the system (if one refers to the existence of different international structures corresponding to the different kinds of power: military, monetary, industrial, etc.) is one of the differences between the present system and past bipolar ones. Another kind of heterogeneity is original: that which results from geopolitical diversity. Past bipolar contests were waged on reasonably homogeneous fields (in the sense that, say, in the system described by Thucydides, both the Greek city-states and the neighboring "barbarians" took part in a single interstate contest). In the present system, the first global one, we find both one worldwide contest, the superpowers' rivalry, *and* tenacious local rivalries or configurations that can be used by the superpowers for their competition (and whose actors can call in the superpowers for their own purposes) but which also have a life of their own and their own rules. Thus, the ability of the superpowers to absorb and to blend all other important conflicts into their own is not unlimited.

Nor does the present system resemble past balance-of-power ones. Today, there are only two dominant military powers capable of projecting their might all over the world; and these powers are locked in a formidable ideological conflict of the sort that has ruled out so far the kinds of fluid alignments and ideologically neutral mechanisms characteristic of balance-of-power systems. The balance of power and the balance of (nuclear) terror are profoundly different: the former required flexible coalitions and allowed for (indeed, demanded) a willingness to use force in behalf of equilibrium if deterrence failed (as it was often bound to fail in a world of anarchy, i.e., separate calculations and uncertain commitments). The balance of terror is not a matter of coalitions (the British, French, and Chinese nuclear forces may complicate Soviet calculations, but they don't enter much into the plans of American strategists); its preservation practically requires abstention from nuclear war (since nobody knows whether and how a resort to nuclear weapons could be kept limited and controlled) as well as great prudence in the use of conventional force.

All past "anarchic" systems, whether bipolar or multipolar (i.e., all truly *international* systems, by contrast with imperial ones) were based on a structure in which military might was the main currency, the distribution of power among actors was fairly clear and easy to evaluate, and the "dynamic density" of relations was relatively limited. This is no longer the case.

2) The present system is marked by a peculiar mix of *resiliency* and *fragility*. In this respect, it resembles balance-of-power systems. But it is a superficial resemblance. In the latter, resiliency was provided by the balancing mechanism's ability to moderate ambitions and conflicts; fragility resulted primarily from the very existence of sovereignty: a jungle of ambitions uncoerced by higher power. The current scene is different in several ways. First, there is the diversity in the structure of power. The nonfungibility of power produces a *"vertical"* fragmentation of the system into partly separate arenas, each one with its hierarchy of players: a factor of resiliency, on the whole—except insofar as several of these arenas can be profoundly affected by moves occurring in one of them (cf. the ripples created by the OPEC decisions of 1973 and 1970) or by internal conditions in the polity of a major actor (cf. the effects of a recession in the United States), and, of course, except insofar as major crises in the strategic–diplomatic arena can have disastrous repercussions in others (cf. the oil embargo of 1973). A thorough study of the relations and exchanges between the different "games" of world affairs remains to be made.

Second, another original aspect is the nature and multiplicity of *restraints* affecting each kind of power: Some restraints result from the risks of rash action (in the nuclear realm as well as because of the "boomerang" effects of the use of economic power in an interdependent world economy), and other restraints result from common norms and procedures (international regimes). At first, these are—again—factors of resiliency. But they also provide irresistible temptations for manipulation and blackmail: of the weak by the powerful, of course, but also of the strong by the weak (cf. client–superpower relations in the Middle East, or the threat of default of debtor countries) and of the mighty by the mighty (cf. threats of first use of nuclear weapons or war-fighting scenarios).

The very density of relations increases the ambiguity of the system.

The dependence of all actors on the system—either, quite starkly, for survival, insofar as a nuclear war destroying the system could also, this time, annihilate all the actors, or for economic development and welfare—is a factor of resiliency. But density also means ideological alignments based on a certain solidarity of domestic regimes, disruptive technological revolutions and demographic explosions, uncertainty about the future of essential resources (such as oil), and increasing vulnerability to events and decisions of external origin. One witnesses therefore countless attempts at harming others or at pushing onto others the bad effects imported from abroad (i.e., expelling immigrant workers, or canceling debts), efforts at re-exporting vulnerability, at reducing the costs of interdependence for oneself, as well as the development in the strategic–diplomatic domain of mutually hostile, hence highly dangerous, alignments.

One more original feature of the system: the "*horizontal*" fragmentation of power into a variety of subsystems also contributes to the mix of resiliency and fragility. The relative autonomy of regional concerns dampens the superpowers' contest, or divides it into reasonably separate compartments. But the inevitable connections between each subsystem and the global cold war can also serve as escalatory factors, either if a confrontation in one arena should lead to a worsening of the superpowers' contest in other areas, or if the superpowers' conflict in one of them should affect their vital interests.

3) Let us move away from comparisons and focus on the chief *characteristics* of the present world political system. It is both "revolutionary" and "moderate": revolutionary because of the bipolar military contest, and because of the continuing ideological confrontation (which persists even though several Communist powers have defected from the Soviet camp, even though the power of attraction of the Leninist model has receded, especially among industrial societies, and despite the presence of highly undemocratic regimes in the "free world" alliances). It is also revolutionary, insofar as the collapse of the (previously porous but visible) barriers between domestic politics and international politics leads to generalized intervention.[11] The system is moderate insofar as it has shown enough flexibility to absorb enormous changes in the distribution of capabilities since 1945, as well as in the number of actors and in the make-up of alignments; also because—until now—major crises have been managed or contained (for instance, except for civil violence, wars in the Middle East have remained limited). Like past international systems, the present one can be described as consisting of a core and a periphery, the (crucial) difference with the past residing in the fact that this periphery is not dominated by the imperial presence of the major powers, but occupied by at least legally independent actors. The *core* is constituted by the superpowers' camps. Its two main features are the nuclear "game" and the alliance systems. Until now, despite profound technological changes, the nuclear game has remained one of mutual deterrence, resting ultimately on the possibility of "mutual assured destruction," whatever strategic doctrine one may concoct in order to avoid it. And, so far, mutual nuclear deterrence has in fact extended to the protection of major allies against conventional attack by the other superpower (although not to the protection of an ally that had itself initiated a war, against conventional retaliation aimed at that ally, as in the cases of North Korea in 1950 and North Vietnam in the 1960's–70's). This is one of the reasons why the alliance systems such as the Warsaw Pact and NATO, and also the United States–Japanese alliance, have survived a number of tests and storms. (There are of course other reasons too: the shared sense of threat, Soviet willingness to use force in order to prevent defections in Eastern Europe, etc.)

As for the *periphery*, it is not possible here to describe the specific features and "rules of the game" of each subsystem. Some have been deeply marked by the active role or interference of both superpowers (Middle East), others have shown a relatively greater autonomy from them (Africa), others still have been functioning either under the (often unwelcome) protection or in the more distant shadow of the United States (OAS, ASEAN). The frequency and intensity of Soviet–American confrontations in these subsystems have varied a great deal: in Africa, the two tense periods have been the early 1960s and the middle and late 1970s, in Central America the early 60s and the present.

There was always a risk that the "core contest" would spill over into all the peripheries and become truly global; i.e., that in each subsystem there would be a struggle for dominance, so to speak, between the truly local (internal and interstate) factors of conflict and the Soviet–American "relation of major tension," which the latter would win. But it is only in the last few years that this potential danger has become a reality because of the increase in the military capabilities of the USSR, especially of its power to project military might at great distances and because of the strong American reaction to it. This new Soviet ability does not, however, eliminate one constant difference in the strategic maps of the two chief adversaries. The principal concern of the USSR remains the security of its camp, that is, real or potential threats on its immediate periphery; hence, its main thrusts and moves concern Europe, the Middle East, and the Far East. The United States, of course, is concerned about its famous back- (or is it front-) yard in Central America and the Caribbean. But its main resources in the contest are devoted to areas separated from its own territory by huge distances: Western Europe, the Far East, the Middle East.

Of the various subsystems, two deserve closer attention: the Middle Eastern one, which, because of its strategic and economic importance to the Western allies, constitutes a sort of second core for the United States, and the Far Eastern one, which constitutes the same for the USSR. It is in the Middle Eastern subsystem that the struggle between indigenous factors of conflict and "imported" ones is most intense, complex, and fluctuating, given both the extraordinary diversity of local hostilities (communal, as in Lebanon or among Palestinians, inter-Arab, Arab–Israeli, Arab–Iranian, etc.) and the importance of the superpowers' interests and commitments. The Far Eastern area is a subsystem in the process of formation (two criteria being a specific configuration of forces and a certain density of relations that form distinctive patterns). It is composed of the two superpowers, Japan, China, and the two Koreas. The centrality of this area to both superpowers now (here, part of the territory of the USSR is included, and part of the American one may be threatened by Soviet weapons deployed there), the increasing importance of the American–Japanese alliance and of China, the fact that some of the major factors of conflict involve at least one of the superpowers (China–USSR, Japan–USSR, and, because of the alliance of the United States with Seoul, North Korea–United States), and the rising role of the Pacific nations in the world economy suggest that this particular subsystem may well deserve to be treated in the future as part of the core. But it is a subsystem with four major actors, not two, and, as a result, its "rules of the game" are quite different from those of the NATO–Warsaw Pact "core."

Until now, nuclear proliferation has proceeded in such a way as to remain under the superpowers' own nuclear umbrella. The British and French deterrents, whatever their independence in theory, are clearly within the core, and China's own strategy and diplomacy are delicately linked to the Soviet–American contest. The next "proliferators" (including the two quasi-nuclear powers, Israel and India) have their own priorities and regional concerns; we shall examine later whether the further spread of nuclear weapons is likely to increase either the fragility or the fragmentation of the system.

The dominant theme of this analysis—the ambiguity of the system—is reinforced if one examines how the international economic system interacts with the international political one. The world economy can be envisaged in two ways. It is, first of all, the air in which the actors breathe. When the quality of the air deteriorates, as it did in the 1970s and early 1980s, their capabilities and the general climate of international relations are obviously affected. In the second place, the world economy is also a separate field, a set of arenas, in which the players act. As such, it has made a contribution both to the moderation of the international system *and* to conflict. The latter is obvious: economic power has been widely used as a tool of the "state of war," either against political adversaries (through boycotts, embargoes, and sanctions) or even against allies or partners, in order to gain temporary advantages or to change the rules of the game (cf. Nixon on August 15, 1971, or OPEC in 1973). Indeed, the very scope of the state's attempts to control the national economy through fiscal and monetary policy, trade legislation, the manipulation of interest rates, a host of nontariff barriers, subsidies and directives for industrial policy, etc., has opened up vast new fronts for interstate competition. On the other hand, in the non-Communist world, the existence of a reasonably open international economy has contributed to moderation in two ways: first, through the operations of "complex interdependence,"[12] which, in the phase of American hegemony, led the United States to define its interest in a way that furthered the development of a partly autonomous transnational society, away from the interstate contests, and also entailed enlightened assistance to other countries, in order to promote absolute increases in prosperity rather than relative national gains. Later, interdependence put definite limits on the mutual manipulations of states or coalitions of states eager to improve their relative positions at the expense of others. Second, this open world economy—partly transnational (and capitalist), partly interstate (and managed)—has required a whole network of international regimes with their own restraints on state actions, their procedures for the settlement of disputes, and the ability, resulting from their very existence, to create a stake in their own survival among the member states (and thus to change the way in which these states define their interests).

4) Obviously, until now the ambiguity of the postwar international system has been benevolent: resiliency has prevailed over fragility, moderation over revolution, economic interdependence and nuclear prudence over all the factors of conflict. The *central question* is whether this will still be the case in the future. What is likely to happen to all the moderating factors? Is it possible for a system of "anarchy" in which states preserve the means to inflict harm on others (one of the possible definitions of sovereignty) and indeed possess unprecedented capabilities for doing so, is it possible especially for a system in which so many causes of conflict ferment, to maintain itself without either self-destruction or what may be called self-transcendence, i.e., the passage to a very different sort of system no longer based on state sovereignty?

Approaches to the future

1) In order to make educated guesses about the future, it is not very useful to begin with a prognosis of the future of the system's *structure* defined as the distribution of capabilities. In the first place, it is unlikely that the coming changes will be such as to challenge the preeminence of the superpowers in the strategic–diplomatic arena. The potential rivals, Western Europe, Japan, China, are not likely to narrow the gap greatly: China's industrial base remains weak and small; the various inhibitions that have reduced Japan's role in that arena may weaken, but even if they should disappear altogether, there are physical limits to Japan's potential might; and there is no sign of a West European ability to overcome the divisions and hangups that have prevented its emergence as an entity (other than in the skinny form of the Economic Community).

To be sure, there may be considerable shifts in the distribution of economic capabilities: the phenomenon of the Asian "new industrialized countries" may not remain exceptional. Thus, regional and functional hierarchies could change a great deal. However, the nonfungibility of power prevents one from drawing any definite conclusions about the effect of these changes in the strategic–diplomatic realm. This effect will depend on what the actors will *want* to do with their resources. We are thus driven back to a consideration of the system as a whole or of the various subsystems (insofar as they limit or shape the specific uses states assign to their power), and to guesses about the domestic evolution of the actors: the nature of their regimes and of state–society relations, which largely determine their decisions about the kinds of capabilities they want, and about what to do with them.

2) If the structure of power is of little help, there remain three different modes of analysis, or ways of speculating about the future, which, I believe, need to be combined. The first is to look at *long-term trends* in the international political system and in the polities. I have, elsewhere,[13] mentioned three main ones. The most obvious is the persistence of the Soviet–American competition on a global scale, with approximate strategic parity (since neither power will allow the other to pull ahead dangerously). The competition would end or lose its saliency only if the USSR gave up its colossal challenge and turned inward as a result of, or in order to cope with, its domestic problems; if, being forced by United States pressure to choose between butter and guns, it settled for butter. The long-term inability of the Soviet system either to improve its economic performance or else to reform drastically enough to remove economic bottlenecks and waste has been stressed by many. What is not clear, however, is how decisive this flaw will be: whether partial adjustments will be successful in preventing paralysis or decline, and also how much the pressure of the external contest will in fact continue to legitimize the regime, preserve the unchallenged priority of the military sector, and inspire creative efforts at reconciling the political system and the need for economic efficiency.

Unless one indulges in a kind of "catastrophic optimism" about the Soviet Union's future, one can still discern only too well all the factors that will keep driving the contest. Two major powers have always, in history, found reasons to clash and attempts to cooperate or to carve up spheres impossible either to negotiate or to maintain. Ideological opposition, in this instance, exacerbates the clashes of power. In the military realm, technology, whether pursued "for its own sake" or so as not to let one's opponent get ahead, will contribute to the rivalry. There are, of course, also conflicting interests: the Soviet insistence on a very high degree of security is incompatible with the American interest in preventing the vassalization of all of the Soviet Union's neighbors; the Soviet interest in preserving the East European *glacis* is incompatible with the Western interest in helping traditional Western-oriented nations regain some autonomy; and nowhere is the struggle of interests more visible than over Germany. Interests create perceptions of threats, but perceptions of threats also create interests: each superpower is likely to continue to act as if every move by the other, even in an area of relatively low priority to itself, *ipso facto* created a need to thwart the move or to prevent a further extension or exploitation of it, in order to protect its own reputation for strength and credibility. Finally, domestic needs feed the contest: the existence of external perils is an important source of legitimacy for the Soviet regime; while the same is certainly not true of the United States, powerful military and economic lobbies there have a stake either in preserving a certain level of hostility or in safeguarding various parts of the world from the threats that emanate directly or indirectly from Moscow or its allies, and the failure or perceived failure of an Administration to "meet the Soviet challenge" guarantees its demise.

A second long-term trend is *nationalism*, which will undoubtedly remain a major force in a world whose units base their legitimacy on the principle of self-determination, and where most actors are and will continue to be engaged in "nation-building." The desire for national independence and self-assertion will be fed by the very diversity and strength of factors that actually negate sovereignty: modern imperialism such as that of the USSR, continuing attempts by various actors to extend or to protect spheres of control (such as the United States in Central America, Vietnam in Cambodia, Khadafi's Libya in parts of Africa, etc.), the presence in many countries of temporary or traditional foreign minorities which provoke resentments and stir prejudices, the absence of control of many developing countries over their economic future because of the grip of multinational corporations or of international organizations (such as the IMF), indeed the frustrating sense many governments have of pushing, in the realm of economics, a multitude of levers that do not respond, because they are either held by someone else or capable of being moved only by combined, hence partly unsatisfactory, action. Thus, there is a kind of symbiosis between nationalism and universal intervention or manipulation.

A third trend is *revolution*—in a great variety of forms: political and social, left-wing or right-wing. The shakiness of the political structures of so many states; the communal conflicts, ideological antagonisms, religious hatreds, and social cleavages in so many countries; the lack of fit between political regimes imposed by past masters (foreign or domestic); and societies undergoing an almost unmanageable process of transformation guarantee endless cycles of revolution, external interventions, and counterrevolutions.

On the whole, however, these long-term trends tell us very little about the future of the international political system, except that there will be a great deal of turbulence. The central question is, of course, how much, how intense, how dangerous—and the trends, by themselves, don't answer it. The fate of the system depends on whether or not the Soviet–American contest will be managed, i.e., on the rivals' capacity to handle crises: Will the superpowers be able to accommodate nationalist demands and will these demands take forms destructive of the world economic order, embroil the rival superpowers, and be accompanied by nuclear proliferation? Will revolutions occur essentially because of domestic conditions or as a result of subversion, will they be accepted by the superpowers or resisted by one or the other of them, and will they take place in areas of such importance to the superpowers as to provoke major confrontations between them? The effects of nationalism and revolution will also depend a great deal on the kinds of leaders countries will produce: in this age of "structural" analysis, personalities matter perhaps more than ever.

3) We should therefore turn to another kind of analysis, namely the prediction of *crises*: Around what flash points could these trends lead to dangerous explosions? As experience has shown, crises (bloody or not) provide moments of truth, they reveal the dynamics, strengths, and weaknesses of a system. Either, as in much of the 19th century, crises produce occasions for the great powers to crank up the various regulatory mechanisms of the balance of power, or they create circumstances which lead to the discovery that these mechanisms don't work (as in the period of the 1860s and early 70s), or they generate points of crystallization for the tightening of alliances (as in the years before 1914) or instants of triumph for unchecked troublemakers (like the Rhineland and Munich crises).

Many long-expected crises never happen (remember the death-of-Tito crisis scenario). What follows is clearly debatable; nevertheless, one can try to locate those possible crises that could have systemwide repercussions. The most dangerous would be a military confrontation in the present core of the system. This could result either from a particular form of weapons deployment deemed physically (and not just politically) intolerable by the other superpower, or from a serious clash in the European theater. Under what conditions could the latter occur? One can imagine major unrest in Eastern Europe, including East Berlin, resulting in Western attempts to help rebels beyond the wall or the iron curtain, or Warsaw Pact attempts to pursue in the West groups fleeing from the East. One can develop a scenario of dangerous instability arising from a drift of the German Federal Republic toward neutralism, encouraged by one side and resisted by the other. The very likelihood of general nuclear war erupting from a major crisis in Europe argues against these scenarios; on the other hand, the importance of the superpowers' stakes and their arsenals make any crisis there particularly dangerous: neither side can afford to see its key alliance system disintegrate. More believable perhaps would be a Soviet decision to move preventively, with or without nuclear weapons, on what remains the USSR's main front, if the general atmosphere, or a crisis elsewhere, had deteriorated so badly as to convince the Kremlin of the high probability of an American attack.

One can also all too easily speculate about typical crises in the Far Eastern and Middle Eastern subsystems. In both cases, it is the infernal machine of ambiguous commitments by the superpowers to third parties (with whom they don't have a formal and effective military alliance) that could result in a conflagration. We have had several rehearsals in the past. In addition, in the Far Eastern system (as in Europe) there are also tight alliances on the American side; but the situation is more fluid, hence more dangerous, than in Europe. Another, but less restrained, effort by China to "punish" Vietnam, leading to Soviet intervention (i.e., to a Soviet decision to cut down a deeply feared and distrusted rival before it becomes too powerful) and to an American counterintervention; another Korean war, with Soviet support for North Korea and Soviet threats aimed at Japan; Soviet attempts to prevent by threats a Japanese rearmament, leading to menacing new deployments by both superpowers; a Soviet decision to punish Israel, should the latter attack a Soviet client (such as Syria), or an American decision to seek a showdown with Syria and the USSR over Lebanon; a Soviet move into Iran, at the request of a pro-Soviet Iranian government, followed by an American intervention there; an American decision to shore up Iraq, followed by (or following) a Soviet one to back Iran militarily—these are the all too plausible crises that could get out of hand, because of the difficulty of limiting the scope of superpower collisions in these areas, and because of the dangerous ability of weaker states to manipulate the superpower contest, to blackmail their big brothers or cousins.

There are other crises with a potential for escalation. It is unlikely that "proxy wars" comparable to what happened in Angola and capable of occurring again in Southern Africa could result in a violent clash between the superpowers' forces themselves, and it is equally unlikely that American moves in Central America would lead to a heavy Soviet commitment (going beyond the provision of military assistance to local clients). But an American military move against Cuba caused by Cuban support of anti-American forces or regimes in Central America might force the Soviets to react there or elsewhere, because of their own need for "credibility." And, in the more distant future, a regional nuclear war between countries other than the current nuclear "big five" might trigger a superpower confrontation, if the "big two" chose sides or if the war affected important clients of one or the other superpowers. Whether a "third party" nuclear war would lead to the superpowers' entanglement or disconnection depends both on the importance of the stakes for them in a given case and on the state of their relations (when they deteriorate, the importance of local stakes increase).

Could a world economic crisis have a disastrous effect on the international political system? Yes, in one or the other of the following two hypotheses. One might be called the 1973 scenario, plus: an act of economic warfare accompanying a regional explosion, but leading, this time, to a military intervention by the threatened Western powers and to a Soviet counterintervention. The other hypothesis is that of a major crisis in the network of international economic and financial institutions (such as a chain of bank collapses following the default of several debtor countries) leading to political turbulence in important developing nations and, thereafter, to new alignments or to violent external diversions sought by these countries' leaders.

"Crisis analysis" has the merit of concentrating the mind on perfectly real perils. But there are two flaws. One is the impossibility of predicting which of these shocks is most likely to happen, or when, and of assigning a meaningful degree of probability to any of them. The other is the impossibility, by definition, of predicting surprises, say, the accidental shooting down by the Soviets of an American civilian airliner with hundreds of passengers aboard, followed by a perfectly imaginable process of emotional as well as political and military escalation.

4) Surprises cannot be forecast (one can only predict that some will happen), but one can try to deal with the other flaw: one can define those *political choices* made by the key actors which could either make the kinds of dangerous crises described above more likely or, on the contrary, help avert them. Thinking about these choices obliges one to conclude (not very hopefully) that the current phase of international politics is particularly important, that a series of decisions to be made in the near future will either switch the train of international affairs on reasonably smooth tracks or else direct it toward disaster.

Three series of choices are of crucial importance. The first, and most important, are those which are presently being made by the superpowers, concerning their contest. They are of two kinds. The first relates to the future of the *nuclear competition*. The trend of the arms race is dismal. Both sides are providing themselves with a new arsenal that undermines crisis stability, i.e., that is likely to heighten tension in a political crisis and to add, as I suggested above, an autonomous source of conflicts to all the political issues which divide them already, such as the conflict over the location of counterforce weapons. The protracted crisis provoked by the ss 20 aimed at the United States and Europe as well as by the NATO decision of December 1979 to put Pershing II and cruise missiles in Western Europe, at a time when there was no sharp political conflict there between East and West (other than Western dismay over Poland) is a first example. The often documented evolution of nuclear strategy from primary reliance on counter-city weapons to the development of accurate counterforce ballistic and cruise missiles, the resulting vulnerability of a sizable fraction of each side's nuclear force (hence the emergence of an incentive to strike first, before one is hit), the recent American desire to build a defensive system which entails the risk of extending the arms race into outer space and to heighten insecurity, the forthcoming proliferation of cheap, slower but powerful and hard-to-verify cruise missiles, all these decisions have drastically changed the nature of the "nuclear question." An arms race with increasing numbers of vulnerable and unverifiable weapons or one in which an advance by one side in the development of defenses might appear to provide an opportunity for a first strike against the lagging side's forces, would be extremely dangerous. Much, therefore, depends on whether the superpowers decide to curb their nuclear competition in space, as well as to reduce their vulnerabilities by either eliminating their MIRV-ed land-based missiles or replacing them with single-warhead ones or (better still) with small, mobile ones that will not be targetable by the other side, and also on whether, in their arms control negotiations, they make a serious effort to stop, while there is still time, the trend toward nuclear war fighting (of which the ability to hit land-based missiles is only one aspect) by trying to curb or even to eliminate land- and sea-based cruise missiles and to limit the number of bombers carrying long-range ones, and by agreeing not to deploy submarines with a counterforce capability.[14] Agreements that leave each side with a considerable amount of freedom to modernize their forces toward more counterforce are of very little use; proposals aimed at obliging the other side to restructure its forces or to end its modernization efforts while protecting one's own plans are political warfare tactics.

The second kind of choice concerns the future of the *political relations between Moscow and Washington*. No single decision or set of decisions is likely to prevent all collisions. Many of these, as we have seen, will tend to result from local moves made by secondary players, capable of enlisting often hesitant superpowers. But how episodic crises will be resolved depends largely on the overall context or flavor of Soviet–American relations, and on what might be called the basic stance chosen by the two rivals. At present, we are on a collision course. The United States seems determined to make Moscow responsible for every challenge to an American position anywhere or to an American ally or client. It often appears to believe that no worthwhile agreement can be signed with the Soviets not only because of their behavior abroad but because of their regime. The Soviets have now reached the conclusion that they are faced with an adversary whose hostility is implacable. The effects of these mutually reinforcing decisions to wage a new cold war, the impact of such a set of self- and mutually fulfilling prophecies on the "core" and on the triangular relationship of Washington, Moscow, and Beijing will increase tension and insecurity. A period of rhetorical and actual confrontation between the superpowers will add to the strains that already weaken the polities in several Western European countries and increase the hesitation of even firmly anti-Soviet Europeans to support American policies outside the NATO sphere; and the Soviets will be tempted to exploit such fissures. As for the Chinese, while they worry that any Soviet–American detente might lead to a kind of euphoric "lowering of the guard" in the United States or in NATO and allow the Soviets to put more pressure, directly or indirectly, on China, high tension between Moscow and Washington, and an American policy that almost automatically supports any force in the Third World that declares itself anti-Soviet or anti-Communist, are likely to push Beijing away from Washington into a subtle, complex, and somewhat unsettling game of balancing. Staying on this collision course would make many of the crises listed above both more probable and more difficult to manage; an erosion of restraints is the most predictable outcome. The alternative tract is that of a return to a mixed strategy on both sides, a mix of competition (which is unavoidable) and cooperation devoid of the illusions harbored by each side in the early 1970s and allowing for better crisis management and prevention.[15]

A second series of choices capable of affecting the possibility and seriousness of crises will be made by other important actors. In *Western Europe*, the choice remains what it has been for almost thirty years: between "more of the same," and greater political and military unity. "More of the same," predicted by several observers[16] means, actually, increasing fragmentation, both within and among the nations of Western Europe, and more tensions between the United States (impatient with its allies' reluctance to support it everywhere and to make a greater effort toward conventional defense) and those allies, dubious about the strategic evolution of the United States (in space, toward fighting nuclear war, and toward a conventional defense of Europe) as well as about Washington's overall world policy. Greater political and military unity in Europe would introduce, on the world stage, a new actor interested in helping moderate the United States–Soviet competition, capable both of stilling recurrent American fears of a Western European drift toward finlandization or neutralization and of closing down one of the Soviets' main avenues of diplomatic intrigue and baiting. But it remains unlikely, partly because of the difficulty of squaring the nuclear circle (i.e., the problem of a German finger on a European trigger, and that of collective decision-making in nuclear matters), partly because of the continuing prevalence of national concerns.

Another important choice concerns *Japan*, primarily the scope and speed of its rearmament. A decision to increase both considerably would probably heighten tension in East Asia; it would worry Japan's former victims (including China) as well as the Soviet Union. Moscow feels threatened by a more militarized Japanese–American alliance no longer aimed at China and seems determined to retaliate by increasing its own conventional and nuclear forces around Japan.

A third important choice is that which will have to be made by *Israel*. The divisions among its Arab neighbors, the savage wars among its enemies, the current hard-line consensus in its public opinion may encourage a kind of tough immobilism, a belief that its opponents are neither capable nor really willing to challenge the gradual absorption into a greater Israel of the territories occupied in 1967. Successful in the short run, such a strategy is likely to backfire in the long run. Syria will not resign itself to the loss of the Golan heights, the Palestinians will not resign themselves to dispersion and annexation, the Arab world in general, especially with the sting and threat of Islamic fundamentalism, will not accept the loss of all of Jerusalem, the USSR will continue to seek ways of challenging the American–Israeli axis. An Israeli decision to exchange territory for peace, entailing both solid guarantees of security for Israel and a divestment of the occupied territories, is unlikely now but necessary in order to prevent the Middle East from becoming the powder keg of the next world war.

The third series of important choices affecting the likelihood, intensity, and manageability of crises will be made in the *world economic system*. I will list them only briefly. The most important decision-maker here remains the United States because of its weight in the world economy and financial system and because of the role of the dollar as the world's main currency for reserves and transactions. Whether the world economy will help fuel or dampen crises will depend on the kinds of decisions taken in four vital areas by the United States and also by the other major industrial powers of the non-Communist world. These areas are: *energy* (reliance on a market that could once more be the victim of political decisions and disruptions in the Middle East, versus the pursuit of policies of conservation, storage, and diversification), *money* (a continuation of the present float, with its frequent and wide fluctuations because of divergent domestic policies and perform-ances, versus an attempt to limit the range of these oscillations by coordi-nation among the major economies and currencies), *the international financial system* (attempts to solve the debt problem by a combination of short-term rescue operations and stringent, socially and politically explosive conditions imposed by the IMF and other lenders, versus an effort at defining a long-term policy aimed both at avoiding imprudent loans and at preventing the recurrence of emergencies), and the *international trade system* (a continuing drift toward protectionism as the way of preventing the traumatic decline of major industries, versus a firmer commitment to liberalism—essential for the access of goods from the developing countries to the markets of the industrial nations—accompanied by domestic adjustment measures on a far greater scale than in the past).

All these choices, obviously, depend to a very large extent on the internal variables which operate in the countries I have mentioned; and the outcome of internal struggles among voters, parties, interest groups, or oligarchs is only slightly, or occasionally, determined by foreign affairs; this is the major predicament of "futurology."

Through the crystal ball, darkly

1) Let us try nevertheless to put elements together. They allow us to see what the international political system is most likely *not* to be. First, it is clear that there is no atrophy of military power. It will continue to be sought by states, both as a means of action on the world stage (at a minimum, as a protection against external meddlers) and as a vital internal instrument for the support or maintenance of (often shaky) regimes in power. Other forms of power will continue to be very important, but they will not replace military might. This does not mean that the history of the international political system will be only that of the distribution of military capabilities and of the interactions of armies and arsenals. On the one hand, the purposes for which military might can be used *effectively* will continue to be the traditional goals of territorial defense and conflict, not the whole range of economic pursuits contemporary states are interested in; and even among the traditional goals, the conquest and subjugation of alien populations are likely to run into formidable obstacles, because of the force of nationalism and of the multiple possibilities, ranging from passive resistance to guerrilla warfare and terrorism, which raise the cost of domination. As for the use of nuclear weapons for purposes of political intimidation, there is no reason why it should be successful when the target country has nuclear weapons of its own or a nuclear protector, given the risk of an uncontrollable nuclear war should the attempt at political coercion backfire; it is difficult to use effectively, for political gains, weapons whose military use is likely to be suicidal. On the other hand, the very *usability* of military power will continue to be constricted by two kinds of restraints: the very uneven ones that result, in certain polities but not in others, from domestic obstacles, institutional or moral, and those which result from the nature of weapons. In peacetime, nuclear weapons will increasingly be useful only as deterrents against a nuclear attack (the credibility of extended deterrence against a conventional attack on allies will diminish) or, in the case of secondary nuclear powers, against a conventional attack by a nonnuclear power unprotected by a nuclear big brother.

Second, the system will become neither multipolar in the global strategic arena (cf. point 1 of the section "Approaches to the Future") nor bipolar in every structure. Even if, miraculously, the superpowers decided to reduce their nuclear arsenals drastically, the gap between them and the other nuclear powers would remain huge (moreover, they would probably try to apply curbs to the secondary nuclear forces before agreeing to the partial disarmament of their own nuclear forces), and their unique capacity to raise vast armies and fleets equipped with the most advanced weapons and endowed with enormous mobility would persist. At the same time, the other structures of power, the other arenas of the international system, will not fold back into the strategic one, and this being the case, there will remain considerable opportunities for action—and mischief—for powers other than the big two. Even in the strategic arena, the fragmentation into regional subsystems, in each of which statesmen have to take into account not only the global balance of terror but also the regional balance of power (i.e., of conventional forces), offers a major role to local hegemons and to middle or even smaller powers. These are obviously less mighty than the superpowers; nevertheless they are able either to bring more resources to bear on one particular front than the global powers, or to manipulate them, or both. Thus, one of the key questions will be that of the relations between the regional strategic arenas, or subsystems, and the global one. (The reader may ask: What about the regional balance of terror, for example, the West Europeans' reference to the "Eurostrategic" balance? It may have a meaning with respect to short-range tactical weapons, but so-called intermediate-range missiles such as ss 20s and Pershing II are "fungible" with long-range ones such as sea-based ICBMs. The notion of a regional nuclear balance between the camps is entirely artificial; the targets are regional, not the weapons that can hit them.)

Third, the separation between domestic and international politics, between the internal operations of governments and their external behavior, will not return. Even in past systems, conduct abroad was always largely determined by factors within; a certain kind of realist theory (certainly not rooted in Thucydides' writings) has been entirely misleading in suggesting a purely "geopolitical" model of decision-making. But conduct abroad was not always, or even usually, aimed at affecting conditions within other countries; and it is in this respect that I foresee a continuation of present practices, both in the various economic arenas of interdependence, and also in the strategic and diplomatic games, because of the persistence of ideological rivalries and transnational movements (manipulated by states), of exceedingly tempting pretexts for intervention in domestic affairs, and even of demands for new, nonexploitative or manipulative interventions, such as for the protection of human rights. A change would require an enormous internal strengthening of, and improved human conditions in, the various units; it is difficult to imagine even massive external economic assistance capable of reaching such a goal.

2) If these are the parameters, or if this is the range within which the possible futures are to be found, then the major question marks that we face are those which follow (and the answers to them will determine which of these possible futures will be realized). They can all be summed up in one set of alternatives: *continuity versus* (a considerable amount of) *discontinuity* in world politics. It is discontinuity that is, in my opinion, desirable. I am convinced that continuity, in the sense of politics as usual, will lead to undesirable, perhaps catastrophic, results, even though the experience of the postwar system so far has not been catastrophic. But the reasons that have kept it manageable, the reasons why its ambiguity has been more benevolent than malignant, are not guaranteed to last.

A *first question* is, precisely, whether the current *bases of moderation* of the system will turn out to be more resilient than fragile, or vice versa. These bases have been of two kinds: the nuclear revolution and economic interdependence or, if you prefer, the will to survive and the will to prosper. But has the nuclear revolution really transformed the nature of world politics radically? Is there going to be no more global "moment of truth"? Has Clausewitz's relevance been relegated to limited wars? In one sense, as many writers have asserted, the nuclear revolution cannot be undone, and we will continue to live with what McGeorge Bundy has called "existential deterrence":

> As long as each side retains survivable strength so that no leader can ever suppose that he could "disarm" his nuclear opponent completely, nuclear war remains an overwhelmingly unattractive proposition for both sides.[17]

But there are those, on both sides, who believe that this revolution can be undone or (rather) that the best way of reenforcing deterrence is to provide oneself with the ability to destroy part of one's opponent's forces, rather than by merely safeguarding one's ability to devastate his cities. And while Bundy is right in saying that

> . . . . most "scenarios" for nuclear warfare between the Soviet Union and the United States reflect nothing more than the state of mind of their authors,[18]

there is no reason to be reassured if these "authors" happen to be the top decision-makers. Bundy's fine essay was a plea for leaving existential deterrence alone. But the rival governments have, for many years now, done exactly the opposite. As a result, there is a clash between the logic of existential deterrence and that of nuclear-war fighting scenarios and no guarantee that the former will always prevail.

As for economic interdependence, the same kind of question can be asked: Has it effected, in the behavior of states, a revolution comparable to the nuclear one? I am relatively more optimistic about this second base of moderation than about the first because the capacity of the developing countries to hurt and disrupt the economies of the advanced ones without grievously hurting themselves is very limited, for many reasons. OPEC has remained exceptional, and is a dubious model. As for the economic solidarity of the industrial countries in the open world economy, it is reinforced by strategic considerations—they are, on the whole, members of an alliance system which is an essential structure of power in the "state of war." However, once more, the success achieved so far in managing crises does not guarantee comparable success in the future. There are other sources of trouble than deliberate acts of economic warfare. Another major world recession could lead to an economic and political collapse of key developing countries that could raise far more havoc than any OPEC. And if the more advanced countries, flooded by immigrant workers coming from developing countries in which they can't find decent employment, react brutally against this flood, the delicate tissue of interdependence might be torn in ways dangerous both for the world economy and for the international political system.

A *second question* immediately follows from this. Will the *logic of sovereignty* (or anarchy) prevail over that of *international regimes* (or collective management), or vice versa? Another way of formulating this question would be: Will states define and calculate their interests, on the whole, in the traditional fashion, which emphasizes the short-run, domestic pressures or priorities and relative gains or will they realize that short-run advantages are increasingly elusive and transitory and that the goals they seek at home and abroad can be obtained only through collective solutions?

Until now, the number of areas in which states have understood that, as Ernst Haas has put it, "hunting hares separately may not be as good as hunting a stag through collective effort"[19] has been limited, and it has not included conflict management. There, traditional attitudes have prevailed partly because the superpowers have so far managed their cold war and because the tolerance of a certain amount of violence has seemed preferable to the constraints on national freedom of action which a set of effective security regimes would entail. The modicum of insecurity inherent in a world of anarchy (cooled by nuclear caution and partly diffused by fragmentation) has been preferred by every major actor to the collective insecurity that might be inherent in a regime controlled by others or permanently subjected to a struggle for control. The alternatives have not been a collective stag hunt or "starving to death."[20] The conditions under which international regimes have spread or survived[21] have been (1) the existence of a dominant power whose norms and procedures for the regime may not have seemed the best solution to all other states, but were accepted because the advantages these states could still derive from the regime exceeded those of refusing to join it (a notion that suggests that the dominant power itself had to define its interest in a sharable, i.e., enlightened way), or (2) the existence of a common good in an area where individual efforts were clearly ineffective or counterproductive, and little was lost by giving up the appearance of sovereignty, or (3) the possibility of a bargain in which, across the board, the benefits outweighed the losses, and the gain in predictability outweighed the burden of restraints on state action (if one analyzes the European Community as an international regime, one sees that these last two conditions have been met).[22] It is therefore rather obvious why such regimes have not spread to the realm of security, why the collapse of the international monetary regime of Bretton Woods has not been followed by the construction of a new one, and why the United States has resisted signing the Law-of-the-Seas agreement reached after many years of complicated bargaining.

A proliferation of international regimes would not change the "ordering principle" of the international system or even "the principles on the basis of which the constituent units are separable from one another."[23] Anarchy and sovereignty would not be abolished, but the significance of both would be profoundly transformed. Indeed, in each "sovereign" domain, there would in effect be two rules, that of the state and that of the regimes (in which the state takes part). We would remain far away from the utopia of a world state, not only because of the possibility of regimes breaking up (or down) when the balance of gains and losses, opportunities and restraints shifts too drastically at the expense of some key members, but also because the insoluble problem of "steering" a world without a single hegemon would not be resolved. There would still be a formidable problem of coordination—both across issues and among states, with much maneuvering aimed either at making it possible for a state that is powerful in one arena to translate some of this power into gains in areas where it is weak, or at blocking such transfers by trying to insulate each regime from the others. Nevertheless, we would be much closer to the world of politics described by the theorists of "complex interdependence" than to that of the "state of war." Steering would become less troublesome if it occurred within the framework and through the procedures and bargains of regimes.

A *third question* brings us back to the level of the *key actors*. Will they undergo the kind of domestic transformations that would make a taming of the logic of sovereignty possible, a strengthening of "existential deterrence," economic interdependence, and international regimes less problematic? In the case of the United States, two kinds of changes would be needed. One concerns the political system: capacity both for greater continuity and for more long-range strategic thinking would be indispensable. Is it achievable, given the four-year presidential term, the weakness of the career civil servants and the priorities of the "in-and-outers," the fragmentation of agencies, the effects of the separation of powers, the flimsy tone and heavy weight of the media? The other changes concern the political style which these institutional features partly shape and help preserve. We would need to break away decisively from the two archetypes of American exceptionalism: the missionary impulse, internationalist though it tends to be, insofar as it does not facilitate the necessary compromises with other peoples' or governments' blemishes, entails a combination of naïveté and excessive expectations, and breeds disappointments and disruptive backlashes. Even more, the impulse to be the world's sheriff needs to be discarded, not only because of the *macho* stands, the virility pose, which it introduces into American diplomacy, not only because of the excessive emphasis on will rather than skill, on resolve and credibility rather than influence and maneuver, but also because of the kind of insecurity it injects into the American public mind—the fear of "loss of nerve," the need to prove one's stamina or toughness by doing silly things (or doing something) even if they aren't worth doing, or if they divert resources, or if the purposes, other than demonstrating strength, are unclear.

As for the USSR, changes would have to go even farther, beyond the point which many of Reagan's advisers have wanted to reach—a turn of the regime inward, toward domestic reform. The USSR would have to transform the very essence of its regime and to overcome some of the most ancient traits of Russian political culture. The regime as a formidable machinery for central and total control (still oiled by an ideology that provides legitimacy), carries an assumption of external hostility, and dictates an imperative of expansion abroad. The least one can say is that it does not make the participation in a host of international regimes easy, nor does it leave much room for providing these with strong, unfettered powers of enforcement. (Although, in my opinion, it would be wrong to believe that it rules all of this out *ab initio*. Simply, in the Soviet calculation of gains and costs, fears of loss of control and of creeping ideological erosion will be weighted very heavily.) As for Russian political culture, with its often almost paranoid fear of external invasion, penetration, defilement, and encirclement, its passionate concern for the absolute security of the fatherland's borders, its chauvinistic feelings toward many other—lesser—breeds, it obviously remains a formidable obstacle. We are very close to a vicious circle. The political regime and public mind of the USSR could be moved away from their profound suspiciousness and attachment to all the trappings of traditional sovereignty if, in a moderate international system, the advantages of moderation, greater openness, and broader cooperation with noncommunist states became visible, but the regime and culture are precisely the reasons that reduce the chances for the development of such a system and the flow of such benefits.

3) Let us, then, at last put the pieces together. There are so many pieces, it is true, that the number of possibilities appears unlimited. But there is a way of reducing this chaos: by presenting three plausible *models* of the future, depending on the way in which the variables combine. The "real world" is likely to resemble one of them, more or less.

The first model is that of an *ideal* world (ideal, that is, within the range of possible ones, which excludes a world government, an end of the international political system). It would have two chief characteristics. One is a general reduction of violence. This would mean, in the relations between the superpowers, reaching an arms control agreement based on these principles: the elimination of unverifiable, nonsurvivable, and counterforce weapons and the primacy of crisis stability. It would also mean a political context of fairly broad cooperation, allowing not only for the prevention or defusing of East–West crises but also for joint action to prevent the inevitable regional conflicts or domestic turbulence in third countries from reaching dangerous levels; i.e., action aimed at insulating the areas of violence and at reducing the intensity, length, and scope of armed conflict. In this context, another subject for joint action would be a strategy aimed at slowing down nuclear proliferation by providing guarantees to states tempted by nuclear weapons for security reasons, and effective sanctions against proliferators through agreements among other suppliers.

Obviously, the other feature of such a system would be the spread of international regimes, including—in the area where they have been least successful so far—security. A global nuclear arms control regime would have to include all the nuclear powers, and it should be designed in such a way as not to reward cheating or breaking out. It would have to entail also mutual information about weapons developments. A global conventional regime might at first be limited to a series of confidence-building measures, but it would be reenforced by a network of regional security regimes that would include agreements of outside arms suppliers to curtail their sales of weapons, and by assurances of countries within the region to keep their own armaments to certain levels and types of weapons. These regimes would need, in order to be effective, to deploy regional or international peace forces whose presence could not be ended at the whim of one of the parties and which would have fairly extensive powers of self-defense, given the prevalence of conflict in most parts of the world. The establishment of regional regimes should, in this model, not wait for and depend on the consent of all the countries of the area: some potential troublemakers may have to be isolated, but at least the tacit consent of both superpowers would be necessary. The solidity of such regional regimes would be buttressed by efforts undertaken at the global (UN) or regional level to resolve the disputes from which violence springs, with the active participation of the superpowers serving, in a sense, as diplomacy's secular arms.

A second model corresponds to a gloomier vision, that of a world in which the superpowers' relationship remains *troubled*, and they as well as other actors are reluctant to give up the advantages of sovereignty in the realm of security except on a temporary, *ad hoc* basis that leaves little room for institutionalization. In this model, the United States and the USSR would continue to sign arms control agreements in order to regulate, and to reduce the costs of, the arms race, but a great deal of qualitative "modernization" would be allowed, including the development of some defensive systems, of weapons that are unverifiable (because of their size and/or mobility), and of survivable counterforce systems. Some nuclear proliferation would also take place, in the absence of a stringent international antiproliferation regime.

In such a world, the main peril for global peace would reside, not in the nuclear arms race, or even in the core, but in the various regional subsystems, in the continuing involvement of the superpowers, enthusiastic or reluctant, but driven by their contest, and in the periodic testing of the limits of their commitments. In other words, this model would resemble the current international political system, or rather the system as it was before the new cold war: troubled global peace, leaving room for occasionally large, but fragmented, regional explosions. It suggests that the tendency of smaller states to resort to force, their capacity to build quite vulnerable and provocative nuclear forces, their ability to exploit the superpowers' rivalry and to trigger the intervention of their respective superpower protector, will increase; at a minimum, regional violence will get much worse. One new feature might be a greater possibility (avoided so far) of limited direct conventional clashes between the superpowers (or also between the USSR and China), through the dynamics of these subsystems.

The third model is a *doomsday* one. It predicts that the constant juggling, the recurrent tense, unsettling improvisation of temporary halts and lasting nonsolutions is unlikely to work in the long run: one can't succeed everywhere, always. It assumes either the failure of further superpower efforts at arms control or the failure of those agreements that might still be reached to reverse the trend toward counterforce and vulnerability. It expects the international political system, despite all of its original features, to end in the same way as past systems, dominated either by two powers or by two armed camps. Sooner or later (just as Pleikus were said to be like streetcars), there comes an Epidamnus or a Potideia, or an accident such as the Sarajevo assassination, and each superpower or camp decides that there is no room for compromise, that it cannot yield without disastrous effects, that waiting until the next crisis will only benefit the adversary, and that it is in any event easier for the *other* side to pull back. . . . The vulnerability of an important part of one's nuclear arsenal, or the hope of gaining a significant advantage by striking first, or the fear that the adversary would gain the advantage unless one preempts, would help make the peaceful settlement of such a crisis impossible. Finally, the model postulates that either a major conventional confrontation in the core area or in one of the other vital subsystems (Middle and Far East) where the USSR has important geographical advantages, or the superpowers' recourse to limited nuclear warfare is bound to prove uncontrollable and will lead to assured mutual destruction.

4) Which model *shall* it be? "Realists" will tend to believe that it must be some form of the second, because the first is too utopian and the perils of the third are too obvious not to be somehow conjured. But I see no room for complacency. First, the history of past systems tells us something that remains valid despite all the original features of the present one. Psychologically, after a series of more or less successfully managed crises that have left frayed nerves and generalized discontent, the willingness to compromise, to restraint, tends to erode, and repressed resentments and regrets take their revenge. The dark side of protracted troubled peace is a kind of gradual, almost imperceptible resignation to submit to the fire next time.

Second, past pluses are rapidly turning into minuses. The changes in the nature of the nuclear arsenal may have the effect that "deterrence," which used to be a form of reassurance, is turning into a kind of provocation; the institutions of international economic interdependence have all been battered by the crises of the past dozen years, and national economic power as an instrument of coercion plays a prominent role alongside the "pooled" economic power or the bargaining kind of economic power found in international regimes. The heterogeneity of the system, that is, its fragmentation into separate compartments because of the nuclear revolution and of the autonomy of local causes of conflicts, seems to inject in the superpowers a desire to overcome these obstacles, to impose the artificial unity of their contest on the world, and to offset local disadvantages in one subsystem with "horizontal escalation" in a more favorable one.

Third, the return to a radical hostility comparable to that of the Stalinist postwar period, symbolized by the breakdown of the Soviet–American dialogue at a time of nuclear parity (which did not exist in the late 1940s) and of incomparably more sophisticated arsenals is an ominous new feature. Another one is the increasing military might of a number of countries in the regional subsystems. With the stakes of regional conflicts rising and the superpowers' rivalry heating up, their willingness and ability to stay out or to keep their involvements limited are likely to be very sorely tested.

The question we face, therefore, changes from "what is most likely to happen" to "what *should* we do to prevent the doomsday model from becoming a reality," since the reasons why, in the past, the international political system resembled the second model are disappearing or cannot be expected to last forever. Obviously, we face a convergence of political and moral imperatives. Both political scientists and—so to speak—professional moralists such as the American bishops have been driven to the conclusion that the political commands of survival, development, moderation are also ethical demands, and that the moral imperatives of peace and justice cannot be separated from a close political and military analysis and strategy. What we should do is work toward the first model, adopt it as a goal, however difficult and distant. As students of political affairs, this means trying to describe as rigorously as we can the kinds of mechanisms which it would require to function, and to specify as sharply as we can the conditions needed to bring it about and to keep it going (a quarter of a century ago, I had called for the formulation of "relevant utopias;" this is the same concern).

But what can we do as citizens? Even the thumbnail sketch I have provided here shows the abyss between where we are and where we ought to get. What is required is nothing less than a bet on the transformation of the superpowers and on a change in the logic of foreign policy. Can one, this time, count on what has never worked before—the power of arguments (remember Norman Angell?), the ability of statesmen to recoil before a "mad momentum" and to reverse it? This time, there may not be any leeway to pour belated regrets into rueful memoirs, and to say "if only I had listened;" but statesmen caught by the iron logic of their roles still act as if they did not have to listen and to innovate—as long as their opponents do not do it first. And so, one comes, reluctantly, to the conclusion that the only path toward the least somber of the three models may be one that passes through a crisis disastrous enough to scare and convert everyone, but not so disastrous as to be fatal to all; and since one cannot wish for such a risk, one's best hope remains the persistence of the second model, despite all the reasons I have given to suggest that one can no longer count on it.

NOTES

1. Immanuel Wallerstein, *The Modern World System*, vols. 1 and 2 (New York: Academic Press, 1974 and 1980).
2. Robert Gilpin, *War and Change in World Politics* (New York: Cambridge University Press, 1981).
3. Robert Keohane, "Theory of World Politics: Structural Realism and Beyond," in

Ada W. Finifter, *Political Science: The State of the Discipline* (Washington, D.C.: APSA, 1983), p. 519.

4. Kenneth Waltz, *Theory of International Politics* (Reading, MA: Addison-Wesley, 1979).

5. For Keohane, see Note 3. Ruggie's critique appears in his "Continuity and Transformation in the World Polity: Toward a Neorealist Synthesis," *World Politics*, January 1983, pp. 261–285.

6. A quarter of a century ago, I had listed state–society relations, transnational forces, and the scope of relations, among the crucial elements of an international system whose transformations determined the passage from one system to another, in Stanley Hoffmann, *Contemporary Theory in International Relations* (Englewood Cliffs: Prentice Hall, 1960).

7. Keohane, "Theory of World Politics: Structural Realism and Beyond," in Ada W. Finifter, *Political Science: The State of the Discipline* (Washington, D.C.: APSA, 1983) p. 513.

8. *Ibidem*, p. 529.

9. Richard Ned Lebow, *Between Peace and War* (Baltimore: Johns Hopkins University Press, 1981).

10. Stanley Hoffmann, *Primacy or World Order*, Part II (New York: McGraw Hill, 1978).

11. This point is developed further in Stanley Hoffmann, *Dead Ends*, Chapters 1 and 2 (Cambridge, MA: Ballinger, 1983).

12. The now classic description is to be found in Robert Keohane and Joseph Nye, *Power and Interdependence* (Boston: Little Brown, 1977).

13. Stanley Hoffmann, *Dead Ends*, Chapter 1.

15. For a much more detailed elaboration, see my and other contributions to *The Making of America's Soviet Policy*, edited by Joseph Nye (New Haven: Yale University Press, 1984).

16. Especially A.W. de Porte, *Europe between the Superpowers* (New Haven: Yale University Press, 1979).

17. McGeorge Bundy, "The Bishops and the Bomb," *New York Review*, June 16, 1983, p. 6.

18. *Ibidem*, p. 4.

19. Ernst Haas, "Postwar Conflict Management," *International Organization*, Fall 1983, p. 235.

20. *Ibidem*, p. 235.

21. See the issue of *International Organizations*, on international regimes, Spring 1962.

22. See my remarks in "Reflections on the Nation-State in Europe Today," *Journal of German Market Studies*, Sept.-Dec. 1982, pp. 21–37.

23. Ruggie, "Continuity and Transformation in the World Polity: Toward a Neorealist Synthesis," *World Politics*, January 1983.